Law's Ideal Dimension

Law's Ideal Dimension

ROBERT ALEXY

OXFORD
UNIVERSITY PRESS

OXFORD
UNIVERSITY PRESS

Great Clarendon Street, Oxford, OX2 6DP,
United Kingdom

Oxford University Press is a department of the University of Oxford.
It furthers the University's objective of excellence in research, scholarship,
and education by publishing worldwide. Oxford is a registered trade mark of
Oxford University Press in the UK and in certain other countries

First Edition published in 2021

Impression: 1

Published in the United States of America by Oxford University Press
198 Madison Avenue, New York, NY 10016, United States of America

British Library Cataloguing in Publication Data

Data available

Library of Congress Control Number: 2020953017

ISBN 978–0–19–879683–1

DOI: 10.1093/oso/9780198796831.001.0001

Printed and bound by
CPI Group (UK) Ltd, Croydon, CR0 4YY

Preface

This volume comprises twenty-one chapters written over a period of thirty-two years. Of these, seventeen have been published previously in English, four of them having been translated from the original German into English by Bartocz Brożek and Stanley L. Paulson (2007), Ruth Adler and Neil MacCormick (1992), Susanne Gaschke (1993), and Kirsten Bock (1998) (see Chapters 11, 17, 19, and 21). The other chapters have all been written in English, a line that is only a half-truth without an acknowledgement of the assistance given to me by Stanley L. Paulson. Stanley has been in residence in Kiel for the past twenty years and has always assisted me on my English-language articles. Indeed, every article from the year 2000 on begins with an asterisk-footnote thanking Stanley for his assistance and advice on matters of English style. And I have enjoyed the same support vis-à-vis the four chapters that are published here for the first time in English. What is more, Stanley has recently gone to the trouble to examine and to refine the English in three fairly early articles of mine. In short, it would simply not have been possible, without Stanley, to publish this volume. My gratitude to him is boundless.

I want also to thank Martin Borowski at the University of Heidelberg and his secretary, Ingrid Baumbusch, for technical assistance. Ms Baumbusch converted the older articles from PDF files into Word files, making my work on the volume a good deal easier.

Robert Alexy
Kiel
September 2020

Acknowledgements

The following chapters were originally published in English as indicated:

1. 'The Nature of Legal Philosophy', *Ratio Juris* 17 (2004), 156–67
2. 'On the Concept and the Nature of Law', *Ratio Juris* 21 (2008), 281–99
3. 'The Dual Nature of Law', *Ratio Juris* 23 (2010), 167–82
4. 'Law, Morality, and the Existence of Human Rights', *Ratio Juris* 25 (2012), 2–14
5. 'An Answer to Joseph Raz', in *Law, Rights and Discourse. The Legal Philosophy of Robert Alexy*, ed. George Pavlakos (Oxford: Hart, 2007), 37–55
6. 'The Ideal Dimension of Law', in *The Cambridge Companion to Natural Law Jurisprudence*, eds George Duke and Robert P. George (Cambridge: Cambridge University Press, 2017), 314–41
7. 'Gustav Radbruch's Concept of Law' (not previously published in English)
8. 'The Construction of Constitutional Rights', *Law & Ethics of Human Rights* 4 (2010), 20–32
9. 'Balancing, Constitutional Review, and Representation', *International Journal of Constitutional Law* 3 (2005), 572–81
10. 'The Existence of Human Rights', *Archives for Philosophy of Law and Social Philosophy*, supplement 136 (2013), 9–18
11. 'The Weight Formula', trans. Bartosz Brożek and Stanley L. Paulson, in *Studies in the Philosophy of Law*, vol. 3, eds Jerzy Stelmach, Bartosz Brożek, and Wojciech Załuski (Kraków: Jagiellonian University Press, 2007), 9–27
12. 'Formal Principles: Some Replies to Critics', *International Journal of Constitutional Law* 12 (2014), 511–24
13. 'Ideal "Ought" and Optimization' (not previously published in English)
14. 'Human Dignity and Proportionality' (not previously published in English)
15. 'Proportionality and Rationality', in *Proportionality. New Frontiers, New Challenges*, eds Vicki C. Jackson and Mark Tushnet (Cambridge: Cambridge University Press, 2017), 13–29
16. 'The Absolute and the Relative Dimension of Constitutional Rights', *Oxford Journal of Legal Studies* 37 (2017), 31–47
17. 'A Discourse-Theoretical Conception of Practical Reason', trans. Ruth Adler and Neil MacCormick, *Ratio Juris* 5 (1992), 231–51
18. 'Problems of Discourse Theory', *Crítica* 20 (1988), 43–65

19. 'Legal Argumentation as Rational Discourse', trans. Susanne Gaschke, *Rivista internazionale di filosofia del diritto* 70 (1993), 165–78
20. Jürgen Habermas's Theory of the Indeterminacy of Law and the Rationality of Adjudication (not previously published in English)
21. 'Law and Correctness', trans. Kirsten Bock, *Current Legal Problems* 51 (1998), 205–21

Contents

PART II CONSTITUTIONAL RIGHTS, HUMAN RIGHTS, AND PROPORTIONALITY

PART III. ARGUMENTATION, CORRECTNESS, AND LAW

Introduction

The twenty-one articles brought together here represent both a further elaboration and systematic connection of the main ideas contained, often in embryonic form, in my three books: *A Theory of Legal Argumentation*,[1] *A Theory of Constitutional Rights*,[2] and *The Argument from Injustice*.[3] Owing to a goodly number of new elements and new connections, the present book is not merely a collection of essays in legal philosophy. Rather, it is a new and comprehensive theory based on the arguments found in the three earlier books.

The collection is divided into three parts. The first concerns the nature of law. This is the theme of *The Argument from Injustice*. Still, there is little in the book on what it means to reflect on the nature of law. Chapter 1, on 'The Nature of Legal Philosophy', addresses this issue. Legal philosophy, in a first step, is defined as reasoning about the nature of law. In a second step, reasoning about the nature of law is understood as reasoning about the necessary properties of law. Finally, in a third step, coercion and the claim to correctness are identified as necessary as well as sufficient, that is, essential properties of law. If this is true, law has a dual nature. It comprises a real as well as an ideal dimension. The existence of a real dimension, defined by authoritative issuance and social efficacy, guaranteed by coercion, is scarcely contested. The case is different, however, with respect to the ideal dimension, defined by the claim to correctness. This claim includes a claim to justice. In *The Argument from Injustice*, law's ideal dimension is sometimes employed, but it plays no systematically important role there. This concept—its place in the title of the book gives expression to its importance in my recent work—is elaborated in Chapter 2, 'On the Concept and the Nature of Law', and Chapter 3, 'The Dual Nature of Law'. In both chapters, I attempt to make more explicit the dual nature thesis, already implicit in *The Argument from Injustice*. In this explication, the distinction between exclusive, inclusive, and super-inclusive non-positivism—inspired by the familiar distinction between exclusive and inclusive positivism—plays a pivotal role. With this distinction, a new field is opened up for the last four articles of Part

[1] Robert Alexy, *A Theory of Legal Argumentation* (1978), trans. Ruth Adler and Neil MacCormick (Oxford: Clarendon Press, 1989).

[2] Robert Alexy, *A Theory of Constitutional Rights* (1985), trans. Julian Rivers (Oxford: Oxford University Press, 2002).

[3] Robert Alexy, *The Argument from Injustice. A Reply to Legal Positivism* (1992), trans. Bonnie Litschewski Paulson and Stanley L. Paulson (Oxford: Clarendon Press, 2002).

Law's Ideal Dimension. Robert Alexy, Oxford University Press.
DOI: 10.1093/oso/9780198796831.003.0001

I of the volume. In 'Law, Morality, and the Existence of Human Rights', Chapter 4, I discuss problems that arise from the fact that non-positivism is possible only if necessary moral elements exist. My thesis is twofold. First, necessary moral elements exist because human rights exist. Second, human rights *qua* moral rights exist because they are justifiable. In this way, Part I of the book, concerning the nature of law, is intrinsically connected with Part II, which bears the title 'Constitutional Rights, Human Rights, and Proportionality'. To understand human rights as moral rights is to identify a decisive element of law's ideal dimension. This identification, however, is only a first step in the justification of non-positivism. The second and far more difficult step is the justification of human rights. An attempt to arrive at such a justification is to be found in Chapter 10, 'The Existence of Human Rights' in Part II of the book. First, however, I should like to invite attention to three additional chapters in the first part. In these chapters I attempt to make clearer, by means of a discussion of theses defended by Joseph Raz (Chapter 5), John Finnis (Chapter 6), and Gustav Radbruch (Chapter 7), what I have said in the preceding four chapters.

In Part II of the book, as already mentioned, I take up constitutional rights, human rights, and proportionality. In Chapter 8, 'The Construction of Constitutional Rights', I defend the construction of constitutional rights as principles against objections raised by proponents of the rule construction. The principles construction implies the necessity of proportionality analysis and, along with this, the necessity of balancing. A standard objection against the principles construction, raised for instance by Jürgen Habermas, is that balancing is irrational. My reply is that balancing is an argument form of rational legal discourse. If rational legal argumentation is possible, then balancing is possible as a rational means of resolving conflicts between constitutional rights and between constitutional rights and collective goods. Thus, the theory of constitutional rights is inextricably connected to the theory of legal argumentation, the theme of my first book and of Part III of the present book. The treatise *A Theory of Constitutional Rights*, has received further elaboration in several of my more recent articles. Two of these elaborations are of special significance: one is philosophical in nature, the other mathematical.

The philosophical elaboration concerns the nature of constitutional rights. Constitutional rights count as positive law, that is to say, positive law at the level of the constitution. This was the starting point of *A Theory of Constitutional Rights*. This fact does not suffice, however, to explain the nature of constitutional rights. Positivity is but one side of constitutional rights, namely their real side. Over and above this real side they also manifest an ideal side. The reason is significant. Constitutional rights are rights that have been recorded in a constitution with the intention of transforming human rights *qua* moral rights into positive law. This intention is often a subjective or actual intention of the framers of the constitution. Still, owing to the claim to correctness, necessarily raised with law and, therefore, with constitutions, this intention is, furthermore, also objective and therefore necessary. Thus, constitutional rights *qua* positive law necessarily have an ideal dimension. The transformation of human rights into constitutional rights is a process of institutionalization. Without constitutional review this process cannot be carried out. Carrying it out, however, raises a problem: the perennial problem of the relation between constitutional rights and democracy. In Chapter 9, 'Balancing, Constitutional Review, and Representation', I try to resolve this problem by means of a classification of constitutional review as, so to speak, an argumentative representation of the people. With this, the theory of argumentation once again makes an entry. In Chapter 10, 'The Existence of Human Rights', I attempt to demonstrate the existence of human rights. The basis of this demonstration is the practice of discourse, essentially defined as a practice of asserting, asking, and arguing.

The mathematical elaboration of the theory of constitutional rights concerns the transformation of the most important element of proportionality analysis, the Law of Balancing as it is found in the *A Theory of Constitutional Rights*, into a mathematical formula, the Weight Formula. This formula is given a systematic presentation in Chapter 11. Chapter 12, 'Formal Principles: Some Replies to Critics', and Chapter 13, 'Ideal "Ought" and Optimization', can be seen as further steps on the path opened up by the Weight Formula. The last three chapters of Part II of the volume, Chapter 14, 'Human Dignity and Proportionality', Chapter 15, 'Proportionality and Rationality', and Chapter 16, 'The Absolute and the Relative Dimension of Constitutional Rights', show that the connection of the mathematical structure of balancing with substantive philosophical arguments leads to insights that are otherwise scarcely possible to imagine.

Part III concerns the relation between argumentation, correctness, and law. The articles it comprises address three themes: the possibility of discursive rationality, the special case thesis, and the idea of correctness. The question of whether discursive rationality is possible is the theme of Chapter 17, 'A Discourse-Theoretical Conception of Practical Reason', and Chapter 18, 'Problems of Discourse Theory'. A key to the positive answer that I offer here is the connection of the idea of an ideal discourse with the concept of real discourse. This, too, counts as a tie of the real with the ideal. If discursive rationality is possible, practical correctness or truth is not a mere illusion. The next step connects general practical rationality with legal rationality. This is the object of the special case thesis. The special case thesis, as developed in *A Theory of Legal Argumentation*, claims that legal argumentation or discourse is a special case of general practical discourse. Legal discourse is a special case of general practical discourse because legal argumentation is not concerned with what is absolutely correct but with what is correct within the framework of the prevailing legal system. This is to say that legal argumentation, too, has a real dimension and an ideal dimension. I discuss various aspects of this in the Chapter 19, 'Legal Argumentation as Rational Discourse', and Chapter 20, 'Jürgen Habermas's Theory of the Indeterminacy of Law and the Rationality of Adjudication'. The latter is a reply to Habermas's critique of my special case thesis. I analyse the implications of the aforementioned arguments for the law in Chapter 21, 'Law and Correctness'. Here the concepts of law and correctness are connected.

PART I

THE NATURE OF LAW

The main theme of Part I of the book is the dual nature of law. The dual-nature thesis says that law necessarily comprises both a real dimension, defined by authoritative issuance and social efficacy, and an ideal dimension, defined by the claim to correctness which includes a claim to justice. This connection between the real and the ideal implies non-positivism.

1
The Nature of Legal Philosophy

The question of the nature of legal philosophy connects two problems. The first concerns the general nature of philosophy, the second, the special character of that part of philosophy we call 'legal philosophy'.

I. The Nature of Philosophy

There are so many schools, methods, styles, subjects, and ideals of philosophy that it is difficult to explain its nature. A general explanation of the nature of philosophy would presuppose that all or at least most of the very different conceptions of philosophy which have appeared in the history of the field have something in common that can be conceived of as the focal meaning or the concept of philosophy.

Perhaps the most general feature of the concept of philosophy seems to be reflexivity. Philosophy is reflective because it is reasoning about reasoning. Philosophy is reasoning about reasoning because its subject, the human practice of conceiving on the one hand of the world, oneself, and other minds, and on the other of human action, is essentially determined by reasons.

Having a conception of the world, oneself, and other minds is to have a conception about what there is. Action, on the other hand, presupposes a conception about what ought to be done or is good. Reasoning about the general question of what there is defines metaphysics *qua* ontology; reasoning about the question of what ought to be done or is good defines ethics. Human practice is not only based—for the most part implicitly—on answers to both questions but it also includes—again, for the most part implicitly—numerous answers to a third question, the question of how to justify our beliefs on what there is and on what ought to be done or is good. This question defines epistemology. Philosophy attempts to make explicit the ontological, ethical, and epistemological assumptions implicit in human practice.

Explicit reflexivity is necessary but not sufficient to explain the nature of philosophy. A teacher who abhors students' chewing gum during his lecture may become reflective by asking himself what the reasons for his attitude are, but this is not enough for him to become a philosopher. Reflexivity must be associated with two other properties if it is to be seen as capturing something genuinely philosophical in nature. The reflection must be reflection about general or fundamental

Law's Ideal Dimension. Robert Alexy, Oxford University Press. © Robert Alexy 2021.
DOI: 10.1093/oso/9780198796831.003.0002

questions, and this reflection must be of a systematic kind. The shortest, most abstract, but nevertheless truly comprehensive definition of philosophy might therefore run as follows: philosophy is general and systematic reflection about what there is, what ought to be done or is good, and how knowledge about both is possible.

This explanation by no means claims to exhaust its subject. Its brevity excludes this, and it may be that even a far more elaborated explanation will never be able to exhaust the nature of philosophy, for behind or between all the concepts one can use to explain its nature there may lie something which cannot be grasped conceptually, despite the fact that philosophy is a conceptual activity. Our explanation, therefore, can only attempt to provide a starting point for an answer to the question about the nature of legal philosophy. One may assume that this question has—as with legal philosophy itself—a certain autonomy, so that we need, indeed, an understanding of the general nature of philosophy only as a first step and not as a final and complete basis on which our understanding of the nature of legal philosophy rests, like a house on its foundations.

My definition of philosophy as general and systematic reflection about what there is, what ought to be done or is good, and how knowledge about both is possible, leads, notwithstanding its extremely abstract and highly tentative character, to three corollaries important for our purposes. First, reflection necessarily has a critical dimension. To reflect on what there is, what ought to be done and is good, and what we can know, is to ask for and to argue about what objectively exists, what is true or right, and what is justified. If one defines normativity as the ability to distinguish what is correct from what is incorrect, these questions are normative questions. Philosophy as a necessarily reflective enterprise therefore necessarily has a normative dimension. The general and systematic character of philosophical reflection leads, second, to an analytic, and third, to a synthetic or holistic dimension of philosophy. The analytic dimension is defined by the attempt to identify and to make explicit the fundamental structures of the natural and social world in which we live and the fundamental concepts and principles by means of which we can grasp both worlds. Without this analytic bite, philosophy could be neither general nor systematic in a substantial sense.

In legal philosophy, the analytic dimension concerns concepts like those of norm, 'ought', person, action, sanction, and institution. The synthetic dimension is defined by the attempt to unite all of this into a coherent whole. A deeply founded and coherent picture of what there is, what ought to be done and is good, and what we can know, is the regulative idea of philosophy or, in simpler terms, its ultimate aim. This implies that philosophy is necessarily holistic. Our definition of philosophy should therefore be complemented by the following, which is implied by the definition: philosophy is normative (or critical), analytic, and holistic (or synthetic). The three concepts of the definition (reflective, general, and systematic), and the three concepts of the corollary (normative, analytic, and holistic), are descriptions of the same things from different perspectives.

II. Pre-Understanding and Arguments

Legal philosophy, as philosophy, is reflection of a general and systematic kind, and it has, exactly like philosophy in general, a normative, an analytic, and a holistic dimension. Its *differentia specifica* consists in its subject: the law. Legal philosophy is not generally directed to the questions of what there is, what ought to be done or is good, and what can be known, but to these questions with respect to the law. Raising these questions with respect to the law is to ask for the nature of law. This seems to lead naturally to the definition of legal philosophy as reasoning about the nature of law.

This, however, seems to cause a problem. It is a circularity problem, which rests on the fact that, on the one hand, legal philosophy cannot be defined without using the concept of law, whereas, on the other, it has the task *qua* reasoning about the nature of law of explaining what law is. How can legal philosophy begin to explore what law is when it is impossible to say what legal philosophy is without knowing what law is? This circularity, however, is not vicious but virtuous in character. It is nothing other than a version of the hermeneutic circle, and it is to be resolved like all variants of this circle: by starting with the pre-understanding suggested by the established practice and elaborating it through critical and systematic reflection.

The pre-understanding of law is not only the pre-understanding of an entity which is highly complex in itself. To this first complexity is added—as a second complexity—that the pre-understanding as such is capable of extreme variations. The scale extends from Holmes's 'bad man',[1] which defines a rather detached external point of view, to Dworkin's judge Hercules,[2] which represents a rather idealistic internal one. Legal philosophy as an enterprise, which, at the same time, is systematic as well as critical, cannot start from just one pre-understanding. It has to consider all of them and, what is more, has to analyse the relation of all of them to all features of law.

The requirement to consider all pre-understandings which are to be found in law and legal philosophy on the one side, and all features of law on the other side, suggests the idea of something like a catalogue of all approaches and all features. But how does one compose such a list? Simply to pick up and collect each approach and each feature which appears in history or today before our eyes would, as Kant says,

1 Oliver Wendell Holmes, 'The Path of the Law', *Harvard Law Review* 10 (1896–97), 457–78, at 459.
2 Ronald Dworkin, *Taking Rights Seriously* (London: Duckworth, 1977), 105.

'not be a *rational system* but merely an aggregate haphazardly collected'.[3] One needs no argument in order to say that this would be incompatible with the systematic and critical character of philosophy. Philosophical reflection demands a system. It is, however, much easier to say that a mere aggregate, or, as Kant sometimes puts it, a 'rhapsody'[4] is not enough than to say how an adequate conceptual system or framework can be constructed. The best answer seems to be not by an abstract theory of legal philosophy but by systematic analysis of the arguments put forward in the discussion about the nature of law. No other procedure seems to fit better the general character of legal philosophy *qua* reasoning about the nature of law.

III. Three Problems

The arguments about the nature of law revolve around three problems. The first problem addresses the questions: in what kind of entities does the law consist, and how are these entities connected such that they form the overarching entity we call 'law'? This problem concerns the concept of a norm and a normative system. The second and the third problem are addressed to the validity of law. The second concerns its real or factual dimension. This is the area of legal positivism. Two centres are to be distinguished here. The first is determined by the concept of authoritative issuance, the second by that of social efficacy. The third problem of the nature of legal philosophy concerns the correctness or legitimacy of law. Here, the main question is the relationship between law and morality. To take up this question is to take up the ideal or critical dimension of law. It is this triad of problems that, taken together, defines the nucleus of the problem of the nature of law.

This tripartition claims to be complete, neutral, and systematic. It is complete when it can absorb all arguments that can be put forward for and against a thesis about the nature of law. The only proof possible for this consists in corroborating our triadic model with respect to as many critical instances as possible. The model is neutral when it adds no preferences to the weights of the arguments it absorbs. The proof is the same as in the case of completeness. It is, finally, systematic when it leads to a coherent picture of the nature of law. In this case, the proof cannot consist of anything else than an elaboration of a coherent account.

The last point can be generalized. Only by elaborating the best theory connecting answers to all three questions about the nature of law can the nature of legal philosophy become as clear as possible. It is, however, not only not the case that one can develop such a perfect theory here but also the case that one may well be sceptical

[3] Immanuel Kant, *The Metaphysics of Morals*, trans. and ed. Mary J. Gregor, in *The Cambridge Edition of the Works of Immanuel Kant. Practical Philosophy* (Cambridge: Cambridge University Press, 1996), 353–603, at 493 (trans. altered); AA 6, 357.

[4] Immanuel Kant, *Critique of Pure Reason*, trans. Werner S. Pluhar (Indianapolis, Ind.: Hackett, 1996), 755; A 832, B 860.

about whether such an ideal of perfection can ever be achieved. Fortunately, it is not necessary to know all in order to know enough. In order to obtain as much as is necessary for our purposes it suffices to use the triadic model as a framework for the discussion of paradigmatic problems.

IV. Four Theses

The consideration of paradigmatic problems vis-à-vis our triadic model shall confirm four theses. This confirmation, again, implies a corroboration of the model. The first thesis says that legal philosophy is not confined to certain special problems connected with law; all problems of philosophy may arise in legal philosophy. In this respect legal philosophy substantially includes the problems of philosophy in general. One can call this the 'general nature thesis'. The second thesis maintains that there are specific problems of legal philosophy. They are due to the specific character of law, which results from the fact that law is necessarily authoritative or institutional as well as critical or ideal. This is the 'specific character thesis'. The third thesis says that there is a special relation between legal philosophy and other provinces of practical philosophy, especially those of moral and political philosophy. One can call this the 'special relation thesis'. A fourth thesis overarches the first three theses. That is, it does not simply join them as a fourth thesis but expresses an idea behind them. It is the idea that legal philosophy can be successful only if it comes up to the level not only of one or two of these theses but to that of all three. This is the 'comprehensive ideal' of legal philosophy.

While the triadic model of the problems of legal philosophy claims to be neutral, the four theses do not. They involve decisions with respect to the solution of these problems. This becomes clear when one contrasts the comprehensive ideal with something like a 'restrictive maxim'. A radical version of such a restrictive maxim maintains, first, that legal philosophy should never get involved in any genuinely philosophical problem; second, that legal philosophy should concentrate its efforts on the institutional or authoritative character of law; and, third, that legal philosophy should delegate critical normative questions to moral and political philosophy, which for their part should be kept, so to speak, beyond reach. The restrictive maxim mirrors a picture of legal philosophy that is fundamentally different from the picture of the field corresponding to the comprehensive ideal. Legal philosophy turns into a juridical theory of law, which is separated from general philosophy as well as from moral and political philosophy.

The choice between the comprehensive ideal and the restrictive maxim is a fundamental choice. The character of legal philosophy is determined by it much more radically than by the choice between legal positivism and non-positivism. The choice between positivism and non-positivism is a choice inside the realm of legal philosophy. The choice between the comprehensive ideal and the restrictive maxim amounts to a choice between philosophy and non-philosophy. This is the background against which our paradigmatic problems have to be considered.

V. Entities and Concepts

The answers given by Kelsen and Olivecrona in the 1930s to the classical question of what entities the law consists of present our first example. Kelsen defines 'law as norm',[5] and norms as 'meaning',[6] and the 'unique sense' of this meaning as 'ought', and 'ought' as a 'category'.[7] This is the language in which abstract entities are described. Kelsen insists that norms—and thus, law—can be reduced neither to physical events nor to psychical processes. They belong not to natural reality but to an 'ideal reality'.[8] Such an ideal reality, which exists in addition to the physical and the psychical world, would be a 'third realm' in the sense of Frege.[9] The opposite position is to be found in Karl Olivecrona, who, with an eye to Kelsen, maintains that '[t]he rules of law are a natural cause—among others—of the actions of the judges in cases of litigation as well as of the behaviour in general of people in relation to each other'.[10] This question—as an ontological question—is not only a question of general philosophical interest, it is also a question which must be answered in order to determine the nature of law, and it is, therefore, a genuine question of legal philosophy.

An adherent of the restrictive maxim might object that the question of the ontological status of norms is, for lawyers, as unimportant as the question of the real or only imagined existence of a mountain in Africa, identified and surveyed by two geographers, is for these two geographers.[11] The reply to this objection is that the realism problem has a different significance for geographers than the meaning problem has for lawyers. The answer to the question as to whether norms are meaning contents or natural causes determines the answer to a further question, namely, whether norms can be conceived as elements of an inferential system and, thereby, as starting points of arguments, or whether they are only elements in a causal network. In the first case, legal reasoning oriented towards correctness is possible, in the second, it would be an illusion. This shows how the self-understanding of legal reasoning and, by means of it, the self-understanding of law depends on ontological presuppositions. There are, naturally, several ways for

[5] Hans Kelsen, *Introduction to the Problems of Legal Theory* (1934), trans. Bonnie Litschewski Paulson and Stanley L. Paulson (Oxford: Clarendon Press, 1992), 13.

[6] Ibid., 11, 14.

[7] Ibid., 24.

[8] Ibid., 15.

[9] Gottlob Frege, 'The Thought: A Logical Inquiry', trans. A. M. Quinton and Marcelle Quinton, in *Philosophical Logic*, ed. P. F. Strawson (Oxford: Oxford University Press, 1967), 17–38, at 29.

[10] Karl Olivecrona, *Law as Fact* (London: Humphrey Milford, 1939), 16.

[11] Rudolf Carnap, 'Pseudoproblems in Philosophy', trans. Rolf A. George, in Carnap, *The Logical Structure of the World and Pseudoproblems in Philosophy* (Chicago, Ill.: Open Court, 2003), 301–43, at 333.

reconstructing these presuppositions. But the mere fact that there exists the necessity of reconstructing them is enough to confirm the thesis that legal philosophy cannot do without arguments that are genuinely philosophical in character.

In any case, the concept of a norm or the 'ought' is a candidate for the most abstract concept of legal philosophy. If one goes one step down from this level of abstraction, the inferential impact of the fundamental concepts of law becomes far more obvious. The distinction between rules and principles is a highly abstract question of the general theory of norms. It has, at the same time, far-reaching consequences for the theory of legal reasoning. If law contains both, then legal reasoning inevitably combines subsumption with balancing.[12] Legal reasoning is thereby essentially determined by structures that are structures of general practical reasoning. This is an important reason for not conceiving of legal reasoning as a province in its own right, separate and distinct from other provinces of reason.

All this shows that fundamental philosophical questions must be answered in order to grasp the nature of law. Reflection about the nature of law cannot succeed when separated from general philosophy.

VI. Necessary Properties

Asking for the nature of something is more than asking for interesting and important properties. Questions about the nature of law are questions about its necessary properties. The concept of necessity leads one to the heart of philosophy. The same is true with its relatives, the concepts of analyticity and the *a priori*. Without these concepts it is impossible to understand the meaning of questions of the type 'What is the nature of Φ?' Without understanding the structure of questions of this kind, one cannot understand the main question of legal philosophy: 'What is the nature of law?' And to fail to understand this question is to fail to know what legal philosophy is.

The possibility of defining the concept of nature as it appears in sentences of the form 'What is the nature of Φ?', namely, by means of the concept of necessity, allows for the substitution of the question 'What is the nature of law?' by the question 'What are the necessary properties of law?' This question leads, by means of the concept of necessity (and its relatives, analyticity, and the a priori), to the specific character of law. The question of what is necessary, when connected with the question of what is specific, turns into the question of what is essential. This is the area of the specific character thesis.

Two properties are essential for law: coercion or force on the one hand, and correctness or rightness on the other. The first concerns a central element of the social

[12] Robert Alexy, 'On Balancing and Subsumption. A Structural Comparison', *Ratio Juris* 16 (2003), 433–48, at 448.

efficacy of law, the second expresses its ideal or critical dimension. It is the central question of legal philosophy to ask how these two concepts are related to the concept of law and, through it, to each other. All—or at least nearly all—questions of legal philosophy depend on the answer to this question.

It is highly contested whether coercion and correctness are necessarily connected with law. This dispute is attended by a meta-dispute about the question of what kind of argument can be given for and against the necessity of such connections. It is impossible to elaborate this here.[13] I will therefore confine myself to some features which seem to be instructive for our question concerning the nature of legal philosophy.

Coercion is the easier case. It seems to be quite natural to argue that a system of rules or norms which in no case authorizes the use of coercion or sanction—not even in case of self-defence—is not a legal system, and this is the case owing to conceptual reasons based on the use of language. Who would apply the expression 'law' to such a system of rules? Conceptual reasons of this kind, however, have little power of their own. Concepts based on the actual use of language are in need of modification once they prove not to be, as Kant says—mentioning, *inter alia*, the concepts of gold, water, and law—'adequate to the object'.[14] Including coercion in the concept of law is adequate to its object, the law, because it mirrors a practical necessity necessarily connected with law. Coercion is necessary if law is to be a social practice that fulfils its basic formal functions as defined by the values of legal certainty and efficiency as well as possible. This practical necessity, which seems to correspond to a certain degree to Hart's 'natural necessity',[15] is mirrored in a conceptual necessity implicit in the use of language. This shows that language, which we use to refer to social facts, is inspired by the hermeneutic principle that each human practice is to be conceived of as an attempt to carry out its functions as well as possible. Unravelling this connection between conceptual and practical necessity makes clear in what sense coercion belongs as a necessary property to the nature of law.

The second central property of law is its claim to correctness. This claim stands in genuine opposition to coercion or force, and it is an essential mark of law that it comprises such a difference.

The necessity of coercion, it has been shown, is based on a practical necessity defined by a means-end relation. In this respect, it has a teleological character. The necessity of the claim to correctness is a necessity resulting from the structure of legal acts and legal reasoning. It has a deontological character. To make explicit this deontological structure implicit in law is one of the most important tasks of legal philosophy.

[13] Robert Alexy, 'The Nature of Arguments about the Nature of Law', in *Rights, Culture, and the Law. Themes from the Legal and Political Philosophy of Joseph Raz*, eds Lukas H. Meyer, Stanley L. Paulson, and Thomas W. Pogge (Oxford: Oxford University Press, 2003), 3–16.

[14] Kant, *Critique of Pure Reason* (n. 4 above), 680; A 728, B 756.

[15] H. L. A. Hart, *The Concept of Law*, 2nd edn (Oxford: Clarendon Press, 1994), 199.

All methods of making the implicit explicit can be applied here. One of them is the construction of performative contradictions.[16] An example of this is a fictitious first article of a constitution which reads as follows: '*X* is a sovereign, federal, and unjust republic.' It is difficult to deny that this article is somehow absurd. The idea underlying the method of performative contradiction is to explain this absurdity as resulting from a contradiction between what is implicitly claimed in acting to frame a constitution—namely, that it is just—and what is explicitly declared—namely, that it is unjust. If this explanation is sound, and if the claim to justice, which is a special case of the broader claim to correctness,[17] is necessarily raised, then a necessary connection between law and justice is made explicit.

It is not difficult to recognize how this argument might be challenged. One simply has to deny that law necessarily raises a claim to correctness. Once this claim disappears, any contradiction between the explicit and the implicit vanishes. The declaration of injustice contained in our first article may then be interpreted as an expression of a claim to power.

This is not the place to discuss the question of whether it is possible for a system of norms to substitute the claim to correctness by a claim to power and nevertheless remain a legal system.[18] This is a question of legal philosophy, not a question about its nature. Here it suffices to say that the discussion about necessary deontological structures implicit in the law belongs to the very nature of legal philosophy.

VII. Law and Morality

If the thesis that law necessarily raises a claim to correctness should prove to be wrong, it would be difficult to contest the positivist's thesis of the separability of law and morality. The opposite, however, is the case if the thesis about the claim to correctness is true. The thesis would then provide a solid basis for the argument that morality is necessarily included in the law.

The inclusion of morality in the law helps to solve problems, but it also creates problems that one might well be able to circumvent if one followed the positivist's separation thesis. The problems which the inclusion of morality can help to solve are, first, the problem of basic evaluations underlying and justifying the law, second, the problem of realizing the claim to correctness in the creation and the application of law, and third, the problem of the limits of law.

[16] Robert Alexy, *The Argument from Injustice. A Reply to Legal Positivism* (1992), trans. Bonnie Litschewski Paulson and Stanley L. Paulson (Oxford: Clarendon Press, 2002), 35–9.

[17] Justice is a special case of correctness, if justice can be defined as correctness of distribution and compensation; see Robert Alexy, 'Giustizia come correttezza', *Ragion pratica* 9 (1997), 103–13, at 105.

[18] Robert Alexy, 'Law and Correctness', trans. Kirsten Bock, *Current Legal Problems* 51 (1998), 205–21, at 213–14 (in this volume: Chapter 21, 312–25, at 319–20).

One aspect of the problem of basic evaluations has already appeared when the relation between law and coercion has been classified as a practical necessity. The concept of a practical necessity is ambiguous. A weak interpretation only refers to a means–end relation, where one treats the choice of the ends merely as a matter of fact or only as hypothetical. This is the import of Hart's concept of 'natural necessity' if one understands the ends only as 'some very obvious generalizations ... concerning human nature and the world in which men live'.[19] The picture begins to change, however, if the general ends of law, like legal certainty and the protection of basic rights, are considered as requirements of practical reason, and it changes completely if these requirements are considered as necessary elements of the law. Such a strong interpretation of the concept of practical necessity would provide an evaluative or normative basis of the law.

The second problem which the inclusion of morality promises to solve is the realization of the claim to correctness within the institutional framework of the law. An example is legal reasoning in hard cases. Once morality is conceived of as included by the law, moral reasons can and must participate in the justification of legal decisions when authoritative reasons run out. The theory of legal reasoning attempts to grasp this by conceiving of legal reasoning as a special case of general practical reasoning.

The third problem, which seems best solved by means of the inclusion of morality in the law, is that of the limits of law. If extreme injustice is not to be considered as law—at least from the point of view of a participant in the legal system—how should this be justified without recourse to moral reasons?[20]

All of this, however, represents only the one side. The other side is, as already mentioned, that the inclusion of morality in the law creates serious problems. One of the main reasons for the authoritative and institutionalized structure of law is the general uncertainty of moral reasoning. Moral disputes tend to be endless. Often in social life a consensus cannot be achieved by discourse. For reasons of practical necessity an authoritative decision must, then, be substituted. This would, however, only be an argument for conceiving of moral reasoning as not belonging to law were it not possible to incorporate moral reasoning into legal reasoning without destroying the necessary authoritative elements of the latter. It is a main task of legal philosophy to consider whether or not this is possible.

A second problem is far more serious. It is the problem of whether moral knowledge or moral justification is possible at all. If the meta-ethical theses of subjectivism, relativism, non-cognitivism, or emotivism should prove to be true, the claim to correctness would have to be interpreted in terms of something like an 'error theory', as Mackie has suggested.[21] This shows that law, by incorporating

19 Hart, *The Concept of Law* (n. 15 above), 192–3.

20 Alexy, *The Argument from Injustice* (n. 16 above), 40–62.

21 John Mackie, *Ethics. Inventing Right and Wrong* (London: Pelican, 1977), 35.

morality *via* the claim to correctness, finds itself encumbered with the epistemological problems of moral knowledge and justification. This is not a small burden.

At the beginning of our deliberations we distinguished three main questions of philosophy: the ontological question of what there is, the ethical or practical question of what ought to be done or is good, and the epistemological question of what we can know. Our way through the fields of legal philosophy has shown that legal philosophy confronts all three kinds of questions. This already seems to be more than can be achieved by one person. But there is more. The reflective and systematic nature of legal philosophy demands that all these questions be connected in a coherent theory, which, for its part, must be as close to law as possible in order to guarantee that what it makes explicit really is the nature of law. In this way, our reflections about the nature of legal philosophy end with the exposition of an ideal.

2

On the Concept and the Nature of Law

The debate over the concept and the nature of law is both venerable and lively. Reaching back more than two millennia, it has acquired in our own days a degree of sophistication hitherto unknown.

I. The Practical and Theoretical Significance of the Debate

There are practical as well as theoretical reasons for the persistence and vivacity of the issue, and these two features are closely connected. To define the concept of law or to determine its nature is to say what law is. Every jurist in every legal system has a more or less clear idea about what law is; were it otherwise, the jurist would not be able to identify what the law requires in a given legal system. In the ordinary run of cases, no problems arise. To engage in reasoning about the concept or the nature of law would be out of place. Things are different, however, in extraordinary cases.

A. Statutory Injustice and the Radbruch Formula

Historically, the single most spectacular class of extraordinary cases concerns statutory injustice. One example is the Eleventh Ordinance, 25 November 1941, issued pursuant to the Statute on Reich Citizenship of 15 September 1935, which stripped emigrant Jews of German citizenship and of all their property.[1] The Eleventh Ordinance had been duly issued and was socially efficacious. According to the positivistic concept of law, which defines law exclusively by appeal to authoritative issuance and social efficacy,[2] that is, as a social fact,[3] the Eleventh Ordinance had, indeed, served to deprive all emigrant German Jews of their citizenship and property.

By contrast, the German Federal Supreme Court[4] and the German Federal Constitutional Court[5] have pursued a non-positivistic line. The jurisprudential

[1] Robert Alexy, 'A Defence of Radbruch's Formula', in *Recrafting the Rule of Law: The Limits of Legal Order*, ed. David Dyzenhaus (Oxford: Hart, 1999), 15–39, at 18–19.

[2] Robert Alexy, *The Argument from Injustice. A Reply to Legal Positivism* (1992), trans. Bonnie Litschewski Paulson and Stanley L. Paulson (Oxford: Clarendon Press, 2002), 3, 14–19.

[3] Joseph Raz, 'Legal Positivism and the Sources of Law', in Raz, *The Authority of Law. Essay on Law and Morality*, 2nd edn (Oxford: Oxford University Press, 2009), 37–52, at 41, 47.

[4] Decisions of the German Federal Supreme Court in Civil Cases (BGHZ), 16, 350 (353–4).

[5] Decisions of the German Federal Constitutional Court (BVerfGE), 23, 98 (106).

Law's Ideal Dimension. Robert Alexy, Oxford University Press. © Robert Alexy 2021.
DOI: 10.1093/oso/9780198796831.003.0003

core of their reasoning is found in Gustav Radbruch's Formula. Here only the first part[6] of the Formula is of interest. It says that

> [t]he positive law, secured by legislation and power, takes precedence even when its content is unjust and fails to benefit the people, unless the conflict between statute and justice reaches such an intolerable degree that the statute, as 'flawed law', must yield to justice.[7]

Perhaps the most important feature of the Radbruch Formula as an expression of a non-positivistic concept of law is that it does not require any sort of complete fit as between law and morality. That is, appropriately issued and socially efficacious norms may well be valid law even where they prove to be severely unjust. It is only when the threshold of intolerable injustice is crossed that appropriately issued and socially efficacious norms lose their legal validity. In this way, the non-positivistic concept of law builds into law an outermost limit.

Along with the term 'intolerable' (*unerträglich*), Radbruch uses the expression 'horrendous' (*horrend*)[8] in order to designate the borderline. The term 'extreme' seems, however, to be more suitable than either 'intolerable' or 'horrible' where expressing the idea of a threshold located at the upper end of a scale is concerned. The shortest conceivable form of the Radbruch Formula would then run as follows:

> Extreme injustice is no law.

Anyone who endorses this formula has not only accepted non-positivism as a theoretical view but is also advocating a substantive legal thesis with direct practical consequences.

B. Law's Open Texture and the Self-Understanding of Jurists

Nowhere is the practical impact of questions about the concept and the nature of law more obvious than in cases of extreme statutory injustice found in a rogue regime. The debate between legal positivism and legal non-positivism has, however, practical consequences not only in spectacular cases but also in the everyday life of law. The everyday life of law is full of hard cases that cannot be decided simply on the basis of what has been authoritatively issued. *Contra legem* decisions are the most conspicuous examples, but jurists also have to have recourse to non-authoritative

[6] On the second part see Alexy, 'A Defence of Radbruch's Formula' (n. 1 above), 15–16.

[7] Gustav Radbruch, 'Statutory Lawlessness and Supra-Statutory Law' (1946), trans. Bonnie Litschewski Paulson and Stanley L. Paulson, *Oxford Journal of Legal Studies* 26 (2006), 1–11, at 7.

[8] Gustav Radbruch, *Vorschule der Rechtsphilosophie* (1948), in *Gustav Radbruch Gesamtausgabe*, ed. Arthur Kaufmann, vol. 3 (Heidelberg: C. F. Müller, 1990), 121–227, at 154.

reasons in cases of gaps, in cases of conflicts between norms that can only be solved by weighing or balancing, and—the most frequent and least spectacular constellation—in cases of vagueness of the language of law or indeterminacy of the intentions of the law-maker. If legal decisions are to be based on reasons, then where authoritative reasons run out, the reasons for legal decisions will have to include non-authoritative reasons. Among these non-authoritative reasons, the most important class consists of reasons referring to justice. Questions of justice are, however, moral questions. This implies that the open texture of law[9] renders a non-arbitrary, justified application of law without moral reasoning impossible.

Now there exists a broad consensus between positivists and non-positivists to the effect that moral arguments are indispensable to legal reasoning or argumentation.[10] The point of disagreement lies in how this is to be interpreted. According to non-positivism the moral arguments that are indispensable for a well-grounded answer to a legal question are necessarily incorporated into the law. Positivism in its weaker version, known as inclusive positivism, rejects the idea that this incorporation is necessary. And, going beyond this, the stronger version of positivism, known as exclusive positivism, maintains that such an incorporation is necessarily excluded, for—so the argument goes—moral reasons *qua* moral reasons are necessarily non-authoritative reasons, and law comprises only authoritative reasons.

This debate is, first and foremost, a debate about the self-understanding of jurists. If law and morality are separated, as positivism insists they must be, then jurists have to distinguish between two points of view in applying the law: the legal point of view and the moral point of view. On the basis of this distinction, moral wickedness has as such no influence on the legal merits of the decision. If, however, law and morality are necessarily connected, then moral wickedness does have an effect on law. Given this condition, morally wicked decisions cannot be legally perfect in all respects. This difference in self-understanding has, unlike the Radbruch Formula, no direct effects on the content of the decisions made. But one may assume that legal decision-making is influenced by the self-understanding of those who decide. In this sense, the difference in self-understanding has indirect consequences. These indirect consequences of the self-understanding of jurists are an essential part of the practical impact of the debate about the concept and nature of law.

C. The Concept of Law as a Concept of a Non-Natural Kind

If the debate about the concept and the nature of law were only of practical significance, it would simply be one more dispute in law, a most abstract dispute certainly, but it would not have any special character. It has, however, a special character, and

[9] See H. L. A. Hart, *The Concept of Law*, 2nd edn (Oxford: Clarendon Press, 1994), 128.

[10] Joseph Raz, 'The Autonomy of Legal Reasoning', *Ratio Juris* 6 (1993), 1–15, at 7–9.

this is due to its theoretical significance. The debate over the concept and the nature of law is a debate over necessary truths about the law. The truth of the controversial claims in question turns in no way on this or that aspect of the historical development of the legal system. That it does not is a reflection of the status of the issue, namely, as one part of a genuinely philosophical debate. The fact that this philosophical debate has practical consequences, that is, consequences for the law of the land, underscores the fact that law and philosophy are necessarily connected.[11]

What has been said thus far, however, will not suffice for one who wishes to understand what is truly at stake in the debate over the concept and the nature of law. The debate is not only philosophical in character but has, as well, a more specific philosophical interest.

The concept of law refers to an entity that connects the real and the ideal in a necessary way. Notwithstanding its anchorage in the real world, law cannot be reduced to a concept referring to a natural kind or object—such as the concepts of water, black holes, or killing. The concept of law is a paradigm concept of a non-natural kind that is intrinsically related to natural kinds. The analysis of such a concept would be of interest for reasons philosophical in nature even if the analysis had no practical legal consequences—which, however, it indeed has.

II. Positivism and Non-Positivism

A. Separation Thesis and Connection Thesis

The controversy between positivism and non-positivism is a dispute about the relationship between law and morality. All positivists defend the *separation thesis.* In its most general form, the thesis says that there is no necessary connection between the law as it is and the law as it ought to be.

In a more precise version, it states that there is no necessary connection between legal validity or legal correctness on the one hand, and moral merits and demerits or moral correctness and incorrectness on the other.[12] By contrast, all

[11] See Robert Alexy, 'On Two Juxtapositions: Concept and Nature, Law and Philosophy. Some Comments on Joseph Raz's "Can There Be a Theory of Law?"', *Ratio Juris* 20 (2007), 162–9, at 166–9.

[12] The separation thesis is sometimes expressed by means of the simple phrase: 'There is no necessary connection between law and morality.' If this is interpreted as shorthand for the more precise version: 'There is no necessary connection between legal validity or legal correctness on the one hand, and moral merits and demerits or moral correctness and incorrectness on the other', this creates no problems. It is, however, possible to interpret the first phrase in such a way that its negation, that is, 'There are necessary connections between law and morality', is compatible with positivism. Raz has done so by referring the concept of a necessary connection to relations between law and morality that have, as such, nothing to do with the moral merits of law or its moral correctness. One of his examples runs as follows: 'Given value pluralism, necessarily no state or legal system can manifest' to the highest degree 'all the virtues or all the vices there are' (Joseph Raz, 'About Morality and the Nature of Law', *The American Journal of Jurisprudence* 48 (2003), 1–15, at 3). If value pluralism is, as Raz proposes,

non-positivists defend the *connection thesis*, which says that there is a necessary connection between legal validity or legal correctness on the one hand, and moral merits and demerits or moral correctness and incorrectness on the other.

B. Exclusive and Inclusive Positivism

Both the separation thesis and the connection thesis lend themselves to a variety of different interpretations. In order to make clear what is at issue in the dispute between positivism and non-positivism, it is well to take a look at the basic positions. The competing positions in our never-ending debate can only be fully understood by way of their opposites.

Within positivism, the distinction between exclusive and inclusive positivism is the most important division where the relation between law and morality is concerned. Exclusive positivism, as advocated most prominently by Joseph Raz, maintains that morality is necessarily excluded from the concept of law.[13] Exclusive positivism stands in a relation of contrariety to non-positivism, which claims that morality is necessarily included in the concept of law, that is to say, necessarily not excluded therefrom. Inclusive positivism, as defended, for instance, by Jules Coleman, counts as the rejection of both exclusive positivism and non-positivism. It says that morality is neither necessarily excluded nor necessarily included. The inclusion is declared to be a contingent or conventional matter[14] turning on what the positive law in fact says.[15] Non-positivism, in arguing not only that morality is

'[d]efined as the existence of a plurality of values which cannot be instantiated in the life of any single human being' (ibid.), than it is, indeed, necessarily true that no legal system can realize or help to realize to the highest degree all competing moral values. This necessity, however, is a logical necessity concerning the relation between legal systems and competing moral values. It has no direct bearing on the problem of positivism, for it has, as such, nothing to do with the relation between legal validity or legal correctness, on the one hand, and moral merits or moral correctness, on the other. In order to bear on this relation, a premise such as 'All values have to be treated equally by law' would have to be added. If such a premise, or its negation, were necessarily connected with law, Raz's example would become relevant to the problem of positivism. But this is not what he maintains. Something similar is true of Raz's other examples of necessary relations between law and morality; see Robert Alexy, 'Agreements and Disagreements', *Anales de la Cátedra Francisco Suárez* 39 (2005), 737–42, at 739–40.

[13] Raz, 'Legal Positivism and the Sources of Law' (n. 3 above), 47.

[14] Jules Coleman, 'Authority and Reason', in *The Autonomy of Law*, ed. Robert P. George (Oxford: Clarendon Press, 1996), 287–319, at 316. The difference between inclusive and exclusive positivism allows for a further distinction, that between a separability thesis and a separation thesis. Inclusive positivism argues only for separability, whereas exclusive positivism insists on separation. For reasons of simplification, however, no use will be made of this distinction. The separation thesis as defined above relates, strictly speaking, to separability, because it does not say that there are necessarily no connections, but only that there are no necessary connections. Separation, however, implies separability. To reject separability is, therefore, to reject separation. This allows for the simpler terminology used here.

[15] It might be noted, in passing, that about half a century earlier, Hans Kelsen had already introduced the main thesis of what is now termed 'inclusive positivism': 'In applying a statute, there may well be room for cognitive activity beyond discovering the frame within which the act of application is to be

not necessarily excluded but also that it is necessarily included, is contrary to both forms of positivism.[16]

C. Exclusive, Inclusive, and Super-Inclusive Non-Positivism

Recently the division between exclusive and inclusive positivism has attracted a great deal of attention. This has not been the case, however, where divisions within non-positivism are concerned. Still, the differences within non-positivism are no less important for the debate over the concept and the nature of law than the differences within positivism.

The differences within non-positivism that are relevant here stem from different effects on legal validity that are attributable to moral defects. Non-positivism can determine the effect on legal validity that stems from moral defects or demerits in three different ways. It might be the case that legal validity is lost in all cases, or it might be the case that legal validity is lost in some cases and not in others, or, finally, it might be the case that legal validity is affected in no way at all.

The first position, according to which every moral defect yields legal invalidity, is the most radical version of non-positivism, and it is only rarely found in the literature. This position might be characterized as 'exclusive non-positivism' in order to express the idea that each moral defect is considered as excluding social

confined; this is not cognition of the positive law, however, but cognition of other norms, which can now make their way into the law-creating process, the norms, namely, of morality, of justice—social value-judgements customarily characterized with the catch-phrases "welfare of the people", "public interest", "progress", and so on. From the standpoint of the positive law, nothing can be said about their validity and whether or not they can be identified. From this vantage-point, all such determinations can only be characterized negatively: they are determinations that do not stem from the positive law itself. In relation to the positive law, the legal act is free of such constraints, that is, the authority called upon to act is free to do so according to his own discretion unless the positive law itself authorizes some metalegal norm such as morality, justice, and so on. This norm, however, would be transformed thereby into a norm of the positive law.' (Hans Kelsen, *Introduction to the Problems of Legal Theory* (1934), trans. Bonnie Litschewski Paulson and Stanley L. Paulson (Oxford: Clarendon Press, 1992), 83).

[16] One may well ask for a more precise determination of the role played by contradiction, on the one hand, and by contrariety, on the other, in the relationship between and among exclusive positivism, inclusive positivism, and non-positivism. The answer is straightforward. 'I' shall represent 'Law includes morality'. Then, prefacing 'I' with the necessity operator '□' yields '□I'. '□I' expresses non-positivism, namely: 'It is necessary that law include morality'. By contrast, exclusive positivism says: 'It is necessary that law not include morality', that is, '□¬I'. '□I' and '□¬I' stand in a relationship of contrariety for the one excludes the other without stemming from its negation. Inclusive positivism is the conjunction of the negation of both exclusive positivism and non-positivism, namely: '¬□¬I & ¬□I', which says: 'It is neither necessary that law not include morality nor necessary that law include morality.' Each of the members of this conjunction stands in a relationship of contradiction to a position not prefaced by negation, that is, in a relationship of contradiction either to exclusive positivism (□¬I) or to non-positivism (□I). The conjunction as a whole, that is, inclusive positivism, stands to both non-positivism and exclusive positivism in a relationship of contrariety. Each of the three excludes the others without stemming from the negation of any of the others. Thus, the conjunction of the subcontraries reflects a triad, which for its part is understood in terms of contrariety.

facts from the sources of legal validity.[17] An example of exclusive non-positivism is the position defended by Deryck Beyleveld and Roger Brownsword. According to their position 'immoral rules are not legally valid'.[18]

This seems, on first glance, to be rather curious. It looks as if morality completely ruled the law. But this, due to 'the inherently controversial nature of moral issues',[19] would amount to anarchism. Beyleveld and Brownsword are, however, well aware of the problem, and they develop a complex theory to delimit what appear to be the pervasive effects of the conflict between law and morality on legal validity.[20] This seems, however, to be a paradigmatic case of an auxiliary construction that serves, at best, to treat the consequences of a mistake instead of curing the disease as such.[21] The disease as such consists in overlooking the dual nature of law. Law comprises a factual as well as an ideal dimension. This precludes any effort to ground the impact of the factual or authoritative dimension on merely auxiliary considerations. The factual dimension, defined by authoritative issuance and social efficacy, like the ideal dimension, defined by moral correctness, belongs to law from the beginning.

The second version of non-positivism, which might be termed 'inclusive non-positivism', claims that exclusive non-positivism as represented by Beyleveld and Brownsword expresses an unjustified bias towards the ideal dimension of law. Therefore, exclusive non-positivism may be reproached for over-idealization. This mistake can be avoided by means of the Radbruch Formula, which claims neither that moral defects always undermine legal validity nor that they never do so. Moral defects undermine legal validity if and only if the threshold of extreme injustice is transgressed. Beneath this threshold the effects of moral defects are confined to legal defectiveness. This is the version of non-positivism that will be defended here.

Accepting the Radbruch Formula is to adhere to a version of inclusive non-positivism which maintains that legal validity is lost in some cases of moral defects or demerits and not in others. There remains, as mentioned, a third version of non-positivism. It maintains that legal validity is in no way at all affected by moral defects or moral incorrectness. On first glance, this version of inclusive non-positivism looks even more curious than exclusive non-positivism. Is it really possible to remain a non-positivist in claiming that legal validity is in no way affected by moral defects? Does one not thereby revert inevitably and unavoidably to

[17] Robert Alexy, 'Effects of Defects—Action or Argument? Thoughts about Deryck Beyleveld and Roger Brownsword's *Law as a Moral Judgment*', *Ratio Juris* 19 (2006), 169–79, at 173. For a related approach, which, however, uses the expressions 'exclusive' and 'inclusive natural law' in a different way, see Massimo La Torre, 'On Two Distinct and Opposing Versions of Natural Law: "Exclusive" versus "Inclusive"', *Ratio Juris* 19 (2006), 197–216, at 200, 207.

[18] Deryck Beyleveld and Roger Brownsword, *Human Dignity in Bioethics and Biolaw* (Oxford: Oxford University Press, 2001), 76.

[19] Deryck Beyleveld and Roger Brownsword, *Law as a Moral Judgment*, 2nd edn (Sheffield: Sheffield Academic Press, 1994), 369.

[20] Ibid.

[21] Alexy, 'Effects of Defects—Action or Argument? Thoughts about Deryck Beyleveld and Roger Brownsword's Law as a Moral Judgment' (n. 17 above), 171.

positivism? A glance at Kant's theory of law might help us in answering this question, a question that appears to be of some significance for the understanding of the nature of non-positivism.[22] Kant begins with claims that are profoundly non-positivistic in character. Especially important are his assumptions to the effect that there exists an 'innate right' to freedom[23] and that there exists a right, based on nothing other than pure reason, to acquire property,[24] both resting 'only on a priori principles',[25] that is, existing independently of any positive law. Kant's second step leads from non-positive or '*natural law*'[26] to positive law. Kant argues that without a transformation into positive law, these non-positive or natural rights would remain completely without effect. For this reason, everyone has the obligation, established a priori by practical reason, to subject itself to positive legislation and the positive administration of law:

> [B]efore a public lawful condition is established individual human beings, peoples and states can never be secure against violence from one another, since each has its own right to do *what seems right and good to it* and not to be dependent upon another's opinion about this. So, unless it wants to renounce any concepts of right, the first thing it has to resolve upon is the principle that it must leave the state of nature, in which each follows its own judgment, unite itself with all others (with which it cannot avoid interacting), subject itself to a public lawful external coercion, and so enter into a condition in which what is to be recognized as belonging to it is determined *by law* and is allotted to it by adequate *power* (not its own but an external power).[27]

The crucial point of Kant's argument is that the transition from non-positive law to positive law is as radical a step as one can conceive. Once a positive legal system is established, every form of resistance or disobedience by appeal to non-positive or natural rights is prohibited—and, Kant adds, 'this prohibition is *unconditional*'.[28] The prohibition applies even in cases in which the legislator 'has empowered the government to proceed quite violently (tyrannically)'.[29]

[22] Another example might well be the interpretation of Aquinas's concept of 'law in a secondary sense' as found in John Finnis, *Natural Law and Natural Rights*, 2nd edn (Oxford: Oxford University Press, 2011), 364–6.

[23] Immanuel Kant, *The Metaphysics of Morals*, trans. and ed. Mary J. Gregor, in *The Cambridge Edition of the Works of Immanuel Kant. Practical Philosophy* (Cambridge: Cambridge University Press, 1996), 353–603, at 393; AA 6, 237.

[24] Ibid., 406; AA 6, 252.

[25] Ibid., 393; AA 6, 237.

[26] Ibid. (trans. altered).

[27] Ibid., 456; AA 6, 312.

[28] Immanuel Kant, 'On the Common Saying: That May be Correct in Theory, but is of No Use in Practice', trans. and ed. Mary J. Gregor, in *The Cambridge Edition of the Works of Immanuel Kant. Practical Philosophy* (n. 23 above), 273–309, at 298; AA 8, 299.

[29] Ibid.

If one were to follow Jeremy Waldron here, one would have to 'leave Kant in the classic, but honest, predicament of the true legal positivist'.[30] But is this true? The basis of Kant's argument in favour of the strict authority of positive law is the '*idea* of a political constitution as such',[31] without which 'establishing public law',[32] that is, assuring the efficacy of rights, would be impossible. This idea—as with, according to Kant, ideas in general—demands 'the greatest perfection possible'.[33] A 'perfect *legal constitution*',[34] however, would require not only perfect positive authority, but also a perfect realization of the non-positive rights. It would demand that a society be established 'in which *freedom under external laws* to the greatest possible extent is combined with irresistible force'.[35] The concept of idea makes it possible for Kant to connect the complete or '[u]nconditional submission'[36] under positive law with a necessary subjugation of positive law to non-positive law. Law as idea is necessarily a part of the concept of law just as law as fact is. Thus, where positive law fails to meet the demands of law *qua* idea, this has the effect of rendering positive law not only morally defective, but also legally defective. When Kant talks about a 'perfect *legal constitution*' or about 'grave defects and gross faults'[37] of a constitution, he has precisely this in mind. A theory of law, however, that not only bases the validity of positive law on principles that are non-positivistic in character—as normative positivism does—but, over and above this, also makes positive law's quality of being *legally* defective necessarily dependent on non-positivistic principles, is a non-positivistic theory of law. To be sure, the fact remains that each and every norm, if only authoritatively issued and socially efficacious, has to be classified by this version of non-positivism as a legally valid norm. That is, every norm based on social facts is a legally valid norm. The connection between law and morality is, therefore, not a classifying one, but only an ideal or qualifying one.[38] This, however, suffices to establish a necessary connection between law and morality, a connection that cannot be reconciled with the positivistic separation thesis. For this reason, it seems to be preferable to conceive of theories such as that of Kant's not as positivistic theories, as Waldron

[30] Jeremy Waldron, 'Kant's Legal Positivism', *Harvard Law Review* 109 (1996), 1535–66, at 1566.
[31] Kant, *The Metaphysics of Morals* (n. 23 above), 505 (trans. altered); AA 6, 372.
[32] Ibid., 506 (trans. altered); AA 6, 372.
[33] Immanuel Kant, *Critique of Pure Reason*, trans. Werner S. Pluhar (Indianapolis, Ind.: Hackett, 1996), 364; A 317, B 374.
[34] Kant, *The Metaphysics of Morals* (n. 23 above), 505 (trans. altered); AA 6, 371.
[35] Immanuel Kant, 'Idea for a Universal History with a Cosmopolitan Purpose', trans. H. B. Nisbet, ed. Hans Reiss, in Kant, *Political Writings*, 2nd edn (Cambridge: Cambridge University Press, 1991), 41–53, at 45 (trans. altered); AA 8, 22. Kant uses both the concept of a 'perfect *legal constitution*' (Kant, *The Metaphysics of Morals* (n. 23 above), 505 (trans. altered); AA 6, 371) and the concept of a 'perfectly *just civil constitution*' (Kant, 'Idea for a Universal History with a Cosmopolitan Purpose', 46; AA 8, 22). These two concepts are connected by the fact that, according to Kant, a constitution that is not perfectly just is not a perfect legal constitution.
[36] Kant, *The Metaphysics of Morals* (n. 23 above), 506; AA 6, 372.
[37] Ibid., 505 (trans. altered); AA 6, 372.
[38] See Alexy, *The Argument from Injustice* (n. 2 above), 26.

proposes, but as non-positivistic theories. Without any doubt, such theories count as fairly extreme versions of non-positivism. They represent the highest degree conceivable of the inclusiveness of non-positivism. For that reason, this version of non-positivism might be termed 'super-inclusive non-positivism'. Owing to its radical character, super-inclusive non-positivism is exposed to objections quite similar to those raised against exclusive non-positivism. Whereas exclusive non-positivism expresses an unjustified bias towards the ideal dimension of law, super-inclusive non-positivism expresses a doubtful bias in favour of law's real or factual dimension. The reproach of over-idealization that has been put forward against exclusive non-positivism has its counterpart in the reproach of paying too little heed to the ideal dimension of law that must be raised against super-inclusive non-positivism.

III. Concept and Nature

The debate within non-positivism as well as the debate between non-positivism and the different forms of positivism is a debate over the concept and the nature of law. The question of how to resolve such a debate depends on what the concept and the nature of a thing is. These questions lead one to the very heart of philosophy. Only certain aspects can be taken up here.

A. Nature

Enquiring into the nature of something is to enquire into its necessary properties. Thus, for the question 'What is the nature of law?' one may substitute the question 'What are the necessary properties of law?' Necessary properties that are specific to the law are essential properties of law.[39] Essential or necessary properties of law are those properties without which law would not be law. They must be there, quite apart from space and time, wherever and whenever law exists. Thus, necessary or essential properties are at the same time universal characteristics of law. Legal philosophy *qua* enquiry into the nature of law is, therefore, an enterprise universalistic in nature.

To be sure, the question as to whether there exist necessary properties of law, properties that define its nature, can be contested and has often been contested. Here the thesis will be defended that law necessarily comprises a real or factual and an ideal or critical dimension. This might be termed the dual-nature thesis. A central element of the real dimension of law is coercion or force. A central element

[39] Robert Alexy, 'The Nature of Legal Philosophy', *Ratio Juris* 17 (2004), 156–67, at 163 (in this volume: Chapter 1, 7–17, at 13).

of its ideal dimension is a claim to correctness, which includes a claim to moral correctness and which, if violated, implies legal defectiveness in normal cases and legal invalidity in extreme cases. With an eye to establishing that both coercion and the claim to correctness are necessary or essential properties of law, appeals to intuitions are of no help at all. Talk about the nature of law makes sense only if arguments are at hand. In this way, the question of the nature of law leads directly to the question of arguments about the nature of law.

B. Concept

At exactly this point a bridge can be constructed between the nature and the concept of law, for arguments about the nature of law stand in a close relation to arguments about the concept of law. Close relations, however, do not exclude differences. According to Joseph Raz, the difference between concept and nature is fundamental. The concept of law is said to be parochial, whereas the nature of law is universal:

> While *the concept* of law is parochial, that is, not all societies have it, our inquiry is universal in that it explores *the nature* of law wherever it is to be found.[40]

The 'parochial nature'[41] of the concept, Raz contends, is not a property specific to the concept of law. Rather, it is a characteristic of all concepts: 'all concepts are parochial'.[42] The reason for this is that they are 'the product of a specific culture'.[43]

Only the concept of law is of interest here. Is it really the case that the concept of law can be distinguished from the nature of law on the ground that the former is parochial, that is, particular, whereas the latter is universal? One has to answer, yes and no. The reason for this mixed reply turns on the twofold character of concepts. To be sure, the genesis of concepts depends on culture. As products of a culture, concepts are socially established rules that concern the meaning of words. To this extent, concepts have a conventional character. They are conventional rules of meaning. But concepts—and this is the other side of the coin—are conventions of a special kind. They claim, as Kant puts it, to be 'adequate to the object'.[44] In this

[40] Joseph Raz, 'Can There Be a Theory of Law?' in *The Blackwell Guide to the Philosophy of Law and Legal Theory*, eds Martin P. Golding and William A. Edmundson (Oxford: Blackwell, 2005), 324–42, at 332.

[41] Ibid., 335.

[42] Joseph Raz, 'On the Nature of Law', *Archives for Philosophy of Law and Social Philosophy* 82 (1996), 1–25, at 5.

[43] Ibid.

[44] Kant, *Critique of Pure Reason* (n. 33 above), 680; A 728, B 756. In this context Kant refers, among other things, to the concepts of water, gold, and law.

way, they are intrinsically related to the correctness or truth of the propositions constructed by means of them. This claim to adequacy necessarily connects the concept of a thing with its nature. With concepts—as part of a practice that is intrinsically connected with truth, justification, intersubjectivity, validity, objectivity, and reality—one strives to grasp the nature of the things to which they refer as perfectly, as correctly, as possible. This is the non-conventional or ideal dimension of concepts. To the degree to which those who use a concept are successful in fulfilling the claim to adequacy necessarily raised by the use of that concept, to that degree the concept corresponds to the nature of its object. And it has universal validity to the degree it corresponds to its object. Thus, the ascription of parochiality to concepts has to be restricted. Concepts, as always on the path to the nature of those things to which they refer, are in part parochial or conventional and in part universal.

This dual nature of concepts explains why an analysis of the concept of law can be, at the same time, an analysis of the nature of law. If 'concept' is understood as 'adequate concept', the question 'What is the concept of law?' can always be substituted for the question 'What is the nature of law?' and vice versa. This is the reason why H. L. A. Hart's *The Concept of Law* can be read as a book about the concept of law and equally well as a book about the nature of law.

This is not to say, however, that the other side of the coin, that is, concepts as conventional rules of meaning, has no role in philosophical analysis. Concepts as conventional rules are indispensable for the identification of the object of analysis. Without a concept of law *qua* conventional rule, we would not know what we are referring to when we undertake an analysis of the nature of law. Moreover, while the analysis of the actual use of language is, as J. L. Austin aptly remarks, '*not* the last word', it provides a starting point for analysis, as a '*first* word'.[45]

IV. The Dual Nature of Law

The basis of non-positivism as defended here is the thesis that the single- most essential feature of law is its dual nature. The thesis of the dual nature of law presupposes that there exist necessary properties of law belonging to its factual or real dimension, as well as necessary properties belonging to its ideal or critical dimension. Coercion is an essential feature found on the factual side, whereas the claim to correctness is constitutive of the ideal dimension.

[45] John L. Austin, 'A Plea for Excuses', in Austin, *Philosophical Papers*, 2nd edn, eds J. O. Urmson and G. J. Warnock (Oxford: Oxford University Press, 1970), 175–204, at 185.

A. Coercion

The necessity of coercion or force is the easier case. It seems to be quite natural to argue, first, that a system of rules or norms that in no case whatever authorizes the use of coercion or sanction—not even in the case of self-defence—is not a legal system, and that, second, this is the case owing to conceptual reasons reflected in the actual use of language. Would anyone be inclined to use the expression 'law' in connection with such a system of rules? Conceptual reasons of this kind, however, have little force of their own. Concepts reflected in the actual use of language are, as already explained, in need of modification once they prove not to be adequate to their object or—to put it in another way—once a divergence from the nature of the objects to which they refer appears. It is of course possible not only to argue for the inadequacy of a concept but also to defend its adequacy. To include coercion in the concept of law is adequate to its object, the law, because it mirrors a practical necessity essentially connected with law.[46] Coercion is necessary if law is to be a social practice that fulfils its basic formal purposes as defined by the values of legal certainty and efficiency. This practical necessity is the reason why the conceptual necessity implicit in the use of language is based not merely on a convention but also on the nature of the thing to which the concept refers. It is, in this sense, an absolute necessity.

The argument presented thus far has, however, a weak point. One might grant that coercion is necessarily connected with legal certainty and efficiency but object that there exists no necessary connection between law and either of these values. This leads to the question of how values, purposes, or functions can be conceived as standing in a necessary relation to law.[47] The answer is that they are so connected because the claim to correctness necessarily connected with law necessarily refers to them. The reasons for this answer can only be sketched here. I will confine myself to the value of legal certainty. The argument starts with the assumption that morality as such does not suffice to resolve problems of social coordination and cooperation.[48] The argument continues with the premise that morality demands a resolution of these problems in order to avoid the moral costs of anarchy. To these two premises the statement is added that those problems can only be resolved by law *qua* enterprise that strives to realize the value of legal certainty. From this it

[46] See Robert Alexy, 'The Nature of Arguments about the Nature of Law', in *Rights, Culture, and the Law. Themes from the Legal and Political Philosophy of Joseph Raz*, eds Lukas H. Meyer, Stanley L. Paulson, and Thomas W. Pogge (Oxford: Oxford University Press, 2003), 3–16, at 8–9.

[47] A famous example of a necessary relation of values, purposes, or functions to the law is Radbruch's connection of justice, purposiveness, and legal certainty *qua* elements of the idea of law with the concept of law; Gustav Radbruch, *Legal Philosophy* (1932), trans. Kurt Wilk, in *The Legal Philosophies of Lask, Radbruch, and Dabin* (Cambridge, Mass.: Harvard University Press, 1950), 43–224, at 107–8. See on this Stanley L. Paulson, 'On the Background and Significance of Gustav Radbruch's Post-War Papers', *Oxford Journal of Legal Studies* 26 (2006), 17–40, at 31–2.

[48] Alexy, 'The Nature of Arguments about the Nature of Law' (n. 46 above), 8.

follows that morality requires law *qua* enterprise that strives to realize the value of legal certainty. Moral correctness, therefore, includes the demand of law *qua* enterprise that strives for legal certainty. This will suffice to establish a necessary connection between law and the value of legal certainty provided that two further theses are true. The first says that law necessarily raises a claim to correctness, the second says that this claim necessarily comprises moral correctness. Something more on this will be said in the next section. Here it shall only be noted that the correctness thesis, if true, plays a central role not only with respect to the ideal or critical dimension of law but also with respect to its factual or real dimension. The reason for this is that moral correctness comprises formal or procedural as well as substantive or material correctness.

As far as the dispute between positivism and non-positivism is concerned, the most pressing problems occur on the substantive side of the claim to correctness, namely, where formal correctness is accompanied by substantive incorrectness, in particular, by extreme substantive incorrectness.[49] In what follows, two questions will be addressed: first, whether moral incorrectness necessarily brings about legal incorrectness, and, second, whether, as per the Radbruch Formula, extreme moral incorrectness necessarily results in legal invalidity.

B. Correctness

With respect to the thesis that the claim of law to correctness is the source of a necessary relation between law and morality, that is, the correctness thesis, three objections arise. According to the first objection, it is not true that law necessarily raises a claim to correctness. There can be law quite apart from such a claim. The answer to this objection consists in demonstrating that the claim to correctness is necessarily implicit in law. The best means of demonstration is by means of the method of performative contradictions.[50] An example of a performative contradiction is the fictitious first article of a constitution that reads: '*X* is a sovereign, federal, and unjust republic.' It is scarcely possible to deny that this article is somehow absurd. The idea underlying the method of performative contradiction is to explain the absurdity as stemming from a contradiction between what is implicitly claimed in framing a constitution, namely, that it is just, and what is explicitly declared, namely, that it is unjust. Much could be said about whether this explanation is sound, and whether it really shows that the claim to justice, which is a special

[49] This does not mean that the problems found on the formal side of the claim to correctness can be neglected. It is the main tenet of positivism that the legal validity of a norm depends on its sources and not on its merits or demerits. Given this tenet, not only substantive but also formal merits and demerits are excluded as criteria of legal validity. See John Gardner, 'Legal Positivism: 5½ Myths', *The American Journal of Jurisprudence* 46 (2001), 199–227, at 208–10.

[50] Alexy, *The Argument from Injustice* (n. 2 above), 35–9.

case of the broader claim to correctness,[51] is necessarily raised. This point will not, however, be elaborated here. The question of whether law necessarily raises a claim to correctness is not the main issue with respect to correctness in the debate over positivism versus non-positivism. No less a proponent of positivism than Joseph Raz, when he argues 'that the law necessarily claims legitimate authority',[52] comes quite close to the thesis that law necessarily raises a claim to correctness.

The second possible objection to the correctness thesis grants the point that law raises a claim to correctness but contests the view that the claim of law to correctness has anything to do with morality. With an eye to meeting this objection, one addresses those cases in which first, the reasons based on positive law—that is, source-based reasons—have run out, and second, reasons based on justice—that is, moral reasons—are available. In order to meet the objection, one has to show that in such cases, the decision at issue has to be grounded on moral reasons. This point, too, will not be elaborated here, for it, too, is not a point crucial for the question of whether positivism or non-positivism is right. A positivist can grant the point that law's claim to correctness comprises a claim to moral correctness but contest the claim that this amounts to a necessary connection between legal validity or legal correctness and morality. Raz's thesis 'that it is essential to the law that it claims to have legitimate, *moral*, authority'[53] seems to fit this reading of law's claim to correctness well.

The third objection is the decisive one. It grants the point that law necessarily raises a claim to correctness and that this claim is necessarily connected with morality, but it goes on to insist that all this is compatible with positivism as well as with non-positivism. It is with this thesis that I should like to take issue.

Perhaps an example will be helpful. Let us imagine a case in which the authoritative material allows for two different interpretations. A single additional argument is available, which is a moral argument that cannot either be reduced or traced back to a source. The moral argument speaks in favour of the first interpretation, rejecting, then, the second interpretation. I think that non-positivists are in agreement here with positivists who, like Joseph Raz, assume that 'judges are subject to morality anyway'.[54] That is, we ought to adopt the first interpretation, backed by the correct moral argument, and not the morally mistaken second interpretation. Still, positivists and non-positivists disagree sharply on how to understand or interpret this.[55] Positivists say that we have to interpret what takes

[51] Justice counts as a special case of correctness, for justice can be defined as correctness of distribution and compensation. See Robert Alexy, 'Giustizia come correttezza', *Ragion pratica* 9 (1997), 103–13, at 105.

[52] Raz, 'On the Nature of Law' (n. 42 above), 16.

[53] Ibid., 6 (emphasis added).

[54] Joseph Raz, 'Incorporation by Law', *Legal Theory* 10 (2004), 1–17, at 12.

[55] Raz describes the reasoning that has to take place in such cases as reasoning 'about how legal disputes should be settled according to law' or as reasoning 'about how courts should decide cases in accordance with law'; Raz 'The Autonomy of Legal Reasoning' (n. 10 above), 2–3. This seems to allow for

place as a law-making act that transforms moral considerations into law on the basis of legal empowerment and legal empowerment alone. If this thesis were true, if from a legal point of view it were merely a question of law-making or issuance based on legal power, then, if the judge chose the morally mistaken interpretation, he would nevertheless be making a legally perfect decision, a decision that counts in all legal aspects as being at the highest level. My rejoinder is that this decision would not be a legally perfect decision in all aspects. Due to the fact that the claim to correctness necessarily raised by law necessarily comprises an ideal dimension as well as an authoritative dimension, a judge who chose a morally mistaken interpretation in a case in which the positive law allows as well for a morally correct interpretation would not be making a legally perfect decision. In such cases, moral incorrectness implies legal incorrectness. To be sure, there are many cases that are far more complex than the simple constellation set out here. This constellation suffices, however, to show that there exists a necessary connection between moral and legal correctness. This connection has, as such, only a qualifying character.[56] Nevertheless, this qualifying connection brings about a fundamental shift in our picture of law.

V. What the Law Is and What It Ought to Be

The question remains of whether there also exists a classifying connection as defined by the Radbruch Formula, which says that extreme injustice is not law. To be sure, the Radbruch Formula cannot be deduced from the correctness thesis. The correctness thesis, taken alone, refers only to legal defectiveness. And legal defectiveness as such does not imply legal invalidity. This is a corollary of the dual nature of law. Law is, at one and the same time, essentially authoritative and essentially ideal. All defects on the ideal side are legal defects, but by no means all of these defects have the wherewithal to undermine what has been established as law by the authoritative side. To take this further step, additional reasons are necessary.

These additional reasons must comprise moral reasons. Moral reasons are normative reasons. The moral or normative reasons standing behind the Radbruch Formula comprise human or fundamental rights. This makes it possible to give expression to non-positivism in normative terms: '[A] non-positivistic concept of

three different interpretations, namely, that the moral reasoning in the open area of law is reasoning 'according to law' or 'in accordance with law', first, because it does not violate the law, or, second, because it is required by some sources of the respective legal system, or, third, because it is required by the law *qua* law. The third reading, however, would lead to non-positivism.

[56] On the concept of a qualifying connection see Alexy, *The Argument from Injustice* (n. 2 above), 26; see also Robert Alexy 'On the Thesis of a Necessary Connection between Law and Morality: Bulygin's Critique', *Ratio Juris* 13 (2000), 138–47, at 144–6.

law must of necessity be applied in order to protect the fundamental rights of the citizen.'[57] It is at exactly this point that one of the main problems of non-positivism comes to light. It can be cast in terms of the following question: 'Is it possible to apply normative arguments in order to determine the nature and the concept of law?' My answer is affirmative.

On first glance, however, a negative answer may seem to be right. To determine the nature of law is to say what the law is, and, as noted, the concept of law has to be defined with an eye to its nature. Is there any basis for considering how the law ought to be as a step in determining what the law is? It comes as no surprise to learn that positivists stress just this point. Raz, for instance, argues that the nature of law is a matter of theory and not of advocacy, and that theory is concerned exclusively with 'how things are'.[58] Similarly, Andrei Marmor insists:

> Once we admit that in order to get to something like the Radbruch formula, you need a normative argument, you rely on a moral argument to tell us something about the law. It is no longer the case that the conclusion is about the nature of law. As simple as that.[59]

Is it really as simple as that?

The reasons as to why it is more complex stem from the fact that it is a part of the nature of law that there exists an observer's perspective as well as a participant's perspective.[60] The difference between these two perspectives is that the observer asks and adduces arguments on behalf of a position that reflects how legal questions are actually decided in a legal system, whereas the participant asks and adduces arguments on behalf of what he deems to be the correct answer to a legal question in the legal system in which he finds himself. The observer's perspective is defined by the question 'How are legal decisions actually made?', the participant's by the question 'What is the correct legal answer?'

These two perspectives correspond to two different views about what the law is: a restricted view and a comprehensive view. According to the restricted view, what the law is depends exclusively on what has actually been issued and is socially efficacious. It is a matter of social fact. According to the comprehensive view, what the law is depends on what it is correctly taken to be. This view constitutes the participant's perspective. What is correctly taken to be the law depends not only on social facts but also on moral correctness. In this way, what the law ought to be finds its way into what the law is. This serves to explain the Radbruch Formula,

[57] Alexy, *The Argument from Injustice* (n. 2 above), 58.

[58] Raz, 'On The Nature of Law' (n. 42 above), 7.

[59] Andrei Marmor, 'Debate', *Anales de la Cátedra Francisco Suárez* 39 (2005), 769–93, at 778.

[60] See, on the one hand, Joseph Raz, 'The Argument from Justice, or How not to Reply to Legal Positivism', in *Law, Rights and Discourse*, ed. George Pavlakos (Oxford: Hart, 2007), 17–35, at 22–5, and, on the other, Robert Alexy, 'An Answer to Joseph Raz', ibid., 37–55, at 45–8.

which says not that 'extreme injustice should not be law' but, rather, that 'extreme injustice is no law'. Much more could and should be said about the difference between the observer's 'is' and the participant's 'is'. Perhaps what has been said will suffice, however, to indicate what non-positivists mean when they claim that their more complex explication is closer to the nature of law than the simpler explication offered by the positivists.

3

The Dual Nature of Law

The law has a dual nature, and it is this thesis that I wish to explicate. The dual-nature thesis sets out the claim that law necessarily comprises both a real or factual dimension and an ideal or critical one. In the definition of law, the factual dimension is represented by the elements of authoritative issuance and social efficacy, whereas the ideal dimension finds its expression in the element of moral correctness. Authoritative issuance and social efficacy are social facts. If one claims that social facts alone can determine what is and is not required by law, that amounts to the endorsement of a positivistic concept of law. Once moral correctness is added as a necessary third element, the picture changes fundamentally. A non-positivistic concept of law emerges. Therefore, the dual-nature thesis implies non-positivism.

To be sure, as thus stated the dual-nature thesis remains abstract and formal. In order to arrive at concrete content and a clear structure, the thesis has to be explicated within a system. The overarching idea of this system is the institutionalization of reason. The political form manifested by the system is democratic or discursive constitutionalism. The system itself is generated in three steps: the argument on behalf of the ideal dimension of law, the argument on behalf of positivity, that is, the real dimension of law, and the reconciliation of the ideal with the real.

I. The Ideal

A. The Claim to Correctness

At a first step, the ideal dimension of law has to be established. My argument turns on the thesis that law necessarily raises a claim to correctness, and that this claim comprises a claim to moral correctness. This claim to correctness is the source of the necessary relation between law and morality.

1. Law is Capable of Making Claims

Against the correctness thesis many objections have been raised. Four are of special significance. The first contests the notion that law is capable of making claims at all. Neil MacCormick puts it this way: '[L]aw claims nothing.'[1] His argument is,

[1] Neil MacCormick, 'Why Law Makes No Claims', in *Law, Rights and Discourse. The Legal Philosophy of Robert Alexy*, ed. George Pavlakos (Oxford: Hart, 2007), 59–67, at 59.

Law's Ideal Dimension. Robert Alexy, Oxford University Press. © Robert Alexy 2021.
DOI: 10.1093/oso/9780198796831.003.0004

first, that law is a 'normative order', secondly, that normative orders are '[s]tates of affairs', and, thirdly, that states of affairs are, in contrast to persons, incapable of having intentions or making claims.[2]

MacCormick is, without doubt, right in maintaining that law as such is incapable of raising, in a literal sense, any claim. In a literal or strict sense, claims can be raised only by subjects having the capacity to speak and to act.[3] Nevertheless, talk about the claim of law to correctness seems to be sensible because this claim is raised by persons, in particular, though not solely,[4] by officials on behalf of the law. Persons raising the claim to correctness on behalf of the law may be characterized as representatives of the law. The rejection of the first objection, therefore, amounts to the following thesis: law can and does raise a claim to correctness because the claim is made by its representatives.

2. The Necessity of the Claim to Correctness

The second objection denies that the claim to correctness is necessarily raised in law. Whether law raises any claims, and which claims, if any, it raises, are said to be empirical questions. One might call this the 'contingency thesis'. If the contingency thesis were true, the dual-nature thesis, which essentially comprises the concept of necessity, would collapse.

One way of answering this objection is to demonstrate that the claim to correctness is necessarily implicit in law. The best means of demonstration is the method of performative contradiction.[5] An example of a performative contradiction is the fictitious first article of a constitution that reads:

> *X* is a sovereign, federal, and unjust republic.

It is scarcely possible to deny that this article is somehow absurd. The idea underlying the method of performative contradiction is to explain the absurdity as stemming from a contradiction between what is implicitly claimed in framing a constitution, namely, that it is just, and what is explicitly declared, namely, that it is unjust. Now, justice counts as a special case of correctness because justice is nothing other than the correctness of distribution and compensation.[6] Thus, our example shows that law and the claim to correctness are not only, as Eugenio Bulygin argues,[7]

[2] Ibid., 60.

[3] Robert Alexy 'My Philosophy of Law: The Institutionalisation of Reason', in *The Law in Philosophical Perspectives*, ed. Luc J. Wintgens (Dordrecht: Kluwer, 1999), 23–45, at 24.

[4] Robert Alexy, 'Thirteen Replies', in *Law, Rights and Discourse* (n. 1 above), 333–66, at 334–5.

[5] Robert Alexy, *The Argument from Injustice. A Reply to Legal Positivism* (1992), trans. Bonnie Litschewski Paulson and Stanley L. Paulson (Oxford: Clarendon Press, 2002), 35–9.

[6] Robert Alexy, 'Giustizia come correttezza', *Ragion pratica* 9 (1997), 103–13, at 105.

[7] Eugenio Bulygin, 'Alexy und das Richtigkeitsargument', in *Rechtsnorm und Rechtswirklichkeit. Festschrift für Werner Krawietz*, eds Aulis Aarnio, Stanley L. Paulson, Ota Weinberger, et al. (Berlin: Duncker & Humblot, 1993), 19–24, at 23–4.

connected by prudential reasons but also—and more importantly by reasons conceptual in nature. This connection is by no means confined to such fundamental acts as framing a constitution. It is present everywhere in the legal system. The absurdity of decisions such as the following makes this explicit:

> The accused is sentenced to life imprisonment, which is an incorrect interpretation of prevailing law.

It might be objected that conceptual considerations of this kind do not address the issue. The question of whether the representatives of law raise a claim to correctness is a question of fact, and it is a fact that there are representatives who do not raise it. Ronald Dworkin's argument, brought against Raz's thesis that law claims legitimate authority, runs in exactly this direction. According to Dworkin it is a matter of fact that 'many officials do not' make such claims.[8] Oliver Wendell Holmes is said to be an example. According to Dworkin, Justice Holmes was not concerned with moral claims but with 'making the cost of acting in certain ways more expensive'.[9] The reply to this objection draws, as replies often do, on a distinction. It is the distinction between an objective or official and a subjective or private raising of the claim to correctness.[10] When Dworkin talks about the 'actual beliefs or attitudes of officials'[11] he refers to the subjective or private side. This misses the decisive point. Subjectively or privately, officials may believe or feel whatever they wish. But as soon as they act on behalf of the law, that is, as representatives of the law, they cannot avoid making the claim objectively or officially.[12] To be sure, a legal system can degenerate into a system based exclusively on the exercise of brute force. Such a system, however, would not be a legal system but, rather, its very opposite, a system of naked power relations.[13] That the claim to correctness is not raised in such a system is, therefore, no argument against its necessity in a legal system.

3. The Content of the Claim to Correctness

One might concede that law is capable of raising claims and that raising claims is necessary for law, and nevertheless insist that this scarcely counts as an argument on behalf of the dual nature of law. One simply has to argue that the content of the claim does not contain anything pointing in an ideal direction.

[8] Ronald Dworkin, *Justice in Robes* (Cambridge Mass.: Harvard University Press, 2006), 200; see also Eugenio Bulygin, 'Alexy's Thesis of a Necessary Connection between Law and Morality', *Ratio Juris* 13 (2000), 133–7, at 134.

[9] Dworkin, *Justice in Robes* (n. 8 above), 200.

[10] Robert Alexy, 'Law and Correctness', trans. Kirsten Bock, *Current Legal Problems* 51 (1998), 205–21, at 206 (in this volume: Chapter 21, 312–25, at 312–13).

[11] Dworkin, *Justice in Robes* (n. 8 above), 200.

[12] See on this John Gardner, 'How Law Claims, What Law Claims', in *Institutionalized Reason. The Jurisprudence of Robert Alexy*, ed. Matthias Klatt (Oxford: Oxford University Press, 2012), 29–44, at 29–33.

[13] Alexy, *The Argument from Injustice* (n. 5 above), 32–4.

Two versions of this argument are conceivable. The first declares that the claim to correctness is trivial or formal, or both. The second version maintains that the content of the claim refers exclusively to the real or factual dimension of law. A variant of the first version is to be found in Joseph Raz's work. Raz maintains that the claim to correctness thesis is nothing other than 'a general thesis about intentional actions and their products'.[14] As such, it applies to each and every case of intentional action, even to the actions of bandits. Here, the claim to correctness or, as Raz prefers to say, to 'appropriateness',[15] may take on such content as, for instance 'being self-enriching'.[16] This example, however, shows that a general claim to appropriateness is essentially different from the claim to correctness. A bandit who claims that his action is self-enriching does not thereby claim that his action, for that reason, has to be accepted by everyone, even by his victims. This is altogether different in case of the claim to correctness. The claim to correctness is a claim that is addressed to all.[17] In this respect, it is similar to the claim to truth. A claim that is addressed to all is, at the same time, a claim to objectivity. As such, both are, indeed, formal. But as a claim that refers to objectivity, the claim to correctness is by no means trivial. Objectivity is not only anything but trivial, it also belongs necessarily to the ideal dimension of law. Thus, the claim to correctness, notwithstanding its formal character, points to the ideal dimension of law.

The second version concerns the question of whether the claim of law to correctness refers exclusively to social facts or also to morals. The objection says that the claim to correctness made by the law concerns only social facts as sources of law, that is, only the real, factual, or authoritative dimension. Now, it is evident that this cannot be true of the claims made by a constitutional convention or by the legislator. But it is also false with respect to judicial decision-making. This is especially clear in cases in which the authoritative reasons—and that is, the source-based reasons—allow for more than one decision. The decision to be made in such an 'open' sphere is the decision of a normative matter that cannot be based on standards of positive law, because if it could be based on such standards, it would not be a decision in an 'open' sphere. If it is to be based on any standard at all, that is, if it is not to be an arbitrary decision, which would contradict the claim to correctness, it must be based on other normative standards. Legal decisions regularly concern questions of distribution and compensation. Questions of correct distribution

[14] Joseph Raz, 'The Argument from Justice, or How not to Reply to Legal Positivism', in *Law, Rights and Discourse. The Legal Philosophy of Robert Alexy*, ed. George Pavlakos (Oxford: Hart, 2007), 17–35, at 27.

[15] Ibid.

[16] Ibid.

[17] This is true without any qualification as far as universal morality is concerned. In the case of a legal system, matters are more complex. Two aspects are to be distinguished. The first concerns internal universality. Decisions and arguments made in a particular legal system claim to be acceptable to all who take the point of view of the legal system in question. The second aspects concerns external universality. Legal systems as such claim to be acceptable to all, that is, to be universally acceptable as a particular, that is, non-universal system.

and compensation are questions of justice because justice is nothing other than correctness in distribution and compensation. Questions of justice, however, are moral questions. In this way, the open texture of law, taken together with the nature of legal questions, implies that the claim to correctness raised in legal decision-making necessarily refers not only to the real or factual but also to the ideal and critical dimension. This applies even in cases in which the authoritative material, say, the wording of a statute, allows for no more than a single decision, a decision that is unjust. In such cases the claim to correctness either amounts to the claim that it is morally justified to adhere to the unjust statute for reasons that address the moral value of legality, or it leads to the claim that it is morally justified to make an exception to it, perhaps even to declare it invalid, on the ground that in this case justice outweighs the moral value of legality. This shows that the claim of law to correctness always has reference not only to social facts but also to morality.[18]

4. The Rationality of the Claim to Correctness

At exactly this point, a fourth objection against the correctness thesis arises. This objection maintains that the claim to correctness, in so far as it refers to morality, is nothing more than an expression of an illusion or an error. '[O]rdinary moral judgments', indeed, include claims to objectivity, but, as John Mackie puts it, 'these claims are all false'.[19] Morality's claim to objectivity therefore has to be confronted with an 'error theory',[20] which says that judgments about what is morally obligatory, forbidden, or allowed, or about what is morally good or bad, or just or unjust, are subjective, relative, or simply reflect the results of mere decisions. For this reason, moral arguments lack rationality and, with it, correctness or truth. The claim of morality to correctness, therefore, is the claim that something is correct that cannot be correct. The claim of law to correctness, the objection continues, must therefore be confined to authoritative or institutional reasons, based exclusively on the real or factual character of law. Otherwise, this claim, in effect, would connect law with irrationality. One might call this the 'irrationality objection'.

B. Discourse Theory

The reply to the irrationality objection is discourse theory. Discourse theory claims that between provability on the one hand and arbitrariness on the

[18] This applies even in cases in which the wording of a statute allows for no more than a single decision, which is just. Here the application of the statute includes the implicit negative assertion that it is not unjust.

[19] John L. Mackie, *Ethics. Inventing Right and Wrong* (London: Pelican, 1977), 35.

[20] Ibid.

other,[21] a third thing exists, namely, rationality or—understood here as the same—reasonableness.[22]

Discourse theory is a procedural theory of practical rationality. According to discourse theory, a practical or normative proposition is correct (or true)[23] if and only if it can be the result of a rational practical discourse.[24] The conditions of discursive rationality can be made explicit by means of a system of principles, rules, and forms of general practical discourse.[25] This system comprises rules that demand non-contradiction, clarity of language, reliability of empirical premises, and sincerity, as well as rules and forms that speak to the consequences, and to balancing, universalizability, and the genesis of normative convictions. The procedural core consists of rules that guarantee freedom and equality in discourse by granting to everyone the right to participate in discourse and the right to question as well as to defend any and all assertions.

Discourse theory is confronted with a number of problems.[26] One of them consists in the fact that discourse is not a procedure that always yields just one right answer. To be sure, certain normative demands are required by discourse theory. The discourse rules give expression to the values of freedom and equality. This serves as a basis for the justification of human rights.[27] Human rights can therefore be considered as discursively necessary. This implies that the denial of human rights is discursively impossible. Along with discursive necessity and discursive impossibility, there exists, however, a broad range of what is merely

[21] See on this Paul Ricoeur, 'Zu einer Hermeneutik des Rechts. Argumentation und Interpretation', *Deutsche Zeitschrift für Philosophie* 42 (1994), 375–84, at 378.

[22] On the relation between the concepts of rationality and reasonableness see Robert Alexy, 'The Reasonableness of Law', in *Reasonableness and Law*, eds Giorgio Bongiovanni, Giovanni Sartor, and Chiara Valentini (Dordrecht: Springer, 2009), 5–15, at 5–7.

[23] Discourse theory would have no problem with substituting 'true' for 'correct'. This can be explained by means of three equivalences. The first concerns a semantic conception of practical truth or correctness. This can be expressed, following Tarski's lines, by the equivalence: (1) The sentence 'Jones ought to tell the truth' is true if and only if Jones ought to tell the truth. Next, the concept of a practical or normative fact is introduced by means of a second equivalence: (2) If and only if Jones ought to tell the truth, it is a practical or normative fact that Jones ought to tell the truth. The third equivalence connects the concepts of truth and fact with the concept of justifiability: (3) Jones ought to tell the truth if and only if it is justifiable that Jones ought to tell the truth. This model of practical truth comprises realistic elements, but it is to be distinguished from a strong or intuitionistic model on a central point. In an intuitionistic model the justifiability of a normative sentence depends on the existence of a normative fact, the perception of which is a matter of intuition. In a discursive model the existence of a normative fact depends on the justifiability of the corresponding sentence. If one wants to attribute realism to discourse theory, it can, therefore, only be a kind of weak realism.

[24] Robert Alexy, 'Problems of Discourse Theory', *Crítica* 20 (1988), 43–65, at 44 (in this volume: Chapter 18, 275–87, at 276).

[25] Robert Alexy, *A Theory of Legal Argumentation* (1978), trans. Ruth Adler and Neil MacCormick (Oxford: Clarendon Press, 1989), 187–206.

[26] A recent extensive analysis of problems in the discourse theory of law can to be found in Carsten Bäcker, *Begründen und Entscheiden. Kritik und Rekonstrukton der Alexyschen Diskurstheorie des Rechts*, 2nd edn (Baden-Baden: Nomos, 2012).

[27] Robert Alexy, 'Discourse Theory and Human Rights', *Ratio Juris* 9 (1996), 209–35, at 221–33.

discursively possible.[28] A judgment is merely discursively possible when one person can justify this judgment without violating any rule or principle of discourse, while another person, at the same time, can do the same with respect to the contradictory of this very judgment. In such a case, incompatible judgments are backed by reasons. Therefore, the disagreement is, as Rawls terms it, a 'reasonable disagreement'.[29] One might call this the 'problem of practical knowledge'.[30]

II. The Real

The problem of practical knowledge requires that one leave the first stage, defined exclusively by the ideals of correctness and discourse, and proceed to a second stage, where legally regulated procedures, first, guarantee the achievement of a decision and, second, provide for their enforcement.[31] This is the step to positivity as defined by authoritative issuance and social efficacy.[32] The insufficiency of the ideal dimension *qua* decision procedure necessitates as its complement the existence of the real, that is, the positive dimension of law.[33] This necessity stems from the moral requirements of avoiding the costs of anarchy and civil war and achieving the advantages of social coordination and cooperation.

[28] On the concepts of discursive necessity, impossibility, and possibility see Alexy, *A Theory of Legal Argumentation* (n. 25 above), 207.

[29] John Rawls, *Political Liberalism* (New York: Columbia University Press, 1993), 55.

[30] Rawls, ibid., 54, speaks in this context of the 'burdens of judgment'.

[31] See on this Kant's 'principle' that one 'must leave the state of nature, in which each follows its own judgment, unite itself with all others (with which it cannot avoid interacting), subject itself to public lawful external coercion, and so enter into a condition in which what is to be recognized as belonging to it is determined *by law* and is allotted to it by adequate *power* (not its own but an external power)'; Immanuel Kant, *The Metaphysics of Morals*, trans. and ed. Mary J. Gregor, in *The Cambridge Edition of the Works of Immanuel Kant. Practical Philosophy* (Cambridge: Cambridge University Press, 1996), 353–603, at 456; AA 6, 312.

[32] Alexy, *The Argument from Injustice* (n. 5 above), 3.

[33] See Gustav Radbruch, *Legal Philosophy* (1932), trans. Kurt Wilk, in *The Legal Philosophies of Lask, Radbruch, and Dabin* (Cambridge, Mass.: Harvard University Press, 1950), 43–224, at 117: 'If no one is able to determine what is just, then someone must stipulate what is to be legal' (trans. altered). Radbruch adds in a footnote: 'That is, one stipulates what *ought to be legal*, one does not stipulate what *is correct*, for that would be self-contradictory', ibid. (trans. altered). This might be interpreted in either of two ways. On the first interpretation, it is meant to express that stipulating what is legal has nothing to do with what is correct. On this interpretation, the quoted statement would be incorrect. Stipulating what is legal necessarily comprises the claim that what is stipulated is correct. The first interpretation, therefore, fails to take account of the dual nature of law. On the second interpretation, the quotation says that authority despite the facts—first, that it claims that what is issued is correct and, second, that it is correct to abide by it—cannot generate the correctness or truth of what is authoritatively issued. On this interpretation, Radbruch's statement would be correct. It would be an expression of the dual nature of law.

III. The Reconciliation of the Ideal and the Real

One might assume that the necessity of positivity implies positivism. This, however, would be incompatible with the claim to correctness. Certainly, the necessity of positivity implies the correctness of positivity. But the correctness of positivity has by no means an exclusive character. To grant to positivity an exclusive character, as Kant, for instance, is inclined to do,[34] would be to underestimate the fact that the claim to substantial correctness—that is, first and foremost, the claim to justice—does not vanish once law is institutionalized. It remains alive behind and in the law. For this reason, one has to distinguish two stages or levels of correctness: first-order correctness and second-order correctness. First-order correctness refers only to the ideal dimension. It concerns justice as such. Second-order correctness is more comprehensive. It refers both to the ideal and to the real dimension. This means that it concerns justice as well as legal certainty (*Rechtssicherheit*). Legal certainty, however, can be achieved only by means of positivity. In this way, the claim to correctness, *qua* second-order claim, necessarily connects both the principle of justice and the principle of legal certainty with law.

The principle of legal certainty is a formal principle. It requires commitment to what is authoritatively issued and socially efficacious. The principle of justice is a material or substantive principle. It requires that the decision be morally correct. Both principles, as principles in general,[35] may collide, and they often do. Neither can ever supplant the other completely, that is, in all cases. On the contrary, the dual nature of law demands that they be seen in correct proportion to each other.

[34] See on this Alexy, *The Argument from Injustice* (n. 5 above), 116–21. In the appendix to the second edition of his *Metaphysical First Principles of the Doctrine of Right* from 1798, the first part of *The Metaphysics of Morals*, Kant restricts his rule 'Obey the authority who has power over you' by means of the following exemption clause: '(in whatever does not conflict with inner morality)'; Kant, *The Metaphysics of Morals* (n. 31 above), 505; AA 6, 371. Kant does not explain to what he refers as being in conflict with inner morality at this place. In his handwritten literary remains, however, we find the following examples: 'e.g. religious coercion. Coercion to unnatural sins: treacherous assassination etc. etc.'; Immanuel Kant, *Reflexionen zur Rechtsphilosophie*, in *Kant's gesammelte Schriften*, vol. 19, ed. Prussian Academy of Sciences (Berlin and Leipzig: Walter de Gruyter, 1934), 443–613, at 595 (trans. R. A.). This does not mean, however, that the effect of such conflicts with inner morality is, as in the case of the Radbruch Formula, the loss of legal validity or legal character. Kant distinguishes between a moral and a strict (or narrow, or pure) concept of law. The moral concept of law 'is related to an obligation corresponding to it'; Kant, *The Metaphysics of Morals* (n. 31 above), 387; AA 6, 230. This obligation (*Verbindlichkeit*) is a moral obligation: '*Obligation* is the necessity of a free action under a categorical imperative of reason', ibid., 377; AA 6, 222. It seems to be this moral obligation to which Kant's exemption clause refers. The law in the strict sense is not affected by this: '[S]trict law, namely that which is not mingled with anything ethical, requires only external grounds for determining choice; for only then is it pure and not mixed with any precepts of virtue. Only a completely external law can therefore be called *strict* (law in the narrow sense)', ibid., 389; AA 6, 232 (trans. altered)). One might think that this applies only to the observer's perspective. Replying to this, however, one can point to Kant's thesis that the judge has to decide on the basis of 'proper (strict) law', ibid., 390; AA 6, 234 (trans. altered). This shows that according to Kant, the concept of strict law is applicable not only from the observer's perspective but also from the participant's perspective.

[35] Robert Alexy, *A Theory of Constitutional Rights* (1985), trans. Julian Rivers (Oxford: Oxford University Press, 2002), 44–110.

To the degree this correct proportion is attained, harmony of the legal system is achieved.

Thus, second-order correctness is a matter of balancing. This shows that balancing has a role to play not only in the creation and application of law, that is, in legal practice, but also at the very basis of law. It is a part of the nature of law.

Second-order correctness is the theme of the third step, which concerns the institutionalization of reason. Two aspects of this institutionalization are to be distinguished: one is substantive, the other procedural.

A. Outermost Border

The first substantive aspect is the postulate of an outermost border of law. This concerns the rejection of Hans Kelsen's thesis that 'any kind of content might be law'.[36] Kelsen illustrates his thesis with the following remark: 'According to the law of totalitarian states, the government is empowered to confine in concentration camps persons with unwanted convictions, religion, or race and to force them to do any sort of work whatever, even to kill them.'[37] Replying to this, the Radbruch Formula[38] has to be introduced. In its shortest form, it runs as follows:

> Extreme injustice is no law.[39]

The dispute about an outermost border of law is a central theme of the debate over legal positivism, a debate that cannot be taken up here. In the present context only the relation between the idea of an outermost border and the dual-nature thesis is of interest.

In order to determine what this relation comes to, two versions of positivism and three versions of non-positivism have to be distinguished. The two versions of positivism are exclusive and inclusive positivism. Exclusive positivism, as advocated most prominently by Joseph Raz, maintains that morality is necessarily excluded from the concept of law.[40] This is, with respect to individual norms, acceptable from the point of view of an observer;[41] from the point of view of a participant, however, it is wrong. A participant in a legal system is characterized in terms

[36] Hans Kelsen, *Pure Theory of Law*, 2nd edn (1960), trans. Max Knight (Berkeley, Calif.: University of California Press, 1967), 198.

[37] Ibid., 40 (trans. altered).

[38] Gustav Radbruch, 'Statutory Lawlessness and Supra-Statutory Law' (1946), trans. Bonnie Litschewski Paulson and Stanley L. Paulson, *Oxford Journal of Legal Studies* 26 (2006), 1–11, at 7.

[39] Robert Alexy, 'A Defence of Radbruch's Formula', in *Recrafting the Rule of Law: The Limits of Legal Order*, ed. David Dyzenhaus (Oxford: Hart, 1999), 15–39, at 17.

[40] Joseph Raz, 'Legal Positivism and the Sources of Law', in Raz, *The Authority of Law. Essays on Law and Morality*, 2nd edn (Oxford: Oxford University Press, 2009), 37–52, at 47.

[41] Alexy, *The Argument from Injustice* (n. 5 above), 27–31.

of the questions and arguments on what counts as the correct answer to a legal question in the legal system in which the participant finds himself. Now, arguments on what counts as the correct answer are impossible without raising a claim to correctness. This implies that the participant necessarily refers to both legal certainty and justice. And this, in turn, is to say that exclusive positivism is precluded.[42]

Inclusive positivism, defended, for instance, by Jules Coleman, is less radical. It says that morality is neither necessarily excluded nor necessarily included. The inclusion is declared to be conventional, that is, a contingent matter, turning on what the positive law in fact says.[43] With this approach, however, one is unable to grasp the necessity of the dual nature of law.

Non-positivism alone is compatible with the dual nature of law. This, however, is not to say that all versions of non-positivism meet its requirements. Two versions of non-positivism do not, namely, exclusive and super-inclusive non-positivism. A third version alone, inclusive non-positivism, adequately represents the dual nature of law.

Exclusive non-positivism is the most thoroughgoing version of non-positivism. It claims that every injustice, every moral defect, of a norm precludes its being legally valid, its being law. Deryck Beyleveld and Roger Brownsword's thesis '[I]mmoral rules are not legally valid'[44] is an example of this view.[45] Resting on an incorrect balance between the principle of legal certainty and the principle of justice, it gives too little weight to the factual or authoritative dimension of law.[46]

Super-inclusive non-positivism goes to the other extreme. It maintains that legal validity is in no way whatever affected by moral defects or moral incorrectness. At first glance, this seems to be a version of positivism, not of non-positivism. This first impression is, however, mistaken, as one sees as soon as one has granted that in addition to a classifying connection between law and morality, there exists a qualifying connection.[47] These two connections are distinguished by the effects of moral defects. The effect of a classifying connection is the loss of legal validity or of legal character. By contrast, the effects of a qualifying connection are restricted to legal defects that do not rise to the level of undermining legal validity or legal character. Aquinas's thesis that a tyrannical law 'is not law simpliciter'[48] or, as John

[42] A more elaborate version of this argument is to be found in Robert Alexy, 'An Answer to Joseph Raz', in *Law, Rights and Discourse*, ed. George Pavlakos (Oxford: Hart, 2007), 37–55, at 45–8, 50–4 (in this volume: Chapter 5, 64–82, at 72–5, 77–80).

[43] Jules Coleman, 'Authority and Reason', in *The Autonomy of Law*, ed. Robert P. George (Oxford: Clarendon Press, 1996), 287–319, at 316.

[44] Deryck Beyleveld and Roger Brownsword, *Human Dignity in Bioethics and Biolaw* (Oxford: Oxford University Press, 2001), 76.

[45] This view is by no means new. See Augustinus, *De libero arbitrio* I, 11, in *Opera. Werke*, vol. 9, trans. and ed. Johannes Brachtendorf (Paderborn: Ferdinand Schöningh, 2006), 86: '*Nam lex mihi esse non videtur, quae iusta non fuerit*' ('For a law that is not just would not seem to me to be a law').

[46] For more details see Robert Alexy, 'On the Concept and the Nature of Law', *Ratio Juris* 21 (2008), 281–99, at 287 (in this volume: Chapter 2, 18–35, at 24).

[47] Alexy, *The Argument from Injustice* (n. 5 above), 26.

[48] Thomas Aquinas, *Summa Theologiae* (Milan: Edizioni Paoline, 1962), 947 (I-II, question 92, art. 1, 4): '*lex tyrannica . . . non est simpliciter lex*'.

Finnis puts it, 'not law in the focal sense of the term "law" ',[49] but only law 'in a secondary sense of that term',[50] that is, defective law, seems to mark a qualifying connection. Another version of super-inclusive non-positivism that can be explained by means of the distinction between classifying and qualifying connections is to be found in Kant's combination of the postulate of '[u]nconditional submission'[51] under positive law with the idea of a necessary subjugation of positive law to non-positive law.[52]

Super-inclusive non-positivism is exposed to objections quite similar to those raised against exclusive positivism. Just as exclusive positivism fails to recognize the ideal dimension of law, so likewise super-inclusive non-positivism fails to attribute to the principle of justice *qua* expression of the ideal dimension of law a weight that suffices to outweigh the principle of legal certainty in extreme cases. It is the thesis of inclusive non-positivism that such weight must be attributed to justice.[53] Inclusive non-positivism claims neither that moral defects always undermine legal validity nor that they never do. Following the Radbruch Formula,[54] inclusive non-positivism maintains that moral defects undermine legal validity if and only if the threshold of extreme injustice is transgressed. Injustice below this threshold is included in the concept of law as defective but valid law.[55] In this way, both sides of the dual nature of law are given their due weight.

[49] John Finnis, *Natural Law and Natural Rights*, 2nd edn (Oxford: Oxford University Press, 2011), 364.

[50] Ibid.

[51] Kant, *The Metaphysics of Morals* (n. 31 above), 506; AA 6, 372.

[52] For more details see Alexy, 'On the Concept and the Nature of Law' (n. 46 above), 288–90 (in this volume: Chapter 2, at 24–27).

[53] This can be reconstructed by means of the Law of Competing Principles; see Alexy, *A Theory of Constitutional Rights* (n. 35 above), 50–4. The principle of legal certainty shall be represented by P_1, the principle of justice by P_2. P symbolizes the relation of precedence, C_i different conditions of precedence. C_1 stands for 'injustice below the threshold of extreme injustice', C_2 for 'extreme injustice'. According to inclusive non-positivism, the following two conditional relations of precedence are valid:

(1) $(P_1 \mathbf{P} P_2)\, C_1$

and

(2) $(P_2 \mathbf{P} P_1)\, C_2$.

P_2 requires, taken alone, the legal consequence that the norm in question is not valid or no law (Q). This, together with (2), implies, according to the Law of Competing Principles, the rule $C_2 \rightarrow Q$. Transformed in words, this rule is the shortest version of the Radbruch Formula: Extreme injustice is no law. In contrast to this, super-inclusive non-positivism and also, in its result, exclusive positivism can be represented by

(3) $(P_1 \mathbf{P} P_2)$,

whereas exclusive non-positivism finds its representation in

(4) $(P_2 \mathbf{P} P_1)$.

(3) and (4), as unconditional relations of precedence, may both be read as expressions of a rejection of balancing in questions concerning the concept and the nature of law. See also Bäcker, *Begründen und Entscheiden* (n. 26 above), 263–5.

[54] See on this Alexy, *The Argument from Injustice* (n. 5 above), 40–62.

[55] Alexy, 'On the Concept and the Nature of Law' (n. 46 above), 287–8 (in this volume: Chapter 2, at 24–5).

B. Democratic Constitutionalism

An outermost border is a necessary but by no means sufficient condition of the institutionalization of reason. In order to bring about the institutionalization of reason, not only does the problem of the confrontation of positivity and correctness at the border have to be resolved but also positivity and correctness have to be connected inside the legal system. This is only possible in the political form of democratic or discursive constitutionalism.

Democracy and constitutional rights are the main elements of democratic constitutionalism. Both are required by discourse theory, and both have a dual nature.

1. Democracy

Democracy is the most important element on the procedural side of the institutionalization of reason. Democracy can be conceived, at the same time, as a decision procedure and as an argumentation procedure. Decision, along the lines of the majority principle, is the real side of democracy. Argumentation, as public discourse, is its ideal side. The only possibility for the political realization of the ideals of discourse theory is the institutionalization of a democracy that unites both sides. The name of this unity is 'deliberative democracy'.

2. Constitutional Rights

Constitutional rights are rights that have been recorded in a constitution with the intention of transforming human rights into positive law—the intention, in other words, of positivizing human rights. Human rights are, first, moral, second, universal, third, fundamental, and fourth, abstract rights that, fifth, take priority over all other norms.[56] Rights exist if they are valid. The validity of human rights *qua* moral rights depends on their justifiability and on that alone. Thus, human rights exist if they are justifiable. Now, human rights are justifiable on the basis of discourse theory because the practice of asserting, asking, and arguing presupposes freedom and equality, and the ideas of freedom and equality imply, together with further premises that can be well established, human rights. Human rights, therefore, are discursively necessary.[57] None of this can be elaborated here.[58] The only point of interest in this context is that human rights as moral rights belong exclusively to the ideal dimension of law. Their transformation into constitutional

[56] Robert Alexy, 'Die Institutionalisierung der Menschenrechte im demokratischen Verfassungsstaat', in *Philosophie der Menschenrechte*, eds Stefan Gosepath and Georg Lohmann (Frankfurt: Suhrkamp, 1998), 244–64, at 246–54.

[57] That human rights *qua* abstract rights are discursively necessary does not imply that their application in concrete cases is always a matter of discursive necessity. There can be reasonable disagreement about what human rights require in a concrete case.

[58] See on this Robert Alexy, 'A Discourse-Theoretical Conception of Practical Reason', *Ratio Juris* 5 (1992), 231–51, at 244–47 (in this volume: Chapter 17, 255–74, at 269–74).

rights, that is, into positive rights, represents the effort to connect the ideal with the real dimension.

In an ideal democracy, the democratic process would always show sufficient respect for constitutional rights. There would be, in principle, no conflict between democracy and constitutional rights. In a real democracy, however, there is conflict. The reality of political life together with the idea of human and constitutional rights, therefore, requires constitutional review. Constitutional review claims to be closer than the parliament to the ideal dimension of law. This claim is justified if constitutional review can be understood as an argumentative or a discursive representation of the people.[59] In this way the dialectic of the real and the ideal, that is, the dual nature of law is present even in the relationship of constitutional review and parliamentary legislation.

3. Legal Argumentation

The establishment of a democratic constitutional state creates an institutional framework for the solution of legal problems. Democratically legitimized legislation, together with constitutional review, is the main instrument. This framework, however, needs to be filled out. The device for doing so is legal argumentation or discourse. The dual nature of legal argumentation is expressed by the special case thesis. This thesis says that legal discourse is a special case of general practical discourse.[60] General practical discourse is a non-institutionalized discourse about practical questions. As a general practical discourse, it comprises all kinds of non-authoritative practical arguments, that is, moral arguments concerning justice and rights as well as ethical arguments concerning individual and collective identity and pragmatic arguments that give expression to means–end rationality. The moral arguments have priority because they represent the universal point of view. This does not, however, mean that their content cannot depend on the other arguments.[61] Legal discourse is a special case of general practical discourse because it is committed to statute, precedent, and legal doctrine. These commitments represent the real or authoritative side of legal discourse.

Habermas has raised a series of arguments against the special case thesis.[62] His central concern is that the special case thesis gives the judiciary so much power that democratic legitimacy is endangered:

> Once the judge is allowed to move in the unrestrained space of reasons that such a 'general practical discourse' offers, a 'red line' that marks the division of powers

[59] Robert Alexy, 'Balancing, Constitutional Review, and Representation', *International Journal of Constitutional Law* 3 (2005), 572–81, at 578–81 (in this volume: Chapter 9, 133–41, at 139–41).

[60] Alexy, *A Theory of Legal Argumentation* (n. 25 above), 211–20.

[61] For some details see Robert Alexy, 'The Special Case Thesis', *Ratio Juris* 12 (1999), 374–84, at 378–9.

[62] Jürgen Habermas, *Between Facts and Norms. Contributions to a Discourse Theory of Law and Democracy* (1992), trans. William Rehg (Cambridge: Polity Press, 1996), 229–37.

> between courts and legislation becomes blurred. In view of the application of the particular statute, the legal discourse of the judge should be confined to the set of reasons that legislators either in fact [have] put forward or at least could have mobilized for the parliamentary justification of that norm. The judge, and the judiciary in general, would otherwise gain or appropriate a problematic independence from those bodies and procedures that provide the only guarantee for democratic legitimacy.[63]

The reply to this rests on two points. The first is that the special case thesis by no means represents a blanket permission 'to move in the unrestrained space of reasons' of general practical discourse. On the contrary, it includes a *prima facie* priority of authoritative reasons.[64] The second point concerns Habermas's proposal that the judge 'should be confined to the set of reasons that legislators either in fact [have] put forward or at least could have mobilized for the parliamentary justification'. The actual intention of the legislator is indeed a highly relevant reason bearing on the interpretation of a stature. But often there are difficulties in recognizing it, or it is vague or inconsistent.[65] The hypothetical intention of the legislator, on the other hand, is a highly problematic construction. It comes close to an invitation to mask the judge's intention as the hypothetical intention of the legislator. Here undisguised general practical argument seems to be preferable. Habermas tries to enhance the impact of the authoritative dimension of law in order to strengthen democracy. The two points just made show, however, first, that the special case thesis offers no reason for such an attempt, and second, that the alternative Habermas proposes is not really an alternative at all. The special case thesis alone makes it possible to strike an adequate balance between the ideal and the real dimension of law in the area of legal argumentation and, what is the same, interpretation.

4. Real and Ideal 'Ought'

In the application of law, rules as well as principles play an essential role. Rules express a definitive or real 'ought', principles a *prima facie* or ideal 'ought'.[66] The theory of principles attempts to develop on this basis a theory of proportionality that essentially includes a theory of balancing. This, again, cannot be elaborated here. In our context, the only point of interest is that principles theory completes

[63] Jürgen Habermas, 'A Short Reply', *Ratio Juris* 12 (1999), 445–53, at 447.

[64] See Alexy, *A Theory of Legal Argumentation* (n. 25 above), 248: 'Arguments which give expression to a link with the actual words of the law, or the will of the historical legislator, take precedence over other arguments, unless rational grounds can be cited for granting precedence to the other arguments.'

[65] See Ronald Dworkin, *A Matter of Principle* (Cambridge Mass.: Harvard University Press, 1985), 34–57.

[66] Robert Alexy, 'Ideales Sollen', in *Grundrechte, Prinzipien und Argumentation. Studien zur Rechtstheorie Robert Alexys*, eds Laura Clérico and Jan-Reinard Sieckmann (Baden-Baden: Nomos, 2009), 21–38.

the variety of considerations we have made on our journey through the different fields of the dual nature of law by a norm-theoretic argument, an argument that has already been present in much of what has been said.

Now the system is closed. The dual nature of law has shown itself to be present—explicitly or implicitly—in all fundamental questions of law. For this reason, it is the single most essential feature of law, and it shows why legal positivism is an inadequate theory of the nature of law.

4

Law, Morality, and the Existence of Human Rights

A central argument against the non-positivistic connection thesis is the argument from relativism.[1] A radical form of this argument has been put forward by Hans Kelsen. According to Kelsen, the thesis 'that an immoral social system is not law presupposes an absolute morality, that is to say, a morality that is valid everywhere and at all times'.[2] This absolute morality must be given '*a priori*'.[3] A merely factually given, that is, contingently given 'common element'[4] would not suffice as the basis of a necessary connection between law and morality, because even if it did exist, which Kelsen denies,[5] it would not establish 'what has to be conceived as good and bad, just and unjust under all circumstances'.[6]

For this reason, the problem of positivism depends on the question of whether there exist *a priori*, absolute, or, as I would prefer to say, necessary moral elements. The question of whether there exist *a priori*, absolute, or necessary moral elements shall be termed the 'existence problem'. In what follows, I will, first, consider the relation between the problem of positivism and the existence problem, and second, defend a solution of the existence problem based on a theory of human rights.

I. Positivism, Non-Positivism, and the Existence Problem

The positivism problem is the question of whether positivism or non-positivism is right, true, or correct. Now, the terms 'positivism' and 'non-positivism' designate very different theses about the relation between law and morality. For this reason, the determination of the relation between the positivism problem and the

[1] Robert Alexy, *The Argument from Injustice. A Reply to Legal Positivism* (1992), trans. Bonnie Litschewski Paulson and Stanley L. Paulson (Oxford: Clarendon Press, 2002), 53–6.

[2] Hans Kelsen, *Pure Theory of Law*, 2nd edn (1960), trans. Max Knight (Berkeley, Calif.: University of California Press, 1967), 68 (trans. altered).

[3] Ibid., 65 (trans. altered).

[4] Ibid., 64 (trans. altered).

[5] Ibid., 'In view of the extraordinary heterogeneity, however, of what men in fact have considered as good and bad, just and unjust, at different times and in different places, no element common to the contents of the various moral orders is detectable' (trans. altered).

[6] Ibid., 65 (trans. altered).

Law's Ideal Dimension. Robert Alexy, Oxford University Press. © Robert Alexy 2021.
DOI: 10.1093/oso/9780198796831.003.0005

existence problem requires some clarification of the concepts of positivism and non-positivism.

A. Three Elements and Two Dimensions

The debate over positivism turns on the relations between and among three elements: first, authoritative issuance, second, social efficacy, and third, correctness of content, which includes moral correctness. In determining the concept or the nature of law, all positivistic theories are confined to the first two elements, that is, they are confined to authoritative issuance and social efficacy.

This implies that positivists must support the *separation thesis* or, at the very least, the *separability thesis*. By contrast, all non-positivistic theories defend the *connection thesis*, which says that the concept of law is to be defined such that moral elements are included.[7] According to non-positivism, law consists not of two elements but of three.

This distinction between and among these three elements can be developed further into the dual-nature thesis.[8] This thesis sets out the claim that law necessarily comprises both a real or factual dimension and an ideal or critical one. The factual dimension is represented by the elements of authoritative issuance and social efficacy, whereas the ideal dimension finds its expression in the element of moral correctness. Authoritative issuance and social efficacy are social facts. If one claims that social facts alone can determine what is and what is not required by law, this claim amounts to the endorsement of a positivistic concept of law. Once moral correctness is added as a necessary third element, a non-positivistic concept of law emerges. Thus, the dual-nature thesis implies non-positivism.

B. Two Forms of Positivism

Within positivism, the distinction between exclusive and inclusive positivism is the most important division where the relation between law and morality is concerned. *Exclusive positivism*, as advocated most prominently by Joseph Raz, maintains that morality is necessarily excluded from the concept of law.[9] If one takes 'I' to stand for 'law includes morality', exclusive positivism can be expressed, using the necessity operator '$\Box$' and the negator '$\neg$', as:

[7] Robert Alexy, 'On the Concept and the Nature of Law', *Ratio Juris* 21 (2008), 281–99, at 284–5 (in this volume: Chapter 2. 18–35, at 21–2).

[8] Robert Alexy, 'The Dual Nature of Law', *Ratio Juris* 23 (2010), 167–82 (in this volume: Chapter 3, 36–50).

[9] Joseph Raz, 'Legal Positivism and the Sources of Law', in Raz, *The Authority of Law. Essays on Law and Morality*, 2nd edn (Oxford: Oxford University Press, 2009), 37–52, at 47.

(1) $\Box\neg I.$

Exclusive positivism stands in a relation of contrariety to non-positivism, which claims that morality is necessarily included in the concept of law. This can be expressed by:

(2) $\Box I.$

Finally, *inclusive positivism*, as defended, for instance, by Jules Coleman, counts as the rejection of both exclusive positivism and non-positivism. It says that morality is neither necessarily excluded nor necessarily included. The inclusion as well as the exclusion is declared to be a contingent or conventional matter,[10] turning on what the positive law in fact says. This can be expressed as follows:

(3) $\neg\Box\neg I \;\&\; \neg\Box I.$

These three positions stand in a relationship of contrariety because each of the three excludes the others without stemming from the negation of any of the others. This can be expressed by a triad that exhausts the logical space of the positivism problem as far as the necessity of the inclusion or exclusion of morality in the concept of law is concerned:

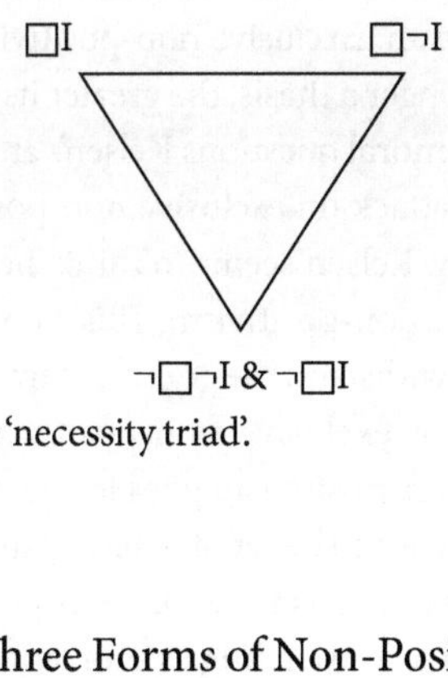

This triad shall be called the 'necessity triad'.

C. Three Forms of Non-Positivism

The differences within non-positivism are no less important for the debate over the concept and the nature of law than the differences within positivism and between positivism and non-positivism, as expressed by the necessity triad. With respect

[10] Jules Coleman, *The Practice of Principle. In Defence of a Pragmatist Approach to Legal Theory* (Oxford: Oxford University Press, 2001), 108.

to the argument from relativism, as put forward by Kelsen, the differences within non-positivism are even more important.

The differences within non-positivism that are relevant here stem from the different effects on legal validity that can be attributed to moral defects. Non-positivism can determine the effect on legal validity that stems from moral defects or demerits in three different ways. It might be the case that legal validity is lost in all cases, or it might be the case that legal validity is lost in some cases and not in others, or, finally, it might be the case that legal validity is affected in no way at all.

The first position, according to which every moral defect, every injustice, yields legal invalidity, is the most radical version of non-positivism. This position might be characterized as '*exclusive non-positivism*' in order to express the idea that each moral defect is considered as excluding social facts from the sources of legal validity. A classical version of this view is expressed by Augustine's statement that 'a law that is not just would not seem to me to be a law'.[11] A recent example is Beyleveld's and Brownsword's thesis 'that immoral rules are not legally valid'.[12]

This version of non-positivism will not be defended here. Exclusive non-positivism gives too little weight to the factual or real dimension of law.[13] Owing to the controversial nature of many moral issues, it would amount to anarchism.[14] With respect to the argument from relativism, another point, however, is more important. Kelsen describes non-positivism as 'the assertion that social norms must have a moral content, must be just in order to be considered as law'.[15] This implies that in case of immoral content, norms are not law at all, they are not valid law. That, however, is exactly the view of exclusive non-positivism. Exclusive non-positivism is the strongest form of non-positivism. Now, the stronger a thesis, the greater its vulnerability. Owing to the controversial nature of many moral questions Kelsen's attack against non-positivism is, I believe, successful as an attack on exclusive non-positivism. Not all answers to moral questions are necessary. Kelsen seems to think, however, that to refute exclusive non-positivism is to refute non-positivism. This, however, is a mistake. There are forms of non-positivism that withstand the argument from relativism.

The radical counterpart of exclusive non-positivism is *super-inclusive non-positivism*. Super-inclusive non-positivism goes to the other extreme. It maintains that legal validity is in no way whatsoever affected by moral defects. At first glance this seems to be a version of positivism, not of non-positivism. This first impression, however, will be seen to be misleading as soon as one sees that there exist two

[11] Augustinus, *De libero arbitrio* I, 11, in *Opera. Werke*, vol. 9, trans. and ed. Johannes Brachtendorf (Paderborn: Ferdinand Schöningh, 2006), 86: '*Nam lex mihi esse non videtur, quae iusta non fuerit.*'

[12] Deryck Beyleveld and Roger Brownsword, *Human Dignity in Bioethics and Biolaw* (Oxford: Oxford University Press, 2001), 76 n 17.

[13] Robert Alexy, 'Effects of Defects—Action or Argument? Thoughts about Deryck Beyleveld and Roger Brownsword's *Law as a Moral Judgment*', *Ratio Juris* 19 (2006), 169–79, at 170–1.

[14] Alexy, 'On the Concept and the Nature of Law' (n. 7 above), 287 (in this volume: Chapter 2, 24).

[15] Kelsen, *Pure Theory of Law* (n. 7 above), 64 (trans. altered). See further Kelsen's interpretation of non-positivism as the 'thesis that law is moral according to its nature', ibid., 68 (trans. altered).

sorts of connection between law and morality: a classifying and a qualifying connection.[16] These two sorts of connection are distinguished by the effects of moral defects. The effect of a classifying connection is the loss of legal validity or of legal character. By contrast, the effect of a qualifying connection is legal defectiveness that does not, however, undermine legal validity or legal character. Kant's combination of the postulate of '[u]nconditional submission'[17] to the positive law with the idea of a necessary subjugation of the positive law to non-positive law can be read as a version of super-inclusive non-positivism.[18] The same applies to the thesis of Aquinas that a tyrannical law is law but 'not law simpliciter'[19] or, as John Finnis puts it, 'not law in the focal sense of the term "law"'.[20]

Returning, for a moment, to exclusive non-positivism: It has been rejected on the ground that it gives insufficient weight to the factual or real dimension of law. It does not give sufficient weight to the real dimension and, by the same token, not to the principle of legal certainty, either, because it holds that moral defects undermine legal validity in all cases. If one puts 'V' for 'is valid', this can be expressed, with the help of the universal quantifier '∀', by:

(4) $$\forall x \neg Vx.$$

Now, super-inclusive non-positivism has to be rejected on the ground that it does not give sufficient weight to the ideal dimension of law. It does not give sufficient weight to the ideal dimension, that is, to the principle of justice, because moral defects in all cases, even in the most extreme cases, leave legal validity untouched. This can be expressed in the following way:

(5) $$\forall x Vx.$$

The only form of non-positivism that gives adequate weight to both the real and the ideal dimension, that is, to both the principle of legal certainty and the principle of justice is *inclusive non-positivism*.[21] Inclusive non-positivism claims neither that moral defects always undermine legal validity nor that they never do. Following the Radbruch Formula,[22] inclusive non-positivism maintains that moral defects undermine legal validity if and only if the threshold of extreme injustice is

[16] Alexy, *The Argument from Injustice* (n. 1 above), 26.

[17] Immanuel Kant, *The Metaphysics of Morals*, trans. and ed. Mary J. Gregor, in *The Cambridge Edition of the Works of Immanuel Kant. Practical Philosophy* (Cambridge: Cambridge University Press, 1996), 353–603, at 506; AA 6, 372.

[18] See Alexy, 'On the Concept and the Nature of Law' (n. 7 above), 288–9 (in this volume: Chapter 2, 25–6); Alexy, 'The Dual Nature of Law' (n. 8 above), 174 (in this volume: Chapter 3, 43).

[19] Thomas Aquinas, *Summa Theologiae* (Milan: Edizioni Paoline, 1962), 947 (I-II, question 92, art. 1, 4): '*lex tyrannica* . . . *non est simpliciter lex*'.

[20] John Finnis, *Natural Law and Natural Rights*, 2nd edn (Oxford: University Press, 2011), 364.

[21] Alexy, 'The Dual Nature of Law' (n. 8 above), 176–7 (in this volume: Chapter 3, 46).

[22] Alexy, *The Argument from Injustice* (n. 1 above), 40–62.

transgressed. Injustice below this threshold is included in the concept of law as defective but valid law. This can be expressed in the following way:

(6) $$\neg\forall x\neg Vx \,\&\, \neg\forall xV$$

or, by means of existential quantifiers,

(6') $$\exists xVx \,\&\, \exists x\neg Vx.$$

With this, a second triad of contraries can be formulated, which counts as an explication of the upper left position in the necessity triad, that is, of □I, as a shorthand for non-positivism:

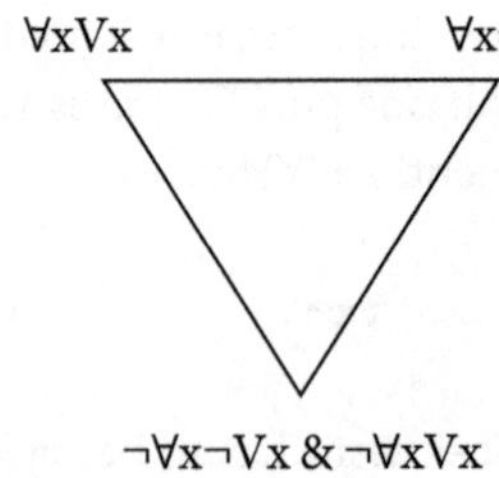

This triad shall be called the 'quantifier triad'. In what follows, only the position at the bottom of the quantifier triad, that is, inclusive non-positivism, defined by the formula

> Extreme injustice is no law.[23]

shall be considered as the object of the argument from relativism.

D. Inclusive Non-Positivism and the Existence Problem

The argument from relativism poses a genuine challenge to the only defensible form of non-positivism, that is, inclusive non-positivism. If there exist no necessary moral elements, for instance, human rights or universal principles of justice, then non-positivism would collapse under its own weight because if such elements did not exist, extreme injustice would not exist either. Existence presupposes objectivity, and moral elements are objective only if they are necessary. If there existed no extreme injustice, the Radbruch Formula would be

[23] Robert Alexy, 'A Defence of Radbruch's Formula', in *Recrafting the Rule of Law: The Limits of Legal Order*, ed. David Dyzenhaus (Oxford: Hart, 1999), 15–39, at 17.

nothing more than an empowerment of those who decide on the validity of law to declare, should they choose, duly issued and socially efficient norms that do not correspond to their factually held moral ideas, preferences, or ideologies to be invalid. The Radbruch Formula would not only lose its sense, still worse, it would turn out to be subjectivity and power shrouded under a mask of objectivity and rationality.

The thesis that there exist necessary moral elements might be termed the 'existence thesis'. The truth of the existence thesis is a necessary condition for the truth of non-positivism. If one lets '¬P' stand for non-positivism and 'E' for the thesis that there exist necessary moral elements, then this relation can be represented as follows:

(7) $$\neg P \rightarrow E.$$

The proposition that the truth of the existence thesis (E) is a necessary condition for non-positivism (¬P) implies the proposition that the denial of the existence thesis (¬E) is a sufficient condition for the truth of positivism (P):

(8) $$\neg E \rightarrow P.$$

Thus, if the existence thesis is false, then positivism prevails. In this case, Kelsen is right. Turning things around, it is, however, not the case that from the truth of the existence thesis one can conclude that non-positivism prevails. The truth of the existence thesis is only a necessary condition, not a sufficient condition, for the truth of non-positivism. It is possible to accept the existence thesis and remain a positivist, that is, one can remain a positivist by simply insisting upon the separation thesis. In order to defend the connection thesis, further arguments are required. These arguments are essentially connected to the claim to correctness, necessarily raised by law. But this shall not be discussed here.[24] In the present context, the only point of importance is that the truth of the existence thesis *qua* necessary condition of the truth of non-positivism would be sufficient for the possibility of non-positivism. This, by itself, makes it clear that the existence problem is one of the main problems of non-positivism.

II. The Existence of Human Rights

In discussing the argument from relativism in *The Argument from Injustice*, I confined myself to the claim that a proposition such as:

[24] See on this Alexy, *The Argument from Injustice* (n. 1 above), 35–9.

> The physical and material destruction of a minority of the population on grounds of race is injustice in the extreme[25]

is rationally justifiable. I did not, however, justify this claim to justifiability. Instead of a justification I referred—apart from discourse theory as taken up in *A Theory of Legal Argumentation*[26]—to an article in which I attempted, for the first time, to offer a justification of human rights.[27] This is something I developed further in the following years, especially in the articles 'Discourse Theory and Human Rights'[28] and 'Menschenrechte ohne Metaphysik?'[29] In what follows I consider whether arguments along these lines suffice to establish the existence of human rights and whether the existence of human rights, established in this way, serves to refute the argument from relativism.

A. Human Rights as Moral Elements

A discussion of the problem of positivism is a discussion of whether 'moral elements'[30] ought to be included in the concept of law or necessarily connected with the nature of law. This gives rise to the question of why these moral elements ought to count as human rights. There are, to be sure, other 'moral elements'. The most important of them is the 'notion of justice' to which I refer in *The Argument from Injustice*.[31] Now the relationship between human rights and justice is a difficult question if one attempts to grasp all aspects of this relation. Here only its basic structure is of interest. This basic structure can be described as follows: every violation of human rights is unjust, but not every injustice is a violation of human rights.[32] If this is true, human rights represent the core of justice, whereas justice comprises more than human rights. This might be called the 'core thesis'.

An alternative to the core thesis is the thesis that human rights and justice are coextensive. It runs as follows: every violation of human rights is unjust, and every injustice is a violation of human rights. This thesis might be termed the

25 Ibid., 54.

26 Robert Alexy, *A Theory of Legal Argumentation* (1978), trans. Ruth Adler and Neil MacCormick (Oxford: Clarendon Press, 1989), 33–208.

27 Robert Alexy, 'On Necessary Relations between Law and Morality', *Ratio Juris* 2 (1989), 167–83, at 180–1.

28 Robert Alexy, 'Discourse Theory and Human Rights', *Ratio Juris* 9 (1996), 209–35, at 220–33.

29 Robert Alexy, 'Menschenrechte ohne Metaphysik?', *Deutsche Zeitschrift für Philosophie* 52 (2004), 15–24.

30 Alexy, *The Argument from Injustice* (n. 1 above), 4.

31 Ibid., 53.

32 Robert Alexy, 'Die Institutionalisierung der Menschenrechte im demokratischen Verfassungsstaat', in *Philosophie der Menschenrechte*, eds Stefan Gosepath and Georg Lohmann (Frankfurt: Suhrkamp, 1998), 244–64, at 251–2.

'equivalence thesis'. For our purposes, it is not necessary to take up the question of which thesis, the core thesis or the equivalence thesis, is true. In both cases, the violation of human rights would be, at the same time, a violation of justice. For this reason, the existence of human rights implies the existence of principles of justice. The 'moral elements', if human rights exist, comprise human rights as well as justice.

To be sure, human rights and justice do not exhaust the realm of what might be called 'morality'. Alongside these two elements, a third element exists. It refers to individual and collective conceptions of the good.[33] These conceptions of the good define individual and collective identities.[34] Now human rights are norms that essentially claim priority with respect to all other norms.[35] If human rights are justifiable, their priority claim is, therefore, also justifiable. For that reason, identity as a moral element may indeed influence the conception of justice,[36] but it cannot restrict the role of human rights and justice in the discussion of the argument from relativity.

B. The Concept of Human Rights

It makes no sense to talk about the existence of something without explaining what it is that is claimed to exist. Now, the concept of human rights is highly contested for reasons both philosophical and political in nature. It is not possible to take up this debate here, and, happily, it is not necessary to do so either. All we need in order to discuss the question of whether human rights exist is a general idea of what human rights are. This general idea can be expressed by means of a definition according to which human rights are, first, moral, second, universal, third, fundamental, and fourth, abstract rights that, fifth, take priority over all other norms.[37] Here the first defining element is of special importance. According to it, human rights are moral rights. Rights exist if they are valid. Now, moral rights are valid if and only if they are justifiable. For this reason, the existence of human rights *qua* moral rights depends on their justifiability, and on that alone.

[33] Questions of human rights and justice are, in Habermas's terminology, moral questions, whereas questions of what is individually and collectively good are 'ethical' questions; see Jürgen Habermas, *Between Facts and Norms. Contributions to a Discourse Theory of Law and Democracy* (1992), trans. William Rehg (Cambridge: Polity Press, 1996), 229–37, 159.

[34] Habermas, *Between Facts and Norms* (n. 33 above), 160, speaks, in the first case, of 'existential' questions, in the second, of '[e]thical-political questions'.

[35] Robert Alexy, 'Discourse Theory and Fundamental Rights', in *Arguing Fundamental Rights*, eds Agustín José Menéndez and Erik Oddvar Eriksen (Dordrecht: Springer, 2006) 15–29, at 18.

[36] Robert Alexy, 'The Special Case Thesis', *Ratio Juris* 12 (1999), 374–84, at 379. It should be added that the good may also influence the interpretation of human rights, especially in cases of balancing.

[37] Alexy, 'Die Institutionalisierung der Menschenrechte im demokratischen Verfassungsstaat' (n. 32 above), 246–54.

C. The Justifiability of Human Rights

The theories about the justifiability of human rights, as well as the theories about the justifiability of moral norms in general, can be classified in many different ways. The most fundamental distinction is that between approaches that generally deny the possibility of any justification of human rights and approaches claiming that some sort of justification is possible. The first approach may be termed 'scepticism', the second 'non-scepticism'. Scepticism will have its roots in forms of emotivism, decisionism, subjectivism, relativism, naturalism, or deconstructivism. Non-scepticism may well include one or more of these sceptical elements, but it insists that there be a possibility of giving reasons for human rights, reasons that lay claim to objectivity, correctness, or truth. Non-positivism presupposes that some version of non-scepticism can be justified.

I have attempted to analyse the possibility of justifying human rights on the basis of distinctions between and among eight non-sceptical approaches. This list comprises first, the religious, second, the intuitionistic, third, the consensual, fourth, the biological, fifth, the instrumental, sixth, the cultural, seventh, the explicative, and eighth, the existential approach. It is impossible to discuss all these approaches here. Suffice it to say that the first six approaches have more defects than strengths.[38] For this reason, I will concentrate on the seventh and the eighth approaches, that is, on the explicative and existential arguments.

1. The Explicative Argument

A justification of human rights is explicative if it consists in making explicit what is necessarily implicit in human practice. A justification that makes explicit what is necessarily implicit in human practice follows the lines of Kant's transcendental philosophy. If the practice is the practice of asserting, asking, and arguing, the justification obtains a discourse-theoretic character. This is the version of the explicative argument that I should like to defend here.

The discursive practice, that is, the practice of asserting, asking, and arguing, or, as Robert Brandom calls it, the practice 'of giving and asking for reasons',[39] presupposes rules of discourse that express the ideas of freedom and equality.[40] The ideas of freedom and equality, however, are the basis of human rights. To recognize another individual as free and equal is to recognize him as autonomous. To recognize him as autonomous is to recognize him as a person. To recognize him as a person is to attribute dignity to him. Attributing dignity to someone is, however, to recognize his human rights. With this, one might think, a justification of human rights has been achieved.

[38] Alexy, 'Discourse Theory and Fundamental Rights' (n. 35 above), 19–21.

[39] Robert Brandom, *Articulating Reasons. An Introduction to Inferentialism* (Canbridge Mass.: Harvard University Press, 2000), 11.

[40] Alexy, 'Discourse Theory and Human Rights' (n. 28 above), 213–16.

2. The Existential Argument

This impression is, however, mistaken. The explicative argument provides, indeed, a necessary part of the justification of human rights, but it is, by itself, not sufficient. Two defects are easily identified. The first concerns the necessity of the discourse rules. It is possible to circumvent this necessity by avoiding any participation in the practice of asserting, asking, and arguing. The price one pays for this, would, however, be high. Never to assert anything, never to ask any question, never to give any reason would be to forbear from participating in what essentially belongs to the form of life of human beings *qua* 'discursive creatures', as Brandom puts it.[41] This price, however, can be reduced considerably by abandoning discourse not generally but only partially. It is possible to have discourses in one's own community and to pass over to propaganda, force, and terror at its borders. The solution to this problem is part of the solution to the second problem of the explicative argument, to which I shall now turn.

This second problem stems from the difference between discourse and action on the one hand and capabilities and interests on the other. Having discursive capabilities does not imply an interest in making use of them. This might be called the 'interest problem'. The interest problem concerns the dimension of discourse as well as the dimension of action—that is, real life as distinct from mere talk. In this second dimension, it is far more pressing. Now human rights are rights that concern not only discourse but also essentially action. The interest in making use of discursive capabilities solely in the sphere of argument might be called a 'weak interest in correctness'. By contrast, the interest in making use of discursive capacities not only in the sphere of argument but also in the realm of action can be characterized as a 'strong interest in correctness'. The strong interest in correctness comprises taking seriously the implications of the discursive capabilities in real life, that is to say, in taking seriously human rights.[42] In this way, the interest in correctness makes it possible for us to arrive at the object of our justification.

It might be objected, however, that this is no justification at all. It has lost its character as a justification, so the objection runs, once the premise concerning the interest is introduced. Indeed, this objection is not without merits. It must, however, be qualified. As with any interest, the interest in correctness is connected with decisions. These decisions concern the fundamental question of whether we accept our discursive capabilities or possibilities. This is the question of whether we want to see ourselves as discursive or reasonable[43] creatures. This is a decision about

[41] Brandom, *Articulating Reasons* (n. 39 above), 26.

[42] A person who takes seriously the implication of the discursive capabilities in real life may be characterized as a 'genuine participant in discourse'; see Alexy, 'Discourse Theory and Human Rights' (n. 28 above), 224.

[43] On the concept of reasonableness and its relation to the concept of rationality, see Robert Alexy, 'The Reasonableness of Law', in *Reasonableness and Law*, eds Giorgio Bongiovanni, Giovanni Sartor, and Chiara Valentini (Dordrecht: Springer, 2009), 5–15, at 5–7.

who we are. With this decision one 'choose[s] oneself' as Kierkegaard puts it.[44] This decision might be called 'existential'. Still, to talk here about justification or substantiation seems to be warranted because this decision is not based on groundless or arbitrary preferences, drawn, so to speak, from nowhere. Rather, the decision has the character of an endorsement of something that has been proven, by means of explication, to be a capability necessarily connected with human beings or, in other words, a necessary possibility. As an endorsement of a necessary possibility the existential argument is intrinsically connected with the explicative argument. One might call this connection the 'explicative-existential justification'.

The explicative argument exhibits the discursive nature of human beings. This discursive nature might be characterized as the ideal dimension of the individual. It is, to use Kierkegaard's words again, 'his ideal self, which he cannot acquire anywhere but within himself'.[45]

The endorsement of the ideal dimension that the individual finds in himself connects objective with subjective elements. The objective dimension consists of two elements, first, the necessary discursive possibilities, and second, their ideal character. This is the *a priori* required by Kelsen.[46] The subjective dimension consists of the existential decision that transforms these ideal possibilities into reality. This means that human rights can only be justified by a connection of objective and subjective elements. This connection can be characterized as a dialectic of the objective and the subjective.

It might be objected that a justification can only be either objective or subjective, and not, so to speak, 'half-objective', and that any contamination with subjective elements eliminates objectivity altogether. The reply to this is that objectivity connected with subjectivity is, certainly, less that pure objectivity, but it is also more than pure subjectivity. For this reason, one can qualify the explicative-existential argument as a justification of human rights, even if it is not a purely objective justification.[47] Due to its objective elements this combined justification, however, provides good reasons for human rights, and this, in turn, suffices to justify them. This

[44] Søren Kierkegaard, *Either/Or*, Part II, trans. and ed. Howard V. Hong and Edna H. Hong (Princeton, N. J. : Princeton University Press, 1987), 258.

[45] Ibid., 259.

[46] Kelsen, *Pure Theory of Law* (n. 2 above), 65.

[47] That the explicative-existential argument consists of a dialectic of objective and subjective arguments is not only a disadvantage. It solves the main problem of all attempts to justify human rights by way of an argument which has the following basic structure:

(1) $\forall x (\Phi x \rightarrow Rx)$.

For 'Φ' all properties can be substituted that are considered as grounds or reasons for granting to individuals (x) human rights (R). In the discussion of human rights many properties has been proposed as such reasons. Examples are the ability to suffer, intelligence, self-consciousness, the freedom to make choices, and autonomy. If one substitutes such a property, for instance autonomy, for Φ, one arrives at a sentence of the form:

(2) All autonomous beings have human rights.

justification establishes their validity *qua* moral rights, which means that human rights exist. When human rights exist, they can be violated.

When human rights can be violated, they can, *qua* abstract rights, be violated either to an extreme degree or to a lesser degree. That human rights can be violated to an extreme degree means that the Radbruch Formula is applicable. If all this is true, the argument from relativism is refuted.

If one confronts this sentence with the question 'Why?', it is difficult to give an answer because autonomy is considered by those who conceive it as a reason for human rights as an ultimate reason. The problem here stems from the fact that Φ-sentences are used in statements that are made from the perspective of an observer. From this perspective it is difficult to explain why autonomy has any normative meaning.

By contrast, the explicative-existential argument is an argument that explores the perspective of a participant of discourses. It does not propose rules from an external point of view but describes rules that are already valid in this practice. In this way, it makes explicit not only the content of these rules but also their internal normativity. With this, it is able to solve the normativity problem.

5
An Answer to Joseph Raz

The recent debate in the English-speaking world on the concept and nature of law has produced a wealth of theories showing that law is a far more complex matter than many had believed earlier. To acknowledge the degree of sophistication achieved in our day is not, however, to accept Joseph Raz's thesis:

> that legal theorists both on the legal positivist and the opposing side have advanced the discussion about the nature of law beyond the point where legal positivism is an illuminating category in such discussions.[1]

Precisely the opposite, I believe, is true. The division between legal positivist and non-positivist theories of the nature of law will be an illuminating category for as long as law exists. The reason for this lies in the dual nature of law, which stems from the fact that law is, on the one hand, factual in nature and, on the other, ideal. The relation between law as fact and law as an ideal is the most important issue in explaining its nature. Non-positivists claim that the factual dimension is internally connected with the ideal dimension; positivists—in any case today, and in considerable numbers—do not grow tired of stressing the important relations between the real and the ideal, but they insist that the ideal remains essentially external to what the law is. In order to answer the question of what the essence of law is, the positivist refers only to facts, while the non-positivist, in contrast, refers to both facts and ideals. I think that this difference is significant enough to warrant the labels 'positivism' and 'non-positivism', rather than 'forget[ting]' them, as Joseph Raz recommends.[2] This is the background against which I would have my rejoinder to Raz's reply to my critique of legal positivism in *The Argument from Injustice* seen.

I. Separation Thesis

According to Raz's first objection, the arguments put forward in *The Argument from Injustice* do not address legal positivism because, Raz contends, I am attacking a thesis

[1] Joseph Raz, 'The Argument from Justice, or How Not to Reply to Legal Positivism', in *Law. Rights and Discourse. The Legal Philosophy of Robert Alexy*, ed. George Pavlakos (Oxford: Hart, 2007), 17–35, at 35.
[2] Ibid.

Law's Ideal Dimension. Robert Alexy, Oxford University Press. © Robert Alexy 2021.
DOI: 10.1093/oso/9780198796831.003.0006

that is not common to the legal positivists. I have called this thesis the 'separation thesis'. At the end of his discussion of my attempt to identify positivism by means of this thesis, Raz presents a 'separation thesis' formulated by Andrei Marmor. Raz believes Marmor's formulation, first, 'to be correct', and, secondly, to be 'possibly ... a fairly important thesis which is common to all the theories within the tradition of legal positivism'.[3] Perhaps it will help in making clear what is at issue if I begin with Marmor's formulation of the separation thesis. It runs as follows:

> This thesis basically maintains that determining what the law is does not necessarily, or conceptually, depend on moral or other evaluative considerations about what the law ought to be in the relevant circumstances.[4]

The separation thesis is expressed in *The Argument from Injustice* as follows:

> All positivistic theories defend the *separation thesis*, which says that the concept of law is to be defined such that no moral elements are included. The separation thesis presupposes that there is no conceptually necessary connection between law and morality, between what the law commands and what justice requires, or between the law as it is and the law as it ought to be. The great legal positivist Hans Kelsen captured this in the statement, 'Thus, the content of the law can be anything whatsoever'.[5]

The second sentence of this quotation from *The Argument from Injustice* is quite close to Marmor's formulation. There might be differences where Marmor's distinction between 'determining what the law is' and 'considerations about what the law ought to be' and my distinction between 'the law as it is and the law as it ought to be' are concerned, but these differences, if they exist at all, seem to be of minor importance. If, however, Marmor's formulation is, as Raz says, successful in getting at the 'common core of the positivist tradition',[6] and if no relevant differences exist between Marmor's formulation and mine, as quoted above, then the reply to positivism in *The Argument from Injustice* hits its target. It does, at any rate, in so far as the concern is with the common core of the positivist tradition as depicted

[3] Ibid., 22.

[4] Andrei Marmor, *Positive Law and Objective Values* (Oxford, Clarendon Press, 2001), 71. Raz adds to this that his 'sources thesis', as presented in *The Authority of Law*, 2nd edn (Oxford: University Press, 2009), 47, is 'a stricter thesis', because it not only says that the law does not necessarily depend on moral arguments, but, what is far more, that such a dependence necessarily does not exist. Marmor's formulation is the contradictory of the connection thesis, which says that what the law is necessarily depends on moral arguments. The separation thesis, as the contradictory of the connection thesis, is indeed the common core of exclusive and inclusive positivism. It is implied by exclusive as well as by inclusive positivism.

[5] Robert Alexy, *The Argument from Injustice. A Reply to Legal Positivism* (1992), trans. Bonnie Litschewski Paulson and Stanley L. Paulson (Oxford: Clarendon Press, 2002), 3.

[6] Raz, 'The Argument from Justice, or How Not to Reply to Legal Positivism' (n. 1 above), 22.

by Marmor's formulation—that is, the separation of the law as it is from the law as it ought to be. Precisely this is, indeed, the main target of my reply. The Radbruch Formula is the most striking example. It says that extreme injustice is no law. Thus, the law in the way it actually stems from its social sources, that is, the 'law as it is', is connected with the 'law as it ought to be'. The former notion then depends on the latter notion.

To be sure, Raz, in objecting that the separation thesis as presented in *The Argument from Injustice* does not correctly identify legal positivism, is not concentrating on the distinction between the 'law as it is' and the 'law as it ought to be'. Rather, the main tenets of Raz's objection are three points connected with this distinction in the paragraph at page 3 of *The Argument from Injustice*, quoted above. These three points concern (1) Kelsen's content-thesis, (2) the idea of a definition of law, and (3) the concept of a necessary connection between law and morality.

A. Kelsen's Statement

Hans Kelsen's famous statement, 'Thus, the content of the law can be anything whatsoever',[7] is adduced as a paradigmatic formulation of the separation thesis as understood in *The Argument from Injustice*. Raz maintains, first, that this statement of Kelsen's is 'manifestly false according to Kelsen's own theory'[8] and, secondly, that, 'even if true, [it] lends no support to Alexy's separation thesis'.[9] Only the first of these two arguments will be considered here. The second argument will be taken up in the context of Raz's general thesis about necessary connections between law and morality.

Kelsen's statement that the content of the law can be anything whatsoever is, Raz claims, false according to Kelsen's own theory because there 'are, according to Kelsen's theory, necessary restrictions on the content of the law'.[10] These necessary restrictions on the content of law are said to follow from Kelsen's concept of law, which implies:

> (a) that the law can consist only of norms, (b) that it must address courts, (c) that it must stipulate for the application of sanctions, and (d) that their application must be conditional on certain conduct taking place.[11]

[7] Hans Kelsen, *Pure Theory of Law*, 2nd edn (1960), trans. Max Knight (Berkeley, Calif.: University of California Press, 1967), 198 (trans. altered); see also Hans Kelsen, *Introduction to the Problems of Legal Theory* (1934), trans. Bonnie Litschewski Paulson and Stanley L Paulson (Oxford: Clarendon Press, 1992), 56.

[8] Raz, 'The Argument from Justice, or How Not to Reply to Legal Positivism' (n. 1 above), 18.

[9] Ibid., 22.

[10] Ibid., 18.

[11] Ibid.

Are these four conditions really restrictions of the *content* of the law?

The concept of content, like the concept of form, is notoriously vague. Perhaps even more importantly, the two concepts are in constant danger of being confused with other concepts. Thus, the distinction between form and content is often conflated with that between abstract and concrete. Kelsen's thesis that law consists of norms is, for instance, more abstract than the thesis that law consists of general norms, because Kelsen's thesis refers to general as well as to individual norms. If, however, one of these theses is formal, both are. Something similar applies in the case of the thesis that law consists of norms that are authoritatively issued, that is, that are issued by some authority or other. This thesis is more abstract than the thesis that the authority must be democratically legitimized in order to be able to issue law.

John Gardner has pointed out that the distinction between form and content is often conflated with a third distinction, namely, that between source-based criteria of legal validity and merit-based criteria.[12] Source-based criteria of legal validity are criteria of a '*merit*-independent type'.[13] This makes it possible to cast Gardner's distinction in slightly more abstract terms by giving it the form, so to speak, of the difference between merit-based and merit-independent criteria of legal validity. The decisive point is that merit-based criteria can be applied not only to the content of law but also to its form. Examples of formal merits are generality and enactment as the result of a democratic procedure.

If, in the light of these three distinctions, we consider the four features of the law that Raz ascribes to Kelsen, the first conclusion is that all of them are formal. The concept of content in Kelsen's famous statement is used as a concept that is contrasted with the concept of form. This becomes quite clear if one reads the sentence following the statement of Kelsen's quoted above: 'There is no human behaviour that would be excluded simply by virtue of its substance from being the content of a legal norm.'[14] This suffices to show that it is not true that Kelsen's statement is false by Kelsen's own lights. Kelsen is referring not to formal features of law as set out by Raz but to its substance.

Even if one were to interpret 'content' in Kelsen's statement as 'merits', not a great deal would change. As already noted, there exist formal merits. But the four restrictions introduced by Raz are so abstract that they hover far above the field where merits and demerits come into play. There seems to be a rule that says the more abstract the formal properties of law, the less significant their moral relevance. Where the cases of consisting of norms and of being addressed to courts are concerned, this seems to be quite clear. Less clear, but clear enough, is the matter in the case

[12] John Gardner, 'Legal Positivism: 5½ Myths', *The American Journal of Jurisprudence*, 46 (2001), 199–227, at 208.

[13] Ibid., 209.

[14] Kelsen, *Pure Theory of Law* (n. 7 above), 198 (trans. altered).

of law's being conditioned on certain conduct. Doubts might arise in the case of sanctions. One can consider the fact that law is connected with sanctions as either a merit or a demerit. This ambivalence, however, shows that the concept of a sanction does not suffice, by itself, to establish a restriction on merits. Therefore, even if for 'content' one were to substitute 'merits', Kelsen's statement would not be rendered false according to his own theory. At most, there would be some doubts respecting sanctions.

B. The Idea of a Definition of Law

Raz's second objection to the separation thesis as per my ascription of it to legal positivism concerns the idea of a definition of law. I do indeed use the concept of a definition in order to explain the separation thesis. Repeating it here:

> All positivistic theories defend the *separation thesis*, which says that the concept of law is to be defined such that no moral elements are included.[15]

Raz's critique begins with the remark that it 'was Hart who convinced many legal theorists that the concentration on defining law ... is unproductive'.[16] He himself 'did not advance a definition of law'.[17] His main reason for this is that 'there is no theoretical justification to focus on the definition of the concepts rather than on their necessary features, some of which may not figure in any sensible definition of them'.[18] The reply to this depends on how one determines the relation between definition, concept, and the nature of things. It is impossible to go into detail here. A handful of remarks must suffice.

Definitions can be introduced for a variety of purposes. A rather unpretentious one is the demarcation of what is defined. An example is the definition of human being as (naturally) a featherless biped. Definitions of this kind can easily be

[15] Alexy, *The Argument from Injustice* (n. 5 above), 3.

[16] Raz, 'The Argument from Justice, or How Not to Reply to Legal Positivism' (n. 1 above), 19. Stanley L Paulson has drawn my attention to the fact that Hart does offer something like a definition of the existence of a legal system—and this in the terms of classical analysis, that is, by means of conditions necessary and jointly sufficient: 'There are therefore two minimum conditions necessary and sufficient for the existence of a legal system. On the one hand, those rules of behaviour which are valid according to the system's ultimate criteria of validity must be generally obeyed, and, on the other hand, its rules of recognition specifying the criteria of legal validity and its rules of change and adjudication must be effectively accepted as common public standards of official behaviour by its officials.' See H. L. A. Hart, *The Concept of Law*, 2nd edn (Oxford: Clarendon Press, 1994), 116. To be sure, the question of whether Hart intended to give a definition in the paragraph quoted as well as the question of how closely Hart's characterization of the existence of a legal system approximates his characterization of law as such remain open. Nonetheless, one can say that Hart's own work raises doubts about the claim that he really considers definitions related to the concept of law in all respects as 'unproductive'.

[17] Ibid.

[18] Ibid., 20.

distinguished from definitions that claim to grasp the essence of what is defined. The definition of human being *qua* rational animal is an example. Definitions of this kind represent a rather pretentious enterprise. For, even if they correctly express our actual common understanding of the concept, they are always in danger of failing. The reason for this is that concepts relate not only to socially established rules of meaning but also to the nature of things. The nature of law consists of its necessary properties. Every definition of the concept of law is in danger of failing to grasp these properties adequately. For this reason, one can never be certain about whether a definition is correct or not, even if it captures perfectly our use of language. This might suggest that one ought to refrain from defining the concept of law at all, and ought to concentrate, instead, on certain essential or necessary features of the law or on a list of such features. But in doing so, a decisive element of our understanding of the nature of law would remain beyond reach. For an explanation of the nature of law it is not enough that some of its necessary properties, or a list of them, be presented. These properties must be fitted together in a system. A definition of law that seeks to grasp the nature of law must represent the attempt to set out the core of such a system. Naturally, this cannot take place at the beginning of an analysis of the nature of law, but perhaps it can take place at the end.[19]

C. Necessary Connections

The remarks about definition, concept, and nature concern method and, to a certain degree, style. Raz's substantial point is that the separation thesis *qua* thesis that the concept of law has to be defined such that no moral elements are included is not a true description of the positivist tradition because, he is arguing, legal positivism is compatible with the existence of necessary connections between law and morality. According to Raz, the number of necessary connections between law and morality is 'indefinite'.[20] Now, it is not possible to work through an indefinite number of things. I will therefore confine myself to four examples presented by Raz.

Raz's first example consists of normative and evaluative concepts that 'are common to moral and non-moral discourse'.[21] It is doubtless true that normative concepts that are common to moral and legal discourse do exist. There are, for instance, moral as well as legal obligations. But the point to be made here is similar to that which has been made with respect to Kelsen's formal properties of law. The

[19] See Immanuel Kant, *Critique of Pure Reason*, trans. Werner S. Pluhar (Indianapolis, Ind: Hackett, 1996), 681; A 731, B 759.

[20] Raz, 'The Argument from Justice, or How Not to Reply to Legal Positivism' (n. 1 above), 21.

[21] Ibid., 19.

mere fact that there exist legal as well as moral obligations says nothing about any moral content that law must necessarily have or not have in order to be valid or invalid. To put it another way, it in no way renders legal validity or legal correctness dependent on any moral merits or demerits.

The last point can be generalized. The separation thesis as ascribed to legal positivism in *The Argument from Injustice* concerns the separation of both legal validity and legal correctness from any moral merits or demerits. It is precisely this that is meant by the separation of the 'law as it is' from the 'law as it ought to be'.[22]

In light of this background, it is not difficult to show that a further example of Raz's fails, again, to distinguish the separation thesis as a thesis about the relation between legal validity or legal correctness on the one hand, and moral merits and demerits or moral correctness and incorrectness on the other. This second example concerns a conceptually necessary relation that law has to morality which black holes do not have:

> it is a conceptual point about the law that it can be morally evaluated as good or bad, and as just and unjust, just as it is a conceptual fact about black holes that propositions like 'this black hole is morally better or more just than that' make no sense.[23]

It is, indeed, a conceptual point about the law that it can be morally evaluated, whereas this is not possible in the case of black holes. To this extent, then, there exists a conceptually necessary relation between law and morality that does not exist between morality and physical objects. But does this relation really count as a connection? It is, in any case, not a connection that makes legal validity or legal correctness dependent on moral merits. The relation between law and the possibility of its moral evaluation is simply a condition of the possibility of such a dependence, a possibility that as such entails nothing whatsoever about any necessary dependence of legal validity or legal correctness on moral merits. Still, I must concede that it is possible to understand the expression 'conceptually necessary connection between law and morality' in such a way that it is not restricted to any dependence on moral merits and demerits but refers also to the possibility of being assessed according to moral criteria. Perhaps I should have been more explicit, namely, in noting that I did not intend to include the latter instead of assuming that this would become clear from the rest of the sentence.

Raz's third example is far more interesting. It directly concerns law's moral merits. Raz's argument runs as follows:

[22] Alexy, *The Argument from Injustice* (n. 5 above), 3.

[23] Raz, 'The Argument from Justice, or How Not to Reply to Legal Positivism' (n. 1 above), 21.

> even if all the law's essential features can be stated without the use of moral concepts it may be the case that that it has those features entails that it has some moral merit.[24]

An example of this—here Raz refers to Fuller—is law's 'reliance on general standards'.[25] Now, law's reliance on general standards does, indeed, restrict the 'ability to act arbitrarily',[26] and avoiding arbitrariness is a moral merit, but is it also true that generality is a necessary or essential feature of law from the point of view of positivism? According to Gardner, it is a 'half-myth' that positivity as such has any moral merits and a myth that legal positivism is necessarily associated with criteria stemming from the rule of law, such as generality.[27] On this point Gardner is right: he is, at any rate, if it is true that according to legal positivism 'whether a given norm is legally valid ... depends on its sources, not its merits'.[28] Law's generality—like the other requirements of Fuller's 'inner morality of law'[29]—is a 'formal moral criteri[on]'.[30] Failure to meet this criterion does not deprive norms of their legal validity if legal validity is understood exclusively as source-based. Being source-based does not imply being general. Generality, therefore, is a contingent property of positive law. It is, as a formal merit, demanded by morality, but it is not implied by positivity. For this reason, it does not provide an example of a connection between law and morality that every legal positivist must accept *qua* legal positivist as a necessary connection.

The fourth example is the most interesting one. It concerns law's claim to legitimate authority. It is one of Raz's main theses about the nature of law 'that necessarily the law claims to have legitimate authority, and that that claim is a moral claim'.[31] Here a necessary connection between law and morality, a connection concerning the merits of law, is indeed at stake. Raz believes that it is possible, on the one hand, to assume that the law is necessarily or essentially connected with a moral claim and, on the other, to defend legal positivism.[32] I think that it is not possible to do both. This issue goes, however, far beyond the question of whether positivism can be identified by means of the separation thesis. It is one of the questions determining which is right, positivism or non-positivism. Raz considers this issue in the third part of his chapter, where he discusses the correctness thesis. I return

24 Ibid., 20.
25 Ibid., 21.
26 Ibid.
27 Gardner, 'Legal Positivism: 5½ Myths' (n. 12 above), 204–8.
28 Ibid., 201.
29 Lon L. Fuller, *The Morality of Law*, rev. edn (New Haven, Conn.: Yale University Press, 1969), 42 and 46–91.
30 Alexy, *The Argument from Injustice* (n. 5 above), 31.
31 Raz, 'The Argument from Justice, or How Not to Reply to Legal Positivism' (n. 1 above), 19.
32 Ibid., 20.

to the issue in section III of the present chapter, where I address the correctness thesis.[33]

II. Participants and Observers

Raz's second objection concerns the distinction between the observer's perspective and the participant's perspective. This distinction plays a central role in my reply to positivism. I do not claim that the separation thesis is wrong from both perspectives. It is wrong only from the perspective of the participant. By contrast, from the observer's perspective it is correct.

It is understood that the participant is found within a certain legal system; the observer, for his part, is referring to that legal system. The difference between their perspectives is that the participant asks and adduces arguments on behalf of what he deems to be the correct answer to a legal question in the legal system in which he is found, whereas the observer asks and adduces arguments on behalf of a position that reflects how legal questions are actually decided in that legal system. Raz objects that there is not really a difference here. One may take a court,

> a litigating lawyer, an academic scholar, or a foreign commentator. Whatever their other aims, when stating what German law is they all normally have the same aim: to state truly how German law is.[34]

There are, indeed, cases in which the observer and the participant can use the same proposition, for instance, the sentence 'In Germany, every person can raise a constitutional complaint on the ground that his constitutional rights have been infringed by public authority.' But as soon as this sentence poses a question of interpretation, the difference between the two perspectives comes to the fore. For example, under what conditions can an omission on the part of the legislator be classified as an infringement of a constitutional right by a public authority against which a constitutional complaint may be raised? This question is highly contested. The participant will give one answer; it claims to be legally correct and is supported by arguments. The answer may well be in opposition to the established practice of the Constitutional Court. The observer, qua observer, can only describe the practice of the Constitutional Court and the debate in which the Court is engaged. He

[33] On three further examples, see Joseph Raz, 'About Morality and the Nature of Law', *The American Journal of Jurisprudence* 48 (2003), 1–15, at 3. One of them is law's inability to commit rape, which is also mentioned in our text. I do not discuss it here as I already have considered it together with the two other examples elsewhere. See Robert Alexy, 'Agreements and Disagreements: Some Introductory Remarks' in *Law and Justice in a Global Society*, eds M. Escamilla and M. Saavedra (Granada: University of Granada, 2005) 737–42, at 739–40.

[34] Raz, 'The Argument from Justice, or How Not to Reply to Legal Positivism' (n. 1 above), 23–4.

cannot engage in argument on the question of which answer is legally correct. As soon as he does that, he ceases to be an observer and becomes a participant. Raz is right in pointing out that a participant not only 'participates in disputation'.[35] As the proposition about constitutional complaints in Germany shows, there are, indeed, sentences that can be used both by observers and participants, but they are embedded in different contexts. The participant's context is defined by the question 'What is the correct legal answer?', the observer's by the question 'How are legal decisions actually made?'

Can one describe perspectives in this way by means of questions? According to Raz a question, or a subject matter identified by it, does not suffice to constitute a perspective. For a perspective Raz seems to be demanding 'different methodologies'.[36] Now it is true that I have not specified different 'method[s] of inquiry'[37] in my explanation of the two perspectives. I think, however, that they are obvious. In the case of the participant, the methods are the rich means of legal argumentation. In the case of the observer, they comprise all the methods of empirical description, namely, for describing the law *qua* social practice. This suggests that Raz's comparison of the distinction between participants and observers with that between 'those interested in physics and those interested in the pay and status of physicists'[38] falls short of the mark. If one wishes to make a comparison in the field of physics, one ought to distinguish those who are asking for the truth of physical theories and those, for example, historians of physics, who are asking for the genesis, the dissemination, and the decline of physical theories without showing any real interest in their truth. It is, I think, not odd to speak in this case about two perspectives.

In my explanation of the participant's perspective, I say that the disputation of participants takes place 'within a legal system'.[39] Raz maintains that this phrase 'adds nothing but confusion to the characterization of the distinction'.[40] Perhaps I ought to have gone into greater detail. Legal systems are not only systems of norms but also systems of procedures.[41] The procedures may or may not be institutionalized. The most general non-institutionalized legal procedure is discourse about what the law of the land says. Whoever adduces an argument on this question takes part in this discourse and is, in this sense, 'within a legal system'.

Raz maintains not only that there is not really any difference between observer and participant but also that even if there were a difference between them, there

[35] Ibid., 23.
[36] Ibid., 24.
[37] Ibid.
[38] Ibid.
[39] Alexy, *The Argument from Injustice* (n. 5 above), 25.
[40] Raz, 'The Argument from Justice, or How Not to Reply to Legal Positivism' (n. 1 above), 23.
[41] See Alexy, *The Argument from Injustice* (n. 5 above), 24–5.

would be 'no reason to expect them not to be able to share the same concepts'.[42] For this reason he finds my claim, namely, that the following sentence, 'as the statement of an observer, contains a contradiction',[43] surprising:

> *A* has not been deprived of citizenship according to German law, although all German courts and officials treat *A* as denaturalized and support their action by appeal to the literal reading of a norm authoritatively issued in accordance with the criteria for validity that are part of the legal system efficacious in Germany.[44]

Raz contends that contradictoriness is a property of propositions, not of the relations between them and those who make them. He therefore considers it odd that being contradictory might depend on whether the proposition is made by an observer or a participant. One would have to agree with Raz on the point about oddity if the statement made by an observer and by a participant did, indeed, express the same proposition. But—the rub—precisely this is not the case. When uttered by an observer, our sentence expresses a different proposition than the same sentence as uttered by a participant. The reason underlying this difference is that the expression 'law' in the first part of the quoted sentence represents one concept when used by the observer and another when used by the participant. When used by the observer it expresses a positivistic concept of law that refers exclusively to social sources or, in other words, to authoritative issuance and social efficacy. When used by a participant it expresses a non-positivistic concept that comprises not only social sources but also moral correctness.

The second part of the quoted sentence refers to a chain of legal sources: (1) a practice of courts and officials, (2) a norm authoritatively issued, and (3) criteria for validity, that is, criteria that are recognized as such in a socially efficacious legal system. If an exercise of state power is grounded in this way on legal sources it is, according to an exclusively source-based concept of law, part of the law of the land. To say, at the same time, that it is, according to that concept, not part of the law of the land involves a contradiction. Things are completely different where the expression 'law' expresses a non-positivistic concept of law that includes morality: in our example, the Radbruch Formula. If the exercise of state power, which is the object of the statement, is extremely unjust, the participant can say that it is not a part of the law of the land, in spite of the fact that it would be deemed to be so if a positivistic concept of law were applied. If the observer and the participant use different concepts of law, then there is not even a hint of oddity in the claim that the sentence is contradictory when uttered by an observer, and not contradictory when uttered by a participant.

42 Raz, 'The Argument from Justice, or How Not to Reply to Legal Positivism' (n. 1 above), 24.
43 Alexy, *The Argument from Injustice* (n. 5 above), 30.
44 Ibid., 29–30.

To be sure, one could pose the question of why the observer and the participant use different concepts of law in the first place. Raz comes quite close to posing this question when he maintains that 'no reason is given here, nor anywhere else in the book, for thinking that "participants" and "observers" are committed by their role to use different concepts'.[45] The reply to this is as follows: if the answer of a participant to the question of what the law is—at least in cases that cannot be solved by simple subsumption—involves considerations about what the law ought to be, then he has to presuppose a concept of law that includes not only a factual but also an ideal dimension. In contrast to this, the observer's answer to the question of what the law is does not in any case involve considerations about what the law ought to be.[46] If it did, the party would not remain an observer. Therefore, he must be presupposing a concept of law that refers only to the factual dimension of law and excludes the ideal dimension. This is a positivistic concept of law.

It is very easy to recognize that the correctness of this reply depends on the question of whether the participant (at least in the class of cases that cannot be solved simply by subsumption) really has to refer to considerations about what the law ought to be in order to be able to say what the law is. This question is the *leitmotif* that connects the three arguments from correctness, from injustice, and from principles.

III. The Argument from Correctness

The argument from correctness is the basis of my reply to positivism. As a reply, the argument would be considerably weakened if it had to be granted that it did not contribute anything to the elucidation of the nature of law. Exactly this is stated by Raz: 'nothing can be learnt from the correctness thesis about the nature of law'.[47] For the argument from correctness—or, as Raz calls it, the correctness thesis:

> is a conceptual thesis not specifically about the law (though it applies to the law) but about the nature of purposes, intentional actions and their products.[48]

Every intentional action commits its agent to 'standards of appropriateness',[49] and on this point one can agree with Raz. What is more, it is true that if the argument

[45] Raz, 'The Argument from Justice, or How Not to Reply to Legal Positivism' (n. 1 above), 25.

[46] This is not to say, however, that the observer's considerations cannot include considerations about what the participants he observes think the law ought to be. One might call such considerations 'indirect' or 'third person' considerations about what the law ought to be by contrast to the direct and first person consideration of the participants.

[47] Raz, 'The Argument from Justice, or How Not to Reply to Legal Positivism' (n. 1 above), 28.

[48] Ibid.

[49] Ibid.

from correctness said no more than this, it would indeed afford 'no specific help in elucidating the nature of law'.[50] But it does say more.

This becomes quite clear as soon as one considers Raz's assessment of what is described in *The Argument from Injustice* as a 'bandit system'.[51] Bandits, if they act intentionally, are indeed committed to the claim that what they do is appropriate. But the general claim to appropriateness that is reflected in all intentional actions is different from the claim to correctness. Raz mentions 'being self-enriching' as a possible standard of the appropriateness of the bandit's action.[52] This is a standard that does not claim to be accepted by all who are affected by the bandits' activities—not, for instance, by their victims—but only by the bandits themselves. The matter is completely different in the case of the claim to correctness. The claim to correctness is a claim that is addressed to all. It is similar to the claim to truth in so far as both are claims to objectivity. As a claim to objectivity in law it does not claim, as universalistic morality does, to be acceptable to all without any further qualification. It claims to be acceptable to all who take the point of view of the legal system in question. This means that law is an enterprise that is intrinsically connected with the idea of objectivity. Objectivity is an essential feature of law, a feature that is not shared by purposeful activity as such, because purposeful activity as such is compatible with the complete subjectivity of the purposes at issue, exactly as the bandit example illustrates.

Raising a claim to correctness *qua* objectivity does not, as such, imply raising a claim to moral correctness. If, however, one adds certain premises that are not easily contested, the claim to moral correctness is indeed implied. This is quite clear in cases in which the authoritative material allows for more than one decision. The decision to be made in such an 'open' sphere is the decision of a normative matter that cannot be based on standards of positive law because if it could be based on such standards, it would not be a decision in an 'open' sphere. If it is to be based on any standard at all, that is, if it is not to be an arbitrary decision, it must be based on other normative standards. Legal decisions often concern questions of distribution and balance. Questions of correct distribution and balance are questions of justice, because justice is nothing other than correctness in distribution and balance. Questions of justice, however, are moral questions. Raz raises the question of how one is to understand the doctrine that the claim to correctness involves the claim that the law is morally correct.[53] Perhaps the preceding remarks suggest the lines along which this might be understood.

Once an argument is adduced, one can always try to construct a counterargument. In the case of the argument from correctness several possibilities are open to

50 Ibid.

51 Alexy, *The Argument from Injustice* (n. 5 above), 33–4

52 Raz, 'The Argument from Justice, or How Not to Reply to Legal Positivism' (n. 1 above), 27.

53 Ibid.

the positivist. Two strategies are of special interest. Both begin with the endorsement of the argument of correctness and continue by contesting the claim that it has any power to undermine positivism. I attempt to counter the first strategy by means of the argument from injustice, the second by means of the argument from principles. Raz contends, however, that my saying in *The Argument from Injustice* that a 'positivist can endorse the argument from correctness and nevertheless insist on the separation thesis'[54] amounts to my conceding that the correctness thesis does not contribute to an argument against positivism.[55] I concede, however, no such thing. Perhaps I should have made the point more clearly, namely, by saying that a 'positivist could endorse' the correctness thesis rather than saying a 'positivist can endorse' it.[56]

IV. The Argument from Injustice

The argument from injustice, in its shortest form, says that extreme injustice is no law. The best-known variant of the extreme injustice thesis is Radbruch's Formula. The Radbruch Formula is a kind of litmus test on the question of whether a theory of law is positivistic or non-positivistic. One who accepts the thesis that extreme injustice is no law has bid farewell to positivism.[57]

Raz's critique of the extreme injustice thesis begins with an analysis of an example that I have used in vindicating the extreme injustice thesis. The example concerns a case in which, on the one hand, Ordinance 11 applies, but, on the other, 'good legal reasons'[58] say that this ordinance ought not to be applied. A judge who grounds his decision on these good legal reasons cannot say that both Ordinance 11 and his decision are, at one and the same time, law. In order to avoid contradiction, he has to say that Ordinance 11 is not law.

Raz argues that this hypothetical situation only shows 'that the law can include a norm that grossly unjust laws are invalid'.[59] This inclusion is said to be a 'matter of social fact'.[60] Therefore, there is nothing 'in the example which is inconsistent with legal positivism'.[61]

[54] Alexy, *The Argument from Injustice* (n. 5 above), 39.

[55] Raz, 'The Argument from Justice, or How Not to Reply to Legal Positivism' (n. 1 above), 27–8.

[56] This applies to the English as well as to the German version.

[57] That adherence to the extreme injustice thesis entails the rejection of positivism does not mean that the rejection of this thesis entails adherence to positivism. By virtue of the argument from correctness it is possible to reject the extreme injustice thesis and to remain a non-positivist.

[58] Alexy, *The Argument from Injustice* (n. 5 above), 42.

[59] Raz, 'The Argument from Justice, or How Not to Reply to Legal Positivism' (n. 1 above), 29–30.

[60] Ibid., 31.

[61] Ibid. Raz refers not only to a power of the court transferred by 'legal rules', but also to a power 'sometimes independently of them, to change law, for example on the ground that it is grossly unjust' (ibid., 30). If this independence of legal rules counts as an independence from social facts, then Raz has, with this, crossed the border into non-positivism, even if the court's power to set aside extremely or grossly unjust laws independently of legal rules only 'sometimes' exists.

The reply misses the point of the example. The point of the example is that the clause 'good legal reasons' refers to authoritative as well as to non-authoritative reasons. The extreme injustice thesis refers to the second class of reasons. The example shows that if there are reasons of the second kind, that is, non-authoritative legal reasons, they affect the concept of law essentially. This appears to be an analytical truth.

Of course, the hypothesis that there are such legal reasons does not count as proof of their existence. Raz, therefore, is right to maintain that in order to argue against legal positivism, it is not enough to show that it would be *morally* right not to follow grossly or extremely unjust law or that it lies beyond the legitimate power—that is, the *morally* legitimate power—of any given authority to issue extremely unjust laws.[62] These two assumptions about moral rightness or legitimacy do not, as such, entail the conclusion that no extremely or grossly unjust law is law, that is, they do not entail the extreme injustice thesis. According to Raz, '[s]uch an inference requires the additional premise that law can never be unjust in these ways'.[63] It does not matter whether this requirement is, indeed, an additional premise that connects the two assumptions with the extreme injustice thesis as conclusion or whether it is simply another way of expressing the conclusion. The decisive point is that 'the whole argument is about the truth of that premise'.[64]

Raz argues that I provide no reason for thinking that the extreme injustice thesis is true or for the claim that owing to the extreme injustice thesis officials, *qua* officials, must believe that they are 'authorized by law' to set aside extremely unjust laws.[65] Perhaps I have still not made my argument clear enough. It can be divided into two parts: a theoretical part and a normative part.

The theoretical part concerns the nature of law. The claim to correctness, which is necessarily raised by law, comprises an institutional or authoritative dimension as well as an ideal or critical one. This implies that it belongs to the nature of law that it has a double character. Law, at the same time, is essentially authoritative and essentially ideal. It is, of course, possible to provide a description of the law of a land that pays heed solely to its institutional or authoritative dimension, and

[62] Raz makes the additional point that the evil flowing from not applying extremely unjust law may sometimes be worse than the evil of applying them (ibid., 32). It is not clear what kinds of cases he has in mind here. I should like simply to remark that there are cases in which, on the one hand, what Raz says about the extent of evil is true, but, on the other, that the extreme injustice thesis, if it applies at all, applies here. Consider a statute requiring that one be sentenced to death on ethnic grounds, and compare a situation in which sentencing one person to death can save a hundred others from being treated in the same way. It shall be assumed that the evil of not applying the statute with respect to one person is, in this constellation, worse than the evil of applying it. But this does not imply that the statute must be considered for that reason alone as valid law, whereas it would not be legally valid for reasons of extreme injustice if sentencing the one saved no one. This shows that the question of the legal validity of a statute has to be separated from considerations concerning the balance of evil in a concrete case.

[63] Ibid., 32.

[64] Ibid.

[65] Ibid., 33.

this is precisely what our observer does. But—and this is the telling point—such a description is restricted to a single necessary aspect of law. In restricting oneself to just one of the necessary aspects of a thing, one cannot grasp its nature.

That the claim to correctness, which is necessarily connected with the law, has two dimensions implies that law is necessarily connected with two kinds of values or principles, those of the authoritative dimension of law and those of its ideal dimension. The most abstract value or principle of the authoritative dimension is legal certainty, the most abstract value or principle attached to the ideal dimension is justice. Law would not be law if it did not comprise these principles, which, as principles or values, say what law ought to be. This implies that it is impossible to say what the law is without saying what it ought to be. Indeed, it is true that law is a social institution. Its being a social institution does not, however, preclude its being a moral entity. Law is a part of reality that refers necessarily to the ideal.

If this is a correct explanation of the nature of law, the theoretical task of explaining the nature of law necessarily includes a normative task. If justice as well as legal certainty is a part of the nature of law, a participant in the legal system, when confronted with extremely unjust law, say Ordinance 11, must ask himself whether justice as a necessary element of law prevents him from applying it, or whether legal certainty prevents him from following the lines of substantive correctness. The answer to this question requires that one strike a balance between these two principles. The result of this balancing or weighing is that the principle of legal certainty precedes justice even if the law is unjust, save for one sort of case: that in which the threshold of extreme injustice is crossed. The reason for the general priority of legal certainty over justice is the moral value and legitimacy of authoritativeness.[66] But if moral reasons are relevant as reasons for abiding by the law, then moral reasons must also be relevant as reasons against abiding by the law; and if reasons of the same kind stand on both sides of a problem, then it is always possible that sometimes those on the one side will prevail, and sometimes those on the other. Thus, the possibility cannot be excluded that the moral reasons on the side of legal certainty will be outweighed by moral reasons on the side of justice. Precisely this is the case when the threshold of extreme injustice is crossed. That happens when human rights are grossly violated.[67] In this way, the Radbruch Formula is vindicated by normative arguments that are embedded in theoretical arguments.

The reproach that I have not offered any argument in favour of the thesis that extreme injustice can never be law is Raz's main point with respect to the extreme injustice thesis. Raz adds to it further objections that are directed against arguments I have put forward in the discussion of this thesis. They address deep philosophical questions, and it goes without saying that I can only offer some brief comments here.

[66] See on this Joseph Raz, 'Incorporation by Law', *Legal Theory* 10 (2004), 1–17, at 8–10.
[67] See Alexy, *The Argument from Injustice* (n. 5 above), 58.

The extreme injustice thesis presupposes that it is possible to know whether a law is, or is not, extremely unjust. In order to show that this is possible, I have connected the concept of rational justification with that of knowledge: 'If there are notions of justice that are rationally justifiable, then one who rationally justifies his view that an action is unjust can be said to know this.'[68] Raz objects that 'one can argue rationally to a mistaken conclusion'.[69] In theoretical discourse this is an obvious truth, but in practical discourse, too, Raz's thesis is correct: it is, at any rate, correct if one understands 'argue rationally' as referring to the degree of rationality that one can actually achieve in real discourses. There will always be the possibility of error. If, however, one reads 'argue rationally' as, in Raz's words, giving 'adequate or completely vindicatory support by reason',[70] then a rather close relation between rational argument and knowledge emerges. This is not the place to discuss how close this relation is, and it is not the place to consider the connection between real and ideal discourses either. I want simply to remark that the concepts of rational argument and knowledge are intrinsically intertwined just as the other concepts found in the objectivity family—truth, correctness, intersubjectivity, reality, and the like—are.

V. The Argument from Principles

The argument from injustice focuses on an exceptional situation, that of a statute that is unjust in the extreme. My reply to positivism adds to this a further argument that concerns the everyday life of law. Specifically, it is an argument that addresses the question of legal argumentation in the open area of the positive law. Due to the complexity of legal argumentation, this argument can be presented in different ways. Perhaps its most interesting version is the argument from principles.

The argument from principles holds, first, that all legal systems, beginning at a minimal level of development, necessarily comprise principles; secondly, that the necessary presence of principles in the legal system leads to a necessary connection between law and some morality or another; and, thirdly, that this, together with the claim to correctness, leads to a necessary connection between law and moral correctness.[71]

Raz's critique of the argument from principles is confined to two points. The first concerns the first step of the argument, that is, the thesis:

[68] Ibid., 52.
[69] Raz, 'The Argument from Justice, or How Not to Reply to Legal Positivism' (n. 1 above), 33.
[70] Joseph Raz, *Engaging Reason* (Oxford: Oxford University Press, 1999), 159.
[71] Alexy, *The Argument from Injustice* (n. 5 above), 74–81.

> that in all legal systems in which there are doubtful cases that give rise to the question of striking a balance, it is legally required to strike a balance and thereby to take principles into account. Thus, in all legal systems of this kind, principles are, for legal reasons, necessary elements of the legal system.[72]

According to Raz, this is merely a special case of a general form of argument establishing 'that every legal system contains various kinds of laws'.[73] The first step of the argument from principles is said to have the same structure as the argument: 'in all legal systems in which deciding a case requires enforcing a duty there are duty-imposing rules'.[74] There is, however, an important difference. The step from the enforcement of a duty to a duty-imposing rule does not involve any interesting shift from one concept to another. There is such a shift, however, in the case of the argument from principles. The argument begins with the possibility of striking a balance, proceeds from this to its necessity, and arrives, finally, at the concept of a principle. It is difficult to say whether this is as 'unexciting'[75] as the step from a duty to a duty-imposing rule. Here it suffices to say that the two arguments have quite different structures, a point that emerges clearly from the fact that the step from the concept of balancing to the concept of a principle is sound only if some fundamental theses of the theory of balancing are true.

Raz's second point, however, has to be taken far more seriously. It concerns the concept of incorporation. The fact that the courts of a country are required, by law, to apply principles no more incorporates these principles into the law of that country than does the requirement that the courts of a country are to apply, as a matter of law, standards drawn from foreign law.[76] Thus, Raz is arguing, conflict-of-law doctrines show that the law can require the application of certain standards without thereby turning these standards into the law of the land.[77] This applies not only to foreign law but also to moral principles.

The validity of this argument depends essentially on what is meant by saying that the courts are required 'by law' to apply principles. In case of foreign law, 'by law' means 'by positive law'. The same is, in principle, true with respect to inclusive positivism because the inclusion must be a matter of positive law if inclusive positivism is to remain a species of positivism.[78] Things look completely different, however, from the standpoint of non-positivism. The clause 'by law' acquires the meaning of the clause 'by the nature of law'. The overarching concept of law, that

[72] Ibid., 74.
[73] Raz, 'The Argument from Justice, or How Not to Reply to Legal Positivism' (n. 1 above), 34.
[74] Ibid.
[75] Ibid.
[76] Ibid.
[77] Raz, 'Incorporation by Law' (n. 66 above), 10.
[78] See Jules Coleman, 'Authority and Reason' in *The Autonomy of Law. Essays on Legal Positivism*, ed. Robert P. George (Oxford: Clarendon Press, 1996), 287–319, at 316.

comprises the authoritative dimension of law as well as the ideal, necessarily and essentially includes moral principles. With respect to the function of 'so-called incorporating laws', Raz has remarked: 'Given that morality applies anyway, their function cannot be to incorporate it.'[79] To this it can be added that morality, by virtue of the nature of law, is already incorporated.

[79] Raz, 'Incorporation by Law' (n. 66 above), 17.

6
The Ideal Dimension of Law

Does law have an ideal dimension? Or can the concept and the nature of law be completely grasped by considering its real dimension alone? The dual-nature thesis sets out the claim that law necessarily comprises both a real or factual dimension and an ideal or critical one. The factual dimension concerns law as fact, that is, as social facts. The social facts to which it refers are authoritative issuance and social efficacy, and each of these is familiar in many different variations and in many different relations to each other. Authoritative issuance as well as enduring social efficacy presuppose institutionalization of one sort or another. For this reason, the real dimension can also be called the 'institutional dimension'. The ideal dimension refers to correctness, primarily to moral correctness. If one claims that social facts alone can determine what is and is not required by law, this amounts to the endorsement of a positivistic concept of law. Once moral correctness is added as a necessary third element, everything changes fundamentally. A non-positivist concept of law emerges. Thus, the dual-nature thesis, in setting out the claim that law necessarily comprises both a real and ideal dimension, implies non-positivism.

I. The Claim to Correctness

The Archimedean point of the thesis that law necessarily has an ideal dimension is the argument from correctness. The argument from correctness states that individual legal norms and individual legal decisions as well as legal systems as a whole necessarily lay claim to correctness. The necessity of raising this claim can be shown by demonstrating that the claim to correctness is necessarily implicit in law. The best means of demonstrating its necessity is the method of performative contradiction.[1] An example of a performative contradiction is the fictitious first article of a constitution that reads:

> *X* is a sovereign, federal, and unjust republic.

It is scarcely possible to deny that this article is somehow absurd. The idea underlying the method of performative contradiction, as applied here, is to explain the absurdity

[1] Robert Alexy, *The Argument from Injustice. A Reply to Legal Positivism* (1992), trans. Bonnie Litschewski Paulson and Stanley L. Paulson (Oxford: Clarendon Press, 2002), 35–9.

Law's Ideal Dimension. Robert Alexy, Oxford University Press. © Robert Alexy 2021.
DOI: 10.1093/oso/9780198796831.003.0007

as stemming from a contradiction between what is implicitly claimed in framing a constitution—namely, that it is just—and what is explicitly declared—namely, that it is unjust. Now, justice counts as a special case of correctness, because justice is nothing other than the correctness of distribution and compensation.[2] Therefore, the contradiction in our example is not only a contradiction with respect to the dichotomy of just and unjust but also a contradiction with respect to the dichotomy of correct and incorrect. What is more, in the aforementioned example of the fictitious first article of a constitution, the contradiction that arises there between what is explicit and what is implicit is necessary. It could be avoided if one were to abandon the implicit claim. But to do this would represent a transition from a legal system to a system of naked power relations, in other words, to something that is, necessarily, no legal system at all.[3]

Many objections have been raised against the argument from correctness, and numerous replies have been offered.[4] This exchange shall not be repeated here in any detail. Only one argument, recently put forward by John Finnis against the thesis that the claim to correctness is necessarily raised in law—it can be called the necessity thesis—shall be considered here.

In the Postscript to *Natural Law and Natural Rights*, Finnis maintains that 'it is possible that some legal systems abstain from claiming to be morally obligatory'.[5] If one substitutes 'correct' for 'morally obligatory', this is a clear negation of the necessity thesis. I criticized this position in 2013.[6] In his reply Finnis puts forward a 'competing argument'[7] which he had already presented in his 'Reflections and Responses'.[8] It runs as follows:

[2] Robert Alexy, 'Giustizia come correttezza' *Ragion pratica* 9 (1997), 103–13, at 105.

[3] Robert Alexy, 'Law and Correctness', trans. Kirsten Bock, *Current Legal Problems* 51 (1998), 205–21, at 213–14 (in this volume: Chapter 21, 312–25, at 319–20), and Alexy, *The Argument from Injustice* (n. 1 above), 32–5.

[4] See, for instance, Eugenio Bulygin, 'Alexy und das Richtigkeitsargument', in *Rechtsnorm und Rechtswirklichkeit. Festschrift für Werner Krawietz*, eds Aulis Aarnio, Stanley L. Paulson, Ota Weinberger, et al. (Berlin: Duncker & Humblot, 1993), 19–24; Robert Alexy, 'Bulygins Kritik des Richtigkeitsarguments', in *Normative Systems in Legal and Moral Theory. Festschrift für Carlos E. Alchourrón and Eugenio Bulygin*, eds Ernesto Garzón Valdés, Werner Krawietz, Georg Henrik von Wright, et al. (Berlin: Duncker & Humblot, 1997), 235–50; Eugenio Bulygin, 'Alexy's Thesis of the Necessary Connection between Law and Morality', *Ratio Juris* 13 (2000), 133–7; Robert Alexy, 'On the Thesis of a Necessary Connection between Law and Morality: Bulygin's Critique', *Ratio Juris* 13 (2000), 138–47; Eugenio Bulygin, 'Alexy Between Positivism and Non-positivism', in *Neutrality and Theory of Law*, eds Jordi Ferrer Beltrán, José Juan Moreso, and Diego M. Papayannis (Dordrecht: Springer, 2013), 49–59; Robert Alexy, 'Between Positivism and Non-positivism? A Third Reply to Eugenio Bulygin', in *Neutrality and Theory of Law*, eds Jordi Ferrer Beltrán, José Juan Moreso, and Diego M. Papayannis (Dordrecht: Springer, 2013), 225–38.

[5] John Finnis, *Natural Law and Natural Rights*, 2nd edn (Oxford: Oxford University Press, 2011), 432 n.13.

[6] Robert Alexy, 'Some Reflections on the Ideal Dimension of Law and on the Legal Philosophy of John Finnis', *The American Journal of Jurisprudence* 58 (2013) 97–110, at 100–1.

[7] John Finnis, 'Law as Fact and as Reason for Action: A Response to Robert Alexy on Law's "Ideal Dimension"', *The American Journal of Jurisprudence* 59 (2014), 85–109, at 91.

[8] John Finnis, 'Reflections and Responses', in *Reason, Morality, and Law. The Philosophy of John Finnis*, eds John Keown and Robert P. George (Oxford: Oxford University Press, 2013), 459–584, at 538.

It seems entirely possible for a regime to proclaim:

> Our law, which satisfies all the (say) Hartian criteria (primary rules restricting violence, theft and fraud, secondary rules of recognition, change and adjudication, etc.), imposes legal duties and confers legal rights that have nothing to do with moral rights. Our law imposes legal obligations that are not moral obligations, and has nothing to do with justice in the moral sense etc., but is instead a structure of ordered power designed to pursue our sectional purposes. We as regime will mercilessly enforce this law.[9]

This proclamation uses the clause 'has (have) nothing to do with' twice. How is this to be understood? A first interpretation would be that the law to which the proclamation refers has no impact on moral rights or justice in the moral sense. It would have no impact if it could neither violate moral rights or justice nor protect them. Finnis connects the proclamation with 'wicked and exploitative regimes',[10] and there is no doubt that wicked and exploitative regimes can violate moral rights and justice. Thus, a negative impact exists. And there exists a positive impact, too. With the words 'rules restricting violence, theft and fraud', the proclamation refers to requirements that are also raised by morality. Therefore, the clause 'has (have) nothing to do with' cannot be understood as saying that contact between the law in question and morality is impossible. For this reason, only a second interpretation is possible, one in which the clause states that the law in question is indifferent to the question of whether moral rights or justice are violated, to whatever degree. It would express a motto like right or wrong, '[o]ur law'![11]

This intended moral indifference, however, does not imply that no claim to correctness is raised. In the proclamation, '[o]ur law' is characterized as 'a structure of ordered power designated to pursue our sectional purposes'.[12] This comes quite close to the counter example raised by Joseph Raz in his critique of the argument from correctness. Raz maintains that the argument from correctness 'is a conceptual thesis not specifically about the law (though it applies to the law) but about the nature of purposes, intentional actions and their products'.[13] With this, the claim to correctness is said to be nothing other than a general claim to appropriateness connected with all intentional actions. As such, it applies, in contrast to what I have said in *The Argument of Injustice*, even to the actions of a system of bandits.[14] Raz mentions 'being self-enriching' as a possible standard of the appropriateness of

[9] Finnis, 'Law as Fact and as Reason for Action' (n. 7 above), 91–2.

[10] Ibid., 92.

[11] Ibid., 91.

[12] Ibid., 91–2.

[13] Joseph Raz, 'The Argument from Justice or How Not to Reply to Legal Positivism', in *Law, Rights and Discourse. The Legal Philosophy of Robert Alexy*, ed. George Pavlakos (Oxford: Hart, 2007), 17–35, at 28.

[14] Alexy, *The Argument from Injustice* (n.1 above), 33.

the bandits' action.[15] '[B]eing self-enriching' seems to belong to the same category as 'designed to pursue our sectional purposes'[16] in Finnis's proclamation, namely, that of maximizing the utility for a certain group. With this, we arrive at the intermediate result that '[o]ur law' raises a claim to correctness that refers to sectional or particular purposes as criteria of correctness.

But this is not the end of the story. It can be contested that sectional purposes are adequate as criteria of correctness in law. Law essentially concerns questions of distribution and compensation. As already remarked, however, questions of correct distribution and compensation are questions of justice. Still, for the authors of the proclamation adduced by Finnis, namely, the '[w]e as regime',[17] there remains a way out. They can explicitly abandon the claim to correctness. For this they might change the characterization of their law as 'a structure of ordered power designed to pursue our sectional purposes'[18] into 'an incorrect structure of ordered power designed to pursue our sectional purposes'. If it were offered seriously and not as a joke, however, this would place the proclamation in the realm of absurdity, side by side with the fictitious first article mentioned above. To be sure, the claim to correctness can be violated, and it is nowhere completely fulfilled. But it is raised just as necessarily in law as the claim to truth is raised in science.[19]

II. Conceptual Analysis and Conceptual Necessities

Finnis connects his argument that the claim to correctness is not necessarily raised in law with a methodological objection consisting of two parts, an argument from fruitlessness and an argument from deficiency.

A. The Argument from Fruitlessness

The argument from fruitlessness is expressed in the following way:

> I do not think that conceptual analyses yield significantly useful fruits in legal, political and moral philosophy. In particular, discussions of what is conceptually possible or impossible, or again of what is or is not conceptually necessary, are virtually always fruitless.[20]

[15] Raz, 'The Argument from Justice' (n. 13 above), 27.

[16] Finnis, 'Law as Fact and as Reason for Action' (n. 7 above), 92.

[17] Ibid.

[18] Ibid.

[19] Robert Alexy, 'An Answer to Joseph Raz', in *Law, Rights and Discourse*, ed. George Pavlakos (Oxford: Hart, 2007), 37–55, at 49 (in this volume: Chapter 5, 64–82, at 76).

[20] Finnis, 'Law as Fact and as Reason for Action' (n. 7 above), 90.

This can be confronted with the thesis that the question of whether there exists a necessary connection between the real and the ideal dimension of law, that is, between law and morality, is of the utmost importance for our understanding of law. To be sure, the thesis that there exists a necessary connection between law and morality can be interpreted in a way that it is of little interest because, being interpreted in this way, it can be accepted by positivists and non-positivists alike.[21] But when it is transformed into a more precise version, in which it states that there exists a necessary connection between legal validity or legal correctness on the one hand and moral correctness and incorrectness on the other,[22] it becomes clear that the concepts of necessity, impossibility, and possibility are indispensable if one wishes to draw a precise and systematic picture of the relation between exclusive positivism, inclusive positivism, and non-positivism.

This can be demonstrated by means of the 'necessity triad'.[23] Within positivism, the distinction between exclusive and inclusive positivism is the most important division where the relation between law and morality is concerned. *Exclusive positivism*, as advocated most prominently by Joseph Raz, maintains that morality is necessarily excluded from the concept of law.[24] If one takes 'I' to stand for 'law includes morality', exclusive positivism can be expressed, using the necessity operator '$\Box$' and the negator '$\neg$', as:

(1) $$\Box\neg I.$$

Exclusive positivism stands in a relation of contrariety to non-positivism, which claims that morality is necessarily included in the concept of law. This can be expressed by:

(2) $$\Box I.$$

Finally, inclusive positivism, as defended, for instance, by Jules Coleman, counts as the rejection of both exclusive positivism and non-positivism. It says that morality is neither necessarily excluded nor necessarily included. The inclusion as well as the exclusion is declared to be a contingent or conventional matter,[25] turning on what the positive law in fact says. This can be expressed as follows:

(3) $$\neg\Box\neg I \;\&\; \neg\Box I.$$

[21] Joseph Raz, 'About Morality and the Nature of Law', *The American Journal of Jurisprudence* 48 (2003) 1–15, at 3; Raz, 'The Argument from Justice' (n. 13 above), 21; Alexy, 'An Answer to Joseph Raz' (n. 19 above), 43–5 (in this volume: Chapter 5, 69–7); Robert Alexy, 'On the Concept and the Nature of Law', *Ratio Juris* 21 (2008), 281–99, at. 285 (in this volume: Chapter 2, 18–35, at 21).

[22] Alexy, 'On the Concept and the Nature of Law' (n. 21 above), 285 n. 4. (in this volume: Chapter 2, 21–2, n 12)

[23] Robert Alexy, 'Law, Morality, and the Existence of Human Rights', *Ratio Juris* 25 (2012), 2–14, at 4 (in this volume: Chapter 4, 51–63, at 53).

[24] Joseph Raz, 'Legal Positivism and the Sources of Law', in Raz, *The Authority of Law. Essays on Law and Morality*, 2nd edn (Oxford: Oxford University Press, 2009), 37–52, at 47.

[25] Jules Coleman, *The Practice of Principle. In Defence of a Pragmatist Approach to Legal Theory* (Oxford: Oxford University Press, 2001), 108.

These three positions stand in a relationship of contrariety because each of the three excludes the others without stemming from the negation of any of the others. All of this can be expressed by means of the necessity triad. It exhausts the logical space of the positivism problem as far as the necessity of the inclusion or exclusion of morality in the concept of law is concerned:

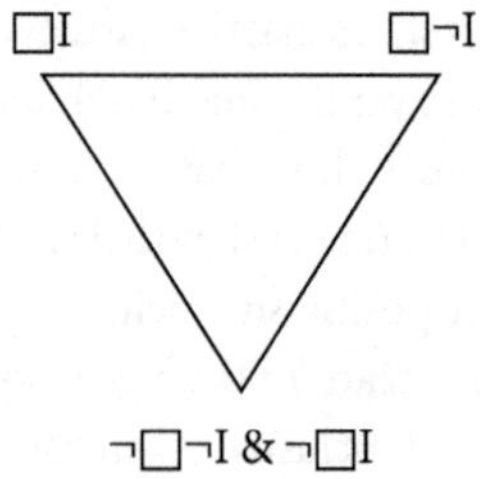

This analysis solves, as such, no normative problem but it enhances, as does analytical clarity in general, the 'process of critical practical reflection',[26] which Finnis sets in a certain opposition to conceptual analysis and the search for necessities. But the question cannot be one of either conceptual analysis or practical reflection. They have to be connected, and the extent to which conceptual analysis is perfect will have a considerable impact on the degree of the perfection of practical discourse or reflection. This suffices to reject the reproach of fruitlessness.

B. The Argument from Deficiency

The second methodological objection, the argument from deficiency, begins with the following thesis:

> Conceptual-analytic arguments regularly become ... a vexatious contest between rival intuitions about concepts supposed to be already fully and rightly established, and about more or less imaginary scenarios supposedly illustrative of the boundaries of those established concepts.[27]

This approach, the wrong way, attributed to me, is answered by Finnis with the right way. It focuses

> on the issues of reality and value that are really at stake, and really of interest. Far more fruitful are reflections and arguments about the *central* kinds of case that come into view when one looks at the main human realities and the main forms

[26] Finnis, 'Law as Fact and as Reason for Action' (n. 7 above), 90.
[27] Ibid., 93.

> of intrinsic human well-being and deprivation—in other words, to characteristically human *needs*—and to the kinds of choice (and thus kinds of practice and institution) intelligently and reasonably responsive to these needs.[28]

In his description of the wrong way, Finnis reproaches conceptual-analytical arguments for beginning from 'intuitions about concepts supposed to be already fully and rightly established'.[29] This is not true. To be sure, conceptual arguments begin with an analysis of the actual use of language. The analysis of the use of language is, however, as J. L. Austin aptly remarked, certainly '*not* the last word', but it provides a starting point for the analysis, or—as Austin puts it—a '*first* word', a first word that 'can everywhere be supplemented and improved upon and superseded'.[30] To this, Finnis's description of conceptual arguments as starting from 'concepts supposed to be already fully and rightly established' does not fit well. Finnis's second point concerns the use of 'more or less imaginary scenarios' as analytical tools. If the analytically oriented debate about the concept of law were to confine itself to confronting the actual use of language with more or less imaginary scenarios, it would, indeed, be a poor debate, but no such confinement is to be found in it. I always have emphasized the point that conceptual arguments have to be connected with normative arguments in order to answer substantive questions relating to the concept and the validity of law—as, for instance, the question of whether extreme injustice can be law.[31]

The basis of this model of conceptual-analytical argumentation is a dual-nature concept of concepts. Concepts are, on the one hand, social conventions about the meaning of words, established by the use of language. That is their real dimension. But, on the other hand, they are social conventions that raise a claim to correctness. That is their ideal dimension. This ideal dimension requires, to put it in Kant's words, that concepts be 'adequate to the object'.[32] The concept of law does not refer to a natural kind—such as the concepts of water, black holes, and killing—but to a non-natural kind in the form of a social kind.[33] The argument from correctness *qua* conceptual-analytical argument requires that normative or practical arguments be given in order to establish the adequacy of the concept of law as a concept of a social kind, normative arguments that are based on the idea of making the best of this social practice in the light of its functions or tasks.[34] These arguments include 'the

[28] Ibid.

[29] Ibid.

[30] John L. Austin, 'A Plea for Excuses', in Austin, *Philosophical Papers*, 2nd edn, eds J. O. Urmson and G. J. Warnock (Oxford: Oxford University Press, 1970), 175–204, at 185.

[31] Alexy, *The Argument from Injustice* (n. 1 above), 20–3, 40, 42–3, 62

[32] Immanuel Kant, *Critique of Pure Reason*, trans. Werner S. Pluhar (Indianapolis, Ind.: Hackett, 1996), 680; A 728, B 756.

[33] Alexy, 'On the Concept and the Nature of Law' (n. 21 above), 284 (in this volume: Chapter 2, 20–1).

[34] Robert Alexy, 'The Nature of Arguments about the Nature of Law', in *Rights. Culture, and the Law. Themes from the Legal and Political Philosophy of Joseph Raz*, eds Lukas H. Meyer, Stanley L. Paulson, and Thomas W. Pogge (Oxford: Oxford University Press, 2003), 3–16 at 7.

issues of reality and value that are really at stake' as well as the 'human *needs*' that Finnis misses in my approach.[35]

Finnis adds the argument that my conception of an 'expedient or adequate concept formation that is justified by normative arguments'[36] is

> not so much about the moral need for law, and law's consequent essential or central-case features but rather about whether or not it is expedient or inexpedient to adopt a boundary line between the legally valid and legally invalid by reference to injustice or at least severe or intolerable injustice.[37]

This sounds as if my theory of law were concentrated only or mainly on one thesis, a thesis Finnis qualifies as 'a subordinate theorem',[38] namely the Radbruch Formula which, in its shortest form, states that extreme injustice is no law.[39] To be sure, the Radbruch Formula is an important touchstone with respect to the question of whether a theory of law is a positivistic or a non-positivistic theory. But it is by no means the only element of the ideal dimension of law. It concerns 'an exceptional situation, that of a statute that is unjust in the extreme'.[40] Not only in law do extreme situations offer the possibility of gaining insights not available in normal situations. What would physics be without extreme situations? But I refer not only to extreme situations. In *The Argument from Injustice* I proceed in my analysis of the participant's perspective in three steps. I begin with the argument from correctness, which is the basis of the other arguments.[41] Then I continue with the argument from injustice that focuses, indeed, on the exceptional situation of extreme injustice.[42] Finally, I elaborate the argument from principles[43] which concerns the 'ideal dimension'[44] in the 'everyday life of the law'.[45] Here, the central argument turns on the connections between the claim to correctness, principles, and legal argumentation.

III. The Necessity of the Real Dimension of Law

A closer analysis of the ideal dimension of law presupposes an analysis of the real dimension. Here, again, the concept of necessity is central. The starting point is the idea

[35] Finnis, 'Law as Fact and as Reason for Action' (n. 7 above), 93.
[36] Alexy, *The Argument from Injustice* (n. 1 above), 40.
[37] Finnis, 'Law as Fact and as Reason for Action' (n. 7 above), 90 n. 22.
[38] Finnis, *Natural Law and Natural Rights* (n. 5 above), 351
[39] Robert Alexy, 'A Defence of Radbruch's Formula', in *Recrafting the Rule of Law: The Limits of Legal Order*, ed. David Dyzenhaus (Oxford: Hart, 1999), 15–39, at 17.
[40] Alexy, *The Argument from Injustice* (n. 1 above), 68.
[41] Ibid., 35–9.
[42] Ibid., 40–68.
[43] Ibid., 68–81.
[44] Ibid., 81
[45] Ibid., 68.

of pure ideality. A purely ideal system of reasons for action would be a system based on nothing other than moral and prudential reflection, rational practical discourse, and spontaneous compliance with the results of reflection and discourse simply owing to their correctness. Such a system would be deficient for three reasons.[46] The first is the problem of practical knowledge.[47] There are a great many practical questions in which no agreement can be arrived at, not even between reasonable persons. That makes legally regulated procedures necessary, procedures that guarantee the arrival at a decision which determines what the law is. This implies the necessity of authoritative issuance as social fact. The second reason is that spontaneous compliance is not enough. If everyone could violate the rules authoritatively issued without any risk, the rules would lose their social efficacy. Therefore, their enforcement is necessary. This necessity includes coercion, incorporating it into the concept of law alongside correctness.[48] Determination and enforcement are to be completed by means of a third reason. Numerous needs and purposes cannot be satisfied by spontaneous action alone. Organization is necessary, and organization presupposes law. For these three reasons, the deficiency of the ideal dimension, if conceived as a purely ideal system of reasons for action, leads to the necessity of positive law, that is, to the necessity of the real dimension. This necessity, however, does not stem from positive law. It stems from the moral requirement of avoiding the costs of anarchy and civil war and achieving the advantages of social coordination and cooperation.

IV. A Conceptual Framework

A. First-Order and Second-Order Correctness

One might assume that the necessity of positivity implies positivism. This, however, would be incompatible with the claim to correctness. To be sure, the moral necessity of positivity implies the correctness of positivity. But the correctness of positivity does not by any means imply that positivity is to be understood as having an exclusive character. To grant positivity an exclusive character would be to fail to take account of the fact that the claim to substantive correctness—first and foremost, the claim to justice—does not vanish once law is institutionalized. It remains alive, standing behind and found in the law, and it is the main task of the theory of the ideal dimension of law to make this explicit. In order to achieve this, one has to distinguish two stages or levels of correctness: first-order correctness and second-order correctness. First-order correctness refers only to the ideal dimension. It

[46] Alexy, 'The Nature of Arguments about the Nature of Law' (n. 33 above), 8.

[47] Robert Alexy, 'The Dual Nature of Law', *Ratio Juris* 23 (2010), 167–82, at 172–3 (in this volume: Chapter 3, 36–50, at 40–2).

[48] Alexy, 'The Nature of Arguments about the Nature of Law' (n. 33 above), 6–9.

concerns justice as such. Second-order correctness is more comprehensive. It refers both to the ideal and to the real dimension. This means that it concerns justice as well as legal certainty. Legal certainty, however, can be achieved only by means of positivity, that is, by determination, enforcement, and organization. In this way, the claim to correctness, *qua* second-order claim, necessarily connects both the principle of justice and the principle of legal certainty with law.

The principle of legal certainty is a formal principle. It requires commitment to what is authoritatively issued and socially efficacious. The principle of justice is, first and foremost, a material or substantive principle. It requires that the decision be morally correct. Both principles, as principles in general,[49] can collide, and they often do. Neither can ever supplant the other completely, that is, in all cases. On the contrary, the dual nature of law requires that they be seen in correct proportion to each other. Thus, second-order correctness is a matter of balancing. This shows that balancing has a role to play not only in the creation and application of law, that is, in legal practice, but also at the very basis of law. It is a part of the nature of law.

The distinction between first-order and second-order correctness is necessary in order to determine the relation between the real and the ideal dimension, but, taken alone, it does not suffice to achieve this. In order to determine the relation between them, this distinction has to be connected with three further distinctions: first, the distinction between the observer's and the participant's perspective, second, the distinction between perspectives and dimensions, and third, the distinction between classifying and qualifying connections.

B. Observer and Participant

The difference between the observer's and the participant's perspective is this. The observer asks questions about and adduces arguments on behalf of a position that reflects how legal questions are actually decided in that legal system, whereas the participant asks questions about and adduces arguments on behalf of what he deems to be the correct answer to a legal question in the legal system in which he finds himself. The observer's perspective is defined by the question 'How are legal decisions actually made?', the participant's by the question 'What is the correct legal answer?'

These two questions require different kinds of argument. The observer is confined to fact-based arguments, whereas the participant, say, a judge, has to adduce, alongside fact-based arguments, normative arguments that are not fact-based. This applies to all cases that, owing to the '*open texture*'[50] of law, cannot be resolved

[49] Robert Alexy, *A Theory of Constitutional Rights* (1985), trans. Julian Rivers (Oxford: Oxford University Press, 2002), 44–110.

[50] H. L. A. Hart, *The Concept of Law*, 2nd edn (Oxford: Clarendon Press, 1994), 128.

solely on the basis of fact-based arguments. These normative arguments can be classified as moral arguments about how the law ought to be. This is not, however, to say that the considerations of an observer

> cannot include considerations about what the participants whom he observes think the law ought to be. One might term such considerations about what persons think the law ought to be 'indirect' or 'third-person' considerations by contrast to the direct or first-person considerations of the participant.[51]

Finnis has characterized this conception of the observer's point of view as so 'inclusive' that it comes close to Hart's thesis that the positivist method allows one to see and 'understand all that law really is—the whole "real dimension" of law including the participant's perspective'.[52]

Thus, Finnis is arguing, the positivist has the possibility of declaring superfluous a participant's perspective, distinguished from the observer's perspective by means of its specific relation to the ideal dimension, where the participant's perspective implies a necessary connection between law and morality. But this is not true. There exists a fundamental difference between the indirect or third-person considerations of an observer about participants and the direct or first-person considerations of the participant himself. Take just one example. Consider a court which has to decide a case with respect to which only one precedent exists. The precedent includes a dissenting vote, and the judges discuss whether, in their new decision, they should follow the dissenter in the earlier case. In order to decide this, they have to answer the question of whether the opinion of the former majority or the opinion of the dissenting judge is correct. This answer requires normative arguments addressed to the issue of the correct legal decision. The position of an observer is completely different. If he is a master at his trade, he can explain without a flaw the former decision and, equally perfectly, he can predict the new one. But he cannot say what would be the correct decision now without shifting from the observer's perspective to the participant's perspective. This implies that it is first, necessary to distinguish the observer's perspective from the participant's perspective and second, to connect the participant's perspective with the ideal dimension.[53]

[51] Alexy, 'Some Reflections on the Ideal Dimension of Law and on the Legal Philosophy of John Finnis' (n. 6 above), 103–4.

[52] Finnis, 'Law as Fact and as Reason for Action' (n. 7 above), 89.

[53] There is one exception that connects even the observer's perspective with the ideal dimension. It concerns the claim to correctness. A system of social rules that does not raise a claim to correctness is not a legal system. This conceptual truth concerns, first, the ideal dimension and is, second, inevitable even for one who qualifies solely as an observer. See Alexy, 'Some Reflections on the Ideal Dimension of Law and on the Legal Philosophy of John Finnis' (n. 6 above), 104.

C. Perspectives and Dimensions

Finnis has qualified the ideas of dual nature and dual dimensions as 'elusive'.[54] To address things like the Radbruch Formula 'in terms of "real" and "ideal" "dimensions of law"' is said to be 'unhelpful'.[55] My concentration on the distinction between the observer's and the participant's perspective in *The Argument from Injustice*, Finnis continues, was 'clearer'.[56] Now the ideas of a real and an ideal dimension, already present in *The Argument from Injustice*,[57] comprise, on the one hand, the complex class of elements to which the observer has to refer when he describes the law, and, on the other, the even more complex class of elements to which the participant has to refer in order to arrive at a correct decision or judgement. Without these two classes of elements, the two perspectives cannot be adequately grasped. For this reason, there exists no question of alternatives where perspectives and dimensions are concerned, as Finnis seems to assume.[58] Rather, the question is one of explication. The two dimensions are necessary for the explication of the two perspectives. Thus, if Finnis's thesis that the idea of dimensions was elusive, the idea of perspectives would be elusive too.

D. Classifying and Qualifying Connections

Finnis and I agree that the participant's perspective is the central perspective.[59] The reason for this is that legal systems are possible without naked or sole observers, but they are not possible without participants. For this reason, the participant's perspective is the true battlefield of the debate between positivism and non-positivism. The mere fact that the positivist's separation thesis is essentially correct from the observer's perspective[60] says nothing on behalf of the positivist's separation thesis.[61]

An answer to the question of how the relation between law and morality or between the real and the ideal dimension is to be determined from the participant's perspective is not possible without the distinction between classifying and

[54] Finnis, 'Law as Fact and as Reason for Action' (n. 7 above), 86.

[55] Ibid., 101.

[56] Ibid., 87.

[57] Alexy, *The Argument from Injustice* (n. 1 above), 81, 128, 130.

[58] Finnis sometimes speaks of a 'double life' of law; see Finnis, 'Law as Fact and as Reason for Action' (n. 7 above), 95–6. Perhaps this can be interpreted as a move away from the alternatives of perspectives and dimensions in the direction of the dual nature thesis, which, again, includes the idea of two dimensions.

[59] Ibid., 102.

[60] Alexy, *The Argument from Injustice* (n. 1 above), 31, 35.

[61] Raz has argued that there exists no difference between the observer's and the participant's perspective; Raz 'The Argument from Justice' (n. 13 above), 22–5. If this were true, we were quite close to the truth of positivism. But it is not true; see Alexy, 'An Answer to Joseph Raz' (n 19 above) 45–8 (in this volume: Chapter 5, 72–5).

qualifying connections between law and morality. The effect of a classifying connection is the loss of legal validity. By contrast, the effect of a qualifying connection is legal defectiveness or incorrectness that does not, however, undermine legal validity.[62] The decisive point here is that the effect of moral defectiveness or incorrectness is *legal* defectiveness or incorrectness. That morally defective laws are morally defective is a trivial truth. The positivist has no problem agreeing with this. But that these laws are, over and above this, also legally defective is not only not trivial but, indeed, of the greatest significance for the relation between the real and the ideal dimension of law, and this not only for theoretical reasons but also for reasons practical in nature. If the defect were merely a moral one, it would be difficult to explain why a higher court—independently of what the positive law says—has legal power to set aside the unjust decision of a lower court in a case in which this unjust decision is every bit as compatible with positive law as a just decision would be.

The positivist's separation thesis states that there is no necessary connection between legal correctness or legal validity on the one hand and moral correctness and incorrectness on the other. This implies that positivism—whether exclusive or inclusive—must deny the existence of both a necessary classifying and a necessary qualifying connection in order to remain positivistic. In contrast to this, the necessity operator '$\Box$' in '$\Box$I', which represents in the necessity triad all forms of non-positivism,[63] refers to classifying as well as to qualifying connections.

The claim to correctness implies that all forms of non-positivism must adhere to the thesis that there exists a necessary qualifying connection between law and morality in all cases. This is different with respect to the classifying connection. Non-positivism can determine the effects of moral defects or incorrectness on legal validity in three diverse ways.[64] It can, first, exclude all morally defective or incorrect norms from the class of legally valid norms. This most radical form of non-positivism can be called 'exclusive non-positivism'. A classical version of this view is expressed by Augustine's statement that 'a law that is not just would not seem to me to be a law'.[65] A recent example is Beyleveld's and Brownsword's thesis 'that immoral rules are not legally valid'.[66] If one employs 'V' for 'is valid', this can be expressed, with the help of the universal quantifier '$\forall$', by:

(4) $$\forall x \neg Vx.$$

[62] Alexy, *The Argument from Injustice* (n. 1 above), 26.

[63] In contrast to this, exclusive positivism is represented in the necessity triad as '$\Box\neg$I' and inclusive positivism as '$\neg\Box\neg$I & $\neg\Box$I'.

[64] Alexy, 'Law, Morality, and the Existence of Human Rights' (n. 23 above), 4–7 (in this volume: Chapter 4, 53–6).

[65] Augustinus, *De libero arbitrio* I, 11, in *Opera. Werke*, vol. 9, trans. and ed. by Johannes Brachtendorf (Paderborn: Ferdinand Schöningh, 2006), 86: '*Nam lex mihi esse non videtur, quae iusta non fuerit.*'

[66] Deryck Beyleveld and Roger Brownsword, *Human Dignity in Bioethics and Biolaw* (Oxford: Oxford University Press, 2001), 76 n. 17.

The second version of non-positivism includes all authoritatively issued and socially efficacious norms in spite of their moral defects in the class of legally valid norms. This can be called 'super-inclusive non-positivism'. With respect to the result of the classifying connection, super-inclusive non-positivism is equivalent to exclusive positivism. But a deep difference remains with respect to the qualifying dimension.[67] Aquinas's thesis that a tyrannical law 'is not law simpliciter'[68] or, as Finnis puts it, 'not law in the focal sense of the term "law"',[69] but only law 'in a secondary sense of that term',[70] that is, defective law, seems to mark a qualifying connection. Another version of super-inclusive non-positivism that can be explained by means of the distinction between classifying and qualifying connections is to be found in Kant's combination of the postulate of '[u]nconditional submission'[71] to the positive law with the idea of a necessary subjugation of positive law to non-positive law.[72] Super-inclusive non-positivism can be expressed in the following way:

(5) $\forall x Vx.$

The third version of non-positivism is inclusive non-positivism. Inclusive non-positivism claims neither that moral defects always undermine legal validity nor that they never do. Its most prominent expression is found in the Radbruch Formula, which in its most compressed form runs as follows: extreme injustice is no law.[73] According to this formula, moral defects undermine legal validity if and only if the threshold of extreme injustice is transgressed. Injustice below this threshold is included in the concept of law as defective but valid law. This can be expressed in the following way:

[67] Finnis, 'Law as Fact and as Reason for Action' (n. 7 above), 89, refers the attribute 'super-inclusive' also to the observer's perspective, and, with this, to positivism, and he criticizes a 'connotation of excess'. This critique would be justified if the concept of super-inclusiveness could indeed sensibly be applied to the observer's perspective. This, however, is not the case. Super-inclusiveness exists only on the side of non-positivism, and the 'connotation of excess' stems from the excessively high weight that super-inclusive non-positivism attributes to the principle of legal certainty in contrast to the excessively low weight attributed to the principle of justice. The result of this is the radical difference between the effect of defects on the level of the qualifying connection and on the level of the classifying connection. It makes no sense to speak of 'super-inclusive positivism' because positivism includes in the concept of law *per definitionem* all positive law. The observer's description of law does not include the balancing just mentioned.

[68] Thomas Aquinas, *Summa Theologiae* (Milan: Edizioni Paoline, 1962), 947 (I-II, question 92, art. 1, 4): '*lex tyrannica ... non est simpliciter lex*'.

[69] Finnis, *Natural Law and Natural Rights* (n. 5 above), 364.

[70] Ibid.

[71] Immanuel Kant, 'The Metaphysics of Morals', trans. and ed. Mary J. Gregor, in *The Cambridge Edition of the Works of Immanuel Kant. Practical Philosophy* (Cambridge: Cambridge University Press, 1996), 353–603, at 506; AA 6, 372.

[72] Alexy, 'On the Concept and the Nature of Law' (n. 21 above), 288–90 (in this volume: Chapter 2, 24–7). On a possible exception to Kant's unconditional submission to the positive law see Alexy, 'The Dual Nature of Law' (n. 46 above), 174, n. 10 (in this volume: Chapter 3, 43, n 34).

[73] Gustav Radbruch, 'Statutory Lawlessness and Supra-Statutory Law' (1946) trans. Bonnie Litschewski Paulson and Stanley L. Paulson, *Oxford Journal of Legal Studies* 26 (2006), 1–11, at 7.

(6) $\neg\forall x \neg Vx \,\&\, \neg\forall x Vx.$

All three versions of non-positivism are represented in the necessity triad by '□I'. They can now be brought together in a second triad, which counts as the explication '□I' in the necessity triad:

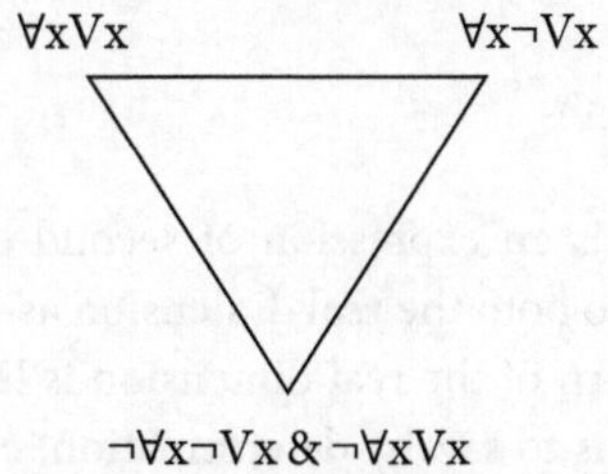

This triad can be called the 'quantifier triad'. The three positions both in the quantifier triad and in the necessity triad stand in a relationship of contrariety, because each excludes the other without stemming from its negation. With this, the instruments for determining the relation between the real and the ideal dimension are at hand.

V. The Relation between the Real and the Ideal Dimension

In order to determine the relation between the real and the ideal dimension of law one has to answer five questions. First, is there an outermost border of law? Second, is legal argumentation based exclusively on authoritative reasons or does it also include non-authoritative reasons? Third, what is the relation between human rights and legal systems? Fourth, is democracy to be understood exclusively as a decision-making procedure or also as a form of discourse? Fifth, do legal systems comprise only rules expressing a real 'ought' or also principles expressing an ideal 'ought'? These five questions shall be answered with the following five theses, the first with the Radbruch Formula, the second with the special case thesis, the third with the thesis that constitutional rights are to be understood as attempts to render positive human rights , the fourth with the deliberative model of democracy, and the fifth with principles theory.

All five theses turn on the same point: the claim to correctness. That is, the claim to correctness is the main reason for all five theses. One could think about drawing a pentagon with one thesis found at each edge and the argument from correctness, like a sun, standing in their midst. One might call this visualization the 'ideal dimension pentagon' but it can, however, only be seen as a heuristic model of a system of the institutionalization of reason that is to be elaborated by means of arguments determining the relation between the real and the ideal dimension in five directions.

A. The Radbruch Formula

The first direction concerns the idea of an outermost boundary of law. The most renowned version of the thesis, namely, that such an outermost boundary exists, is the Radbruch Formula. In its shortest form, as already mentioned, it runs as follows:

> Extreme injustice is no law.[74]

The Radbruch Formula is an expression of second-order correctness. Second-order correctness refers to both the real dimension as well as the ideal dimension of law. The central concern of the real dimension is legal certainty, arrived at by means of positivity, that is to say, by determination, enforcement, and organization. By contrast with this, the central concern of the ideal dimension is substantive justice. In this way, the claim to correctness necessarily connects both the principle of justice and the principle of legal certainty with law.

Second-order correctness requires that the problem of unjust law be resolved by means of balancing. The relation between the principles of justice and legal certainty on the one hand, and the Radbruch Formula on the other, is determined by the first of the two laws found in principles theory, the Law of Competing Principles. The Law of Competing Principles says, in its less technical formulation, that

> [t]he circumstances under which one principle takes precedence over another constitute the conditions of a *rule* which has the same legal consequences as the principle taking precedence.[75]

The Radbruch Formula is nothing other than the rule of which this law speaks. The conditions of this rule are the circumstances under which the principle of justice takes precedence over the principle of legal certainty, namely extreme injustice. Its legal consequences are the consequences that would be required by the preceding principle, the principle of justice, if it were taken alone, namely lack of legal validity from the beginning. The picture changes below the threshold of extreme injustice. Under these circumstances the principle of legal certainty takes precedence over the principle of justice. A new rule emerges. It states that injustice below the threshold of extreme injustice does not exclude legal validity.[76]

[74] Alexy, 'A Defence of Radbruch's Formula' (n. 38 above), 17.

[75] Robert Alexy, *A Theory of Constitutional Rights* (1985), trans. Julian Rivers (Oxford: Oxford University Press, 2002), 54 (new emphasis).

[76] On a more technical analysis see Robert Alexy, 'Legal Certainty and Correctness', *Ratio Juris* 28 (2015), 441–51, at 445.

The Radbruch Formula represents inclusive non-positivism. The two other forms of non-positivism also can be reconstructed in the light of the Law of Competing Principles. Exclusive non-positivism gives precedence to justice over legal certainty under all circumstances, and super-inclusive non-positivism gives precedence to legal certainty over justice, again under all circumstances. That is to say, both establish an abstract or absolute relation of precedence by contrast to the conditional relation of precedence established by inclusive non-positivism.[77] Such abstract or absolute relations of preference, however, express a bias in favour of either the ideal or the real dimension, both of which are incompatible with second-order correctness.[78] For this reason, law's claim to correctness requires inclusive non-positivism as expressed by the Radbruch Formula and justified by balancing.

Finnis has raised two objections against this balancing approach. The first says that

> it confuses *Is* and *Ought* to assimilate (as Alexy does) the real dimension with 'the principle of legal certainty', a principle in tension with 'the principle of justice'. If the one principle is in tension with the other, they are in the same plane or realm, which in Alexy's terminology is the 'ideal'.[79]

The problem here stems from the term 'assimilate'. If I were to identify the principle of legal certainty with the real dimension, Finnis would be right. But I do not identify them. The real dimension consists of law as fact. By contrast with this, the principle of legal certainty is a reason that requires compliance with what has been authoritatively issued and is socially efficacious. This is to say that the real dimension is the subject of the principle of legal certainty, which demands, as a norm, that this subject be taken as seriously as is possible. The principle of legal certainty and the principle of justice are both required by second-order correctness, and they are, *qua* principles, that is to say, *qua* norms, both found at the normative level. Thus, a confusion of 'is' and 'ought' is precluded.

The second objection against the balancing approach maintains that 'the idea that one could weigh *by reason* such incommensurables as "ideal" and "real/factual" "dimensions"'.[80] is a mistake. Now the weighing or balancing takes place between the principle of legal certainty and the principle of justice. The second law of principles theory, the Law of Balancing, shows that and how reasonable balancing between these two principles is possible. The Law of Balancing reads as follows:

77 See on this Alexy, *A Theory of Constitutional Rights* (n. 75 above), 52–3.

78 Alexy, 'On the Concept and the Nature of Law' (n. 21 above), 290 (in this volume: Chapter 2, 27).

79 Finnis, 'Law as Fact and as Reason for Action' (n. 7 above), 101.

80 Ibid., 108.

> The greater the degree of non-satisfaction of, or detriment to, one principle, the greater must be the importance of satisfying the other.[81]

According to the Law of Balancing one has to determine on the one hand, how great the non-satisfaction of or interference with the principle of legal certainty is, and on the other, how great the importance of satisfying the principle of justice is. An example is the bank deposit decision of the German Federal Court of Justice for Civil Cases. This decision concerns the question of whether a Jewish woman who emigrated has, on the basis of Section 3 of the Eleventh Ordinance, 25 November 1941, issued pursuant to the Statute on Reich Citizenship, lost her claim to securities left in a bank deposit of a German bank. The Court declared Section 3 of the Eleventh Ordinance, which provided for the devolution of such property to the Reich, as 'void from the outset',[82] and this can be reconstructed as a balancing led by reason. The injustice was extreme. Since, according to the Radbruch Formula, only extreme injustice and not, then, every instance of injustice leads to invalidity, the interference with the principle of legal certainty can be described as relatively light. By contrast with this, the interference with the principle of justice would be very serious if the Jewish woman, expropriated for reasons 'racial' in nature, were not to get her property back. Therefore, the Law of Balancing requires that the case be decided according to the rule: extreme injustice is no law. In order to contest the rationality of balancing in this case, one would have to contest the classifications of the interferences with the two principles, that is, the classification of the interference with the principle of justice as very serious, and the classification with the principle of legal certainty as only light or medium. It seems that it would be impossible to contest this with rational arguments. This implies that commensurability is established by rational discourse.[83]

Finnis's objection to, he claims, a confusion of 'is' and 'ought' as well as his incommensurability objection concern the justification of the Radbruch Formula by way of balancing and are, in this sense, indirect objections. To these indirect objections he adds two objections that concern the Radbruch Formula directly. The first concerns the practice, the second the theory of the Radbruch Formula. The objection from practice classifies the formula as 'simplistic',[84] 'somewhat rough and

[81] Alexy, *A Theory of Constitutional Rights* (n. 75 above), 102. This Law of Balancing can be developed further by means of the Weight Formula, but this refinement is not necessary in the present context. See on this Robert Alexy, 'The Weight Formula', trans. Bartosz Brożek and Stanley L. Paulson, in *Studies in the Philosophy of Law*, vol. 3, eds Jerzy Stelmach, Bartosz Brożek, and Wojciech Załuski (Kraków: Jagiellonian University Press, 2007), 9–27, at 25 (in this volume: Chapter 11, 154–74, at 172).

[82] Decisions of the German Federal Court of Justice in Civil Cases (BGHZ) 16, 350 (354) (trans. R. A.).

[83] Alexy, 'The Weight Formula' (n. 81 above), 18 (in this volume: Chapter 11, 163–4).

[84] Finnis, 'Law as Fact and as Reason for Action' (n. 7 above), 106.

ready',[85] and nothing more than a 'rule of thumb'.[86] The formula over-simplifies 'matters by offering too short a short-cut through the forest'.[87] Finnis's counter-model is characterized as follows:

> It is better, I think, to proceed on the assumption that the moral consequences of significant injustice in the making or content of purportedly and intra-systematically valid legal rules are to be assessed by reference to all the considerations of justice that bear on the situation in which the question of the rule's application (present or past) arises for consideration.[88]

It is striking that Finnis refers here to 'significant injustice' and not, as the Radbruch Formula has it, to 'extreme injustice', and that he asks not for legal consequences but for 'moral consequences'.[89] But this shall not be elaborated here. At this point, the only question of interest is whether Finnis's all-things-considered fashion ought to be preferred to the 'all-or-nothing fashion'[90] of the Radbruch Formula.

Finnis attempts to illustrate the lack of soundness of the all-or-nothing fashion by looking to a case to which I, indeed, have given 'pride of place'[91] in *The Argument from Injustice*.[92] It is the decision of the German Federal Constitutional Court in 1968 on citizenship. The Eleventh Ordinance, 25 November 1941, issued pursuant to the Statute on Reich Citizenship, stripped emigrant Jews not only of property, as in the bank deposit case mentioned above, but also of citizenship on the ground of race. The Federal Constitutional Court was to decide whether, according to this directive, a Jewish lawyer had forfeited German citizenship by emigrating to Holland shortly before the outbreak of the Second World War. In 1942, he was deported from Amsterdam, and since his whereabouts were not known, he was presumed dead, ruling out the possibility of restoration of German citizenship in accordance with Article 116(2) of the post-war Constitution of the Federal Republic of Germany. The Court reached the conclusion that the lawyer had never lost his German citizenship, arguing that the 'conflict' of the Eleventh Ordinance 'with justice [had] reached such an intolerable degree that the Ordinance must be held to be null and void, that is, invalid from the outset'.[93] And the Court adds: 'Moreover,

85 Ibid., 107.

86 Ibid., 107, 109.

87 Ibid., 101.

88 Ibid., 107.

89 On the last point see Alexy, 'Some Reflections on the Ideal Dimension of Law and on the Legal Philosophy of John Finnis' (n. 6 above), 109–10.

90 Finnis, 'Law as Fact and as Reason for Action' (n. 7 above), 108.

91 Ibid., 105.

92 Alexy, *The Argument from Injustice* (n. 1 above), 5–7.

93 Decisions of the German Federal Constitutional Court (BVerfGE) 23, 98 (106); English quotation in Alexy, *The Argument from Injustice* (n. 1 above), 6.

the Ordinance did not become legally valid in virtue of having been observed over a number of years.'[94]

Finnis's argument that all of this is 'simplistic'[95] is based on Article 116(2) German Basic Law of 23 May 1949, which runs as follows:

> Former German citizens who, between 30 January 1933 and 8 May 1945, were deprived of their citizenship on political, racial, or religious grounds, and their descendants, shall be regranted German citizenship on application. They shall be considered as not having been deprived of their German citizenship if they established their domicile in Germany after 8 May 1945 and have not expressed a contrary intention.

Finnis is right in his argument that there exists the possibility of interpreting Article 116(2) as a denial of the Radbruch Formula.[96] The first sentence speaks about *regranting* German citizenship. One can regrant only what has been taken away. The second sentence does not say that they have not been deprived of their German citizenship, as the Federal Constitutional Court maintains. It only states that they shall be *considered* as having not been deprived of it. But this possibility of interpretation has two weak points. The first is that other interpretative possibilities exist. The Court's argument, turning over five pages, has it that the intent of the framers of the Constitution had two sides.[97] On the one hand, they wanted to conceive of the Eleventh Ordinance as null and void from the beginning. In the bank deposit case this presented no problems. But in the citizenship case it did. Not all Jewish emigrants, after the Nazi Regime, wanted to be considered as Germans any longer. The Court stresses several times that their will has to be respected, that is, that German citizenship may not be imposed on them against their will.[98] This, however, does not imply that the Eleventh Ordinance is to be considered as legally valid. It only implies that it is to be considered as if it were legally valid. This is a paradigmatic case of a legal fiction. And it is a fiction justified by the human rights of those concerned. As a first step, their human rights require a holding of invalidity from the beginning. As a second step, their human rights require the fiction of validity for all those who do not want the consequences that stem from the holding of invalidity. Concerning the result, this may have some similarity with Finnis's all-things-considered fashion. For systematic reasons, however, it is completely different. The Radbruch Formula remains the basis and one that cannot be replaced by the cluster of reasons that is relevant according to the all-things-considered

94 Ibid.; trans. altered: 'legally valid' instead of 'efficacious', because '*wirksam*', here, does not refer to social efficacy (*soziale Wirksamkeit*), but to legal validity (*rechtliche Wirksamkeit*).

95 Finnis, 'Law as Fact and as Reason for Action' (n. 7 above), 106.

96 Ibid.

97 BVerfGE 23, 98 (108–112).

98 BVerfGE 23, 98 (107, 108, 110–111).

fashion. This fashion is a completely open hermeneutical maxim that can only complement the Radbruch Formula in the context of its application but cannot replace it.

This immediately leads to Finnis's theoretical or philosophical objection to the Radbruch Formula. Finnis insists that the Radbruch Formula and, with it, inclusive non-positivism, is not 'a truth about the nature or essence of law'.[99] 'It is not a truth about law, a truth of the philosophy of law (legal theory).'[100] My reply to this is that it is a truth about the nature and essence of law and, with this, a truth of the philosophy of law. In section II above, I have pointed out that the analysis of the concept of law, *qua* concept referring to social kinds, requires a connection of analytical and normative arguments. Normative arguments concern the nature and the essence and, with this, the concept of law[101] when they refer to those normatively necessary requirements that are necessarily connected with law. The claim to correctness, necessarily connected with law as a conceptual matter,[102] connects the normative requirements of legal certainty and justice necessarily with law, and these two requirements, taken together, include the Radbruch Formula in the concept and nature of law. And the question of the concept and nature of law is the main question of legal philosophy.[103]

B. The Special Case Thesis

The second field in which the real and the ideal dimension of law are connected is legal argumentation. This connection is expressed by the special case thesis. This thesis states that legal argumentation or legal discourse is a special case of general practical argumentation or discourse.[104] General practical discourse is a non-institutionalized discourse about practical questions. As a general practical discourse, it comprises all kinds of non-authoritative practical arguments, that is, moral arguments concerning justice and rights as well as ethical arguments concerning individual and collective identity, and pragmatic arguments that give expression to means–end rationality. The moral arguments have priority because they represent the universal point of view. This does not, however, mean that their content cannot depend on the other arguments.[105] Legal discourse is a special case of general practical discourse because it is committed to statute,

[99] Finnis, 'Law as Fact and as Reason for Action' (n. 7 above), 108.

[100] Ibid., 107.

[101] On the relation between the concepts of nature and essence and the concept of concept, see Alexy, 'On the Concept and the Nature of Law' (n. 21 above), 290–2 (in this volume: Chapter 2, 27–9).

[102] Alexy, 'The Nature of Arguments about the Nature of Law' (n. 34 above), 12.

[103] Robert Alexy, 'The Nature of Legal Philosophy', *Ratio Juris* 17 (2004), 156–67, at 162–4 (in this volume: Chapter 1, 7–17, at 13–15).

[104] Robert Alexy, *A Theory of Legal Argumentation* (1978), trans. Ruth Adler and Neil MacCormick (Oxford: Clarendon Press, 1989), 211–20.

[105] Robert Alexy, 'The Special Case Thesis', *Ratio Juris* 12 (1999), 374–84, at 378–9.

precedent, and legal doctrine. These commitments represent the real dimension of legal discourse or argumentation. The ideal dimension comprises general practical argumentation.

An elaborated explication of the relation between the real and the ideal in legal argumentation cannot be given here. This would require an answer to the question 'what is to count as a rational justification within the validly prevailing legal order?'[106] This, however, could only be answered by means of a theory of legal reasoning or argumentation.[107] Only two points are of interest. The first is that the claim to correctness raised in legal argumentation is a claim to second-order correctness. This means that it concerns justice as well as legal certainty. The second point is that the special case thesis by no means represents, as Habermas fears, a blanket permission 'to move in the unrestrained space of reasons'[108] of general practical discourse. On the contrary, it includes a *prima facie* priority of authoritative reasons. This *prima facie* priority finds its expression in the following rule of legal discourse:

> Arguments which give expression to a link with the actual words of the law, or the will of the historical legislator, take precedence over other arguments, unless rational grounds can be cited for granting precedence to the other arguments.[109]

The structure of this rule is quite different from that of the Radbruch Formula. But its function is the same. Both serve to determine the relation between the real and the ideal dimension of law.

C. Human Rights

The third area in which the relation between the real and the ideal dimension is of pivotal importance is the field of human and constitutional rights. Human rights are characterized by five properties. They are: first, moral, second, universal, third, fundamental, and fourth, abstract rights, that, fifth, take priority over all other norms with respect to their moral validity.[110] Here only the first of these five properties is of interest: the moral character of human rights.

The moral character of human rights consists in their having, *qua* moral rights, only moral validity. This means that human rights as such belong exclusively to the ideal dimension of law. Now, a right is morally valid if it can be justified. Rights

[106] Alexy, *A Theory of Legal* Argumentation (n. 104 above), 220.
[107] Ibid.
[108] Jürgen Habermas, 'A Short Reply', *Ratio Juris* 12 (1999), 445–53, at 447.
[109] Alexy, *A Theory of Legal* Argumentation (n. 104 above), 248.
[110] Alexy, 'Law, Morality, and the Existence of Human Rights' (n. 23 above), 10 (in this volume, Chapter 4, 59).

exist, as norms in general,[111] if they are valid. Thus, the existence of human rights depends on their justifiability and on nothing else. Elsewhere, I have attempted to show that human rights are justifiable and that they, therefore, exist.[112] This cannot be undertaken here. In the present context, the only question to be addressed is the relation between human rights and constitutional rights.

Constitutional rights are part of positive law, namely positive law at the level of the constitution.[113] As such, they belong to the real dimension of law. The relation between constitutional rights and human rights would belong to the relations between the real and the ideal dimension of law if there be a necessary connection between human rights and constitutional rights.

The key to this necessary connection is the concept of correctness. Constitutions, as with law in general, necessarily raise a claim to correctness. This is one side of the argument. The other side is that human rights—since their existence consists in their justifiability—are necessarily connected with the concept of correctness because what is justifiable is correct. This and the priority of human rights require to transform human rights into positive law at the constitutional level. For this reason, constitutional rights can be considered as attempts to transform human rights *qua* ideal rights into positive law, that is, into real rights. The ideal dimension remains alive after the transformation into the real dimension. And this has far-reaching consequences for the interpretation of constitutional rights and their role in the legal system, but this cannot be elaborated here.

D. Democracy

Democracy, at one and the same time, can be conceived, as a decision-making procedure and as an argumentation procedure. Making decisions, in the manner familiar from the majority principle, is the real side of democracy. Argumentation, as public discourse, is necessarily connected with the claim to substantive correctness. For this reason, it is the ideal side of democracy. The only possibility for the realization of second-order correctness in political life, especially in public law-making, is the institutionalization of a democracy that unites both sides. The name given to this unity is 'deliberative democracy'.

[111] Hans Kelsen, *Pure Theory of Law*, 2nd ed. (1960), trans. Max Knight (Berkeley, Calif.: University of California Press, 1967), 10.

[112] Robert Alexy, 'The Existence of Human Rights', *Archives for Philosophy of Law and Social Philosophy*, supplement 136 (2013), 9–18, at 13–8 (in this volume: Chapter 10, 142–53, at 147–53).

[113] Including rights in constitutions is only one way of transforming them into positive law. International and supra-national covenants, conventions, or charters are further possibilities here.

E. Principles Theory

In the application of law, rules as well as principles play an essential role. Rules express a definitive or real 'ought', principles a *prima facie* or ideal 'ought'. The principles of a legal system, taken together, constitute what might be called a 'world of the ideal Ought'.[114] The theory of principles attempts to develop on this basis a theory of proportionality that connects balancing with correctness. This, again, cannot be elaborated here. In our context, the only point of interest is that principles theory completes the system of the five directions of the ideal dimension of law.

[114] Alexy, *A Theory of Constitutional Rights* (n. 75 above), 82.

7

Gustav Radbruch's Concept of Law

In the twentieth century, two legal philosophers in the German-speaking countries excelled over all the others and their philosophies remain topics of lively debate in the global discussion today. I have in mind Hans Kelsen and Gustav Radbruch. I will be concerned here with Radbruch.[1]

The elaboration of Radbruch's legal philosophy culminates in two developments. The first is the systematic presentation of his position in *Legal Philosophy* (1932) the new edition of his treatise *Outlines of Legal Philosophy* (1914).[2] In the preface to the new edition Radbruch remarks, with an eye to the first edition, that the text of 1932 is in fact 'a new book rather than a new edition'.[3] The second culminating development is represented by the article 'Statutory Lawlessness and Supra-Statutory Law', published in 1946, where Radbruch introduces his formula, well known as 'the Radbruch Formula', which says, in a word, that extremely unjust law is no law.[4] With this, Radbruch clearly takes a stand as a non-positivist. The Radbruch Formula is not only one of the most widely discussed doctrines in legal philosophy, it is also of the greatest practical significance, as its application by German courts after the defeat of National Socialism in 1945 and after the collapse of the German Democratic Republic in 1989 shows.[5] One of the main problems in interpreting Radbruch is to determine whether these two texts, that of 1932 and that of 1946, stand in a relation of discontinuity or of continuity. This question, too, will be answered here. The focus shall be both Radbruch's system as it is developed in the *Legal Philosophy* of 1932 and its relation to the formula of 1946. The analysis will lead, practically by itself, to a continuity thesis, which shows that Radbruch, already in 1932, was a non-positivist,[6] and that his alterations in the system, far from

[1] On Radbruch's biography, see Robert Alexy, 'Gustav Radbruch (1878-1949)', *Christiana Albertina* 58 (2004), 47–51.

[2] On the relation of the *Outlines of Legal Philosophy* of 1914 to the *Legal Philosophy* of 1932, see Ralf Dreier, 'Kontinuitäten und Diskontinuitäten in der Rechtsphilosophie Radbruchs', in *Die Natur des Rechts bei Gustav Radbruch*, eds Martin Borowski and Stanley L. Paulson (Tübingen: Mohr Siebeck, 2015), 183–228, at 190–212.

[3] Gustav Radbruch, *Legal Philosophy* (1932), trans. Kurt Wilk, in *The Legal Philosophies of Lask, Radbruch, and Dabin* (Cambridge, Mass.: Harvard University Press, 1950), 43–224, at 47.

[4] Gustav Radbruch, 'Statutory Lawlessness and Supra-Statutory Law' (1946), trans. Bonnie Litschewski Paulson and Stanley L. Paulson, *Oxford Journal of Legal Studies* 26 (2006), 1–11, at 7.

[5] See on this Robert Alexy, 'A Defense of Radbruch's Formula', in *Recrafting the Rule of Law: The Limits of Legal Order*, ed. David Dyzenhaus (Oxford: Hart, 1999), 15–39, at 18–22.

[6] On Radbruch's non-positivism before 1932, see Stanley L. Paulson, 'Zur Kontinuität der nichtpositivistischen Rechtsphilosophie Radbruchs', in *Die Natur des Rechts bei Gustav Radbruch*, eds Martin Borowski and Stanley L. Paulson (Tübingen: Mohr Siebeck, 2015), 151–82, at 158–77.

Law's Ideal Dimension. Robert Alexy, Oxford University Press. © Robert Alexy 2021.
DOI: 10.1093/oso/9780198796831.003.0008

disrupting it, were modest in character. Nevertheless, they have had far-reaching consequences.

I. Gustav Radbruch's System

The system of Radbruch's legal philosophy consists of three triads: the law triad, the idea triad, and the triad of purpose or, if you will, the purpose triad.

A. The Law Triad

Radbruch gives expression to the law triad in the following statement, which he emphasizes with italics: '*Law is the reality whose sense is to serve the value of law, the idea of law.*'[7] The reference to the value of law alongside the idea of law has no independent significance for the content of the statement. It serves simply to hint at the neo-Kantian background[8] of Radbruch's concept of law. This observation is confirmed by the fact that Radbruch refers in many formulations solely to the idea of law.[9] This leading statement of Radbruch's connects three elements: reality, the idea of law, and sense. With the concept of reality, Radbruch refers to the positivity of law, that is, to its issuance and its efficacy. This is the real dimension of law. With the concept of the idea of law, Radbruch juxtaposes this real dimension with an ideal dimension,[10] the centre of which is justice as the 'specific idea of law'.[11] Our analysis of the second triad, the idea triad, will show that the idea of law is not exhausted by justice. On the contrary, it includes, as its 'second element', purposiveness, and, as its 'third element', legal certainty.[12] This implies that Radbruch's alternative formulation of the law triad, which says, also emphasized using italics and repeated at another point in the text,[13] that '*law is the reality whose sense is to serve justice*'[14] must be interpreted either as an abridged version accentuating the specific character of justice or as a version in which the concept of justice is used with a sufficiently broad meaning to include purposiveness and legal certainty. There is textual support for both of these interpretations.[15]

[7] Radbruch, *Legal Philosophy* (n. 3, above), 73 (trans. altered).

[8] See on this Ralf Dreier and Stanley L. Paulson, 'Einführung in die Rechtsphilosophie Radbruchs', in *Gustav Radbruch. Rechtsphilosophie*, eds Ralf Dreier and Stanley L. Paulson, 2nd edn (C. F. Müller: Heidelberg 2003), 237–53, at 238–41

[9] Radbruch, *Legal Philosophy* (n. 3 above), 52, 69, 107.

[10] On the distinction between the real and the ideal dimension of law, see Robert Alexy, 'The Dual Nature of Law', *Ratio Juris* 23 (2010), 167–82, at 168, 173 (in this volume: Chapter 3, 36–50, at 36–7, 42).

[11] Radbruch, *Legal Philosophy* (n. 3 above), 90.

[12] Ibid., 108.

[13] Ibid., 88.

[14] Ibid., 75 (trans. altered).

[15] See ibid., 90: 'specific idea of law' and 119: 'just judge'.

A legal positivist can accept the notion that there exists a lack of accord between positivity and ideality without thereby abandoning his positivism. He need only maintain that the law as such is confined to positivity, a restriction that does not preclude its being criticized from the point of view of ideality, understood as a point of view external to law, which is to say, a moral point of view. Radbruch's argument against the positivist's separation thesis is the third element of the law triad, the sense thesis. What Radbruch would have us understand by this thesis becomes clear in his application of it to the relation between science and truth. That science has the sense of 'serving the truth' means that scientific 'labours, regardless of their success or failure, … all at least aim at the truth and claim to be true'.[16] That is, to have the sense of serving the truth is to raise the claim to be true. With this, a bridge is constructed between the neo-Kantian concept of sense and the concept of claim that stems from analytical philosophy.[17] Radbruch himself already anticipated this in remarking that '[l]aw, by its nature, raises the claim to justice'.[18] The phrase 'by its nature' is of special significance here. Its import is that law *necessarily* raises a claim to justice. With another of his formulations, Radbruch clearly enters the centre stage in the contemporary debate over the concept of law, which turns on the question of whether law, first, necessarily raises a claim to correctness and, second, whether this claim as a claim to correctness includes moral correctness.[19] The statement in question reads: 'Justice means correctness as related especially to the law'.[20] And justice is, indeed, nothing other than the correctness of distribution and compensation,[21] and the law is essentially concerned with distribution and compensation. For these reasons Radbruch can be considered as an early representative of the claim to correctness thesis, and, as such, he is necessarily a non-positivist, at least a super-inclusive non-positivist.[22]

[16] Ibid., 50 (trans. altered).

[17] See on this Dreier and Paulson, 'Einführung in die Rechtsphilosophie Radbruchs' (n. 8 above), 241.

[18] Radbruch, *Legal Philosophy* (n. 3 above), 64.

[19] See, for instance, Eugenio Bulygin, 'Alexy und das Richtigkeitsargument', in *Rechtsnorm und Rechtswirklichkeit. Festschrift für Werner Krawietz*, eds Aulis Aarnio, Stanley L. Paulson, Ota Weinberger, et al. (Berlin: Duncker & Humblot, 1993), 19–24; Robert Alexy, 'Bulygins Kritik des Richtigkeitsarguments', in *Normative Systems in Legal and Moral Theory. Festschrift für Carlos E. Alchourrón and Eugenio Bulygin*, eds Ernesto Garzón Valdés, Werner Krawietz, Georg Henrik von Wright, et al. (Berlin: Duncker & Humblot, 1997), 235–50; Eugenio Bulygin, 'Alexy's Thesis of the Necessary Connection between Law and Morality', *Ratio Juris* 13 (2000), 133–7; Robert Alexy, 'On the Thesis of a Necessary Connection between Law and Morality: Bulygin's Critique', *Ratio Juris* 13 (2000), 138–47; Eugenio Bulygin, 'Alexy Between Positivism and Non-positivism', in *Neutrality and Theory of Law*, eds Jordi Ferrer Beltrán, José Juan Moreso, and Diego M. Papayannis (Dordrecht: Springer, 2013), 49–59; Robert Alexy, 'Between Positivism and Non-positivism? A Third Reply to Eugenio Bulygin', in *Neutrality and Theory of Law*, eds Jordi Ferrer Beltrán, José Juan Moreso, and Diego M. Papayannis (Dordrecht: Springer, 2013), 225–38.

[20] Radbruch, *Legal Philosophy* (n. 3 above), 76 (trans. altered).

[21] Robert Alexy, 'Giustitia come correttezza', *Ragion pratica* 9 (1997), 103–13, at 105.

[22] On the three forms of non-positivism, exclusive, inclusive, and super-inclusive non-positivism, see Robert Alexy, 'Law, Morality, and the Existence of Human Rights', *Ratio Juris* 25 (2012), 2–14, at 4–7 (in this volume: Chapter 4, 51–63, at 53–6); Robert Alexy, 'Law and Morality: A Continental European Perspective', in *International Encyclopedia of the Social and Behavioral Sciences*, ed. James D. Wright, 2nd edn, vol. 13 (Oxford: Elsevier, 2015), 479–82, at 479–80.

Is Radbruch's statement that law is the reality whose sense is to serve the idea of law—or its specification that law is the reality whose sense is to serve justice—properly considered as his definition of law? This proposal cannot be endorsed as it stands. For Radbruch, with direct reference to the specification, the justice version, goes on to say: 'With this, a determination of the concept of law would seem to be indicated, but a determination of the concept itself has not yet been given.'[23] Now the statement that law is the reality whose sense is to serve the idea of law can be designated as the 'basic statement' in Radbruch's legal philosophy. Radbruch attempts to reach a definition of law from his second version, the justice version, when he writes: 'we define law as the *complex of general precepts for human beings' living together*'.[24] The bridge from the basic statement to this definition is said to be the neo-Kantian theorem of the 'material qualification of the idea'.[25] I shall not, however, pursue this. Here only one point is of interest. It concerns the demands that ought to be made on definitions. It is a postulate of rationality that a definition, in its *definiens*, uses concepts that are as precise as possible. 'Reality' in the basic statement is not very precise. 'Precept' is more concrete, 'norm', however, would be more precise than 'precept'. But these are technical questions, not the main problem of Radbruch's 'determination of the concept of law'. The main problem is that his determination does not meet, or meets only poorly, an essential demand on definitions. Definitions, and the concepts defined by them, must, as Kant puts it, be 'adequate to the object'.[26] This presupposes that they capture not only the necessary properties of the object but also its essential properties.[27] The two essential properties of law are power in the form of decisions and coercion, and correctness, as including justice.[28] In Radbruch's 'determination of the concept', power is, indeed, represented by what he terms a 'precept', albeit not very clearly. Weighing more heavily is the fact that the sense of 'serving justice' or the claim to correctness, including justice, is only present in the general character of precepts in an altogether emaciated form.[29] In short, Radbruch's definition of law as a complex of general precepts for human beings' living together does not capture the essence of law. This, however, means that Radbruch's basic statement, for example in the justice version, is his real definition of law, although the 'idea of law' version predominates for reasons systematic in nature. This is supported by textual evidence. Thus, in section 1 of *Legal Philosophy*, one reads that the 'concept of law can only be determined as something given, the sense of which is to realize

[23] Radbruch, *Legal Philosophy* (n. 3 above), 76 (trans. altered).

[24] Ibid., (trans. altered).

[25] Ibid.

[26] Immanuel Kant, *Critique of Pure Reason*, trans. Werner S. Pluhar (Indianapolis, Ind.: Hackett, 1996), 680; A 728, B 756.

[27] Robert Alexy, 'On the Concept and the Nature of Law', *Ratio Juris* 21 (2008), 281–99, at 290–92 (in this volume: Chapter 2, 18–35, at 27–9).

[28] Ibid., 292–6 (Chapter 2, 29–33).

[29] On this, see Andreas Funke, 'Überlegungen zu Gustav Radbruchs "Verleugnungsformel"', *Archives for Philosophy of Law and Social Philosophy* 89 (2003), 1–16, at 14.

the idea of law'.[30] This concerns the *determination* of the concept of law. But what is the determination of a concept if not its definition? Something similar is found in section 9, where Radbruch talks about the 'concept of law' as 'urging' us to take up the 'idea of law'.[31] Here concept and idea are directly connected. This connection has consequences for the classification of something as law, that is, consequences for the legal character or legal nature, which Radbruch describes as follows: 'As a matter of fact, we decide by the standard of purported justice alone whether a precept is legal in nature at all, whether it accords with the *concept* of law.'[32] Thus, the basis statement clearly proves to be a non-positivistic definition of law. Still, it is not to be denied that Radbruch's definition of law as the complex of general precepts for human beings' living together has the character of a definition. This is, however, a secondary matter, to be placed behind Radbruch's real definition of law, which says: '*Law is the reality whose sense is to serve the value of law, the idea of law.*'[33] Here, in neo-Kantian terminology, Radbruch has identified the Archimedean point around which debates over the concept of law revolve and will continue to revolve for as long as philosophical questions are entertained.

B. The Idea Triad

It has already been remarked that the idea of law refers not only to justice. It includes, as further elements or 'sides',[34] purposiveness and legal certainty.[35] Occasionally, Radbruch, speaks of 'three principles'[36] instead of the more familiar three elements or three sides. This is of considerable importance for determining, by means of balancing, the relation of the three elements of the idea of law to each other.[37]

1. Justice

Justice often takes the place of the greater idea of law in Radbruch's basic statement, a fact that invites attention to the particular importance that he attaches to it. This high-level systematic ranking is connected, however, with a minimal content. Justice is understood as equality,[38] and as equality it is defined in a purely formal way. The two classical elements of formal justice are found here, albeit not always

30 Radbruch, *Legal Philosophy* (n. 3 above), 52 (trans. altered).
31 Ibid., 107 (trans. altered).
32 Ibid., 110 (trans. altered). On this, see Robert Alexy, *The Argument from Injustice. A Reply to Legal Positivism* (1992), trans. Bonnie Litschewski Paulson and Stanley L. Paulson (Oxford: Clarendon Press, 2002), 34.
33 Ibid., 73 (trans. altered).
34 Ibid., 111 (trans. altered).
35 Ibid., 108
36 Ibid., 110.
37 Robert Alexy, 'Legal Certainty and Correctness', *Ratio Juris* 28 (2015), 441–51, at 444–7.
38 Radbruch, *Legal Philosophy* (n. 3 above), 74.

clearly separated. The first is the general form. Radbruch says in this connection that 'it is essential to a legal precept ... that the claim to generalizability be raised'.[39] 'Generalizability' is not thereby understood as referring to some test of universalizability. The claim of legal precepts to generalizability is confined to the claim of having a 'general character'.[40] This is nothing more than a demand set by the logical form of the legal norm, requiring that legal norms have the form: for all *x*, if *x* is an *F*, then it is obligatory that *x* is a *C*,[41] where '*F*' refers to the operative fact and '*C*' to the legal consequences. Nothing is said here about the content of the norm. The second classical element of formal justice is the Aristotelian demand[42] 'that equals be treated equally, and that unequals be treated differently according to their differences'.[43] Radbruch correctly emphasizes that with this the question of 'who is to be treated as equal and who as unequal' is not yet answered.[44] But this, so Radbruch in 1932, reaches beyond what justice can say. Justice determines only 'the form of what is right'.[45] And at exactly this point, Radbruch takes a step that is fraught with consequences for his system: 'In order to acquire the content of law, a second notion must be added, purposiveness.'[46]

2. Purposiveness

'Purposiveness' is generally understood as speaking to the suitability of a means for the realization of an end. Purposiveness in Radbruch's philosophy is, however, altogether different. It refers not to means but to ends, and not just to any end but only to those ends that are 'capable of absolute value'.[47] Three kinds of such ends or purposes are said to exist: 'individual human personalities, collective human personalities, and human artefacts'.[48] The question of whether and how, on this basis, the content of justice can be determined shall be considered in the context of the triad of purpose, which consists of these three purposes. It turns out that this triad serves as the link between Radbruch's legal philosophy before 1933 and after 1945. Before turning to this, however, it is well to turn to the third element of the idea triad, that of legal certainty.

39 Ibid., 76 (trans. altered).
40 Ibid., (trans. altered).
41 See Robert Alexy, *A Theory of Legal Argumentation* (1978), trans. Ruth Adler and Neil MacCormick (Oxford: Clarendon Press, 1989), 222.
42 Aristotele, *Politics*, in *The Complete Works of Aristotle. The Revised Oxford Translation*, ed. Jonathan Barnes, vol. 2 (Princeton, N.J.: Princeton University Press, 1984), 1986–2129, at 2031 (1280a): 'For example, justice is thought by them to be, and is, equality—not, however, for all, but only for equals. And inequality is thought to be, and is, justice; neither is this for all, but only for unequals.'
43 Radbruch, *Legal Philosophy* (n. 3 above), 90 (trans. altered).
44 Ibid., 75.
45 Ibid., 91 (trans. altered).
46 Ibid., (trans. altered).
47 Ibid., 92 (trans. altered).
48 Ibid., (trans. altered).

3. Legal Certainty

The third element of the idea of law, legal certainty, serves to compensate for the weaknesses of the first two elements. These weaknesses are epistemic in character. Here one can speak of the problem of practical knowledge.[49] Practical knowledge concerns knowledge about what is obligatory, forbidden, and permitted, and what is good and bad. If, in law, this could be known in all cases 'with scientific discernibility',[50] the principle of legal certainty would play a relatively small role. The determinations of positive law would not be real determinations. Rather, they would have merely a declaratory character. The real field of legal certainty would no longer be a matter of determination but of enforcement. This leads directly to the question of the degree to which purposiveness can give justice a discernibly recognizable content. This turns on the third triad, the triad of purpose.

C. The Triad of Purpose

Radbruch presents the three purposes in manifold ways. The distinction, already mentioned, between individual human personalities, collective human personalities, and human artefacts is specified as a distinction between '*individual values*, *collective values*, and *artefact values*'[51] as well as between '*individualistic*, *supra-individualistic*, and completely *transpersonal* views'.[52] Corresponding to these there is the triad of liberty, nation, and culture.[53] Three points are of interest. The first is that liberty and, with it, 'human rights, constitutional rights, and the individual's right to freedom'[54] are assigned to the individualistic view, whereas the supra-individualistic view is connected with the aphorism 'self-interest yields to the common good'.[55] The second point is that the three views collide.[56] The third and, of the three, systematically most important point, is that in Radbruch's *Legal Philosophy* of 1932 the resolution of these collisions is not a matter of cognition but a matter of decision: 'One has to decide whether one wants to grant the first place in the hierarchy of values to the individual values, the collective values, or the artefact values.'[57] This rejection of cognition is characterized by Radbruch as a 'relativistically self-imposed moderation'.[58] This relativism, reaching to the entire system of purposes, has far-reaching consequences. In particular, it led to the widely shared

[49] Alexy, 'The Dual Nature of Law' (n. 10 above), 173 (in this volume: Chapter 3, 42).
[50] Radbruch, *Legal Philosophy* (n. 3, above), 116 (trans. altered).
[51] Ibid., 92 (trans. altered).
[52] Ibid., 92–3 (trans. altered).
[53] Ibid., 94.
[54] Ibid., 102 (trans. altered).
[55] Ibid., 106 (trans. altered).
[56] Ibid., 92
[57] Ibid., (trans. altered).
[58] Ibid., 108 (trans. altered).

reading of Radbruch's legal philosophy before 1933 as positivistic.[59] If justice as such is merely formal, that is, devoid of substance, and if purposiveness, which is supposed to provide for substance or content, can only offer alternatives that contradict each other, on the ground that it is 'impossible to answer the question of the purpose of law other than by the enumeration of the manifold partisan views about it',[60] then the decisive role falls to the third element of the idea of law, that of legal certainty. Legal certainty requires, then, that when 'no-one is able to recognize what is just, someone must determine what shall be legal'.[61] This leads, so Radbruch states, to a 'basic norm' that is, to be sure, non-positivistic with respect to its justification but positivistic with respect to its content: 'If in a community there is a supreme ruler, what he commands is to be obeyed.'[62] For the judge, this implies being completely subjected to the positive law. Radbruch puts it this way: 'It is the professional duty of the judge to give effect to the will of the statute, to sacrifice his own sense of justice to the authoritative command of the law, to ask only what is legal, and never whether it is also just.'[63] It is the principle of legal certainty that is supposed to justify this: 'However unjust the law may be in its content, by its very existence . . . it always fulfills *one* purpose, namely that of legal certainty.'[64] This suffices to render a merely 'legal judge' as, in the end, a 'just judge'.[65]

Something different obtains, however, with respect to the individual, since 'the complete validity of all positive law cannot be demonstrated as applying to every individual'.[66] '[T]here may be "shameful laws" that conscience refuses to obey.'[67] As an example, Radbruch points to the Socialist Act of 1878. Here the reason for suspending validity is, once again, the idea of law with its three sub-principles of justice, purposiveness, and legal certainty. In the case of an individual, however, they are weighed in a different way. There arises, however, a contradiction if the validity that is suspended in the case of the individual is legal validity: From the standpoint of the individual something is legally allowed that is prohibited from the standpoint of the judge.[68] The contradiction is resolved when, for the

[59] For example, in 1992 I took the position that Radbruch before 1933 was a positivist; Robert Alexy, *Begriff und Geltung des Rechts* (Freiburg: Karl Alber, 1992), 80. In the English translation, however, this was modified as follows: 'Before the era of National Socialism in Germany, Radbruch was a legal positivist—not in terms of justification, to be sure, but in terms of result, at any rate where the judge is concerned'; Alexy, *The Argument from Injustice* (n. 32 above), 45. See also Arthur Kaufmann, *Rechtsphilosophie*, 2nd edn (Munich: C.H. Beck, 1997), 41–4.

[60] Radbruch, *Legal Philosophy* (n. 3 above), 116 (trans. altered).

[61] Ibid., 117 (trans. altered).

[62] Ibid., (trans. altered); see further 125, 205.

[63] Ibid., 119 (trans. altered).

[64] Ibid., (trans. altered).

[65] Ibid., (trans. altered).

[66] Ibid., 118 (trans. altered).

[67] Ibid., (trans. altered).

[68] Dreier speaks here of a 'split validity doctrine'; Ralf Dreier, 'Gustav Radbruchs Rechtsbegriff', in *Gesellschaft und Gerechtigkeit. Festschrift für Hubert Rottleuthner*, ed. Matthias Mahlmann (Baden-Baden: Nomos, 2011), 17–44, at 31, see also 28. Neumann characterizes the splitting by means of the concept of a 'relational validity doctrine'; Ulfrid Neumann, 'Zum Verhältnis von Rechtsgeltung und

individual, only moral validity is suspended while legal validity is retained.[69] Then the question arises, however, of how this divergence can be explained by the idea of law. This, however, is not something I wish to pursue further here. It suffices to state that in *Legal Philosophy* (1932), despite certain restrictions with an eye to the individual, legal certainty—and with it, positivity—has absolute priority for the judge.

II. The Radbruch Formula

This absolute priority is revoked by the Radbruch Formula. The formula—Radbruch introduces it in 1946—cannot be analysed in detail here. Rather, the sole question that I wish to address here is the relation of the formula to Radbruch's system in 1932. The Formula has two parts, intolerability and disavowal, but only the first of these will be considered.[70] It reads:

> The conflict between justice and legal certainty may well be resolved in this way: The positive law, secured by legislation and power, takes precedence even when its content is unjust and fails to benefit the people, unless the conflict between statute and justice reaches such an intolerable degree that the statute, as 'flawed law', must yield to justice.[71]

Rechtsbegriff. Wandlungen in der Rechtsphilosophie Gustav Radbruchs', in *Die Natur des Rechts bei Gustav Radbruch*, eds Martin Borowski and Stanley L. Paulson (Tübingen: Mohr Siebeck, 2015), 129–49, at 139. According to the relational validity doctrine, validity is a two-place predicate '("binding for ... ")'; ibid., 131. With the removal of the splitting, validity becomes a one-place predicate; ibid. One can, indeed, say this. The subsumption of a norm (n) under a one-place validity predicate (Vn), however, implies its subsumption under a two-place validity predicate which is preceded by an universal quantifier that refers to the validity addressees (x), which have to be distinguished from the norm addressees: $\forall x\,(Vnx)$.

[69] Radbruch's remark directed to the 'criminal out of conviction' points in this direction: 'From the perpetrator, duty demands the crime, from the judge, duty demands punishment, and perhaps duty even demands that the punishment imposed for the crime committed out of duty be accepted, this for the sake of law's inviolability, legal certainty.' Radbruch, *Legal Philosophy* (n. 3 above), 119–20 (trans. altered).

[70] The disavowal formula is a direct application of the basic definition 'Law is the reality whose sense is to serve ... the idea of law' to norms which do not even represent 'an attempt at justice', Radbruch, 'Statutory Lawlessness and Supra-Statutory Law' (n. 4 above), 7, that is, to norms that do not even raise a claim to correctness or justice. The 'nature of law' is denied to them, ibid. This corresponds exactly to the statement from 1932, already quoted, which says: 'As a matter of fact, we decide by the standard of purported justice alone whether a precept is legal in nature at all, whether it accords with the *concept* of law"; Radbruch, *Legal Philosophy* (n. 3 above), 110 (trans. altered). Radbruch seems to repeat with his disavowal formula only what he already has said in 1932. Greater continuity than that is not conceivable.

[71] Radbruch, 'Statutory Lawlessness and Supra-Statutory Law' (n. 4 above), 7. In his *Primer* of 1948, Radbruch speaks instead of an 'intolerable degree' of 'horrendously unjust laws'; Gustav Radbruch, *Vorschule der Rechtsphilosophie*, in *Gustav Radbruch Gesamtausgabe*, ed. Arthur Kaufmann, vol. 3 (Heidelberg: C. F. Müller, 1990), 121–227, at 154 (trans. R. A.). In the newspaper article 'Exclusive Lesson on the Administration of Justice' from 1947, he uses the formulation 'cases of an appalling contradiction between law and justice'; Gustav Radbruch, 'Privatissimum der Rechtspflege', in *Gustav Radbruch Gesamtausgabe*, ed. Arthur Kaufmann, vol. 14 (Heidelberg: C. F. Müller, 2002), 150–3, at 152. If one replaces all these characterizations by the term 'extreme', which indicates a scale, Alexy, 'On the

It can be immediately recognized that the three elements of the idea of law, justice, legal certainty, and purposiveness, are still in play. The use of the expression 'flawed law' shows, by contrast with the talk of the loss of the 'nature of law'[72] in the disavowal formula, that the intolerability formula is solely concerned with the loss of legal validity. Thus, nothing, with a sole exception, is different from the state of affairs in 1932. The exception consists in the fact that the intolerability formula, when a certain degree of injustice is reached, revokes legal validity. Thus, the old thesis that the judge is committed to the positive law 'however unjust'[73] its content may be, is abandoned and replaced by the new thesis to the effect that although he is committed to unjust positive law, this commitment nevertheless comes to an end when the threshold of intolerable or extreme injustice is reached. This represents a discontinuity with respect to the degree to which legal certainty prevails. Does it also represent a discontinuity in the system?

In order to answer this question, the reasons for introducing the threshold of extreme injustice have to be taken into account. These reasons consist of human rights. In 1932, they stood in the triad of purpose as individual values with a rank equal to the collective values and artefact values. That is, one could decide in favour of them or against them. After initial steps in the 1930s,[74] this complete 'relativistically self-imposed moderation'[75] is abandoned in 1945 in the short article 'Five Minutes of Legal Philosophy'. Here Radbruch says:

> There are principles of law ... that are weightier than any legal enactment, so that a law in conflict with them is devoid of validity... To be sure, their details remain open to question, but the work of centuries has in fact established a solid core of them, and they have come to enjoy such far-reaching consensus in the so-called declarations of human and civil rights that only the dogmatic sceptic could still entertain doubts about some of them.[76]

In his *Primer*, Radbruch adds to this partly cultural and partly consensual justification[77] a justification that refers to 'the inner freedom of the ethical decision',[78] that

Concept and the Nature of Law' (n. 27 above), 282. (in this volume: Chapter 2, 19), Radbruch's intolerability formula can be transformed into the short form 'Extreme injustice is no (valid) law'.

[72] Radbruch, 'Statutory Lawlessness and Supra-Statutory Law' (n. 4 above), 7.

[73] Radbruch, *Legal Philosophy* (n. 3, above), 119.

[74] Gustav Radbruch, 'Der Relativismus in der Rechtsphilosophie' (1934), in *Gustav Radbruch Gesamtausgabe*, ed. Arthur Kaufmann, vol. 3 (Heidelberg: C. F. Müller, 1990), 17–22, at 22;; Gustav Radbruch, 'Der Zweck des Rechts' (1937/38), in *Gustav Radbruch Gesamtausgabe*, ed. Arthur Kaufmann, vol. 3 (Heidelberg: C. F. Müller, 1990), 39–50, at 43, 49.

[75] Radbruch, *Legal Philosophy* (n. 3, above), 108 (trans. altered).

[76] Gustav Radbruch, 'Five Minutes of Legal Philosophy', trans. Bonnie Litschewski Paulson and Stanley L. Paulson, *Oxford Journal of Legal Studies* 26 (2006), 13–15, at 14–15.

[77] See on this Robert Alexy, 'The Existence of Human Rights', *Archives for Philosophy of Law and Social Philosophy*, supplement 136 (2013), 9–18, at 14–15 (in this volume: Chapter 10, 142–53, at 148–9).

[78] Radbruch, *Vorschule der Rechtsphilosophie* (n. 71 above), 146 (trans. R. A.).

is, to autonomy. Radbruch's justification of human rights shall not, however, be considered here. What is important here is their role in his system. Radbruch ascribes an 'absolute nature' to them.[79] The concept of absoluteness implies the concept of necessity. In 1932, it was only possible to determine the content of justice by appeal to human rights. Now this appeal has become necessary, at any rate with respect to their core. If, however, it is necessary to determine the content of justice by appeal to human rights, then human rights, to the extent that their content is necessary to determinations of justice, belong, therefore, to justice.[80] This implies that justice is no longer merely formal, which means, in turn, that at least some of the individual values are transported from the triad of purposes into justice as the first element of the idea of law.[81] One might call this the 'transport theorem'. Here 'transport' gives expression to an absolute substantive limit that is imposed on what had heretofore been seen as a comprehensive relativism that knew a possible transport but by no means a necessary one. Thanks to this development, Radbruch no longer counts as a non-positivist who, under the aspect of content, allows anything, at any rate with respect to the judge.[82] He has, in other words, abandoned super-inclusive non-positivism in favour of a merely inclusive non-positivism.[83] There are systems that collapse with small changes. Radbruch's system, however, is not endangered by this momentous transport. Rather, it is strengthened. That this is possible marks the eminence of Radbruch's system. That this possibility became reality is the eminence of Radbruch.

[79] Ibid., (trans. R. A.).

[80] The thesis of the 'individualistic content of the idea of justice' from 1937 already aimed at this; Radbruch, 'Der Zweck des Rechts' (n. 74 above), 49 (trans. R. A.).

[81] This transport is made possible by the close relationship between justice and human rights, which, to be sure, does not go so far as to hold that every injustice is a violation of human rights, but consists in the fact that every violation of human rights is an injustice. On this issue, see Robert Alexy, 'Die Institutionalisierung der Menschenrechte im demokratischen Verfassungsstaat', in *Philosophie der Menschenrechte*, eds Stefan Gosepath and Georg Lohmann (Frankfurt: Suhrkamp, 1998), 244–64, at 251–2.

[82] This statement refers to the relation between *Legal Philosophy* of 1932 to the writings after 1945. With respect to the greater œuvre of Radbruch, Ralf Dreier has established the following more comprehensive thesis: 'Radbruch was at no time a legal positivist in the sense of a conceptual separation between law and justice.' Dreier, 'Kontinuitäten und Diskontinuitäten in der Rechtsphilosophie Radbruchs' (n. 2 above), 228 (trans. R. A.). Stanley L. Paulson, 'Zur Kontinuität der nichtpositivistischen Rechtsphilosophie Radbruchs' (n. 6 above), 155, goes in the same direction.

[83] Alexy, 'Law and Morality: A Continental European Perspective' (n. 22 above), 479–80. In this context, Martin Borowski aptly remarks that one can ask 'whether Radbruch's already initially non-positivistic concept of law has turned into *another* non-positivistic concept of law'. See Martin Borowski, 'Begriff und Geltung des Rechts bei Gustav Radbruch', in *Die Natur des Rechts bei Gustav Radbruch*, eds Martin Borowski and Stanley L. Paulson (Tübingen: Mohr Siebeck, 2015), 229–65, at 236 (trans. R. A.), see also 257–8.

PART II

CONSTITUTIONAL RIGHTS, HUMAN RIGHTS, AND PROPORTIONALITY

The main subject of Part II is constitutional rights. Two aspects are paramount. The first is the relation between constitutional rights and human rights. Constitutional rights are defined as attempts to transform human rights, which, as such, have only moral validity, into positive law. This is required by the claim to correctness. The second aspect is the relation between constitutional rights and proportionality analysis. Proportionality analysis includes balancing. The structure of balancing is reconstructed by a mathematical formula, the Weight Formula. The thesis is that balancing is the most rational method of the application of constitutional rights, when it is connected with argumentation. Again, the claim to correctness, and with it law's ideal dimension, enters the stage.

8
The Construction of Constitutional Rights

There are two fundamentally different constructions of constitutional rights: the rule construction and the principles construction. Neither of these constructions is at any point realized to the fullest extent, but they nevertheless represent two opposing ideas on which the solution of nearly all questions of the doctrine of constitutional rights turns. Questions pertaining to constitutional rights are not simply questions in a particular area of law. The answers given to such questions have consequences for the structure of the entire legal system. The spectrum extends from the third party or horizontal effect, that is, the bearing of constitutional rights on private law, right up to the relation between the legislature and the practice of constitutional review, behind which the tension between constitutional rights and democracy is found. The question of which construction, the rule construction or the principles construction, is to be preferred is, therefore, by no means a problem of theoretical interest alone. It also has far-reaching practical import. For this reason, it is a basic question of constitutionalism.

I. The Rule Construction

A. Rules and Principles

The basis of both the rule and the principles construction is the norm-theoretic distinction between rules and principles.[1] Rules are norms that require something definitively. They are *definitive commands*. Their form of application is subsumption. If a rule is valid and applicable it is definitively required that exactly what it demands be done. If this is done, the rule is complied with; if this is not done, the rule is not complied with. By contrast, principles are norms requiring that something be realized to the greatest extent possible, given the factual and legal possibilities at hand. Thus, principles are optimization requirements. As such, they are characterized by the fact that they can be satisfied to varying degrees, and that the appropriate degree of satisfaction depends not only on what is factually possible but also on what is legally possible. Rules aside, the legal possibilities are determined essentially by opposing principles. For this reason, principles, each taken

[1] See Robert Alexy, *A Theory of Constitutional Rights* (1985), trans. Julian Rivers (Oxford: Oxford University Press, 2002), 47–9.

Law's Ideal Dimension. Robert Alexy, Oxford University Press. © Robert Alexy 2021.
DOI: 10.1093/oso/9780198796831.003.0009

alone, always comprise a merely *prima facie* requirement. The determination of the appropriate degree of satisfaction of one principle relative to the requirements of another principle is balancing. Thus, balancing is the specific form of the application of principles.

The distinction between rules and principles is at the heart of a theory that might be called 'principles theory'. The principles theory is the system drawn from the implications of the distinction between rules and principles. These implications affect all areas of the law. As far as constitutional rights are concerned, one may speak of the 'principles theory of constitutional rights' as well as of their 'principles construction'. The debate over the principles theory is, first of all, a debate over weighing or balancing—and, therefore, since balancing is the core of the proportionality test, a debate over proportionality analysis.

B. The Postulate to Avoid Balancing

The counterpart of the principles construction, the rule construction, can be seen as an attempt to avoid the problems connected with balancing. Constitutional rights norms are considered as rules that are applicable, in essence, without balancing. This does not mean that the application of constitutional rights is conceived, in all instances, as an unproblematic subsumption. Subsumption, here as elsewhere in the law, can be rather difficult, and may require intermediate steps as well as further arguments of different kinds in order to justify these intermediate steps.[2] Thus, it can be very doubtful whether a certain statement is an expression of one's opinion, protected by the freedom of speech, or whether a certain activity is an exercise of religion, or whether a certain valuable advantage counts as property, as protected by the constitution. It is decisive for the rule construction that not only such questions as these but, going beyond them, all other questions that may arise in the application of constitutional rights be resolved in essence *without* balancing.

This solution, freedom from balancing, may acquire either a positivistic or a non-positivistic character. An example of a positivistic construction, free of balancing, is Ernst Forsthoff's postulate that all questions connected with the application of constitutional rights be resolved by means of the traditional canons of interpretation,[3] that is, by appealing, above all, to the wording of the constitutional rights provisions, the intentions of those who framed the constitution, and the systematic context of the provision being interpreted. Today the best-known version of a non-positivistic construction, free of balancing, is found in the work of Ronald

[2] See Robert Alexy, *A Theory of Legal Argumentation* (1978), trans. Ruth Adler and Neil MacCormick (Oxford: Clarendon Press, 1989), 221–30.

[3] Ernst Forsthoff, 'Zur Problematik der Verfassungsauslegung', in Forsthoff, *Rechtsstaat im Wandel*, 2nd edn (Munich: C. H. Beck, 1976), 153–74, at 173.

Dworkin. According to him, the application of constitutional rights is not a matter of striking a balance. Rather, it concerns 'the very different question of what morality requires'.[4] If the principles construction is defined as a proportionality construction that includes balancing essentially, then this, too, is a rule construction, albeit one of a special kind.

C. Problems of the Rule Construction

The problems of the rule construction emerge most clearly in connection with the question of the limits of constitutional rights. Here only two constellations will be considered: that of a constitutional right with a statutory reservation, and that of a constitutional right guaranteed without this reservation.

The simplest form of a statutory reservation is present, for example, when a constitutional rights provision guarantees, in a first step, constitutional rights such as the right to life and to bodily integrity, and, in a second step, then empowers the legislature by means of a clause such as '[t]hese rights may only be interfered with on a statutory basis'[5] to limit these rights. If one follows the rule construction and takes these provisions literally, the limitation clause makes possible any interference with life and bodily integrity as long as the interference is based on a statute. Thus, the constitutional right is reduced to a special statutory reservation. It loses the power it would otherwise have had to bind the legislator. From the standpoint, then, of substantive law, such a constitutional right simply has no bearing on the legislator. This, however, stands in contradiction to the binding force of constitutional rights on the legislature. One may attempt to avoid this situation by adding more rules. The systematically most demanding attempt here is the prohibition to infringe on the core content of a constitutional right, as found in Article 19(2) German Basic Law. Even here, however, the legislature remains completely free at every point beneath the threshold of the core content. Moreover, it is highly unlikely that the core content can be determined at all in a manner that is free from balancing.[6]

No less serious are the problems of the rule construction in case of constitutional rights guaranteed without a statutory reservation, that is, constitutional rights with respect to which the constitution explicitly provides for no limits. In the German Basic Law this is the case, for instance, with freedom of religion and of science. If one were to subsume, as an isolated instance, religious suppression, when required by a particular religious faith, and medical experiments with human beings, when advancing scientific progress, this type of isolated instances of subsumption would

[4] Ronald Dworkin, *Is Democracy Possible Here?* (Princeton, N. J.: Princeton University Press, 2006), 27; see Kai Möller, 'Balancing and the Structure of Constitutional Rights', *International Journal of Constitutional Law*, 5 (2007), 453–68, at 458–61.

[5] See Article 2(2)(3) German Basic Law.

[6] See Alexy, *A Theory of Constitutional Rights* (n. 1 above), 192–6.

be allowed. The alternative of not classifying these measures as religious acts or scientific research would contradict the wording of the constitutional rights provisions. If, however, the rights to freedom, life, and bodily integrity of those concerned are employed as reasons for imposing limitations, one inevitably confronts the need to balance. In this way, the postulate of systematic interpretation warrants, indeed requires that one move beyond the scope of the rule model.

II. Principles Construction and Proportionality Analysis

The principles construction attempts to resolve these and a great many additional problems by conceiving of constitutional rights as principles, that is, as optimization requirements.

The significance of constitutional rights as principles stems from their connection to the principle of proportionality. This connection is as close as it could possibly be. It consists in a relation of mutual implication. The principle of proportionality with its three sub-principles of suitability, necessity, and proportionality in the narrower sense follows logically from the definition of principle, just as the definition of principle follows from the principle of proportionality with its three sub-principles.[7] This means that the principle of proportionality is valid if constitutional rights have the character of principles and that constitutional rights have the character of principles if the principle of proportionality determines the application of constitutional rights. The core of the principles construction consists in this necessary connection between constitutional rights and proportionality.

III. Objections to the Principles Construction

To the principles construction as well as to the principles theory in general a great many objections of various sorts have been raised, and it is impossible to discuss all of them here. But because the objections, despite their diversity, have a certain systematic relation to each other, a short general account of them shall be offered before taking up the most central objection. A classification into seven groups seems to be advisable. The first group comprises the *norm-theoretic* objections. Here the concern is over such questions as whether there exist legal principles at all,[8] whether and how principles can be distinguished from rules,[9] whether

[7] Ibid., 66–9.

[8] Larry Alexander, 'Legal Objectivity and the Illusion of Legal Principles', in *Institutionalized Reason. The Jurisprudence of Robert Alexy*, ed. Matthias Klatt (Oxford: Oxford University Press, 2012), 115–31, at 121–3.

[9] Ralf Poscher, 'Einsichten, Irrtümer und Selbstmissverständnis der Prinzipientheorie', in *Die Prinzipientheorie der Grundrechte*, ed. Jan-Reinard Sieckmann (Baden-Baden: Nomos, 2007), 59–79, at 65, 70.

principles are norms,[10] and whether a basic opposition of rules to principles is not misguided, in light of the extraordinary variety of norms.[11] The objections of the second group may be designated as *argumentation-theoretic*. Here the central issue is whether balancing is properly seen as rational argumentation or whether it must be classified as a non-rational or irrational method.[12] The objections of the third group turn on the question of whether the principles construction counts as a danger to constitutional rights, eliminating as it does their strict validity as rules.[13] Objections of this kind concern the doctrine of constitutional rights. They may, therefore, be termed *doctrinal* objections. Whereas the doctrinal objections appeal to the danger of too little force in constitutional rights, the opposite, the danger of too much force, stands at the centre of the objections of the fourth group. These objections claim that the optimization thesis leads to a proliferation of constitutional rights, leading in turn to an over-constitutionalization of the legal system. The institutional consequence is said to be a 'gradual transition from a parliamentary, legislative state to a constitutional court-based, jurisdiction state'.[14] One may refer here to *institutional* objections. The fifth group consists of *interpretation-theoretic* objections. They concern the question of whether and how the principles construction can be established as a correct interpretation of a catalogue of constitutional rights as understood in positive law.[15] Is it possible to justify the universal validity of the principle or proportionality construction,[16] or is it to be applied, at best, only occasionally and on an ad hoc basis? The objections of the sixth group concern *validity-theoretic* questions. These objections reproach the principles theory for jeopardizing the superior rank of the constitution and the subjection of the executive and judiciary to statutory law.[17] The hierarchical

[10] Jan Henrik Klement, 'Vom Nutzen einer Theorie, die alles erklärt', *Juristenzeitung* 63 (2008), 756–63, at 760.

[11] Poscher, 'Einsichten, Irrtümer und Selbstmissverständnis der Prinzipientheorie' (n. 9 above), 73–4.

[12] See Jürgen Habermas, *Between Facts and Norms. Contribution to a Discourse Theory of Law and Democracy* (1992) trans. William Rehg (Cambridge: Polity Press, 1996), 259;; Bernhard Schlink, 'Der Grundsatz der Verhältnismäßigkeit', in *Festschrift 50 Jahre Bundesverfassungsgericht*, vol. 2, eds Peter Badura and Horst Dreier (Tübingen: Mohr Siebeck, 2001), 445–65, at 460.

[13] See on this Habermas, *Between Facts and Norms* (n. 12 above), 258–9, who maintains that with the principles construction a 'firewall' is collapsing.

[14] Ernst-Wolfgang Böckenförde, 'Fundamental Rights as Constitutional Principles. On the Current State of Interpreting Fundamental Rights', in Böckenförde, *Constitutional and Political Theory. Selected Writings*, eds Mirjam Künkler and Tine Stein (Oxford: Oxford University Press, 2017), 235–65, at 259.

[15] Matthias Jestaedt, 'Die Abwägungslehre—ihre Stärken und ihre Schwächen', in *Staat im Wort. Festschrift für Josef Isensee*, eds Otto Depenheuer, Markus Heintzen, Matthias Jestaedt, et al. (Heidelberg: C. F. Müller, 2007), 253–75, at 260, 262–3, 275; Poscher, 'Einsichten, Irrtümer und Selbstmissverständnis der Prinzipientheorie' (n. 9 above), 79; Klement, 'Vom Nutzen einer Theorie, die alles erklärt' (n. 10 above), 761, 763.

[16] So, for instance, David M. Beatty, *The Ultimate Rule of Law* (Oxford: Oxford University Press, 2004), 162: 'Proportionality is a universal criterion of constitutionality.'

[17] Jestaedt, 'Die Abwägungslehre—ihre Stärken und ihre Schwächen' (n. 15 above), 268, 275; Poscher, 'Einsichten, Irrtümer und Selbstmissverständnis der Prinzipientheorie' (n. 9 above), 76; Klement, 'Vom Nutzen einer Theorie, die alles erklärt' (n. 10 above), 759.

structure of the legal system is said to collapse in the whirl of balancing.[18] The seventh group, finally, is formed by *science-theoretic* objections. The principles theory is said to consist of 'statements that for reason of their abstractness do not say anything at all',[19] statements that are capable of explaining each and every decision taken, but without 'any directive power for decisions to be taken in the future'.[20] For this reason, so it is argued, the principles theory cannot suffice as a doctrine of constitutional rights.[21]

IV. The Rationality of Balancing

A. The Central Role of the Rationality Problem

The argumentation-theoretic objections that concern the rationality of balancing count as the most important group. If balancing were by its nature irrational, it would have to be rejected, and with it, principles *qua* norms that require something irrational.[22] The norm-theoretic debate would have lost its point. Moreover, if balancing were irrational, it would not make sense to argue on behalf of balancing as the applicable criterion on the question of the admissibility of limitations on constitutional rights. The doctrinal objections would win hands down. The same would apply to the institutional critique. To be sure, the situation is more complex in the case of the interpretation-theoretic arguments. If balancing should prove to be irrational, one would adhere to it at most in instances where a constitution explicitly required a proportionality test, as, for instance, in the case of Article 52(1)(2) of the Charter of Fundamental Rights of the European Union. Even here, however, one may ask whether a norm that requires something irrational might not be corrected more appropriately by way of interpretation. The validity-theoretic objection would carry the day, too. Who would care to assent to an irrational restriction on the validity of a norm? The irrationality of balancing would, finally, be grist to the mills of all science-theoretic objections. For these reasons, the rationality problem shall take the centre stage in what follows. To be sure, a refutation of the irrationality objection does not imply the refutation of any of the other objections. The rationality of balancing is not a sufficient condition for the rebuttal of the other objections, but it is, in any case, a necessary condition.

[18] Jestaedt, 'Die Abwägungslehre—ihre Stärken und ihre Schwächen' (n. 15 above), 269–70.

[19] Ibid., 269 (trans. R. A.).

[20] Klement, 'Vom Nutzen einer Theorie, die alles erklärt' (n. 10 above), 756 (trans. R. A.); Ralf Poscher, *Grundrechte als Abwehrrechte. Reflexive Regelung rechtlich geordneter Freiheit* (Tübingen: Mohr Siebeck, 2003), 76; Jestaedt, 'Die Abwägungslehre—ihre Stärken und ihre Schwächen' (n. 15 above), 269.

[21] Poscher, *Grundrechte als Abwehrrechte* (n. 20 above), 77–8.

[22] This applies in any case to optimization relative to the legal possibilities. Optimization relative to the factual possibilities might be retained even in the case of irrationality of balancing.

B. The Irrationality Objection

Many authors have contested the rationality and, with it, the objectivity of balancing—especially emphatically by Habermas and Schlink. Habermas's central point is that there exist 'no rational standards' for balancing:

> Because there are no rational standards for this, weighing takes place either arbitrarily or unreflectively, according to customary standards and hierarchies.[23]

Where Habermas speaks about arbitrariness and unreflected customs, Schlink employs the concepts of subjectivity and decision:

> In the test of proportionality in the narrower sense, it is only the subjectivity of those performing the test that can, in the end, be effective ... The operations of evaluation and balancing required by the test of proportionality in the narrower sense can be achieved ... in the end, only in a decisionistic manner.[24]

Is this true? Is balancing really non-rational or irrational, arbitrary, subjective, and decisionistic? Does balancing indeed mean that rationality, correctness, and objectivity are abandoned? It is difficult to answer these questions without knowing what balancing is. And to find out what balancing is, some insight into its structure is presupposed.

C. Pareto-Optimality

It has already been noted that balancing is the subject of the third sub-principle of the principle of proportionality. This is the principle of proportionality in the narrower sense, which concerns optimization relative to the legal possibilities at hand. By contrast, the subject of the first two sub-principles, the sub-principles of suitability and necessity, is optimization relative to the factual possibilities. In this respect, they are concerned with the question of whether the factual possibilities allow for the avoidance of costs to constitutional rights without bringing about costs contrary to the aims of the legislator. The issue, in other words, is Pareto-optimality.[25] This is far less problematic than balancing, which is concerned with the question of which side has to bear the costs. For this reason, the principles of

[23] Habermas, *Between Facts and Norms* (n. 12 above), 259.

[24] Bernhard Schlink, 'Freiheit durch Eingriffsabwehr—Rekonstruktion der klassischen Grundrechtsfunktion', *Europäische Grundrechte-Zeitschrift* 11 (1984), 457–68, at 462 (trans. R. A.); see further Schlink, 'Der Grundsatz der Verhältnismäßigkeit' (n. 12 above), 460.

[25] Alexy, *A Theory of Constitutional Rights* (n. 1 above), 105, 398–9.

suitability and necessity shall not be discussed here.[26] In any case, the mere fact that the principles construction is able to grasp this aspect, too, is a strong argument on behalf of its correctness.

D. The Law of Balancing

The basic idea of optimization relative to the legal possibilities at hand can be expressed by a rule that might be called the 'Law of Balancing'. A statement of this rule runs as follows:

> The greater the degree of non-satisfaction of, or detriment to, one principle, the greater must be the importance of satisfying the other.[27]

The Law of Balancing shows that balancing can be broken down into three stages. The first stage is a matter of establishing the degree of non-satisfaction of, or detriment to, the first principle. This is followed by a second stage, in which the importance of satisfying the competing principle is established. Finally, the third stage answers the question of whether or not the importance of satisfying the competing principle justifies the detriment to, or non-satisfaction of, the first principle. If it were not possible to make rational judgments about first, intensities of interference, second, degrees of importance, and third, their relationship to each other, the objections raised by Habermas and Schlink would be justified.

E. The Weight Formula

In order to show that rational judgments about intensity of interference and degree of importance are possible, I turn first to a decision of the German Federal Constitutional Court on health warnings.[28] The Court characterizes the obligation of tobacco producers to place health warnings respecting the dangers of smoking on their products as a relatively minor or light interference with the freedom to pursue one's profession. By contrast, a total ban on all tobacco products would count as a serious interference. Between such minor and serious cases, others of moderate intensity of interference can be found. In this way, a scale can be developed with the stages 'light', 'moderate', and 'serious'. Our example shows that the intensity of interference can be determined by means of this scale.

[26] See on this Laura Clérico, *Die Struktur der Verhältnismäßigkeit* (Baden-Baden: Nomos, 2001), 26–139.

[27] See Alexy, *A Theory of Constitutional Rights* (n. 1 above), 102.

[28] Decisions of the German Federal Constitutional Court (BVerfGE) 95, 173.

The same is possible on the side of the competing reasons. The health risks resulting from smoking are high. Thus, the reasons justifying interference weigh heavily. If in this way the intensity of interference is established as minor, and the degree of importance of the reasons for the interference as high, then the outcome of examining proportionality in the narrower sense can well be described—as the German Federal Constitutional Court has in fact described it—as 'obvious'.[29]

The teachings drawn from the *Tobacco* Judgment are corroborated if one looks at other cases. A rather different case is represented by the *Titanic* Judgment. The widely-published satirical magazine, *Titanic*, described a paraplegic reserve officer, first, as a 'born murderer' and then, in a later edition, as a 'cripple'. A German Court ruled against *Titanic* and ordered the magazine to pay damages to the officer in the amount of DM 12,000. *Titanic* brought a constitutional complaint. The Federal Constitutional Court undertook a 'case-specific balancing'[30] between the freedom of expression of the magazine and the officer's general right of personality. This case, too, can be reconstructed by means of the triadic scale: light, moderate, and serious.

However, the triadic scale is not by itself enough to demonstrate that balancing is rational. A demonstration requires that it is possible to embed such classifications in an inferential system that is understood as implicit in balancing and that, in turn, is intrinsically connected with the concept of correctness. In the case of subsumption under a rule, such an inferential system can be expressed by means of a deductive scheme, called 'internal justification', that is constructed with the help of propositional, predicate, and deontic logic and integrated into the theory of legal discourse.[31] It is of great importance, both for the theory of legal discourse and the theory of constitutional rights, that in the case of balancing a counterpart to this deductive scheme exists.[32] This is the Weight Formula.

The core and, at the same time, the simplest form of the Weight Formula runs as follows:

$$W_{i,j} = \frac{I_i}{I_j}$$

In this formula, one finds that the variables for the abstract weights of the competing principles (W_i, W_j) and for the reliability of the empirical assumptions concerning what the measure in question means in the concrete case for the non-realization of the one principle and the realization of the other principle (R_i, R_j) are

29 BVerfGE 95, 173 (187).

30 BVerfGE 86, 1 (11).

31 Alexy, *A Theory of Legal Argumentation* (n. 2 above), 221–30.

32 Robert Alexy, 'On Balancing and Subsumption. A Structural Comparison', *Ratio Juris* 16 (2003), 433–49, at 448.

still lacking. But this can be left out of consideration here, so that the simplest form just mentioned may stand for the complete form:[33]

$$W_{i,j} = \frac{I_i \cdot W_i \cdot R_i}{I_j \cdot W_j \cdot R_j}$$

In the simplest as well as in the complete form, I_i stands for the intensity of interference with the principle P_i, in our case, the principle granting the freedom of expression of *Titanic*. I_j stands for the importance of satisfying the competing principle P_j, which, in our case, is the principle granting the personality right of the paraplegic officer. Finally, $W_{i,j}$ stands for the concrete weight of the principle whose violation is being examined, in our case, that of P_i. The Weight Formula gives expression to the point that the concrete weight of a principle is a relative weight. It does this, in the simplest form, by defining the concrete weight as the quotient of the intensity of interference with this principle (P_i) and the concrete importance of the competing principle (P_j).

Now, the objection is clear that one can only talk about quotients in the presence of numbers, and that numbers are not used in the balancing carried out in constitutional law. The reply to this objection might begin with the observation that the vocabulary drawn from logic, which we are using in order to express the structure of subsumption, is also not used in judicial reasoning, but that this vocabulary is nevertheless the best means available to make explicit the inferential structure of rules. The same would apply to an expression of the inferential structure of principles by means of numbers that are substituted for the variables of the Weight Formula.

The three values of the triadic model, light, moderate, and serious, can be represented by *l*, *m*, and *s*. Certainly, the triadic model by no means exhausts the possibilities of graduation. Balancing would be possible once one had a scale with two values, say, *l* and *s*. Balancing is impossible only if everything has the same value.[34] Moreover, there are numerous possibilities for refining the scale. A double-triadic scale is of special interest. It works with nine steps or values: (1) *ll*, (2) *lm*, (3) *ls*, (4) *ml*, (5) *mm*, (6) *ms*, (7) *sl*, (8) *sm*, (9) *ss*. It is of utmost importance that the possibilities of refinement are limited. All classifications are judgments. Everybody understands a statement such as 'the infringement is light (*l*)' or a statement such as 'the infringement is a serious moderate infringement'. But how should the statement 'the infringement is a serious light infringement of moderate kind (*lsm*)' be understood, which is made possible by adding a third triad? A justification can

[33] See generally Robert Alexy, 'The Weight Formula', trans. Bartosz Brożek and Stanley L. Paulson, in *Studies in the Philosophy of Law*, vol. 3, eds Jerzy Stelmach, Bartosz Brożek, and Wojciech Załuski (Kraków: Jagiellonian University Press, 2007), 9–27, at 20–6 (in this volume: Chapter 11, 154–74, at 165–73).

[34] See on this Aharon Barak, *The Judge in a Democracy* (Princeton, N.J.: Princeton University Press, 2006), 166: 'One cannot balance without a scale.'

only be given for what one understands, and the justifiability of statements about intensities is a condition of the rationality of balancing. This implies that graduation in the province of constitutional rights can work only with relatively crude scales. In the end, it is the nature of law, here the nature of constitutional law that sets limits to the degree to which the graduation can be refined and altogether excludes the applicability of any infinitesimal scale.[35] Calculable measurements by way of a continuum of points between 0 and 1 cannot have any application.

Even crude, discrete scales, however, cannot dispense with the allocation of numbers if the inferential structure of balancing is going to be expressed by the Weight Formula. There are various possibilities for allocating numbers to the three values of the triadic model. A rather simple and at the same time highly instructive possibility consists in taking the geometric sequence 2^0, 2^1, and 2^2, that is, 1, 2, and 4.[36] In the *Titanic* Judgment, the Federal Constitutional Court considered the intensity of infringement (I_i) with the freedom of expression (P_i) as serious (*s*); it considered the importance of satisfying the right to personality (P_j) of the officer (I_j), in the matter of describing him as 'born murderer', given its highly satirical context, as only moderate (*m*), perhaps even as light (*l*). If we insert the corresponding values of our geometric sequence for *s* and *m*, then the concrete weight of P_i ($W_{i,j}$) is, in this case, $4/2$, that is, 2. If, conversely, I_i were *m* and I_j were *s*, the value would be $2/4$, that is, ½. The priority of P_i is expressed by a concrete weight greater than 1; the priority of P_j by a concrete weight less than 1. In all stalemate cases the value is 1.

The description of the officer as a 'cripple', however, was considered by the Court as a severe (*s*) interference with the right of personality. This gave rise to a stalemate, with the consequence that *Titanic*'s constitutional complaint was not successful in so far as it related to damages stemming from the description 'cripple'. By contrast, freedom of expression enjoys priority in the case of the description 'born murderer' with the consequence that the damages were in so far as they related thereto disproportional, hence unconstitutional. The constitutional complaint was to this extent successful.

The rationality of an inferential structure essentially depends on the question of whether it connects premises that, again, can be justified. In the Weight Formula the premises are represented by numbers which stand for judgments. An example is the judgment that the public description of a severely disabled person as a 'cripple' is a serious interference with that person's personality right. This judgment raises a claim to correctness, which can be justified in a discourse. The commensurability

[35] Robert Alexy, 'Verfassungsrecht und einfaches Recht—Verfassungsgerichtsbarkeit und Fachgerichtsbarkeit', *Veröffentlichungen der Vereinigung der Deutschen Staatsrechtslehrer* 61 (2002), 7–30, at 25–6.

[36] The greatest advantage of the geometric sequence consists in its providing for the best representation of the over-proportional increase of the power of rights as correlated with an increasing intensity of interference, a fact that serves as the basis for the refutation of the objection concerning the dissolution of the power of constitutional rights. See Alexy, 'The Weight Formula' (n. 33 above), 22–3 (in this volume: Chapter 11, 167–9).

of the assessments on both sides of the balance is granted if the discourse is conducted on the basis of a common point of view: the point of view of the constitution.[37] The Federal Constitutional Court justifies its assessment with the argument that the description as a 'cripple' is nowadays considered as an expression of disrespect and humiliation.[38] Naturally, one can carry on a dispute about this, as about so many questions in the law. But contestability does not imply irrationality. If this were the case, not only balancing but legal reasoning as such would be for the most part irrational. Precisely the opposite, however, is the case. Justifiability, despite the fact that it cannot be identified with provability, implies rationality, and, with it, objectivity, understood as lying between certainty and arbitrariness.

The end is attained. Balancing turns out to be an argument form[39] of rational legal discourse.[40] This suffices to refute the irrationalism objection as an objection specifically directed against balancing. Of course, one might enquire quite generally into the possibility of rational legal argument, and one could also think about undertaking a reply to the objections of the other six groups on the basis of what has been elaborated here. This, however, will have to await another occasion. Here it suffices to say that the irrationalism objection, on which everything else depends, can be dismissed. Having done so, we might well be in a position to say that an important step along the way towards a full defence of the principles construction of constitutional rights has been taken.

[37] Alexy, 'The Weight Formula' (n. 33 above), 18 (in this volume: Chapter 11, 163–4).

[38] BVerfGE 86, 1 (13).

[39] See Alexy, *A Theory of Legal Argumentation* (n. 2 above), 92. This, perhaps, is the point of Barak's thesis that 'balancing introduces order into legal thought'. See Barak, *The Judge in a Democracy* (n. 34 above), 173; see also 164.

[40] As an inferential scheme expressed by the Weight Formula, balancing is a formal structure that contains, as such, no substance whatever. The application of the Weight Formula, however, requires that content—made explicit by judgments about the intensity of interference, abstract weight, and the reliability of empirical assumptions—is substituted for the variables of the Weight Formula. For this reason, one can say that balancing is procedurally substantive.

9

Balancing, Constitutional Review, and Representation

Discursive constitutionalism is a theory which stems from the connection of five different concepts: (1) constitutional rights, (2) balancing, (3) discourse, (4) constitutional review, and (5) representation. The system formed by these five concepts is highly complex. The picture of it that shall be presented here is concentrated on the concepts of balancing, constitutional review, and representation.

I. Balancing

One of the main topics in the current debate about the interpretation of constitutional rights is the role of balancing or weighing. In the actual practice of many constitutional courts, balancing plays a central role. In German constitutional law balancing is one part of what is required by a more comprehensive principle. This more comprehensive principle is the principle of proportionality (*Verhäl tnismäßigkeitsgrundsatz*). The principle of proportionality consists of three sub-principles: the principles of suitability, of necessity, and of proportionality in the narrower sense. All these principles give expression to the idea of optimization. Interpreting constitutional rights in the light of the principle of proportionality is to treat constitutional rights as optimization requirements, that is, as principles, not simply as rules. As optimization requirements, principles are norms requiring that something be realized to the greatest extent possible, given the factual and legal possibilities.[1]

The principles of suitability and necessity concern optimization relative to what is factually possible. They thereby express the idea of Pareto-optimality. The third sub-principle, the principle of proportionality in the narrower sense, concerns optimization relative to the legal possibilities. The legal possibilities are essentially defined by competing principles. Balancing consists in nothing other than optimization relative to competing principles. The third sub-principle can therefore be expressed by a rule that states:

[1] Robert Alexy, *A Theory of Constitutional Rights* (1985), trans. Julian Rivers (Oxford: Oxford University Press, 2002), 47.

Law's Ideal Dimension. Robert Alexy, Oxford University Press. © Robert Alexy 2021.
DOI: 10.1093/oso/9780198796831.003.0010

> The greater the degree of non-satisfaction of, or detriment to, one principle, the greater must be the importance of satisfying the other.

This rule might be called the 'Law of Balancing'.[2]

A. Two Objections

The phenomenon of balancing in constitutional law leads to so many problems that I cannot provide a list of them here, much less a discussion. I will confine myself to two objections.

The first objection has been raised by many authors. Their objection rejects the idea that balancing is a rational procedure. It is said to be a rhetorical figure that allows for unlimited subjectivity. The reasons for this are, as Habermas puts it, that 'there are no rational standards' for balancing.[3]

The second objection is more subtle. It concerns a conceptual problem. Once again, we can refer to Habermas, who has presented a highly interesting version of the problem. Habermas maintains that the balancing approach takes legal rulings out of the realm defined by such concepts as right and wrong, correctness and incorrectness, and also justification, and into a realm defined by such concepts as adequate and inadequate, and discretion. 'Weighing of values' is said to be able to yield a judgment as to its '*result*' but is not able to '*justify*' that result:

> The court's judgment is then *itself* a value judgment that more or less adequately reflects a form of life articulating itself in the framework of a concrete order of values. But this judgment is no longer related to the alternatives of a right or wrong decision.[4]

This second objection is at least as serious as the first one. It amounts to the thesis that the loss of the category of correctness is the price to be paid for balancing or weighing. If weighing is only able to produce results but is unable to justify these results, then weighing would need to be located in a realm outside the region defined by the concepts of truth, correctness, knowledge, justification, and objectivity. The inhabitants of this region are judgments or propositions *qua* entities that lend themselves to assignments of truth or falsity, correctness or incorrectness. These entities, in other words, give expression to what, in fact, is the case, to what can be characterized as actually being known and not merely believed. By the same

[2] Ibid., 102.

[3] Jürgen Habermas, *Between Facts and Norms. Contribution to a Discourse Theory of Law and Democracy* (1992), trans. William Rehg (Cambridge: Polity Press, 1996), 259.

[4] Jürgen Habermas, 'Reply to Symposium Participants, Benjamin N. Cardozo School of Law', *Cardozo Law Review* 17 (1996), 1477–557, at 1531.

token, these entities lend themselves to justification rather than to merely rhetorical support. This region might be termed the empire of objectivity.

If balancing, from the beginning, were excluded from the sphere of objectivity, the balancing approach would suffer a fatal blow. Constitutional review is necessarily connected to a claim to correctness.[5] If balancing or weighing were incompatible with correctness, objectivity, and justification, it would have no place in constitutional law.

Is balancing intrinsically irrational and subjective? Does balancing truly mean we are compelled to bid farewell to correctness, objectivity, and justification—and, thus, to reason, too?

B. The Structure of Balancing

It is difficult to answer these questions without knowing what balancing is. To know what balancing is presupposes insight into its structure. The Law of Balancing shows that balancing can be broken down into three stages. The first stage involves establishing the degree of non-satisfaction of, or detriment to, a first principle. This is followed by a second stage in which the importance of satisfying the competing principle is established. Finally, in the third stage, it is established whether the importance of satisfying the latter principle justifies the detriment to or non-satisfaction of the former. If it were not possible to make rational judgments about, first, intensity of interference, secondly, degrees of importance, and, thirdly, their relationship to each other, then the objections raised by Habermas would be justified. Everything turns, then, on the possibility of making such judgments.

In order to show that rational judgments about intensity of interference and degrees of importance are possible, I shall take up a decision of the German Federal Constitutional Court on health warnings.[6] The Court characterizes the duty of tobacco producers to place health warnings respecting the dangers of smoking on their products as a relatively minor or light interference with freedom to pursue one's profession (*Berufsausübungsfreiheit*). By contrast, a total ban on all tobacco products would count as a serious interference. Between such minor and serious cases, others of moderate intensity of interference can be found. In this way, a scale can be developed with the stages '*light*', '*moderate*', and '*serious*'. Our example shows that valid assignments following this scale are possible.

The same is possible on the side of the competing reasons. The health risks resulting from smoking are great. The reasons justifying the interference, therefore, weigh heavily. If in this way the intensity of interference is established as

[5] Robert Alexy, 'Law and Correctness', trans. Kirsten Bock, *Current Legal Problems* 51 (1998), 205–21, at 209–14 (in this volume: Chapter 21, 312–25, at 315–20).

[6] Decisions of the German Federal Constitutional Court (BVerfGE) 95, 173.

minor, and the degree of importance of the reasons for the interference as high, then the outcome of examining proportionality in the narrower sense may well be described—as the German Federal Constitutional Court, in fact, described it—as 'obvious'.[7]

The teachings of the *Tobacco* Judgment are corroborated if one looks at other cases. A rather different one is the *Titanic* Judgment. The widely published satirical magazine, *Titanic*, described a paraplegic reserve officer, first, as a 'born murderer' and then, in a later edition, as a 'cripple'. A German court ruled against *Titanic* and ordered the magazine to pay damages to the officer in the amount of DM 12,000. *Titanic* brought a constitutional complaint. The Federal Constitutional Court undertook a 'case-specific balancing'[8] between the freedom of expression of the magazine (Article 5(1)(1) German Basic Law) and the officer's general right to personality (Article 2(1) in connection with Article 1(1) German Basic Law). I will show that this case, too, can be reconstructed by means of the triadic scale: light, moderate, and serious.

However, the triadic structure, as such, is not enough for a demonstration that balancing is rational. For this it is necessary that an inferential system be understood as implicit in balancing which, in turn, is intrinsically connected with the concept of correctness. In the case of subsumption under a rule, such an inferential system can be expressed by means of a deductive scheme called 'internal justification', which is constructed with the help of propositional, predicate, and deontic logic. It is of central importance for the theory of legal discourse that, in the case of the balancing of principles, a counterpart to this deductive scheme exists.[9] We will call it the 'Weight Formula'.

The simplest form of the Weight Formula goes as follows:

$$W_{i,j} = \frac{I_i}{I_j}$$

Let 'I_i' stand for the intensity of interference with the principle P_i, for example, the principle granting the freedom of expression of *Titanic*. 'I_j' stands for the importance of satisfying the competing principle P_j—in our case, the principle granting the personality right of the paraplegic officer. And let '$W_{i,j}$' stand for the concrete weight of P_i. The Weight Formula makes the point that the concrete weight of a principle is a relative weight. It does this by making the concrete weight the quotient of the intensity of interference with this principle (P_i) and the concrete importance of the competing principle (P_j).

[7] BVerfGE 95, 173 (187).

[8] BVerfGE 86, 1 (11) (trans. R. A.).

[9] Robert Alexy, 'On Balancing and Subsumption. A Structural Comparison', *Ratio Juris* 16 (2003), 433–48, at 448.

Now, the objection is clear that one can only talk about quotients in the presence of numbers, and that numbers are not used in the balancing carried out in constitutional law. The reply to this objection might begin with the observation that the logical vocabulary we are using in order to express the structure of subsumption is not used in judicial reasoning but that this vocabulary is, nevertheless, the best means available to make explicit the inferential structure of rules. The same applies to the expression of the inferential structure of principles by numbers that are substituted for the variables of the Weight Formula.

The three values of our triadic model—light, moderate, and serious—shall be represented by '*l*', '*m*', and '*s*'. There are various possibilities for assigning numbers to *l*, *m*, and *s*. A rather simple and, at the same time, highly instructive possibility consists in taking the geometric sequence 2^0, 2^1, and 2^2, that is, 1, 2, and 4. On this basis, *l* has the value 1, *m* the value 2, and *s* the value 4. The Federal Constitutional Court considered the intensity of interference (I_i) with the freedom of expression (P_i) in the *Titanic* Judgment as serious (*s*), and the importance of satisfying the right to personality (P_j) of the officer (I_j) in the matter of describing him as a 'born murderer'—given its highly satirical context—as only moderate (*m*), perhaps even as light (*l*). If we insert the corresponding values of our geometric sequence for *s* and *m*, than the concrete weight of P_i ($W_{i,j}$) is, in this case, $\frac{4}{2}$ that is, 2. If I_i were *m* and I_j were *s*, the value would be $\frac{2}{4}$, that is, $\frac{1}{2}$. In stalemate cases this value is 1. The precedence of P_i is expressed by a concrete weight greater than 1: the precedence of P_j by a concrete weight less than 1. The description of the officer as 'cripple' was considered as serious. This gave rise to a stalemate, with the consequence that *Titanic*'s constitutional complaint was not successful in so far as it related to damages stemming from the description 'cripple'.

The rationality of an inferential structure essentially depends on the question of whether it connects premises that, again, can be justified. The structure expressed by the Weight Formula would not be a structure of rational reasoning if the character of the input were such as to exclude it from the realm of rationality. This, however, is not the case. The input that is represented by numbers is a judgment. An example is the judgment that the public description of a severely disabled person as 'cripple' is a 'serious breach'[10] of that person's personality right. This judgment raises a claim to correctness, and it can be justified as the conclusion of another inferential scheme in a discourse. The Federal Constitutional Court carries out this discourse with the argument that the description of the paraplegic as a 'cripple' was humiliating and disrespectful. The Weight Formula transfers the correctness of this argument, together with the correctness of arguments that concern the intensity of the interference with the freedom of expression, to the judgment about the weight of *Titanic*'s right in the concrete case, which, again, implies—together with

[10] BVerfGE 86, 1 (13) (trans. R. A.).

further premises—the judgment expressing the ruling of the court. This is a rational structure for establishing the correctness of a legal judgment in a discourse. The basic elements of this structure are judgments or propositions. This means that the nature of balancing is characterized by something that could be characterized as 'propositionality'. In this way, Habermas' objection that balancing necessarily takes one out of the area of justification, correctness, and objectivity is rejected.

The judgments or propositions that are connected by the Weight Formula have to be justified by means of further arguments. This is to say that the Weight Formula is a form of argument. Forms of arguments define the logical structure of moves in discourse, and they show how different moves are connected with each other.

The third of the five concepts that form the conceptual system of discursive constitutionalism is discourse. Now it is clear how balancing is connected with discourse. Balancing is not possible without discourse, and the forms of arguments or inferential schemes of discourse necessarily include the structure of balancing as made explicit by the Weight Formula. On this basis, one can counter Habermas's irrationality objection by saying that balancing is as rational as discourse. If practical discourse were not rational, there would be no practical rationality at all.

Balancing is not only necessarily connected with discourse but also with constitutional rights.[11] From this it follows that constitutional rights are necessarily connected with discourse. The question then arises: what does this mean for the fourth concept of the conceptual system of discursive constitutionalism, the concept of constitutional review?

II. Constitutional Review

Constitutional review is an expression of the priority or superiority of constitutional rights over and against parliamentary legislation. Its logical basis is the concept of contradiction. The declaration of a statute as unconstitutional implies that it contradicts at least one norm of the constitution. This contradiction at the level of norms is accompanied by a contradiction at the level of judgments about norms. The judgment of the constitutional court is, in most cases, explicit. It has the form 'the statute *S* is unconstitutional'. The judgment of the parliament—at least during the process of legislation, that is, before the pleading at the constitutional court begins—is usually only implicit. It has the form 'the statute *S* is constitutional'. These two kinds of contradictions show that constitutional review is essentially propositional and, therefore, argumentative or discursive.

Constitutional review, however, consists of more than assertions concerning constitutionality. The constitutional court not only says something but also does

[11] Alexy, *A Theory of Constitutional Rights* (n.1 above), 69–86.

something. It typically has the power to invalidate unconstitutional acts of the parliament. This kind of participation in legislation means that the activity of constitutional courts has not only a propositional or discursive character but also an institutional or authoritative one.

The issue of balancing is the chief problem connected with the methodological dimension of constitutional review. The main problem pertaining to its institutional dimension emerges as the question of how to justify the legal power of a constitutional court to invalidate acts of parliament. With this question we have arrived at the perennial problem of the relation between constitutional review and democracy.

III. Representation

Constitutional review represents an exercise of state authority. In a democratic state in which—as stated in Article 20(2)(1) of the Basic Law of the Federal Republic of Germany—'all state authority proceeds from the people', constitutional review can be legitimate only if it is compatible with democracy. The exercise of state authority by the parliament is legitimate because the parliament represents the people. This representation is democratic because the members of parliament are selected and controlled by free and general elections. Matters are, at least in general, different in the case of constitutional review. The judges of the constitutional court have, as a rule, no direct democratic legitimation, and the people have, normally, no possibility of control by denying them re-election. Is this compatible with democracy?

The only way to reconcile constitutional review with democracy is to conceive of it, too, as representation of the people. This approach, however, seems to be blocked by two obstacles. First, representation seems necessarily connected with elections, and second, if representation should be possible without elections, why should this kind of representation have priority over representation based on elections?

A. Argumentative Representation

The key to the solution of these problems and, thereby, to the solution of the general problem of constitutional review, is the concept of argumentative representation. Representation is a dyadic relation between a *repraesentandum* and a *repraesentans*. In the case of parliamentary legislation, the relation between the *repraesentandum*—the people—and the *repraesentans*—the parliament—is essentially determined by election. Now, it is possible to draw a picture of democracy that contains no more than a system of decision-making centred around the concepts of election and majority rule. This would be a purely decisionistic model of democracy. An adequate concept of democracy must, however, comprise not only decision but also argument. The inclusion of argument in the concept of democracy makes democracy deliberative. Deliberative democracy is an attempt to institutionalize discourse as far as possible as a means of public decision-making. For this reason, the connection between the people and the parliament must not only be determined by decisions expressed in elections and votes, but also by argument. In this way, the representation of the people by the parliament is, at the same time, volitional or decisionistic as well as argumentative or discursive.

The representation of the people by a constitutional court is, in contrast, purely argumentative. The fact that representation by parliament is volitional as well as discursive shows that representation and argumentation are not incompatible. On the contrary, an adequate concept of representation must refer—as Leibholz puts it—to some 'ideal values'.[12] Representation is more than—as Kelsen proposes—a proxy,[13] and more than—as Carl Schmitt maintains—rendering the *repraesentandum* existent.[14] To be sure, it includes elements of both, that is, representation is necessarily normative as well as real, but these elements do not exhaust this concept.[15] Representation necessarily lays claim to correctness. Therefore, a fully fledged concept of representation must include an ideal dimension, which connects decision with discourse. Representation is thus defined by the connection of normative, factual, and ideal dimensions.

B. Conditions of True Argumentative Representation

A critic of constitutional review might well object that this all boils down to an over-idealization. He will maintain that purely argumentative representation is a chimera. Once the ideal is substituted for the real, the constitutional court is free to declare each argument, an argument representing the people. There would be no limits and no control. Constitutional review could depart as far as it wished from what people really think and demand and nevertheless lay claim to represent them. The path of discursive constitutionalism that begins with constitutional rights and continues with balancing, discourse, and constitutional review ends with an illusion, in which the legitimation of everything is possible.

[12] Gerhard Leibholz, *Das Wesen der Repräsentation und der Gestaltwandel der Demokratie im 20. Jahrhundert*, 3rd edn (Berlin: Walter de Gruyter, 1966), 35. See ibid., 32: 'The one and only sphere of value which allows for a representation is an ideally determined one' (trans. R. A.).

[13] Hans Kelsen, *Pure Theory of Law*, 2nd edn (1960), trans. Max Knight (Berkeley, Calif.: University of California Press, 1967), 299: '"Representation" means the same as proxy' (trans. altered).

[14] Carl Schmitt, Verfassungslehre (1928), 5th edn (Berlin: Duncker & Humblot, 1970), 209: 'Representation is not a normative event, not a process, not a procedure, but something *existential*' (trans. R. A.).

[15] This becomes quite clear by Schmitt when he says that only an 'increased kind of being' is able of an existence; ibid., 210 (trans. R. A.).

This objection can be rejected if it is possible to show, first, that constitutional review as argument or discourse does not allow for everything, and second, that constitutional review as representation can be connected to what people really think. Constitutional review as argument does not allow for everything in so far as good from bad or better from worse constitutional arguments can be distinguished from one another. The analysis of the examples presented above shows that rational argument and, thereby, objectivity is possible in constitutional argumentation to a considerable degree. It shows, too, that the existence of cases in which the arguments lead to a stalemate represents no danger at all for constitutional review. In cases of stalemate the legislator has discretion, and the discretion of the legislator is necessary if the constitution is not to decide each and every legal question.[16] All we need is a class of cases that is sufficiently broad in scope, cases in which judgments about intensity of interference can be backed by arguments that are recognized as good, or, at least, plausible, by all those who accept the constitution.

The existence of good or plausible arguments is enough for deliberation or reflection, but not for representation. For this, it is necessary that the court not only claims that its arguments are the arguments of the people; a sufficient number of people must, at least in the long run, accept these arguments for reasons of correctness. Only rational persons are able to accept an argument on the ground that it is correct or sound. This shows that there are two fundamental conditions of true argumentative representation: (1) the existence of sound or correct arguments, and (2) the existence of rational persons, that is, persons who are able and willing to accept sound or correct arguments for the reason that they are sound or correct. One might call these persons, by analogy to John Rawls's concept of the liberal person,[17] 'constitutional persons'. Constitutional review can be successful only if the arguments presented by the constitutional court are sound and only if a sufficient number of members of the community are able and willing to exercise their rational capacities.

If these conditions are fulfilled, the answer to the question, raised above, as to why purely argumentative representation shall have priority over representation based on election and re-election is no longer difficult. Discursive constitutionalism, as a whole, is an enterprise of institutionalizing reason and correctness. If there exist sound and correct arguments as well as rational persons, reason and correctness are better institutionalized with constitutional review than without it.

[16] Alexy, *A Theory of Constitutional Rights* (n. 1 above), 388–425

[17] John Rawls, *Political Liberalism* (New York, N.Y.: Columbia University Press, 1993), 290.

10
The Existence of Human Rights

Human rights are understood, worldwide, to be the basis of society. This broad agreement is found not only in philosophical circles but also in politics and law. Numerous human rights covenants as well as the incorporation of human rights into a great many constitutions can be read as an expression of the triumphant march of human rights in the period after the Second World War. In a word, their existence seems to be beyond question.

Still, there are doubts about whether the belief in the existence of human rights amounts to anything more than a collective error or illusion. Fundamental criticism, directed at the assumption that human rights exist, is found not only in the dark regions of political, ideological, and religious extremism but also in highly respectable philosophical writings. Alasdair MacIntyre's claim that 'there are no such rights, and belief in them is one with belief in witches and in unicorns'[1] is an example. This—along with the fact, often corroborated in the history of ideas, that widespread consensus is by no means a guarantee of truth—is reason enough to raise the question of the existence of human rights, in short, the existence question.

I. The Theoretical and Practical Significance of the Existence Question

The question of whether human rights exist has far-reaching consequences for legal philosophy, for the theory of constitutional rights, and for politics.

In legal philosophy, the answer to the question of what law is, that is, to the question of the concept and the nature of law, essentially depends on whether human rights exist. Hans Kelsen has adduced an argument against the non-positivistic thesis of a necessary connection between law and morality, namely, the argument that 'an absolute moral order excluding the possibility of the validity of another moral order does not exist'.[2] One might call this the 'argument from relativism'.[3] Human rights are the core of justice. Every violation of human rights is unjust, even if not every injustice is a violation of human rights. The core thesis implies

[1] Alasdair MacIntyre, *After Virtue*, 2nd edn (London: Duckworth, 1985), 69.

[2] Hans Kelsen, *Pure Theory of Law*, 2nd edn (1960), trans. Max Knight (Berkeley, Calif.: University of California Press, 1967), 63.

[3] Robert Alexy, *The Argument from Injustice. A Reply to Legal Positivism* (1992), trans. Bonnie Litschewski Paulson and Stanley L. Paulson (Oxford: Clarendon Press, 2002), 53–5.

Law's Ideal Dimension. Robert Alexy, Oxford University Press. © Robert Alexy 2021.
DOI: 10.1093/oso/9780198796831.003.0011

that if human rights do not exist, then additional absolute, universal, or necessary criteria of justice do not exist either. Neither the Radbruch Formula,[4] which in its shortest form says that extreme injustice is no law,[5] nor the thesis that law necessarily raises a claim to correctness, essentially a claim to justice,[6] would make sense any longer. Non-positivism would have to yield to positivism.

The consequences of the existence question for the theory of constitutional rights concern the basic understanding of constitutional rights as well as the basic understanding of constitutional review. If human rights did not exist, constitutional rights would amount to nothing more than what has been recorded, written down, in the constitution. In that case, everything might have been different because constitutional rights would have an exclusively positivistic character. Originalism and textualism would be the only promising candidates for a theory of constitutional interpretation. If, however, it should be the case that human rights exist, then the picture changes fundamentally. Constitutional rights could then be understood as an effort to transform human rights into positive law. This, in turn, would imply that the ideal character of human rights remains present in the interpretation of constitutional rights. The domain of general practical argumentation in constitutional interpretation would have to be extended accordingly. Originalism and textualism would be confronted with a rationalism in law that is based on human rights.

Finally, with respect to politics the main consequence of the existence question concerns the problem of cultural relativism. If human rights did not exist, that would count as a strong argument for strong forms of cultural relativism. By the same token, the existence of human rights would count as a good reason against strong forms of cultural relativism. Should human rights exist, a common basis of law would then exist that, as the concept of a basis implies, might well be compatible with a considerable scope accorded to cultural diversity. A common basis along these lines seems to be indispensable for a global legal order of whatever kind. All of this shows that the question of the existence of human rights has real theoretical and practical significance.

II. The Concept of Human Rights

The answer to the question of whether human rights exist depends on what human rights are. To begin with, human rights are rights. With respect to their structure, rights in general can be divided into first, claim rights, second, liberties, and third,

[4] Gustav Radbruch, 'Statutory Lawlessness and Supra-Statutory Law' (1946), trans. Bonnie Litschewski Paulson and Stanley L. Paulson, *Oxford Journal of Legal Studies* 26 (2006), 1–11, at 7.

[5] Robert Alexy, 'The Dual Nature of Law', *Ratio Juris* 23 (2010), 167–82, at 175 (in this volume: Chapter 3, 36–50, at 44).

[6] Ibid., 171 (Chapter 3, 40).

immunities as well as powers.[7] Here, only human rights as claim rights shall be of interest. Claim rights are three-place relations of which the first element is the beneficiary or *holder* of the right (*a*), the second is the *addressee* of the right (*b*), and the third is the *subject-matter* of the right (*G*).[8] If *a* has against *b* a right to *G*, *b* has a duty to *a* with respect to *G*, and vice versa.[9] This implies that the concept of a right is intrinsically connected with the concept of the 'ought'.

Human rights, as rights, are characterized by five properties. The first is *universality*. The beneficiary or holder of human rights is every human being *qua* human being. Universality on the side of the addressees is more complex. Some human rights as, for instance, the right to life are addressed to all who can be addressees of duties, that is, to all human beings but also against all states and organizations. Other human rights such as the right to participate in the process of political will-formation, especially the right to vote, are addressed only to the state to which the holder enjoys citizenship or in which he resides.

The second property of human rights is the *fundamental* character of their subject-matter. Human rights do not protect all conceivable sources and conditions of well-being but only fundamental capacities, interests, and needs. The question of which capacities, interests, and needs are fundamental determines the content of human rights. Nevertheless, this question will not be discussed here. The solution to the problem of the content of human rights presupposes that they exist, and an answer to the question of existence requires nothing more than the assumption that human beings have at least some fundamental needs, interests, or capacities such as, for instance, life, including good health, freedom, and self-determination.

The third property, too, concerns the subject-matter of human rights. This property is their *abstractness*. The right to good health is an example of an abstract right. It is easy to agree that all have a right to good health, but on the question of what that means in a concrete case, protracted controversy is possible. The distinction between human rights as abstract rights and their application in concrete cases will be of overriding significance for the question of their existence.

The fourth and the fifth properties concern neither the holder nor the addressees nor the subject-matter of human rights but rather their validity. Human rights as such have only moral validity. For that reason, the fourth property of human rights is their *morality*. A right is morally valid if it can be justified against each and every person who is willing to take part in a rational discourse. In this sense, moral validity is universal validity. The universality of the structure of human rights as rights of all against, in principle, all is thus complemented by a universality of validity. A right that is valid is a right that exists. This implies the basic thesis of the theory

[7] See on this Robert Alexy, *A Theory of Constitutional Rights* (1985), trans. Julian Rivers (Oxford: Oxford University Press, 2002), 120–59.

[8] Ibid., 120–1.

[9] Ibid., 132.

of the existence of human rights presented here. It runs as follows: The existence of human rights consists in their justifiability, and in nothing else. To be sure, the moral validity of human rights can be accompanied by positive validity consisting in due enactment and social efficacy. Examples are the International Covenant on Civil and Political Rights of 19 December 1966, the European Convention on Human Rights and Fundamental Freedoms of 4 November 1950, the Charter of Fundamental Rights of the European Union of 7 December 2000 and 12 December 2007, and the Basic Law of the Federal Republic of Germany of 23 May 1949. But such transformations of human rights into positive law never count as ultimate solutions. They are attempts to give institutional shape, secured by positive law, to what is valid solely owing to its correctness. For that reason, constitutional rights have to be defined as rights that have been recorded in a constitution with the intention of transforming human rights into positive law—the intention, in other words, of rendering positive human rights.[10]

This leads to the fifth property of human rights, their *priority.* Human rights *qua* moral rights cannot be invalidated by rules of positive law. On the contrary, human rights are standards for the assessment of positive law. This is to say that human rights conventions and catalogues of constitutional rights as well as decisions of human rights courts and decisions of constitutional courts can violate human rights. With this, the list of the five properties that distinguish human rights from all other rights is complete. Human rights are first, universal, second, fundamental, third, abstract, and fourth, moral rights that, fifth, take priority over all other norms.

For the question of the existence of human rights, the fourth defining element, the morality of human rights, is of special importance. Rights exist if they are valid. Human rights *qua* moral rights are valid if they are justifiable. Thus, the question of the existence of human rights turns out to be the question of their justifiability.

III. The Justification of Human Rights

A. The Principles Structure of Human Rights

Human rights are abstract rights. They refer *simpliciter*, for example, to freedom and equality, life and property, and free speech and protection of personality. As abstract rights, human rights inevitably collide with other human rights and with collective goods such as protection of the environment and public safety. Human rights, therefore, stand in need of balancing. Balancing is the central dimension of proportionality analysis. Proportionality analysis presupposes that the rights

[10] Robert Alexy, 'Discourse Theory and Fundamental Rights', in *Arguing Fundamental Rights*, eds Agustín José Menéndez and Erik Oddvar Eriksen (Dordrecht: Springer, 2006), 15–29, at 17.

involved have the structure of principles. This, in turn, implies that human rights have the structure of principles.[11]

The principles structure of human rights has far-reaching consequences for their justifiability. A justification of human rights does not require that an answer be given to all human rights questions. It only requires that sufficient reasons be given for what has to be balanced, that is, for human rights *qua* principles. This reduces the burden of justification considerably. If all questions about the assessment of claims respecting human rights had to be resolved in order to justify human rights, a justification of human rights could never be achieved. It could never be achieved because in many cases balancing leads to 'reasonable disagreement'.[12] This is a central theme in the theory of discretion as a part of the theory of proportionality.[13] Here, a single point is of interest. The restriction of the justification to human rights *qua* principles implies, indeed, considerable flexibility with respect to what, in the justification of human rights, is justified. It allows even for a certain degree of cultural discretion.[14] This is not to say, however, that flexibility or variability is unlimited. The most important limitation stems from a fundamental rule of balancing, namely, that the power of rights increases over-proportionally with an increasing intensity of interference.[15] In cases that concern the core of human rights, this often has the consequence that only one solution is compatible with human rights. For this reason, flexibility is by no means to be equated with arbitrariness. This suffices to qualify human rights *qua* principles as objects of justification.

B. Scepticism and Non-Scepticism

Theories about the justifiability of human rights, as well as theories about the justifiability of moral norms in general, can be classified in many different ways. The most fundamental distinction is that between those theories that generally deny the possibility of any justification of human rights and those theories claiming that some sort of justification is possible. The first approach may be termed 'scepticism', the second 'non-scepticism'. Scepticism has its roots in forms of emotivism, decisionism, subjectivism, relativism, naturalism, and deconstructivism. Non-scepticism may well include one or more of these sceptical elements, but it insists that there be a possibility of giving reasons for human rights, reasons that lay claim to objectivity, correctness, or truth.

11 On the concept of principle see Alexy, *A Theory of Constitutional Rights* (n. 7 above), 47–8.

12 See John Rawls, *Political Liberalism* (New York, N.Y.: Columbia University Press, 1993), 55.

13 Alexy, *A Theory of Constitutional Rights* (n. 7, above), 414–25.

14 Julian Rivers, 'Proportionality, Discretion and the Second Law of Balancing', in *Law, Rights and Discourse. The Legal Philosophy of Robert Alexy*, ed. George Pavlakos (Oxford: Hart, 2007), 167–88, at 178–80.

15 Alexy, *A Theory of Constitutional Rights* (n. 7, above), 103; Robert Alexy, 'On Balancing and Subsumption', *Ratio Juris* 16 (2003), 433–49, at 446.

C. Justification and Thesis

Often certain properties are adduced as reasons for having human rights. To be a human being, to have the capacity to suffer, to have intelligence, self-consciousness, the capacity to make choices or plans, and autonomy—these are all examples. The logical form of arguments that turn on the possession of such properties is:

All individuals possessing the property Φ have human rights.

Often this simple form is extended by means of intermediate steps. It is possible, for instance, first to appeal to autonomy as a reason for being a person, and then second, to appeal to being a person as a reason for having human dignity, and then third, to appeal to human dignity as a reason for having human rights. Fundamental here is that the first step remains the decisive step. It is the step from a Φ-property to a normative conclusion, which is arrived at either directly or by means of intermediate steps. This step includes a transition from 'is' to 'ought'. Such a transition is not valid without justification. Why, for instance, is being a human being or having the capacity to suffer a reason for having human rights? This question can be raised even in the case of autonomy. Why should the mere fact that other individuals are able both to judge what is morally right and wrong and to act accordingly be a reason for granting them human rights? To be sure, autonomy plays an important role in the justification of human rights, but the simple transition from the concept of autonomy to the concept of human rights, as performed in a Φ-sentence, is nothing more than an assertion or a thesis that stands, just as with any thesis, in need of justification.

D. Eight Justifications

The attempts to justify human rights differ greatly. Eight approaches shall be distinguished here.

The first is the *religious* approach. A religious justification of human rights draws its support from a very strong foundation. He who believes that human beings are created by God in his own image will have a good reason for attributing dignity to human beings. Dignity is a solid basis for human rights. With this background, the thesis that all individuals who are human beings have human rights is well grounded. The argument has, however, a decisive weakness. It counts as an argument only for those who believe in God and his creation of man in his own image. The same applies to every other kind of religious argument.

The second approach is the *biological* or, more precisely, the socio-biological approach. According to this model, morality is a form of altruism. Certain forms of altruistic behaviour, such as, in particular, caring for one's own children and helping relatives but also reciprocal altruism generating mutual help, are said to promote the genetic pool of individuals, whereas mutual indifference or even aggression does not have this effect in those contexts.[16] Now it has to be granted that the tendency to maximize one's reproductive success may in some cases lead to respect and help vis-à-vis some persons, but it is a pattern of behaviour—to use Günther Patzig's words—'often accompanied by indifference and even hostility towards outsiders'.[17] This, however, is incompatible with the universal character of human rights.

The third approach is the *intuitive* approach. The intuitive model claims that human rights are justified because their existence or validity is evident. Evidence, however, does not count as a reason if it is possible not to share the evidence without thereby rendering oneself vulnerable to any reproach other than that one does not conceive the evidence as evident. If the intuitive model is not embedded in arguments, it is nothing more than emotivism. If, however, it is embedded in arguments, it is no longer the intuitive model.

According to the fourth approach, the *consensual* approach, human rights are justified if they find universal agreement. If, however, this consensus consists in nothing other than the fact of a mere congruence of beliefs, then the consensual approach is tantamount to a form of collective intuitive approach. A universal consensus on human rights, especially if it is achieved as the result of a discourse, ought not to be dismissed. Still, such a consensus does not exist, and if it did, it would always be in danger of dissolution. For these reasons, the argument of consensus, if not connected with the idea of rational argumentation or discourse, cannot provide a satisfactory justification of human rights. If, however, this argument is connected with rational argumentation, it is no longer a purely consensual approach, referring exclusively to the facticity of a congruence of beliefs.

The fifth approach is the *instrumental* one. A justification of human rights is instrumental if it is argued that the acceptance of human rights is indispensable for the maximization of individual or collective utility. This approach appears in elementary forms as well as in highly sophisticated models. An example for an elementary version is the argument: 'If you do not want to be killed, you must respect other's right to life.' If it is possible for individuals or collectives to increase their utility by violating the human rights of others, the elementary argument breaks down. History shows that this possibility cannot be ruled out. Highly sophisticated models have been developed in the theory of rational choice, for instance, by James Buchanan and David Gauthier. These theories, however, must either work with provisos that exclude unacceptable outcomes, as Gauthier does when he says that

[16] Richard Dawkins, *The Selfish Gene*, 30th anniversary edn (Oxford: Oxford University Press, 2006), 93–108, 166–88.

[17] Günther Patzig, 'Can Moral Norms be Rationally Justified?' *Angewandte Chemie. International Edition* 41 (2002), 3353–58, at 3355.

'[r]ights provide the starting point for, and not the outcome of, agreement',[18] or their proponents must be willing to accept outcomes that, to put it in Buchanan's words, 'may be something similar to the slave contract, in which the "weak" agree to produce goods for the "strong" in exchange for being allowed to retain something over and above bare subsistence, which they may be unable to secure in the anarchistic setting'.[19] Buchanan's model is a purely instrumental model, but the possibility of a slave contract shows that it is not compatible with human rights. Gauthier's model may be compatible, but this is entirely owing to reasons addressing elements that can be justified only within a non-instrumental approach. None of this means that the instrumental approach is of no value with respect to the justification of human rights. In so far as it can provide reasons for respecting human rights,[20] it should be incorporated into a more comprehensive model. The more comprehensive model, however, must be governed by principles that purely instrumental reasoning cannot generate.

The sixth approach is the *cultural* one. It claims that the public conviction that human rights exist represents an achievement in the history of human culture. Gustav Radbruch presents a combination of a cultural argument with a consensual argument when—with an eye to 'principles of law ... that are weightier than any legal enactment'—he says:

> To be sure, their details remain open to question, but the work of centuries has in fact established a solid core of them, and they have come to enjoy such far-reaching consensus in the so-called declarations of human and civil rights that only the dogmatic sceptic could still entertain doubts about some of them.[21]

The cultural model, similar to the instrumental model, is useful but not sufficient. Human rights are not the result of the history of all cultures. The mere fact that 'the work of centuries' has established human rights in one or more cultures is not enough to justify their universal validity, which is a part of their concept.

The defects in the six approaches considered thus far are greater than their strengths. For this reason, the justification of human rights proposed here is based not on these first six approaches, but on a seventh and an eighth approach. The seventh approach is explicative, the eighth existential. A justification of human rights is *explicative* if it consists in making explicit what is necessarily implicit in human practice. A justification that makes explicit what is necessarily implicit in human practice follows the lines of Kant's transcendental philosophy. If the practice is the practice of asserting, asking, and arguing, the justification obtains a

[18] David Gauthier, *Morals by Agreement* (Oxford: Clarendon Press, 1986), 222.

[19] James M. Buchanan, *The Limits of Liberty* (Chicago, Ill.: University of Chicago Press, 1975), 60.

[20] See Robert Alexy, 'Discourse Theory and Human Rights', *Ratio Juris* 9 (1996), 209–35, at 219–20.

[21] Gustav Radbruch, 'Five Minutes of Legal Philosophy', trans. Bonnie Litschewski Paulson and Stanley L. Paulson, *Oxford Journal of Legal Studies* 26 (2006), 13–15, at 14–15.

discourse-theoretic character. This is the version of the explicative argument that I should like to defend here.

The discursive practice, that is, the practice of asserting, asking, and arguing, or, as Robert Brandom calls it, the practice 'of giving and asking for reasons',[22] presupposes rules of discourse that express the ideas of freedom and equality. This implicit normative content can be made explicit by means of statements that explicitly negate it.[23] Examples of such statements are:

> If my reasons do not convince you, you are dismissed

and

> For me, the reason *R*, to which I am appealing in support of my assertion, is not a good reason; but in light of your low intelligence, you ought to accept it as a good reason for this assertion.

The absurdity of these two utterances points to the necessity of the implicit rules against which they offend. In the first example, this rule is the postulate of discursive freedom, in the second, the postulate of discursive equality. The ideas of freedom and equality, however, are the basis of human rights. To recognize another individual as free and equal is to recognize him as autonomous. To recognize him as autonomous is to recognize him as a person. To recognize him as a person is to attribute dignity to him. Attributing dignity to someone is to recognize his human rights. With this, one might well think, a justification of human rights has been achieved.

This impression, however, is mistaken. The explicative argument provides, to be sure, a necessary part of the justification of human rights, but it is not by itself sufficient. For this reason, the explicative argument has to be supplemented by a further argument, the eighth. This is the *existential* argument.

The necessity of connecting the explicative argument with the existential one stems from two defects in the explicative argument. The question of whether human rights can be justified, that is, the question of their existence, depends then on whether the existential argument can handle the defects found in the explicative argument.

The first defect concerns the necessity of the rules of discourse *qua* rules of discourse. The necessity of the rules of discourse *qua* rules of discourse is limited in two respects. In the first respect a relatively small problem arises, but in the second, a very considerable problem. The first respect concerns the possibility of circumventing the necessity of the rules of discourse completely, namely, by avoiding any participation in the practice of asserting, asking, and arguing. The price one pays for this is, however, high. Never to assert anything, never to ask a question, never to

[22] Robert Brandom, *Articulating Reasons* (Cambridge, Mass.: Harvard University Press, 2000), 11.
[23] For a more elaborated account, see Alexy, 'Discourse Theory and Human Rights' (n. 20 above), 216.

offer any reason, is to forbear from participating in what belongs essentially to the most general form of life of human beings[24] *qua* 'discursive creatures', as Brandom puts it.[25] None of this completely rules out the option of doing forever without any assertion, any question, or any argument. But it comes close to such an exclusion.[26]

Far more serious than the problems stemming from the possibility of circumventing the rules of discourse completely by avoiding any participation in the practice of asserting, asking, and arguing is the problem stemming from the possibility of abandoning discourse not completely or generally but only partially. It is possible that one may have discussions solely in one's own community and to lapse into propaganda, force, and terror directed towards outsiders. The price paid for is much lower than the price for completely abandoning any form of discourse. This defect of the explicative argument can only be repaired by means of the existential argument.

Thus far, only the defects of the explicative argument that concern the rules of discourse *qua* rules of discourse have been considered. Human rights, however, are essentially rules that concern not only discourse but also real social life, that is, the realm of action. The necessity of treating the other as free and equal in discourse does not imply the necessity of accepting him as free and equal in social life. It is, for instance, possible to engage in discussion with slaves.

This problem as well as the problem of abandoning discourse partially stems from the difference between capabilities on the one hand and interests on the other. The explicative argument can only establish the discursive capabilities. Having discursive capabilities, however, does not imply an interest in making use of them. This might be called the 'interest problem'. The interest problem concerns the dimension of discourse as well as the dimension of action. The interest in making use of discursive capabilities solely in the sphere of discourse might be called a 'weak interest in correctness'. By contrast, the interest in making use of discursive capabilities not only in the sphere of argument but also in the realm of action can be characterized as a 'strong interest in correctness'. The strong interest in correctness is a matter of taking seriously the discursive capabilities in real life. This, again,

[24] On the concept of the most general form of life, see Alexy, 'Discourse Theory and Human Rights' (n. 20 above), 217–18; Robert Alexy, 'A Discourse-Theoretical Conception of Practical Reason', *Ratio Juris* 5 (1992), 231–51, at 241–2 (in this volume: Chapter 17, 225–74, at 266–7).

[25] Brandom, *Articulating Reasons* (n. 22 above), 26.

[26] It might be objected that this argument turns on an 'is'–'ought' fallacy. That the most general form of life of human beings includes the practice of asserting, asking, and arguing can be considered, from the point of view of an observer, a matter of fact. The postulates of freedom and equality are, by contrast, norms, and norms cannot be derived from facts. This objection misses, however, the point of the explicative argument. The explicative argument is an argument that explores the perspective of a participant in the practice of discourse. The 'is'–'ought' objection would arise only if the explicative argument were an argument made from the external perspective of an observer. This, however, is not the case. The explicative argument brings to light norms that are valid in a practice in which the party offering the explication is already a participant. If one wishes to speak of a transition in this case, it is a transition not from an 'is' to an 'ought' but from an implicit 'ought' to an explicit 'ought'.

includes the interest in solving social conflicts by means of discursively generated and discursively controlled rules.[27] One who wishes to solve social conflicts through discursively generated and discursively controlled rules recognizes as free and equal the other individuals, and this is to take seriously their human rights. In this way, the interest in correctness makes it possible to arrive at the object of our justification—to arrive, in other words, at human rights.

It might be objected, however, that this is no justification at all. It has lost its character as a justification, so the objection runs, once the premise concerning interests is introduced. And this objection is not without merit. It must, however, be qualified. As with any interest, the interest in correctness is connected with decisions. These decisions concern the fundamental question of whether we want to see ourselves as discursive, reasonable creatures. This is a decision about who we are. With this decision one 'choose[s] oneself' as Kierkegaard puts it.[28] This decision is an existential decision. Still, to talk here about justification or substantiation seems to be warranted because this decision is not based on groundless or arbitrary preferences, drawn, so to speak, from nowhere. Rather, the decision has the character of an endorsement of something that has been proven, by means of explication, to be a capability necessarily connected with human beings—or, to put it another way, a necessary possibility. As an endorsement of a necessary possibility, the existential argument is intrinsically connected with the explicative argument. One might call this connection the 'explicative-existential justification'.

The explicative argument exhibits the discursive nature of human beings. This discursive nature might be characterized as the ideal dimension of the individual. It is, to use Kierkegaard's words again, 'his ideal self, which he cannot acquire anywhere but within himself'.[29] For this reason, the existential argument concerns not only the endorsement of a necessary possibility of some kind or other. It concerns, over and above this, the endorsement of a possibility or capability that defines, *qua* ideal dimension, the higher dimension of our self, or, to put it in Kant's terms, its 'highest vocation'.[30]

This endorsement of the ideal dimensions that the individual finds within himself connects objective with subjective elements. The objective dimension consists of two elements: first, the necessary discursive capabilities and, second, their ideal character. The subjective dimension consists of the existential decision that transforms these ideal possibilities into reality. This means that human rights can only

[27] On this issue, see Alexy, 'Discourse Theory and Human Rights' (n. 20 above), 223–4.

[28] Søren Kierkegaard, *Either/Or*, Part II, trans. and eds Howard V. Hong and Edna H. Hong (Princeton, N.J.: Princeton University Press, 1987), 258.

[29] Ibid., 259.

[30] Immanuel Kant, 'Critique of Practical Reason', trans. and ed. Mary J. Gregor, in *The Cambridge Edition of the Works of Immanuel Kant. Practical Philosophy* (Cambridge: Cambridge University Press 1996), 137–271, at 210; AA 5, 87. See Robert Alexy, 'Normativity, Metaphysics and Decision', in *New Essays on the Normativity of Law*, eds Stefano Bertea and George Pavlakos (Oxford: Hart, 2011), 219–28, at 227–8.

be justified by a connection of objective and subjective elements. This connection can be characterized as a dialectic of the objective and the subjective.

Against this position, a final objection might be raised. The objection would have us believe that a justification can only be either objective or subjective, and not, so to speak, 'half-objective', and that any contamination with subjective elements eliminates objectivity altogether. The reply to this is that objectivity connected with subjectivity is most certainly less than pure objectivity, but it is also more than pure subjectivity. For this reason, one can qualify the explicative-existential argument as a genuine justification of human rights, even though it is not a purely objective justification. Owing to its objective elements this objective-subjective justification provides, however, good reasons for human rights, and this, in turn, suffices to justify them. This justification establishes their validity *qua* moral rights, which is to say that human rights exist.

11
The Weight Formula

In the application of law there are two basic operations: subsumption and balancing. While subsumption has been reasonably well clarified, there are still a great many open questions where balancing is concerned. These questions invite attention to three problems: the structure of balancing, its rationality, and its legitimacy. Between and among those problems there are close connections. The legitimacy of balancing in law turns on its rationality. The more rational balancing is, the greater its legitimacy. The rationality of balancing is determined, however, by its structure. If its analysis were to show that balancing cannot be anything but arbitrary decision, the rationality of balancing together with its legitimacy would be called into question in the application of law, particularly in constitutional law. The core of the problem of balancing in law is, therefore, the problem of the structure of balancing.

I. The Norm-Theoretic Basis: Rules and Principles

The distinction between rules and principles forms the norm-theoretic basis of subsumption on the one hand and balancing on the other.[1] Rules are norms that require something definitively. They are *definitive commands*. Most rules require that certain conditions be fulfilled for their application. They are, then, conditional norms. Rules, however, can also be categorical in form. An example would be an absolute prohibition of torture. The decisive point is that if a rule is valid and applicable, it is then definitively required that exactly what it demands be done. If exactly what is demanded is done, the rule is complied with; otherwise, the rule is not complied with. Thus, rules are those norms that can only be either complied with or not complied with. By contrast, principles are norms requiring that something be realized to the greatest extent possible, given the factual and legal possibilities. Thus, principles are *optimization requirements*. As such they are characterized by the fact that they can be satisfied to varying degrees. What is more, the appropriate degree of satisfaction depends not only on what is factually possible but also on what is legally possible. Rules aside, the legal possibilities are determined essentially by opposing principles.

[1] See on this Robert Alexy, *A Theory of Constitutional Rights* (1985), trans. Julian Rivers (Oxford: Oxford University Press, 2002), 44–69; Robert Alexy, 'On the Structure of Legal Principles', *Ratio Juris* 13 (2000), 294–304, at 295.

Law's Ideal Dimension. Robert Alexy, Oxford University Press. © Robert Alexy 2021.
DOI: 10.1093/oso/9780198796831.003.0012

II. The Principle of Proportionality in the Narrower Sense

As with distinctions generally, norm-theoretic distinctions, too, may have a greater or smaller theoretical and practical significance. The significance of the distinction between rules and principles stems from the fact that the most important standard of substantive constitutional law, the principle of proportionality, is implied by the very nature of principles, and vice versa. The principle of proportionality with its three sub-principles of suitability, necessity, and proportionality in the narrower sense, follows logically from the definition of principle, just as the latter follows from the former.

Principles require that something be realized to the highest possible degree, relative to both the factual and legal possibilities. The sub-principles of suitability and necessity express the requirement of optimization relative to the factual possibilities.[2] In this respect, they are concerned not with balancing as such but with avoiding those interferences with constitutional rights that can be avoided without costs for other principles.[3] They are concerned, in other words, with Pareto-optimality.[4] By contrast, the principle of proportionality in the narrower sense concerns the optimization relative to the legal possibilities. This is the field of balancing, and this field alone is of interest here.

The core of balancing is constituted by a relation that might be termed the 'Law of Balancing', which can be formulated as follows:

> The greater the degree of non-satisfaction of, or detriment to, one principle, the greater must be the importance of satisfying the other.[5]

The Law of Balancing shows that balancing can be broken down into three stages. The first stage involves establishing the degree of non-satisfaction of, or detriment to, the first principle. This is followed by a second stage, in which the importance of satisfying the competing principle is established. Finally, at the third stage it is established whether or not the importance of satisfying the latter principle justifies the detriment to, or non-satisfaction of, the former principle.

This fundamental structure shows what a radical sceptic towards balancing, for example, Jürgen Habermas or Bernhard Schlink, must call into question when they claim that balancing, '[b]ecause there are no rational standards', must take

[2] See on this Laura Clérico, *Die Struktur der Verhältnismäßigkeit* (Baden-Baden: Nomos, 2001), 26–111.

[3] See on this and on the relationship between the principles of suitability and of necessity on the one hand and the principle of proportionality in the narrower sense on the other Alexy, *A Theory of Constititional Rights* (n. 1 above), 397–414.

[4] Ibid., 105.

[5] Ibid., 102.

'place either arbitrarily or unreflectively, according to customary standards and hierarchies',[6] or when they say that

> [i]n the test of proportionality in the narrower sense, it is only the subjectivity of those performing the test that can, in the end, be effective ... The operations of evaluation and balancing required by the test of proportionality in the narrower sense can be achieved ... in the end, only in a decisionistic manner.[7]

They must, in other words, contest the claim that rational judgments about intensity of interference and degrees of importance are possible. It is, however, not at all difficult to find cases in which these types of judgments are indeed possible. Thus, the duty of tobacco producers to place health warnings regarding the dangers of smoking on their products is a relatively minor or light interference with freedom to pursue one's profession. By contrast, a total ban on all tobacco products would count as a serious interference. Between such minor and serious cases, others of moderate intensity of interference can be found. An example would be a ban on cigarette machines along with the introduction of restrictions of the sale of tobacco to selected shops. Following examples such as these, a scale can be developed with the stages 'light', 'moderate', and 'serious'. The examples show that valid assignments at different points on the scale are possible or, turning things around, take the case of a person who classifies, on the one hand, a total ban on all tobacco products as a light interference with the tobacco producers' freedom to pursue their profession, while this same person considers, on the other hand, the duty to set down health warnings as a serious interference. It would not be easy to take such judgments seriously.

The use of a three-stage scale is also possible for the competing reasons. The reason for the duty to place health warnings on tobacco products is to protect the population from the health risks of smoking. The German Federal Constitutional Court seemed not to have exaggerated in its decision on health warnings in considering it, 'according to the current state of medical knowledge, as certain' that smoking may cause cancer or vascular diseases.[8] The weight of the reasons justifying the interference is, therefore, serious. In a word, they weigh heavily. If, in this way, the intensity of interference is established as minor and the degree of importance attributed to the reasons for interference is high, it is then an easy enough matter to reach the conclusion at hand. The serious reason for interference serves

[6] Jürgen Habermas, *Between Facts and Norms. Contribution to a Discourse Theory of Law and Democracy*, trans. William Rehg (Cambridge: Polity Press, 1996), 259.

[7] Bernhard Schlink, 'Freiheit durch Eingriffsabwehr—Rekonstruktion der klassischen Grundrechtsfunktion', *Europäische Grundrechte-Zeitschrift* 11 (1984), 457–68, at 462 (trans. R. A.); Bernhard Schlink, 'Der Grundsatz der Verhältnismäßigkeit', in *Festschrift 50 Jahre Bundesverfassungsgericht*, vol. 2, eds Peter Badura and Horst Dreier (Tübingen: Mohr Siebeck, 2001), 445–65, at 460–2.; Bodo Pieroth and Bernhard Schlink, *Grundrechte* (Heidelberg: C.F. Müller, 1985), 74.

[8] Decisions of the German Federal Constitutional Court (BVerfGE) 95, 173 (184) (trans. R. A.)

to justify the light interference. Thus, the duty to place health warnings on tobacco products does not violate the tobacco producers' right to pursue their profession, as guaranteed in Article 12(1) of the German Basic Law. This result, stemming from an examination of proportionality in the narrower sense, is not only plausible. It is, given the light intensity of interference and the serious weight of the reasons for it and following here the Federal Constitutional Court, downright 'obvious'.[9]

Now one could well claim that the example here does not say very much. The case concerns, on the one hand, economic activities. Here it is easy to apply scales because they boil down to cost-benefit analysis. On the other hand, the question at hand concerns a matter of life and death; where empirical investigations show that the risks are fairly high, the classification, addressed to a highly important matter, can be based on quantifiable facts. These considerations are not applicable in areas where quantifiable factors such as costs and probabilities play no significant role.

To deal with this objection, a case shall be considered that concerns the classic conflict between freedom of expression and personality rights. A widely circulating satirical magazine, *Titanic*, described a paraplegic reserve officer who had successfully carried out his responsibilities, having been called to active duty, first as a 'born murderer' and in a later edition as a 'cripple'. The Düsseldorf Regional Court of Appeals ruled against *Titanic* in an action brought by the officer and ordered the magazine to pay damages in the amount of DM 12,000. *Titanic* brought a constitutional complaint. The Federal Constitutional Court undertook 'case-specific balancing'[10] between the freedom of expression of those associated with the magazine (Article 5(1)(1) of the Basic Law) and the officer's general personality right (Article 2(1) in connection with Article 1(1) of the Basic Law). To this end, the intensity of interference with these rights was determined, with the one set in relation to the other. The judgment in damages was treated as representing a 'lasting' or *serious* interference with freedom of expression, irrespective of the fact that it was not decided in a criminal trial but only in a civil proceeding. This conclusion was justified, above all, by the argument that awarding damages could affect the future willingness of those producing the magazine to carry out their work in the way they had done until that time.[11] The description 'born murderer' was then placed in the context of examples of satire published by the *Titanic*. Here several persons had been described, in a 'recognizably humorous' way, from 'puns to silliness', as having had this or that surname at birth—for example, Richard von Weizsäcker, then Federal President, was described as a 'born Citizen'.[12] The context precludes a reading of such a description as an 'unlawful, serious, illegal breach of personality'.[13] The interference with the right to personality was thus treated as

[9] BVerfGE 95, 173 (187).
[10] BVerfGE 86, 1 (11).
[11] BVerfGE 86, 1 (10).
[12] BVerfGE 86, 1 (11).
[13] BVerfGE 86, 1 (12).

having at most a *moderate*, perhaps only a *light* or *minor* intensity. Corresponding to this, the importance of protecting the officer's right to personality through an award of damages was *moderate*, perhaps only *light* or *minor*. These assessments completed the first part of the judgment. In order to justify an award of damages as a serious interference with the constitutional right to freedom of expression, the impairment of the right to personality, which was supposed to be compensated for by damages, would have had to have been evaluated as having been at least as serious. According to the assessment of the Federal Constitutional Court, however, it was not. That meant that the interference with the freedom of expression was disproportionate, which meant in turn that calling the officer a 'born murderer' was not a ground for awarding damages.

The case of the description of the officer as a 'cripple', however, was considered to be a different matter. According to the assessment of the Federal Constitutional Court, this description did count as a '*serious* breach of the paraplegic's personality right'.[14] The importance of protecting the officer by means of a judgment for damages was, therefore, great. This was justified by the fact that describing a severely disabled person as a 'cripple' is currently seen as 'humiliating' and as expressing a 'lack of respect'. Thus, serious interference with freedom of expression was countered by the great importance accorded to the protection of personality. In this situation, the Federal Constitutional Court came to the conclusion that 'the balancing here did not give rise to a flaw leading to the detriment of freedom of expression'.[15] Thus, *Titanic's* constitutional complaint was only justified to the extent that it related to damages for the description 'born murderer'. As far as the description 'cripple' was concerned, it was unjustified.[16]

Of course, one can argue about whether the description 'born murderer' really represents nothing more than a moderate or minor interference. For present purposes, however, the significant point lies elsewhere. It can hardly be doubted that the awarding of damages and the description of someone as a 'cripple' are both very intensive interferences with the relevant principles. Indeed, with respect to the severely disabled, one can move to a characterization of this that goes beyond the Court's. The Federal Constitutional Court rightly held that describing a paraplegic as a 'cripple' was humiliating and disrespectful. Such public humiliation and lack of respect reaches to and undermines the very dignity of the victim. This is not only serious, it is a very serious indeed, an extraordinarily serious impairment. One has reached an area in which impairments can scarcely ever be justified by any strengthening of the reasons for the interference. This corresponds to the law of diminishing marginal utility.[17] The *Titanic* case is thus an example of the fact

[14] BVerfGE 86, 1 (13) (emphasis by R. A.).
[15] Ibid., (trans. R. A.).
[16] BVerfGE 86, 1 (14).
[17] See Alexy, *A Theory of Constitutional Rights* (n. 1 above), 103.

that scales, intelligently set in relation to each other, are possible, even in the case of immaterial goods such as personality and free speech. The case also illustrates the power inherent in constitutional rights *qua* principles to set limits by means of balancing, limits that are firm and clear, albeit not ascertainable without balancing.

The *Tobacco* Judgment and the *Titanic* Judgment show that rational judgments about degrees of intensity and importance are possible, at least in some cases, and that such judgments may be set in relation to each other for the sake of justifying an outcome. Of course, such judgments presuppose standards that are not themselves to be found in the Law of Balancing. Establishing that a judgment against the *Titanic* to pay damages is a serious interference with freedom of expression is to make assumptions about what freedom of expression means and how it may be threatened. On the other hand, the judgment that the description 'cripple' is a serious interference with personality requires assumptions about what it means to be a person and have dignity. This, however, does not mean, in Habermas's words, that 'weighing takes place either arbitrarily or unreflectively, according to customary standards and hierarchies'.[18] The assumptions underlying judgments about intensity of interference and degree of importance are not arbitrary. Reasons for them are given, and they may well be sound. It is also questionable whether these assumptions are made by the German Federal Constitutional Court 'unreflectively, according to customary standards and hierarchies'. It is true that the standards follow a line of precedent. But talk of 'customary standards' would be justified only if the existence of precedent, and not the correctness of the standards at issue, were the only matter relevant to the decision. Furthermore, one could talk of an 'unreflective' application only if this application did not take place in the course of argumentation because arguments are the public expression of reflection. But there is no lack of argument here. All this applies to the *Tobacco* Judgment as well.

III. The Triadic Scale

Up to this point, nothing apart from examples has been considered. The examples have shown that there are cases in which the balancing of colliding principles provides for a result in a rational way. This suffices to refute the thesis that owing to a lack of rational standards, balancing is able to yield all imaginable results in all cases. This will not suffice, however, if one wants to come to terms with the structure of balancing. In order to be able to arrive at a general conclusion about the *possibility* of rational balancing, a conclusion that goes well beyond the examples, a closer look at the system standing behind the classifications considered thus far is required.

[18] Habermas, *Between Facts and Norms* (n. 6 above), 259.

All the judgments about intensity of interference and degree of importance considered thus far follow a three-grade or triadic model. To be sure, this scheme of three steps or grades is not necessary for balancing. Balancing is possible as soon as one has arrived at two steps, and the number of steps, moving upwards, is open. Thus, what follows here will also apply, with certain modifications, if one reduces the number of steps to two or increases them to more than three. The only proviso, as will be explained below, is that the number not become too great. Compared with the alternatives, the triadic scale has the advantage of fitting the practice of legal argumentation particularly well. In addition, the triadic scale can be extended in a highly intuitive way.

As the examples show, the three stages can be represented by the terms 'light', 'moderate', and 'serious'. Representation is facilitated if these stages are identified by the letters '*l*', '*m*', and '*s*', respectively. Here '*l*' stands not just for the common term 'light', but also for other expressions such as 'minor' or 'weak', and '*s*' stands for 'high' and 'strong' as well as for 'serious'.

According to the Law of Balancing, the objects of evaluation as *l*, *m*, or *s* count, on the one hand, as the degree of non-satisfaction of, or detriment to, the one principle and, on the other, as the importance of satisfying the other principle. In the first part of the Law of Balancing there is found the double concept of non-satisfaction and detriment. This expresses the dichotomy of defence and protection. As far as defensive constitutional rights are concerned, the action submitted to the proportionality test is an interference. Interferences count as detriments. Instead of 'degree of detriment', one could use the term 'intensity of interference'. This shall be done in what follows. It is a mark of the flexibility of language that one can designate each interference, at the same time, as 'non-satisfaction'. The expression 'non-satisfaction' appears, however, in a more natural light when protective rights are at stake because they—unlike defensive rights—require not omissions but positive action. Here, too, however, one can speak of 'detriments' or even of 'interferences', which, again, is a mark of the flexibility of language. Where a principle requires protection and no protection is granted, one can speak not only of the 'non-satisfaction' of this principle but also of an 'interference' with it—in fact, an 'interference through non-satisfaction'.

Against this background, the following can be established. 'P_i' shall be used as a variable for the principle whose violation—to use, again, the words of the Law of Balancing—through non-satisfaction or detriment is to be examined. 'IP_i' shall represent the intensity of the interference with P_i. Interferences are always concrete interferences. Thus, intensity of interference is a concrete quantity. As such it is different from the abstract weight of P_i, which shall be represented by 'WP_i'. The abstract weight of a principle P_i is the weight that P_i has relative to other principles, independently of the circumstances of any case. Many constitutional principles do not differ in their abstract weights. Some, however, do. The right to life, for instance, has a higher abstract weight than general freedom of action. If the abstract weight of colliding principles is equal, it can be disregarded in balancing. As the first object of balancing, the Law of Balancing points only to the intensity of interference. This shows that it is tailored to the situation in which the abstract weights are equal, that is to say, play no role at all. The question of what is to be done where the abstract weights differ will be addressed later. Here it suffices to note that in order to avoid confusion, it is always well to make clear whether one is talking about abstract or concrete quantities. In case of IP_i, no additional information is necessary, for the intensity of interference is necessarily concrete. It does no harm, however, to make explicit the concreteness of IP_i by adding '*C*'. '*C*' stands for all the circumstances of the case that are relevant to the decision. '*C*' plays a pivotal role in the Law of Competing Principles, which, however, cannot be discussed here.[19] In any case, the first object of evaluation as *l*, *m*, or *s*, that is to say, the intensity of interference, can be represented by 'IP_iC'.

'IP_iC' expresses three different aspects. 'P_i' makes explicit that the principle P_i is in play. '*I*' says that what is at stake is the intensity of interference with P_i, and, finally, '*C*' stands for the fact that a concrete case is at hand. It enhances the exposition to represent these three aspects in a single complex expression as 'IP_iC'. Otherwise, only *one* quantity, the intensity of interference, will be of concern. This clearly suggests that it is appropriate to write 'I_i' instead of 'IP_iC' in all those cases in which nothing turns on stressing the three aspects. I_i is in no respect different from IP_iC: $I_i = IP_iC$. 'I_i' may be termed the 'concise version' of the detailed version 'IP_iC'.[20] The letter '*I*' expresses that the intensity of interference is of concern. The index '*i*' makes clear that an interference with P_i is at stake, and the fact that 'I_i' represents a concrete value follows from the very nature of the notion of intensity of interference.

Parallel notations can be recommended with respect to abstract weight. The abstract weight of P_i has already been noted as 'WP_i'. If one wishes to make the abstract character explicit, one can add—analogous to '*C*'—the letter '*A*'. The detailed denotation of the abstract (*A*) weight (*W*) of P_i is, then, 'WP_iA'. The concise version takes on, correspondingly, the form 'W_i'. It has already been mentioned that the abstract weight—expressed by 'WP_iA or 'W_i'—plays a role in balancing only if it has a value different from that of the abstract weight of the colliding principle. If the abstract weights on both sides are equal, they cancel each other out.

According to the Law of Balancing, the second object of evaluation as *l*, *m*, or *s* is the 'importance of satisfying' the other principle. By contrast to the intensity of interference, the degree of importance need not necessarily be exclusively conceived of as a concrete quantity. One can form a concept of importance that combines the concrete and the abstract. In this case, the importance of satisfying the

[19] See Alexy, *A Theory of Constitutional Rights* (n. 1 above), 54.

[20] The detailed version is used in Robert Alexy, 'Die Abwägung in der Rechtsanwendung', *Annual Report of the Institute for Law at the Meiji Gakuin University* 17 (2001), 69–83, at 77.

colliding principle depends both on how intensive the interference with the colliding principle would be had it not been given priority and on how high its abstract weight is. As already remarked, however, the fact that the first part of the Law of Balancing concerns only the intensity of interference shows that this law as a whole is constructed in such a way as to capture the constellation in which the abstract weights are equal and play, for that reason, no role whatsoever. This suggests interpreting the 'importance' as contained in the Law of Balancing initially as referring exclusively to concrete importance.

Thus, everything boils down to the question of what the concrete importance of satisfying the colliding principle—as addressed by the Law of Balancing—is. Because the Law of Balancing exclusively concerns the relation between the two colliding principles, it can only depend on the effects that the omission or non-performance of the measure that interferes with P_i would have for the fulfilment of the colliding principle, represented here by P_j. The concrete importance of satisfying P_j is determined, then, by the results that would be brought about for P_j by forbearing from any interference with P_i. This can be illustrated by means of the *Titanic* case. Only the description of the paraplegic officer as a 'cripple' shall be considered. In order to determine the intensity of interference with freedom of expression, one simply has to ask how intensively the prohibition of this expression combined with an award of damages interferes with freedom of expression. That is what the Constitution would require of this constitutional right if it were to permit the prohibition contained in the judgment of the Düsseldorf Higher Regional Court of Appeals along with its award of damages. In order to establish the concrete importance of satisfying the principle of protecting personality, one has to ask, in reverse, what omitting or failing to implement the interference with freedom of expression, that is, treating the description 'cripple' as permitted and therefore not subject to damages, would mean for the protection of personality. This is none other than the cost to the protection of personality if freedom of expression were to be preserved here. The importance of the principle of protecting personality in the *Titanic* case can thus be derived from the intensity with which non-protection through non-interference in *Titanic*'s freedom of expression would interfere with the officer's personality right. This can be generalized and stated as follows: the concrete importance of P_j is determined by the intensity with which the non-interference with P_i interferes with P_j.

The question concerning the notation arises again. One might consider using a new letter to refer to the importance—say, '*U*', alluding to urgency—and to refer to the concrete importance of the colliding principle—analogous to 'IP_iC'—as 'UP_jC'. This would have the advantage of approximating the ordinary usage of language, as per the wording of the Law of Balancing.[21] Systematic analysis, however, suggests a

[21] For this reason in earlier works in case of the colliding principle another letter has been chosen than in case of the intensity of interference; see Alexy, 'Die Abwägung in der Rechtsanwendung' (n. 20 above), 73.

different solution. The concept of the concrete importance of P_j is, as shown, identical to the concept of the intensity of interference with P_j by omitting the interference with P_i. The point is the intensity of a hypothetical interference through non-interference. This is most clearly expressed when, on the side of the colliding principle too, '*I*', that is, the symbol for the intensity of interference, is employed. Thus, the counterpart of 'IP_iC' is 'IP_jC'. Again, this detailed description can be replaced by a concise one, that is, 'I_j'. $IP_jC = I_j$ is also valid here. In what follows, only the concise expressions will be used.[22]

The objects of evaluation as *l*, *m*, or *s* have now been established. In setting out the Law of Balancing, it was stated that it breaks down the balancing process into three steps. The first two can now be carried out, namely, in the triadic model: evaluating I_i as *l*, *m*, or *s* and evaluating I_j as *l*, *m*, or *s*. The question then arises: how is the third step, in which the evaluations are to be set in relation to each other, to be carried out in the triadic model?

It might be objected that evaluations of this kind cannot be comprehended in relation to each other at all because what is colliding is incommensurable.[23] In the *Titanic* case, for instance, it might be claimed that the description as 'born murderer' and the court order to pay damages in the amount of DM 12,000 are two social facts that have about as much in common as apples and oranges. This, however, does not speak to the decisive point. The question is not the direct comparability of certain entities but the comparability vis-à-vis their importance to the constitution which, of course, leads indirectly to their comparability. The concept of comparability of importance to the constitution contains two elements that are together sufficient to bring about commensurability. The first is a common point of view: that of the constitution. It is, of course, possible to have a dispute about what is valid from this point of view. Indeed, this occurs regularly. It is, however, always a dispute about what is correct on the basis of the constitution. Incommensurability does indeed come into being immediately once the common point of view is given up. This would be the case, for example, if one interpreter of the constitution were to say to the other that from his point of view, one thing is valid, from the other's point of view, the opposite, so that each is right from his own point of view, with the result that neither can be wrong or even criticized because a common point of view, from which something could be proven wrong, neither exists nor could exist. Discourse that amounts to more than empty rhetoric, that is, rational discourse addressed to a correct solution, would then be rendered impossible. The opposite, of course, is valid, too. If rational discourse about what is correct on the basis of the constitution is possible, then a common point of view is possible, too. It becomes

[22] In what follows the letter '*U*' will be used for a quantity that is composed of the concrete importance in the sense of the intensity of interference (*I*) and the abstract weight (*W*).

[23] See on this T. Alexander Aleinikoff, 'Constitutional Law in the Age of Balancing', *The Yale Law Journal* 96 (1987), 943–1005, at 972–6.

real as soon as rational discourse, oriented to the regulative idea of what is correct on the basis of the constitution, commences. He who wishes to undermine the possibility of evaluations by appeal to the impossibility of a common point of view must, therefore, be prepared to claim that rational discourse about evaluations within a constitutional framework is impossible. This claim has to be refuted, even if its refutation cannot be taken up here.[24] The second element that brings about commensurability is a scale, of whatever kind, representing the classes for the evaluation of the constitutional gains and losses. The triadic scale *l*, *m*, *s* is an example. Its use, on the basis of the common point of view of the constitution, brings about commensurability.

Once commensurability is created by both point of view and scale, the question of how the third step of balancing can be carried out proves to be easy. There are three constellations in which the interference with P_i is more intensive than that with P_j:

(1) I_i: *s*, I_j: *l*
(2) I_i: *s*, I_j: *m*
(3) I_i: *m*, I_j: *l*

In these cases P_i precedes P_j. According to the Law of Competing Principles, already mentioned, the conditional relation of precedence $(P_i \mathbf{P} P_j)C$ is valid.[25] These three cases of the precedence of P_i are matched by three cases of the precedence of P_j:

(4) I_i: *l*, I_j: *s*
(5) I_i: *m*, I_j: *s*
(6) I_i: *l*, I_j: *m*

In these cases, $(P_j \mathbf{P} P_i)C$ is valid. In addition to these six cases, which can be decided on the base of the triadic scale, there are three stalemate situations:

(7) I_i: *l*, I_j: *l*
(8) I_i: *m*, I_j: *m*
(9) I_i: *s*, I_j: *s*

In case of a stalemate, balancing determines no result. This is an instance, in other words, of discretion in balancing, that is, an instance of discretion stemming from the structure of norms *qua* principles, in short, an instance of 'structural discretion'. Discretion in balancing is of the greatest importance for the delimitation of

[24] See on this Robert Alexy, *A Theory of Legal Argumentation* (1978) trans. Ruth Adler and Neil MacCormick (Oxford: Clarendon Press, 1989), 33–4, 177–220.
[25] Alexy, *A Theory of Constitutional Rights* (n. 1 above), 54.

the competences of that part of the judiciary that exercises a constitutional review power on the one hand, and those of the legislator and of courts of ordinary jurisdiction on the other. But this cannot be discussed here.[26]

The three steps or classes of the triadic model represent a scale that attempts to systematize classifications found both in everyday practice and legal argumentation. Such a three-class system is far removed from a metrification of intensities of interference and degrees of importance on a cardinal scale running over a continuum from 0 to 1, and it has to be far removed, for intensities of interference and degrees of importance are not capable of metrification on such a scale.[27] It is true that it is often possible to use a refined triadic model—an eligible candidate, as will be shown, is a double-triadic model—but there are limits. Gradation in terms of light, moderate, or serious is often difficult enough as it is. In some cases, one can just barely distinguish light and serious, indeed, in some cases even that seem impossible.[28] Thus, legal scales can only be made for work with relatively crude divisions—and not even that in every instance. In the end, it is the nature of constitutional law that sets limits on just how finely drawn the gradation can be and that altogether excludes the applicability of any infinitesimal scale.[29] Calculable measurements by way of a continuum of points between 0 and 1 cannot, then, apply.[30] What is possible, however, is an illustration of the structure underlying the triadic model with the help of numbers.

IV. The Formula

There are two fundamentally different possibilities for relating I_i and I_j to each other. The first consists in using arithmetic, the second in using geometric sequences. There are many ways in which the triple *l*, *m*, *s* can be represented as an arithmetic sequence. A very simple example is the sequence 1, 2, 3. On this basis, one can present a formula that determines the weight of a principle in the circumstances of the case at hand—in short, its concrete weight—as follows:

$$W_{i,j} = I_i - I_j$$

[26] See on this Robert Alexy, 'Verfassungsrecht und einfaches Recht—Verfassungsgerichtsbarkeit und Fachgerichtsbarkeit', *Veröffentlichungen der Vereinigung der Deutschen Staatsrechtslehrer* 61 (2002), 7–33.

[27] Alexy, *A Theory of Constitutional Rights* (n. 1 above), 99.

[28] Given this impossibility, any difference between intensities of interference disappears. Balancing based on intensities can no longer be performed. The scale *l*, *s* is the minimal scale.

[29] Alexy, 'Verfassungsrecht und einfaches Recht—Verfassungsgerichtsbarkeit und Fachgerichtsbarkeit' (n. 26 above), 25–6.

[30] Not excluded, however, is the application of such scales in ideal models, which represent what would be the case if infinitesimal scaling in law were possible; see on this Nils Jansen 'Die Abwägung von Grundrechten', *Der Staat* 36 (1997), 27–54, at 29.

This formula can be termed the 'Difference Formula'.[31]

The only symbol in the Difference Formula that has not been introduced thus far is '$W_{i,j}$'. '$W_{i,j}$' is not to be confused with 'W_i'. 'W_i', as already noted, stands for the abstract weight of P_i. The detailed notation, 'WP_iA', expresses this clearly. '$W_{i,j}$', on the other hand, stands for the concrete weight of P_i, that is, for the weight of P_i in the circumstances of the case at hand. In the detailed notation this reads as follows:

'$WP_{i,j}C$'[32]

The Difference Formula shows that the concrete weight of a principle is a relative weight. It shows this by determining the concrete weight as the difference between the intensity of interference with this principle (P_i) and the concrete importance of the colliding principle (P_j), where the latter represents the intensity of the hypothetical interference with P_j through the omission of the interference with P_i, that is, through non-interference with P_i. This relativity is expressed by '$W_{i,j}$'. The concrete weight of P_i is the concrete weight of P_i relative to P_j.

If one substitutes the numbers 1, 2, and 3 in the Difference Formula, one acquires solutions that are, *prima facie*, convincing. The nine possible constellations of the triadic model, as presented above, are now to be reconsidered. In the first three constellations, in which P_i precedes P_j—representing them here in a simplified way—then $W_{i,j}$ acquires the following positive values:

(1) $s, l = 3–1 = 2$
(2) $s, m = 3–2 = 1$
(3) $m, l = 2–1 = 1$

In cases in which P_j takes precedence over P_i, then $W_{i,j}$ acquires negative values:

(4) $l, s = 1–3 = –2$
(5) $m, s = 2–3 = –1$
(6) $l, m = 1–2= –1$

In all three stalemate cases, the concrete and thus relative weight of P_i is 0:

(7) $l, l = 1–1 = 0$
(8) $m, m = 2–2 = 0$

[31] On the representation of the relation of the weights of values or principles with the help of subtraction and addition see Heinrich Hubmann, *Wertung und Abwägung im Recht* (Köln: Heymann, 1977) 26–7, 162.

[32] With the detailed notation the Difference Formula has the following form: $WP_{i,j}C = IP_iC–IP_jC$.

(9) $s, s = 3 - 3 = 0$

This illustration of the relations in the triadic model, facilitated by the use of numbers, has the advantages of simplicity and a highly intuitive plausibility. What is more, it aptly expresses that the stalemate case is a case in which no principle, owing to equal standing, can have any effect, negative or positive, on the other principle. Still, there is a pivotal feature of principles that the Difference Formula is not in a position to capture. This becomes clear once the illustration of the triadic model by means of an arithmetic sequence is compared with an illustration provided by means of a geometric sequence.

It is both simple and at the same time highly instructive to adopt the geometrical sequence 2^0, 2^1, and 2^2, that is 1, 2, and 4. This sequence is essentially different from the arithmetic one in that the distances between the stages increase instead of remaining equal in all cases. This makes it possible to represent the fact that the power of principles increases over-proportionately with an increasing intensity of interference, a fact that corresponds to law of diminishing marginal utility.[33]

The geometrical character of the scale provides for a definition of the concrete weight of P_i not through a Difference Formula but through the Quotient Formula. It reads:

$$W_{i,j} = \frac{I_i}{I_j}$$

This formula is the core of a more expansive formula that shall be termed the 'Weight Formula'. In its complete form the Weight Formula includes not only the intensities of interference but also the abstract weights of the colliding principles and the degrees of the reliability of the empirical assumptions on what the measure in question means for the non-realization of P_i and the realization of P_j. This means that in the case of a conflict between two principles, the concrete or relative weights of both principles will depend on three pairs of factors, thus, on six factors altogether. They are, however, only to be introduced where the respective factors, constituting pairs, are unequal. Where they are equal, they cancel each other out. The formula presented above can thus be understood as expressing a situation in which the abstract weights and the degrees of reliability have been reduced for reasons of equality. Confined to the intensities of interference, the formula is then not different from the complete formula. Rather, it is, after reduction, the same. In this sense, the Quotient Formula in what follows is called the 'Weight Formula'.

Even the complete version of the formula, including, then, three pairs of factors, will speak only to a collision of two principles. Complexity increases as soon as

33 See Alexy, *A Theory of Constitutional Rights* (n. 1 above), 103.

more than two principles come into play. One can attempt to grasp this with the help of a formula that goes well beyond the formula that is complete with respect to two principles. This formula will be called the 'Extended Weight Formula'. Before any extension of the simple Weight Formula that concerns exclusively the intensities of interference can be carried out, however, this formula itself will have to be submitted to closer scrutiny.

The Weight Formula is acceptable only if the values of $W_{i,j}$ in different constellations adequately serve to reconstruct balancing. The simple triadic scale shall be considered first. In all cases in which P_i takes precedence over P_j, the value of $W_{i,j}$ is greater than 1:

(1) $s, l = 4/1 = 4$
(2) $s, m = 4/2 = 2$
(3) $m, l = 2/1 = 2$

If P_j takes precedence over P_i, it goes below 1:

(4) $l, s = 1/4 = \frac{1}{4}$
(5) $m, s = 2/4 = \frac{1}{2}$
(6) $l, m = 1/2 = \frac{1}{2}$

In all stalemate cases the concrete weight of P_i is the same, namely 1:

(7) $l, l = 1/1 = 1$
(8) $m, m = 2/2 = 1$
(9) $s, s = 4/4 = 1$

On first glance, this representation seems to have no advantage over that provided by the arithmetic sequence. The bigger differences (*s, l*; *l, s*) have, by comparison with the smaller ones (*s, m*; *m, l*; *m, s*; *l, m*), a double or a half value respectively. One might even assume, here, that 0 illustrates the stalemate better than 1 does.

The picture changes, however, if the triadic model is extended to a double-triadic model. The arithmetic sequence then augments to the sequence 1 to 9, the geometric sequence to 2^0 to 2^8. These sequences represent in each instance the values *ll*, *lm*, *ls*, *ml*, *mm*, *ms*, *sl*, *sm*, *ss*, where, for example, *ll* stands for a light light, that is, a very light interference, *ss* for a seriously serious, that is, a very serious inference, and *ml* for a light moderate inference, that is, for an inference just above the threshold between light and moderate. The difference between the Difference Formula and the Quotient Formula becomes clear when one compares the cases of the least and highest justification of an interference with a constitutional right. In the double-triadic model, the least justified interference is represented by the combination *ss*, *ll*. An example is a seven-year term of imprisonment, which is a very serious (*ss*) interference with freedom. Where this prison term stems from having thrown a cigarette stub into the street, this counts as a very light (*ll*) reason for the prison term. The Difference Formula leads on the basis of the values 9 (*ss*) and 1 (*ll*) to 8 as the concrete weight of the constitutional guarantee of freedom (Article 2(1) and Article 2(2)(2) of the Basic Law). By contrast, the Quotient Formula leads on the basis of the values 2^8 (*ss*) and 2^0 (*ll*)—which is the most extreme constellation in the double-triadic model of an unjustified interference with a constitutional right—to a swelling of the concrete weight up to 256.[34] Conversely, the strongest justification of an interference is represented by *ll*, *ss*. According to the Difference Formula this means –8, according to the Quotient Formula 1/256 or 0.00390625. With the Quotient Formula the values in the extreme constellations approach, on the one hand, zero, and, on the other, infinity. This corresponds to the notion that there may well exist something approximating unlimited injustice. Of course, such tendencies can also be reconstructed by means of the Difference Formula. One need only extend the scale to which it applies in the directions of zero and infinity. In this way, however, the difference scale as such becomes intricate. The simple sequence 1, 2, 3 represents *l*, *m*, and *s* in a way that clearly mirrors the crude structure of our capacity to classify interferences according to their intensity. The same also holds for the representation of the double-triadic model by means of the sequence 1 to 9. It is doubtful, however, whether such a correspondence would still exist if the sequence were extended in the directions of zero and infinity. The geometric sequence stays clear of such problems. It fits the triadic structures as well as the increasing power of resistance on the part of rights with an increasing intensity of interference.

It has already been mentioned that not only the intensity of interference but also the abstract weights can play a role in balancing. This possibility becomes actual whenever they differ. As long as the abstract weights are equal, they cancel each other out. But when they have different weights, the result of balancing may well turn on this difference.

The relation between the intensities of interference (I_i, I_j) and the abstract weights (W_i, W_j) can obtain in the form of three basic constellations. In the first, the abstract weights are different while the intensities of interference are equal. In this constellation the intensities of interference cancel each other out. Everything, then, turns on the abstract weights. This constellation is the opposite of the second, far more frequent and hence, in practical terms, far more important basic constellation, in which the abstract weights are equal while the intensities of interference are

[34] One could point to even more extreme cases such as, for instance, life imprisonment for having coughed during a lecture. This case, indeed, is more extreme than that of the cigarette stub. The double-triadic model is, however, not prepared to grasp this difference in extremeness. To this end, there would have to be further differentiations in the sphere of the extreme. Such further differentiations seem altogether possible. It would be an attempt to construct the idea that one's capacity to discriminate increases as one moves towards the extremes, whereas it decreases as one moves towards the middle.

different. In the third basic constellation both the abstract weights and the intensities of interference are different. All four values, then, count. These correlations can be expressed by the following extended version of the Weight Formula:

$$W_{i,j} = \frac{I_i \cdot W_i}{I_j \cdot W_j}$$

If this formula is adequate, it can serve as the basis for still another conceptual clarification. The products $I_i \cdot W_i$ and $I_j \cdot W_j$ express something that, often in addition to or in the place of $W_{i,j}$ and W_i or W_j, is called 'weight'. The expression 'weight' thus acquires three different meanings. Equivocation does not cause any harm as long as the context makes it possible to decide clearly what is meant. In the discussion concerning balancing, however, this is not always the case. For this reason, terminological clarification is necessary. There are two possibilities. One can term the product $I_i \cdot W_i$ both the 'non-relative concrete weight' or the 'importance of P_i'. The former is complicated but clear. It places the non-relative concrete weight ($I_i \cdot W_i$) distinctly between the relative concrete weight ($W_{i,j}$) and the abstract weight (W_i). Compared with that, the term 'importance' is more elegant and quite close to the ordinary use of language. It is possible to understand the Law of Balancing as not having explicit reference to abstract weights, for the reason that these cancel each other out owing to the equality of weights. One ought for reasons of clarity to refrain, therefore, from designating I_j without further explanation as 'importance', as has been done in the formulation of the Law of Balancing presented above. If one chooses this approach, the non-relative concrete weight can be defined as importance (U_i, U_j) in the following way:

$$U_i = I_i \cdot W_i$$

$$U_j = I_j \cdot W_j$$

'U_i' and 'U_j' as allusions to urgency are employed here, owing to the fact that 'I_i' and 'I_j' have already been engaged for the representation of the intensity of interference. In this way, the triple meaning of the term 'weight' can be given expression.

It also seems advisable to express also the values of W_i and W_j by means of triadic scales that are represented by geometric sequences. Everything that has been said about the values of I_i and I_j also applies, then, to those of W_i and W_j. This does not come about as a matter of course but is rather an expression of the assumption that both the abstract weight and the intensity of interference have to be assigned the same weights in the determination of the concrete or relative weight represented by $W_{i,j}$. Here the chameleonic concept of weight is being used on the meta-level. This equal-weight assumption provides for the possibility of comprehensive compensation. A light (l) interference (I_i) with a principle of a high (s) abstract weight (W_i)

has the same importance (U_i) as a serious (s) interference (I_j) with a principle of a low (l) abstract weight (W_j), brought about by its omission. In this way, a stalemate emerges.

The third pair of variables of the complete Weight Formula has already been mentioned, too. It refers to the degree of reliability of the empirical assumptions concerning what the measure in question means for the non-realization of the one principle and the realization of the other principle. In its *Co-determination* Judgment the German Federal Constitutional Court has aptly stated, where empirical prognoses are concerned, that the legislator takes as the basis of his estimate of proportionality that neither the assumption that in all cases certainty be required nor the assumption that uncertainty be granted at will is correct.[35] The most prominent among the criteria for determining the required degree of reliability is that of importance, as defined by intensity of interference and abstract weight of the constitutional right in the case at hand. Against this background and parallel to the Law of Balancing presented above, an Epistemic Law of Balancing can be formulated. It reads:

> The more heavily an interference with a constitutional right weighs, the greater must be the certainty of its underlying premises.

This second Law of Balancing carries the predicate 'epistemic', for it has reference not to the substantive importance of the reasons underlying the interference but rather to their epistemic quality. The first Law of Balancing, which, as explained, defines the third sub-principle of the principle of proportionality, can be termed, if one wishes to give expression to the difference between it and its epistemic counterpart, the 'Substantive Law of Balancing'.

A triadic scale seems also to suggest itself in the case of the Epistemic Law of Balancing. In its *Co-determination* Judgment, the Federal Constitutional Court has attempted to distinguish three different degrees of intensity of review: an 'intensive review of content', a 'plausibility review', and an 'evidential review'.[36] This corresponds to the three epistemic classes, namely: (r) reliable or certain, (p) plausible or defensible, and (e) not evidently false. The reliability of the empirical assumptions concerning what the measure in question means for the non-realization of P_i and the realization of P_j in the circumstances of the case at hand can be represented by 'R_i' and 'R_j', or, in the detailed version, as 'RP_iC' and 'RP_jC'. In order to give expression to the notion that the power of defence as well as the power of infringement decreases with increasing uncertainty of the premises backing the respective side, r is assigned the value of 2^0, p the value 2^{-1}, and e the value 2^{-2}. Of course, a

[35] BVerfGE 50, 290 (332).

[36] BVerfGE 50, 290 (333) (trans. R. A.).

refinement of the triad, for instance as a double-triad, is possible here, too. The complete Weight Formula would then read as follows:

$$W_{i,j} = \frac{I_i \cdot W_i \cdot R_i}{I_j \cdot W_j \cdot R_j}$$

In order to illustrate how this formula works, two constellations shall be considered. In both of them, the abstract weights (W_i, W_j) shall be equal, thereby making things a bit simpler. In the first case, both the interference that would occur with P_i if the measure under consideration were performed and the interference that would occur with P_j if it were not performed are serious (s). The assumption that P_i would meet with a serious interference may be classified as certain (r), the corresponding assumption with respect to P_j, however, only as plausible (p). Under these conditions $W_{i,j}$ is determined as follows:[37]

$$W_{i,j} = \frac{4 \cdot 1}{4 \cdot \frac{1}{2}} = 2$$

Thus, P_i takes precedence.

In the second constellation, too, the interference with P_i shall be certain (r), whereas the damage for P_j that would result from refraining from interference with P_i can only plausibly (p) be assumed to occur. Such an assignment of values to the epistemic pair of variables R_i, R_j can be found in the *Cannabis* Judgment.[38] Now, the German Federal Constitutional Court considered the prohibition against the possession and use of cannabis products as constitutional. From this, along with the inequality of the values R_i and R_j, it follows that the assignment of values to I_i and I_j or to W_i and W_j must be unequal. The details of the Court's complex distinctions and arguments cannot be considered here. It shall only be noted that the assumption of an interference of only moderate intensity together with a highest importance of the avoidance of the dangers connected with cannabis products would create a possibility to compensate the only medium reliability, p, of the empirical premises backing the liability. $W_{i,j}$ would, then, acquire the following value:

$$W_{i,j} = \frac{2 \cdot 1}{4 \cdot \frac{1}{2}} = 1$$

[37] Its detailed version runs: $WP_{i,j}C = \frac{IP_iC \cdot WP_iA \cdot RP_iC}{IP_jC \cdot WP_jA \cdot RP_jC}$

[38] BVerfGE 90, 145 (182): 'The opinion of the legislature that no means equally effective but less intrusive than the threat of criminal penalties are at its disposal is also *defensible* from the standpoint of the current state of knowledge, as the above ... indicated sources makes clear' (emphasis by R. A).

With that, we would have a stalemate. This means that the liability for the possession or use of cannabis products is a matter of the discretion of the legislator.

V. The Extended Formula

Thus far, only the collisions between two principles have been considered. These can be completely grasped by means of the Weight Formula. Often there are, however—on one side or both—additional principles at stake. Because only one decision can be taken in these cases, all relevant principles must be related to each other in one way or other. The question is whether this can be achieved by incorporating cumulative effects in the Weight Formula. The simplest version would be a plain additive cumulation. Here, only the side of the limits to constitutional rights shall be considered.[39] If the additive cumulation is admitted, the following formula is obtained:

$$W_{i,j-n} = \frac{I_i \cdot W_i \cdot R_i}{I_j \cdot W_j \cdot R_j + \ldots I_n \cdot W_n \cdot R_n}$$

This formula can be termed 'Extended Weight Formula'.

It is a general question of the theory of argumentation whether the cumulation of arguments can be represented as addition. If one leaves this question aside, the main problem of the Extended Weight Formula is posed by the question of what can be cumulated under what conditions. The direction in which an answer to this question would be found is easy enough to recognize. The cumulated principles may not overlap substantively. Their objects of optimization must be substantively different. Hence, the rule that heterogeneity is a presupposition of additive

[39] If one also takes into consideration the constitutional right whose violation is being examined (P_i), then cumulation inevitably leads to constitutional rights holism. All constitutional rights that are ever negatively affected by whatever interferes with P_i would have to be set beside P_i. The traditional scheme, according to which an interference with a single constitutional right has to be examined, would dissolve. This dissolution would be at its most radical if the possibility of cumulation were extended to all constitutional principles, not only to those referring to constitutional rights. All those principles speaking against the measure under consideration would then take, so to speak, joint action against all those principles speaking for it. The constitutional right whose violation is being examined would then no longer be a single combatant but rather the leader of a more or less all-encompassing corps. The concrete weight of the constitutional right whose violation is being examined would become the concrete weight of this principle *in the total system* of the constitution. This can be expressed by the following formula:

$$W_{i-m,j-n} = \frac{I_i \cdot W_i \cdot R_i + \ldots I_m \cdot W_m \cdot R_m}{I_j \cdot W_j \cdot R_j + \ldots I_n \cdot W_n \cdot R_n}$$

This formula shall be termed the 'Complete Extended Weight Formula'.

cumulation is valid. Sometimes this rule can be applied easily. Thus, the general freedom of action can, in general, be identified easily enough as already contained in specific constitutional rights. Or—the other way around—one can well imagine cases in which an interference is grounded on several principles that do not overlap. This may suggest itself when one principle protects collective goods and another protects individual rights. But even here caution is advised. In view of the complex relation[40] between individual rights and collective goods the possibility of substantive overlap always has to be taken into account. The mere fact that what convenes are, on the one side, individual rights, and, on the other, collective goods, does, as such, not guarantee heterogeneity.

The problem would be simple if heterogeneity were an all-or-nothing matter. This, however, is not the case. Principles can overlap substantively more or less. All of this, however, is no reason at all not to begin with the analysis of the relatively simple relations, as are to be observed in the case of collision between two principles, and, moreover, not a good reason not to undertake steps, on the basis of this analysis, into the more complex regions of collisions between bundles of principles.

[40] See Robert Alexy, 'Individual Rights and Collective Goods' in *Rights*, ed. Carlos Nino (Aldershot: Dartmouth, 1992), 163–81.

12

Formal Principles: Some Replies to Critics

I. The Problem

The principles theory of constitutional rights is confronted with numerous objections.[1] Under the aspect of democratic constitutionalism the institutional objection is of special importance. It says that the optimization thesis—without which principles theory would not be principles theory—leads to a ballooning of constitutional rights, leading in turn to an over-constitutionalization of the legal system. According to Ernst-Wolfgang Böckenförde, the institutional consequence is a 'gradual transition from a parliamentary, legislative state to a constitutional court-based, jurisdiction state'.[2] In short, principles theory is reproached for being unable to determine in an adequate way the relation between constitutional rights and constitutional review on the one hand, and democracy on the other.

Principles theory has, from its beginning, attempted to counter this objection with a theory of discretion. In this theory, the concept of formal principle plays a pivotal role. This concept, however, is still highly contested. The controversy over formal principles is not only an important part of the debate between opponents and proponents of principles theory but has reached to a lively dispute about formal principles even inside the camp of principles theory. Martin Borowski recently characterized the formal principles as an element of principles theory that has 'remained oddly enigmatical',[3] and he refers to them with the metaphor of 'the last great white patch on the map of principles theory'.[4] I will attempt to defend the thesis that an analysis of formal principles is possible that implies an adequate theory of legislative discretion. The basis of this model is the Weight Formula. I shall begin with a presentation of some basic elements of principles theory.

[1] On a classification of these objections into seven groups see Robert Alexy, 'The Construction of Constitutional Rights', *Law & Ethics of Human Rights* 4 (2010), 20–32, at 24–6 (in this volume: Chapter 8, 121–32, at 124–6).

[2] Ernst-Wolfgang Böckenförde, 'Fundamental Rights as Constitutional Principles. On the Current State of Interpreting Fundamental Rights', in *Böckenförde, Constitutional and Political Theory. Selected Writings*, eds Mirjam Künkler and Tine Stein (Oxford: Oxford University Press, 2017), 235–65, at 259.

[3] Martin Borowski, 'Formelle Prinzipien und Gewichtsformel', in *Prinzipientheorie und Theorie der Abwägung*, ed. Matthias Klatt (Tübingen: Mohr Siebeck, 2013), 151–99, at 151 (trans. R. A.).

[4] Ibid., (trans. R. A.).

Law's Ideal Dimension. Robert Alexy, Oxford University Press. © Robert Alexy 2021.
DOI: 10.1093/oso/9780198796831.003.0013

II. Some Basic Elements of Principles Theory

A. Rules and Principles

The basis of principles theory is the norm-theoretic distinction between rules and principles.[5] Rules are norms that require something determinate. They are *definitive commands.* Their form of application is subsumption. By contrast, principles are *optimization requirements.* As such, they demand 'that something be realized to the greatest extent possible given the legal and factual possibilities'.[6] Rules aside, the legal possibilities are determined essentially by opposing principles. For this reason, principles, each taken alone, always comprise merely *prima facie* requirements. The determination of the appropriate degree of satisfaction of one principle relative to the requirements of other principles is brought about by means of balancing. Thus, balancing is the specific form of application of principles.

B. Proportionality

The nature of principles as optimization requirements leads immediately to a necessary connection between principles and proportionality analysis. The principle of proportionality, which in the last decades has received ever greater international recognition in the practice and theory of constitutional review,[7] consists of three sub-principles: the principle of suitability, the principle of necessity, and the principle of proportionality in the narrower sense. All three sub-principles express the idea of optimization. For this reason, the nature of principles implies the principle of proportionality and vice-versa.

The principles of suitability and necessity refer to optimization relative to the factual possibilities. Optimization relative to the factual possibilities consists in avoiding avoidable costs.[8] Costs, however, are unavoidable when principles collide. Balancing then becomes necessary. Balancing is the subject of the third sub-principle of the principle of proportionality, namely, the principle of proportionality in the narrower sense. This principle expresses what optimization relative to the legal possibilities means. It is identical with a rule that can be called 'Law of Balancing'.[9] It states:

5 Robert Alexy, *A Theory of Constitutional Rights* (1985), trans. Julian Rivers (Oxford: Oxford University Press, 2002), 47–8.

6 Ibid., 47.

7 See, for instance, David M. Beatty, *The Ultimate Rule of Law* (Oxford: Oxford University Press, 2004); Alec Stone Sweet and Jud Mathews, 'Proportionality Balancing and Global Constitutionalism', *Columbia Journal of Transnational Law* 47 (2008), 72–164; Aharon Barak, *Proportionality. Constitutional Rights and their Limitations* (Cambridge: Cambridge University Press, 2012).

8 See on this Robert Alexy, 'Constitutional Rights and Proportionality', *Chinese Yearbook of Constitutional Law* (2010), 221–35, at 222–4.

9 Alexy, *A Theory of Constitutional Rights* (n. 5 above), 102.

The greater the degree of non-satisfaction of, or detriment to, one principle, the greater must be the importance of satisfying the other.

C. Weight Formula

Nearly everywhere in constitutional adjudication, the Law of Balancing is found in various different formulations. It expresses the essence of balancing and is of great practical importance. The analysis of formal principles and legislative discretion requires, however, a more precise and complete description of the structure of balancing. In order to achieve this, the Law of Balancing has to be elaborated further. The result of such a further elaboration is the Weight Formula.[10] It runs as follows:

$$W_{i,j} = \frac{I_i \cdot W_i \cdot R_i}{I_j \cdot W_j \cdot R_j}$$

$W_{i,j}$ represents the concrete weight of the principle P_i relative to the colliding principle P_j. The Weight Formula defines this concrete weight as the quotient of three factors standing, so to speak, on each side of balancing. I_i and I_j are of special importance. I_i stands for the intensity of interference with P_i. I_j represents the importance of satisfying the colliding principle P_j. I_j, too, can be understood as intensity of interference, that is, as the intensity of interference with P_j through non-interference with P_i. W_i and W_j stand for the abstract weights of the colliding principles P_i and P_j. When the abstract weights are equal, which is often the case in collisions of constitutional rights, they cancel each other out.

I_i and I_j, and also W_i and W_j, concern the substantive dimension of balancing. R_i and R_j have a completely different character. They refer to the reliability of the empirical and normative assumptions concerning, first and foremost, the question of how intensive the interference with P_i is, and how intensive the interference with P_j would be if the interference with P_i were omitted. Over and above this, the reliability of empirical and normative assumptions can also relate to the classification of the abstract weights, that is, to W_i and W_j. The decisive point is that reliability is a factor that does not refer to the things, in our case the intensity of interference and the abstract weights, that is, it is not an ontic factor. Rather, it is a factor that refers to the knowledge of things, that is, it is an epistemic factor. This distinction between ontic and epistemic factors will turn out to be of utmost importance for the theory of formal principles and legislative discretion.

[10] Robert Alexy, 'The Weight Formula', trans. Bartosz Brożek and Stanley L. Paulson, in *Studies in the Philosophy of Law*, vol. 3, eds Jerzy Stelmach, Bartosz Brożek, and Wojciech Załuski (Kraków: Jagiellonian University Press, 2007), 9–27, at 25 (in this volume: Chapter 11, 154–74, at 172).

Since 2003,[11] reliability has been represented on both sides of the Weight Formula by just one variable: R_i and R_j, and in some publications I have defined R_i and R_j as referring only to 'empirical assumptions'[12]. This does not fit well, however, with the fact that already in the Postscript of *A Theory of Constitutional Rights*, that is, in 2002, I stressed the systematic importance of the distinction between empirical epistemic discretion and normative epistemic discretion.[13] This does not fit well with the formulation of the second Law of Balancing either, that is, the formulation of the epistemic Law of Balancing. It states:

> The more heavily an interference in a constitutional right weighs, the greater must be the certainty of its underlying premises.[14]

This law refers not to empirical premises but, in a quite general way, to 'underlying premises'. Now the decisive point is that the concept of underlying premises comprises normative premises as well as empirical premises. R_i and R_j must therefore be understood as referring to normative premises as well as to empirical premises. This can be expressed by the following equation:

$$R_i = R_i^e \cdot R_i^n$$

This equation might be called the 'reliability equation'.

I have characterized the Weight Formula as presented above as the 'complete Weight Formula'.[15] It can continue to bear this name. In a great number of cases, empirical reliability alone is a problem. Then there is no practical necessity of explicitly applying the reliability equation. However, as soon as both empirical and normative reliability are in question, R_i and R_j have to be substituted by the respective products on the right side of the reliability equation. In this way, a new version of the Weight Formula enters the stage:

$$W_{i,j} = \frac{I_i \cdot W_i \cdot R_i^e \cdot R_i^n}{I_j \cdot W_j \cdot R_j^e \cdot R_j^n}$$

This version might be designated as the 'refined complete Weight Formula'. A considerable number of authors have suggested that a fourth variable should be

[11] Robert Alexy, 'On Balancing and Subsumtion. A Structural Comparison', *Ratio Juris* 16 (2003), 433–49, at 446. On an earlier notation see Alexy, *A Theory of Constitutional Rights* (n. 5 above), 419.

[12] Alexy, *A Theory of Constitutional Rights* (n. 5 above), 419; Alexy, 'On Balancing and Subsumption' (n. 11 above), 446; Alexy, 'The Weight Formula' (n. 10 above), 25. (in this volume: Chapter 11, 171)

[13] Alexy, *A Theory of Constitutional Rights* (n. 5 above), 414–25.

[14] Ibid., 418.

[15] Alexy, 'The Weight Formula' (n. 10 above), 25 (in this volume: Chapter 11, 172).

inserted into the Weight Formula.[16] To the degree in which these proposals are compatible with the reliability equation and the refinement of the Weight Formula achieved thereby, I agree with them.

A formula like the Weight Formula, which expresses a quotient of two products, is sensible only if all of the factors can be represented by numbers. This is the problem of graduation. Elsewhere,[17] I have proposed a discrete, that is, a non-continuous triadic scale, in which geometric sequences are implemented. This scale assigns the values 'light', 'moderate', and 'serious' to the intensity of interference and to the abstract weights. These values are expressed by the numbers 2^0, 2^1, and 2^2, that is, by 1, 2, and 4. Where the epistemic side is concerned, that is R_i and R_j, or, in the refined version of the Weight Formula, R_i^e and R_i^n as well as R_j^e and R_j^n, one can work with the stages 'reliable' or 'certain' (*r*), 'plausible' (*p*), and 'not evidently false' (*e*), to which the numbers 2^0, 2^{-1}, and 2^{-2}, that is, 1, ½, and ¼, are to be assigned.[18] If the epistemic values are 1, the substantive values remain untouched. If the epistemic values are lower than 1, the impact of the substantive values is reduced accordingly. The lowest epistemic value occurs when the reliability of both the empirical and the normative premises is to be assessed as not higher than 'not evidently false'. In this case, the epistemic side receives the value $1/16$. Such an extremely bad epistemic quality destroys the power of even the strongest substantive reasons for interference with constitutional rights nearly completely. This shows that the reliability equation has a high intuitive plausibility.

By means of these triads, most of the decisions of constitutional courts can be grasped. Where they do not suffice, that is, where one has to introduce still more attenuated graduations, they can be extended to double-triadic scales.[19] Much more could be said about the Weight Formula. For a discussion of formal principles, however, what has been said ought to suffice.

III. The Concept of Formal Principle

Formal principles are principles. Principles are optimization requirements. Thus, the definition of optimization requirements as 'norms which require that something be

[16] See, for instance, Johannes Badenhop, *Normtheoretische Grundlagen der Europäischen Menschenrechtskonvention* (Baden-Baden: Nomos, 2010), 366–7; Mattias Klatt and Moritz Meister, *The Constitutional Structure of Proportionality* (Oxford: Oxford University Press, 2012), 132; Matthias Klatt and Johannes Schmidt, 'Epistemic Discretion in Constitutional Law', *International Journal of Constitutional Law* 10 (2012), 69–105, at 91; Jorge A. Portocarrero Quispe, *Der autoritative Charakter der Grundrechtsabwägung* (Baden-Baden: Nomos, 2014), 163–4.

[17] Alexy, *A Theory of Constitutional Rights* (n. 5 above), 409–10, 419; Alexy, 'The Weight Formula' (n. 10 above), 20–6 (in this volume: Chapter 11, 165–73).

[18] Alexy, 'The Weight Formula' (n. 10 above), 25 (in this volume: Chapter 11, 171).

[19] Ibid., 22–3 (Chapter 11, 168–9).

realized to the greatest extent possible given the legal and factual possibilities'[20] applies to formal principles in the same way as to substantive principles. The difference between these two kinds of principle is confined to that to which the word 'something' in the definition refers, that is, to the object of optimization. The *differentia specifica* of substantive principles is that their objects of optimization are certain contents, as, for instance, life, freedom of speech, existential minimum, and protection of the environment. By contrast, the optimization objects of formal principles are legal decisions regardless of their content. Formal principles require that the authority of duly issued and socially efficacious norms is optimized. Authoritative issuance and social efficacy are the defining elements of legal positivism.[21] This implies that formal principles refer to the real or factual dimension of law.

This real or factual aspect can, however, be connected with ideal elements. The principle of democracy is an example. Democracy is an attempt to institutionalize the ideals of discourse *qua* public deliberation as far as possible.[22] Nevertheless, it is a formal principle. It refers, as far as representative democracy, not direct democracy, is concerned, to the decisions made by parliament according to the majority rule. Democracy, however, is not just one decision procedure among others. It is the most rational and legitimate procedure of law-making. For this reason, the principle of democracy lends not only special weight to the decisions of parliament. It requires, over and above this, that 'the democratically legitimated legislature should take as many important decisions for society as possible'.[23] With this requirement, the principle of democracy refers not only to the authority of decisions made from within the scope of parliamentary competences. It also demands that this scope be as broad as possible. This is of special importance for the relation between constitutional rights and democracy.

IV. Principles and Balancing in General

T. R. S. Allen has argued that 'a purely *formal* principle of democracy lacks ... any independent weight'.[24] This raises the question of whether formal principles can participate in balancing as described by the Weight Formula. I will, first, take up this question with respect to formal and substantive principles in general. The question of balancing democracy and constitutional rights will be taken up later.

[20] Alexy, *A Theory of Constitutional Rights* (n. 5 above), 47.

[21] Robert Alexy, *The Argument from Injustice. A Reply to Legal Positivism* (1992), trans. Bonnie Litschewski Paulson and Stanley L. Paulson (Oxford: Clarendon Press, 2002), 3–4, 13–19.

[22] Robert Alexy, 'The Dual Nature of Law', *Ratio Juris* 23 (2010), 167–82, at 177–8 (in this volume: Chapter 3, 36–50, at 47).

[23] Alexy, *A Theory of Constitutional Rights* (n. 5 above), 417.

[24] T. R. S. Allen, 'Constitutional Rights and the Rule of Law', in *Institutionalized Reason. The Jurisprudence of Robert Alexy*, ed. Matthias Klatt (Oxford: Oxford University Press, 2012), 132–51, at 135–6.

Now the question is: can a formal principle be balanced against a substantive principle, and vice versa?

It is easy to find cases in which a formal principle can, and even must, be balanced against a substantive principle. After National Socialism was defeated in 1945, as well as after the collapse of the German Democratic Republic in 1989, courts in Germany were confronted in a number of cases with the problem of statutory injustice. They applied the Radbruch Formula, which, in its shortest form, runs as follows:

> Extreme injustice is no law.[25]

This formula is the result of balancing the substantive principle of justice against the formal principle of legal certainty.[26] Balancing rests on two laws. The first has already been introduced. It is the Law of Balancing, which finds its elaborated form in the Weight Formula. The second is the Law of Competing Principles,[27] which says that according to the concrete weight of the colliding principle P_i, established by the Weight Formula ($W_{i,j}$), a concrete relation of preference has to be established with respect to the conditions of the case. The Radbruch Formula rests on the distinction between two conditions of precedence. The first, C_1, is injustice below the threshold of extreme injustice. The second, C_2, is extreme injustice. Under the first condition, C_1, the formal principle of legal certainty takes precedence over the substantive principle of justice. Under the second condition, C_2, the substantive principle of justice takes precedence over the formal principle of legal certainty. According to the Law of Colliding Principles, the consequence of the precedence of the principle of justice over the principle of legal certainty under the condition of extreme injustice is that under this condition the consequence required by the prevailing principle of justice applies, and this is exactly what the Radbruch Formula states.

It is of the utmost importance that all this be intrinsically connected with the Weight Formula. The formal principle of legal certainty has precedence over the substantive principle of justice if and only if it has a higher concrete weight than this principle. Now, under the condition of injustice below the threshold of extreme injustice, the interference with the principle of justice does not have the highest intensity. I would classify it, on the basis of the triadic scale, at best as medium—and in cases of less severe injustice even as light. The value of legal certainty below the threshold of extreme injustice is, however, high. If each and every injustice were to lead to legal invalidity, the function of the legal system to coordinate behaviour and

25 Robert Alexy, 'A Defense of Radbruch's Formula', in *Recrafting the Rule of Law: The Limits of Legal Order*, ed. David Dyzenhaus (Oxford: Hart, 1999), 15–39, at 17.

26 Alexy, 'The Dual Nature of Law' (n. 22 above), 177 (in this volume: Chapter 3, 46).

27 Alexy, *A Theory of Constitutional Rights* (n. 5 above), 54.

to secure the advantages of social coordination and cooperation would be endangered. According to the Weight Formula, a principle with a high weight justifies an interference with a principle with a medium or light weight. If, however, the injustice is extreme, the interference with the principle of justice would be serious. By contrast, one has to assume only a medium or light interference with the principle of legal certainty. Extreme injustice occurs only in extreme situations of legal systems, and it concerns by no means all legal norms, but only those specific to the rough legal system.[28] All this means that balancing formal and substantive principles is not only possible but, indeed, is also necessary in law.

Something similar applies when a legal system allows *contra legem* decisions, at least in some areas of law, as the German system does. A statute is not automatically overruled when a competing substantive principle has greater weight than its own underlying substantive principle on the facts of the case. A *contra legem* decision, such as the incorporation of an exemption into the statute in deciding a particular case, requires that the competing substantive principle has a greater weight than the substantive principle underlying the statute together with formal principles like the principles of legal certainty, democracy, and the separation of powers, which all require that what is authoritatively issued be respected.[29] This shows that formal principles can not only be balanced on their own against colliding substantive principles, as with the grounding of the Radbruch Formula. They can also be balanced in combination with substantive principles against colliding substantive principles. One might call the first of these the 'pure substantive-formal model' of balancing principles and the latter the 'mixed substantive-formal model', or, shorter, 'the combination model'.

V. The Wrong Way

One might well think that these two models also apply to the relation between constitutional rights and the formal principle of democracy. Indeed, in *A Theory of Constitutional Rights*, first published 1985, I endorsed the combination model:

> A formal or procedural principle is, for example, the principle which says that the democratic legislature shall take decisions which are significant for society as a whole. This procedural principle, *together with* a substantive principle serving some secondary public interest, can be balanced against a constitutional principle guaranteeing an individual right.[30]

[28] Alexy, *The Argument from Injustice* (n. 21 above), 66–8.
[29] Alexy, *A Theory of Constitutional Rights* (n. 5 above), 58.
[30] Ibid., 82 (new emphasis).

More recently, Borowski has argued in favour of the combination model:

> The consideration of the formal principle has the effect of adding weight to one of the two substantive principles.[31]

For this reason,

> in addition to the substantive principles 'i' and 'j' a formal principle 'f' must be inserted into the Weight Formula.[32]

Both the pure substantive-formal and the combination model, however, lead to serious problems where constitutional rights are concerned. This is especially clear in the case of the pure substantive-formal model. If the principle of democracy on its own were able to justify an interference with a constitutional right, it would be possible to say: 'The interference is not justified by any substantive principle, that is, not justified by any substantive reason, but it is none the less permissible, for the democratically legitimated legislature can take more decisions when it is permitted to take this decision than when it is not.' An interference with a constitutional right, an interference that is not justified by any substantive reason, is not only disproportional, it is also arbitrary. To acknowledge a competence on the part of the democratically legitimated legislature to interfere with constitutional rights simply because it is democratically legitimated would undermine the priority of the constitution over ordinary parliamentary legislation.

Things are more complex in the case of the mixed substantive-formal or combination model. Nevertheless, this model has, basically, the same defects as the pure formal-substantive model. If one were to insert formal principles into the Weight Formula alongside the substantive principles, constellations like the following would become possible. On the one side, the interference with a constitutional right is serious (s), that is, I_i has the value 4. On the other side, the importance of satisfying the colliding principle is moderate (m), that is, I_j has the value 2. This is a clear case of disproportionality, and, with this, of unconstitutionality. Now it is possible to attribute to the formal principle of the legislature's decision-making competence, standing on the side of the colliding substantive principle, a high weight, that is, P_f receives the value 4. This would transform the unconstitutional decision into a constitutional one. If this were possible, disproportional interferences with constitutional rights would be permissible, for the reason that the democratically legitimated legislature can take more decisions when it is permitted to take this

[31] Martin Borowski, 'The Structure of Formal Principles—Robert Alexy's "Law of Combination"', *Archives for Philosophy of Law and Social Philosophy*, supplement 119 (2010), 18–35, at 34.

[32] Borowski, 'Formelle Prinzipien und Gewichtsformel' (n. 3 above), 184 (trans. R. A.).

decision than when it is not. As in the case of the pure formal-substantive model, this would undermine the priority of the constitution over ordinary parliamentary legislation.

Does this mean that the democratically legitimated legislature never has discretion where constitutional rights are concerned? The answer is: no. The substantiation of this answer is possible on the basis of an analysis of the concept of discretion.

VI. Two Kinds of Discretion

There are two kinds of discretion: substantive or structural discretion and epistemic discretion. The substantive discretion of the legislature comprises everything that constitutional norms neither definitely prohibit nor command. What is neither prohibited nor commanded is left free.[33] Thus, the scope of substantive discretion is identical with what the constitution has definitely left free. The question of epistemic discretion arises whenever knowledge of what is definitively prohibited, commanded, or left free by constitutional norms is uncertain. In such cases the legislature has epistemic discretion to the degree to which it has competence to determine what is definitively prohibited, commanded, or left free. Substantive discretion, which exists in three forms,[34] is much less problematic than epistemic discretion. That the legislature is free where no obligations exist is not in need of justification. For this reason, formal principles play no role with respect to substantive discretion. That the legislative has competence to decide whether it is free or not in cases in which it is uncertain whether it is free or not is, however, much less obvious. Here, formal principles play the decisive role. In what follows only epistemic discretion shall be considered.

VII. Second-Order Epistemic Optimization

Epistemic discretion has to be further classified into two kinds: into empirical and into normative epistemic discretion. Empirical epistemic discretion causes many fewer problems than does normative epistemic discretion. Therefore, empirical epistemic discretion shall be at the centre of our considerations.[35]

Empirical uncertainty can be a problem in all three stages of proportionality analysis. The *Cannabis* Decision of the German Federal Constitutional Court offers an example. The central question of this decision is which dangers

33 Alexy, *A Theory of Constitutional Rights* (n. 5 above), 130–1.
34 Ibid., 395–414.
35 On normative epistemic discretion see ibid, 415–16, 420–2.

are connected with the use of cannabis products, and by which measures these dangers can be combatted. The legislature has justified its ban on cannabis products, sanctioned by criminal penalties, with the assumption of a high danger for health and social life which can only be adequately combatted by criminal prohibition.[36] The other side argued that the high danger assumed by the legislature does not exist. The danger is at best small, and the measures chosen by the legislature are neither suitable nor necessary. Now one could take the view that the Court should only permit interference if the truth of those empirical assumptions on which suitability, necessity, and the extent of the danger depend is established. But the Court proceeds differently. It does not establish the truth or falsity of the legislature's empirical premises, but their uncertainty: 'Scientifically based knowledge, which necessarily points to the correctness of one or the other strategies, is not available.'[37] The Court nonetheless permits the interference with the constitutional right. This is the result of giving the legislature discretion with respect to the knowledge of relevant facts, in other words an empirical epistemic discretion, and locating the legislature's empirical assumptions underlying the ban of cannabis within this discretion.

The *Cannabis* Judgment clearly exposes the main problem with all epistemic discretion. If the legislature is permitted to base its interference with constitutional rights on uncertain premises, then it is possible that the protection afforded by constitutional rights will be refused on the basis of false assumptions, even though constitutional rights have in reality been breached.

The solution is provided by a third model of the role of formal principles in balancing, a model that stands between the pure substantive-formal model and the combination or mixed substantive-formal model. This third model can be called the 'epistemic model'. The basis of the epistemic model is the idea of second-order balancing. Balancing according to the lines of the Weight Formula is first-order balancing. Second-order balancing is concerned with justifying the incorporation of epistemic reliability, that is, of R_i and R_j, in the Weight Formula.[38] Constitutional rights as principles require the greatest possible realization relative to what is factually and legally possible. The realization of constitutional rights increases when they can only be limited on the grounds of premises the truth of which is assured. If premises below the level of certainty were nevertheless admitted, the realization of constitutional rights would increase where the premise most favourable for the right was chosen. Discretion of legislature would be excluded in this case, too. In this sense, constitutional rights require not only substantive optimization but also epistemic optimization.[39] The decisive point of second-order balancing is

36 BVerfGE 90, 145 (174).
37 BVerfGE 90, 145 (182–3) (trans. R. A.).
38 In the refined Weight Formula R_i is substituted by $R_i^e \cdot R_i^n$, and R_j by $R_j^e \cdot R_j^n$.
39 Alexy, *A Theory of Constitutional Rights* (n. 5 above), 416.

that constitutional rights as epistemic optimization requirements collide with the formal principle of the democratically legitimated legislature. If this collision could be solved by establishing an absolute precedence for the substantive constitutional rights principle as against the formal principle of democratically legitimated legislature, in wide areas of law the consequences would be inacceptable. In reasonably complex contexts, like commercial, security, and environmental law, empirical premises that are reliably true, are practically never available. Thus, an absolute precedence for the substantive constitutional rights principle in cases of empirical uncertainty would lead to far-reaching legislative paralysis.[40] This would be a disproportional interference with the formal principle of the democratically legitimated legislature. This disproportionality is established by means of a second-order balancing. This is a balancing of a substantive principle with a formal principle. In this respect it corresponds to the pure substantive-formal model, presented above. But it is a special case of substantive-formal balancing because it takes place not inside the Weight Formula but on a meta-level, where it is concerned with the question of which variables with which kind of scales have to be inserted into the Weight Formula.[41]

According to the Law of Competing Principles, balancing results in a conditional relation of precedence.[42] The three stages of the epistemic scale can be considered as such conditions of precedence. If the epistemic value of an empirical assumption is 'reliable' or 'certain' (*r*), the constitutional rights principle for which this classification is favourable has precedence over the formal principle. This implies that the number 2^0, that is, 1, has to be inserted into the formula, which means that the substantive result on the side of the constitutional right is not at all influenced by any formal or procedural considerations as required by formal principles. If, however, the epistemic value is only 'plausible' (*p*) or even 'not evidently false' (*e*), the formal principle has precedence in second-order balancing over the substantive principle, which, taken in isolation, requires the value 'reliable' or 'certain' (*r*) in cases of interference. However, this precedence

40 Ibid., 417.

41 In the Postscript of *A Theory of Constitutional Rights*, I have formulated a 'Law of Combination' which runs as follows: 'Procedural formal principles can override substantive constitutional rights principles only in connection with other substantive principles'; ibid., 423. At first glance, this can be read as an acknowledgement of the combination or mixed substantive-formal model. In a more recent publication I have proposed that this admittedly unhappy formulation should be understood in a way in which the clause 'in connection with' refers to 'a second-order relation of a formal principle to a first-order relation between substantive principles'; Robert Alexy, 'Comments and Responses', in *Institutionalized Reason. The Jurisprudence of Robert Alexy*, ed. Matthias Klatt (Oxford: Oxford University Press, 2012), 319–56, at 331. This, too, is in need of clarification. As a balancing relation, the second-order relation is a relation between a formal and a substantive principle. This second-order balancing relation is related to a first-order balancing relation which is deeply determined by the results of striking a balance between a formal and a substantive principle at the second level, but in which the formal principle does not directly participate.

42 Alexy, *A Theory of Constitutional Rights* (n. 5 above), 53–4.

does not, as such, determine the concrete weight ($W_{i,j}$) of the colliding substantive principle. This concrete weight is determined by all eight variables of the refined Weight Formula. The precedence of the formal principle in cases of merely plausible or even not evidently false empirical assumptions only means that these assumptions are not excluded from balancing. They are admitted on the basis of the formal principle. This admission, however, is linked to their power to reduce the weight of the substantive values of the substantive variables to which they are attached. What concrete effects the inclusion of the epistemic variables into the Weight Formula has depends on the values substituted for all the other variables. The number of constellations is great. If one takes the refined Weight Formula with four variables on each side, that is, with eight variables altogether, one receives, on the basis of the two triadic scales, 3^8, that is, 6561 constellations. The second-order balancing results in nothing other than opening the door for premises below the level of certainty or full reliability to balancing according to the lines of the Weight Formula. Which role they play there with respect to the final result depends on all the other values.

Incorporating substantive as well as epistemic variables into the Weight Formula is nothing other than connecting the first, that is, the substantive Law of Balancing with the second, that is, the epistemic Law of Balancing. It is of the utmost systematic significance that the protases of the two Laws of Balancing are identical. Both refer to the weight of the interference with the constitutional right as defined by the combination of the intensity of interference and the abstract weight, or, more exactly, by the product of I_i and W_i. This shows that the constitutional rights principle in issue presents the Archimedean point of balancing.[43] This speaks against approaches, like Sieckmann's 'model of competing conceptions of law'[44] and Klatt and Schmidt's 'two-level model',[45] which separate the balancing of substantive principles from the balancing of formal principles. In second-order or meta-balancing, the balancing of formal principles is necessarily a balancing with a colliding substantive principle,[46] and with the result of this balancing, the incorporation of epistemic variables and their scales in the Weight Formula, the formal principles are represented in first-order balancing according to this formula.

[43] Ibid., 419.

[44] Jan Sieckmann, *Recht als normatives System* (Baden-Baden: Nomos, 2009), 200–4 (trans. R. A.).

[45] Klatt and Schmidt, 'Epistemic Discretion in Constitutional Law' (n. 16 above), 100.

[46] It is remarkable that Sieckmann describes the balancing at his second stage as balancing of formal principles in which, nevertheless, substantive principles can play a role: 'On the other hand, substantive principles can become relevant besides formal principles. A high intensity of interference with a constitutional right can, for instance, justify a more extensive constitutional review'; Sieckmann, *Recht als normatives System* (n. 44 above), 204 (trans. R. A.).

VIII. Formal Principles and Discretion

Martin Borowski has argued that

> [t]he variable '*R*', which Alexy inserts into the Weight Formula, is neither a formal principle nor does it establish discretion.[47]

It is, indeed, true that the variable *R* is not a formal principle. But it is false that it does not establish discretion. The *Cannabis* Decision of the German Federal Constitutional Court may serve to explain this. The Court classified the assumption of the legislature that the dangers connected with cannabis products are high as arguable or plausible. On the other hand, it concedes that the contrary thesis, namely, that the dangers are low, held by Judge Sommer in his dissenting vote,[48] is plausible, too. This means that the court classified both the high danger premise and the low danger premise as plausible (*p*). These epistemic classifications both concern the variable R_j in the Weight Formula. The high danger premise and also the low danger premise are the bases of quite different substantive classifications of the importance of an interference with the constitutional right concerned, here with the right to liberty, that is, they lead to different values of the variable I_j. The high danger assumption requires the value serious (*s*), the low danger assumption the value light (*l*). If one assumes first, that the abstract values, W_i and W_j, are equal, that is, that they can be reduced, second, that the intensity of interference with freedom is moderate (*m*), third, that it is certain (*r*) that this interference is caused by the ban on cannabis products, and fourth, that normative epistemic values play no role, one receives the following two results of inserting all this into the Weight Formula. In the case of the high danger assumption this runs as follows:

$$W_{i,j} = \frac{2 \cdot 1}{4 \cdot \frac{1}{2}} = 1$$

With the concrete weight 1, the result is a stalemate, that is, the legislature has structural discretion. The ban on cannabis products remains within the discretion of the legislature. It is, therefore, constitutional. The low danger assumption leads to the opposite result. In numbers:

$$W_{i,j} = \frac{2 \cdot 1}{1 \cdot \frac{1}{2}} = 4$$

47 Borowski, 'Formelle Prinzipien und Gewichtsformel' (n. 3 above), 174 (trans. R. A.).
48 BVerfGE 90, 145 (220).

The number 4 expresses that the constitutional right has precedence over combatting the danger. This means that the ban on cannabis products is disproportional, and therefore unconstitutional.

According to Borowski, the insertion of the variable *R* into the Weight Formula does not establish discretion. Our example, however, shows that and also how inserting this variable into the Weight Formula establishes discretion. When two opposing assumptions have the same epistemic value, here the value plausible (*p*), that is, ½, then an epistemic stalemate exists. Now the decisive point is that in cases of epistemic stalemate the *legislature* has epistemic discretion. With respect to the *Cannabis* Decision this means the legislature is free to decide whether it wants to follow the high danger line, that is, to conceive the ban as constitutional, or to follow the low danger line and to conceive the ban as unconstitutional.[49] With this, the variable *R*, indeed, establishes discretion. It establishes discretion in all cases of epistemic stalemate. If the formal principle did not exist, the substantive constitutional rights principle would either exclude interferences on the basis of only plausible or only not evidently false premises or require that the most favourable premise always be adopted, that is, in the *Cannabis* case, the low danger assumption. What is more, this discretion is indirectly[50] established by the principle of democratically legitimated legislature. It is this formal principle that requires that the reliability variable *R* be inserted into the Weight Formula. Much more could be said about the role of formal principles in balancing. But what has been presented here suffices to indicate how formal principles can influence the balancing of constitutional rights without becoming either a victim of the Scylla of the combination or mixed substantive-formal model, that is, the model that simply adds formal principles into the Weight Formula as reinforcements of substantive principles, or a victim of the Charybdis of the separation model, which attempts to place the balancing of formal principles at a stage where substantive principles are not at home.

[49] Klatt and Schmidt have argued that this reconstruction of the *Cannabis* Decision grants 'the legislature a classification discretion which is far too wide'; Klatt and Schmidt, 'Epistemic Discretion in Constitutional Law' (n. 16 above), 102. This objection is based on their thesis that balancing is necessary already on the level of classifying the intensities of interferences. They call this the 'classification balancing'; ibid., 81. According to Klatt and Schmidt, this classification balancing has the result that the legislature has in the *Cannabis* case no epistemic discretion. The legislature must insert into the Weight Formula the value serious (*s*) for the concrete importance of the dangers connected with the drug, that is, it has to follow the high danger thesis when it determines the value for I_j; ibid., 83. The two authors are well aware that the epistemic values for the high danger thesis as well as for the low danger thesis are the same. Nevertheless, they exclude discretion on the basis of different degrees of danger, that is, on the content of the two competing assumptions. It seems, however, not to be plausible to make the selection of assumptions with equal epistemic values dependent on their content. Their content is a factor that has to be inserted into the Weight Formula, which connects it with all other relevant aspects. See also Matthias Klatt and Johannes Schmidt, *Spielräume im Öffentlichen Recht* (Tübingen: Mohr Siebeck, 2010), 25–7.

[50] See Alexy, 'Comments and Responses' (n. 41 above), 331.

13
Ideal 'Ought' and Optimization

The basis of principles theory is the norm-theoretic distinction between rules and principles. In *A Theory of Constitutional Rights* I define principles as *optimization requirements*. As such, they require 'that something be realized to the greatest extent possible given the legal and factual possibilities'.[1] Rules aside, the legal possibilities are determined essentially by opposing principles. For this reason, principles, each taken alone, always comprise merely *prima facie* requirements. The determination of the appropriate degree of satisfaction of one principle relative to the requirements of other principles is brought about by means of balancing. Thus, balancing is the specific form of the application of principles. By contrast, rules are norms that require something determinate. They are *definitive commands*. Their form of application is subsumption.

Against the definition of principles as optimization requirements, Aulis Aarnio and Jan-Reinard Sieckmann raised, more than twenty years ago, the objection that the concept of optimization requirement is ill-suited for distinguishing between rules and principles. The obligation to optimize has a definitive character. It can only either be fulfilled or not fulfilled, and its complete fulfilment is always obligatory.[2] Aarnio puts this point as follows: 'Either one does or one does not optimize. For example, in the case of conflict between two value principles, the principles must be brought together in the optimum manner, and only in the optimum manner.'[3] He and Sieckmann are right. Optimization requirements are rules. In my reply, ten years later, I introduced the distinction between optimization commands and commands to be optimized. Drawing on this distinction, I classified optimization commands as rules and commands to be optimized as principles. The first is clear and true, but the second leads to problems and is, therefore, in need of explication. The basis of this explication will be the thesis that principles express an 'ideal "ought"',[4] a thesis found in this paper and, indeed, in my very first article on principles theory, stemming from 1979.[5] It is of the greatest importance

[1] Robert Alexy, *A Theory of Constitutional Rights* (1985), trans. Julian Rivers (Oxford: Oxford University Press, 2002), 47.

[2] Jan-Reinard Sieckmann, *Regelmodelle und Prinzipienmodelle des Rechtssystems* (Baden-Baden: Nomos, 1990), 65.

[3] Aulis Aarnio, 'Taking Rules Seriously', *Archives for Philosophy of Law and Social Philosophy*, supplement 42 (1990), 180–92, at 187.

[4] Robert Alexy, 'On the Structure of Legal Principles', *Ratio Juris* 13 (2000), 294–304, at 300.

[5] Robert Alexy, 'Zum Begriff des Rechtsprinzips', *Rechtstheorie*, supplement 1 (1979), 59–87, at 79–82.

Law's Ideal Dimension. Robert Alexy, Oxford University Press. © Robert Alexy 2021.
DOI: 10.1093/oso/9780198796831.003.0014

for principles theory that there exists a necessary connection between optimization requirements and the ideal 'ought'. To say it in the words I used in my reply to Aarnio and Sieckmann: 'The ideal "ought" implies the optimization command and *vice versa*. These are two sides of the same coin.'[6]

Poscher, in 2007, raised the objection that principles *qua* ideal 'ought' are not necessary.[7] The 'interpretation of principles as optimization requirements does not require that commands actually be optimized but only that they constitute non-normative objects of optimization'.[8] This non-necessity thesis is connected with a non-existence thesis, which maintains that 'principles that do not have the structure of rules ... [do] not exist'.[9] I have attempted to refute the non-existence thesis as well as the non-necessity thesis by means of an index model of the ideal 'ought', published in 2009.[10] This model, too, has been criticized by Poscher[11] and by Sieckmann.[12] Poscher's critique stems from a point of view outside principles theory, whereas Sieckmann's critique comes from a point of view within principles theory. My reply to both begins with a presentation of the index model.

I. The Index Model of the Ideal 'Ought'

The basis of the index model is the distinction between two kinds of deontic modalities. Those of the first group concern the ideal 'ought'. They are expressed, for instance, in the following way:

(1) $$O_i\, p$$

The other deontic modalities can certainly also be indexed in this way, that is to say, $F_i\, p$ and $P_i\, p$ are possible as well. The modalities of the second group concern the real 'ought'. They are expressed as follows:

(2) $$O_r\, p$$

[6] Alexy, 'On the Structure of Legal Principles' (n. 4 above) 301.

[7] Ralf Poscher, 'Einsichten, Irrtümer und Selbstmissverständnis der Prinzipentheorie', in *Die Prinzipientheorie der Grundrechte. Studien zur Grundrechtstheorie Robert Alexys*, ed. Jan-Reinard Sieckmann (Baden-Baden: Nomos, 2007), 59–79, at 69.

[8] Ralf Poscher, 'The Principles Theory. How Many Theories and What is Their Merit?' in *Institutionalized Reason. The Jurisprudence of Robert Alexy*, ed. Matthias Klatt (Oxford: Oxford University Press, 2012), 218–47, at 233.

[9] Ibid., 235.

[10] Robert Alexy, 'Ideales Sollen', in *Grundrechte, Prinzipien und Argumentation. Studien zur Rechtstheorie Robert Alexys*, eds Laura Clérico and Jan-Reinard Sieckmann (Baden-Baden: Nomos, 2009), 21–38.

[11] Ralf Poscher, 'Theorie eines Phantoms—Die erfolglose Suche der Prinzipientheorie nach ihrem Gegenstand', *Rechtswissenschaft* 1 (2010), 349–72.

[12] Jan-Reinard Sieckmann, 'Prinzipien, ideales Sollen und normative Argumente', *Archives for Philosophy of Law and Social Philosophy* 97 (2011), 178–97.

The other deontic modalities can also be indexed in this way.

The ideal 'ought', expressed by '$O_i p$', is an 'ought' that abstracts from any countervailing 'ought', be it a right or a duty. This abstraction means that it is not yet related to limited possibilities of the normative world.[13] In this sense, it expresses an ideal. This abstraction from countervailing reasons implies that the ideal 'ought' is only a *prima facie*[14] or *pro tanto* 'ought'.[15] By contrast, the real 'ought', expressed by '$O_r p$', is a definitive 'ought' or an 'ought' all things considered. In this way, '$O_i p$' and '$O_r p$' count as a formal reconstruction of the distinction between rules and principles.

This formal reconstruction would be of little value if the index model offered no more than a new notation. This, however, is not the case. The notation presented is the basis for two rules that express in a formal way an insight of principles theory that is so fundamental that one might speak of them as the two 'basic axioms of principles theory'. They run, formulated with the help of the possibility operator '$\Diamond$', as follows:

(3) $$\Diamond (O_i p \,\&\, O_i \neg p)$$

(4) $$\neg \Diamond (O_r p \,\&\, O_r \neg p)$$

The formulation at (3), we can call it 'axiom 1' or the 'first axiom', states that a contradiction of norms at the ideal level is possible in the sense that both norms retain their validity. The formulation at (4), we can call it 'axiom 2' or the second axiom, states that a contradiction of norms at the real level is not possible in the sense that both norms retain their validity. This makes explicit the different structures for resolving conflicts of principles and rules. Competing principles and their implications in concrete cases remain valid even if they are outweighed by another principle. That is, the competition is resolved by means of the dimension of weight, not by means of the dimension of validity. By contrast, a conflict of rules is resolved by means of the dimension of validity in that one of the conflicting rules is declared to be completely invalid or in that an exception clause is read into it,[16] which is to declare it as partially invalid.[17] It is of greatest importance that both the conflict that arises in connection with the ideal 'ought' and the conflict that arises in connection with the real 'ought' are conflicts of norms. Thus, we arrive at an initial intermediate result. The ideal 'ought' and, with it, principles, exist if there exist conflicts of norms that arise in connection with the ideal 'ought', and principles are

[13] The optimization relative to the factual possibilities concerns not limitation but extension.

[14] See Alexy, *A Theory of Constitutional Rights* (n. 1, above), 57–9.

[15] See S. L. Hurley, *Natural Reasons. Personality and Polity* (Oxford: Oxford University Press, 1989), 130.

[16] See Alexy, *A Theory of Constitutional Rights* (n. 1 above), 49–50.

[17] See Christoph Kallmeyer, *Ideales Sollen. Eine Analyse der Prinzipienkonstruktion* (Baden-Baden: Nomos, 2016), 157.

necessary if the solution of these conflicts can be adequately understood only on the basis of the first axiom.

II. The Law of Competing Principles

Along with the two axioms, there are two laws that are constitutive for principles theory: the Law of Competing Principles and the Law of Balancing, which is further elaborated by the Weight Formula. In order to answer the question of whether there exist conflicts of norms in the context of the ideal 'ought', it is well to have a look at the Law of Competing Principles. For this law, two concepts are constitutive. The first is the relation of precedence. This relation is symbolized by 'P'. The second is the condition of precedence. It is symbolized by 'C'. The result of each application of the Weight Formula can be expressed on the basis of these two concepts. The standard form is:

$$(5) \qquad (P_i \mathbf{P} P_j)C$$

This formula expresses a conditional relation of precedence. It is to be read as follows: 'Principle P_i precedes principle P_j under the condition C'. The decisive point is that this conditional relation of precedence implies a rule. Precisely this implication is expressed by the Law of Competing Principles, which runs as follows:

> If principle P_i takes precedence over principle P_j in circumstances C: $(P_i \mathbf{P} P_j)C$, and if P_i gives rise to legal consequences Q in circumstances C, then a valid rule applies which has C as its protasis and Q as its apodosis: $C \rightarrow Q$.[18]

In order to illustrate this, it might be useful to turn to a case. The case in question is a decision of the German Federal Constitutional Court that concerns the classic conflict between freedom of expression and personality right.[19] Specifically, the case concerns a paraplegic reserve officer who had successfully carried out his responsibilities, having been called to active duty. A widely published satirical magazine, *Titanic*, described him first as a 'born murderer' and in a later edition as a 'cripple'. The Düsseldorf Higher Regional Court of Appeal ruled against *Titanic* in an action brought by the officer and ordered the magazine to pay damages in the amount of DM 12,000. In its constitutional complaint, appealing to this decision, the *Titanic* was successful insofar as the Constitutional Court's decision relates to damages for the description 'born murderer'. As far as the description 'cripple' was

[18] Alexy, *A Theory of Constitutional Rights* (n. 1 above), 54.
[19] Decisions of the German Federal Constitutional Court (BVerfGE) 86, 1.

concerned, the constitutional complaint was rejected. Only the first point shall be considered in what follows.

Principles can be more or less abstract. The most abstract version of the principle of freedom of expression is the requirement of a state of affairs[20] in which freedom of expression is realized to the greatest extent possible. One can call principles of this kind 'principles at the highest level of abstraction'.[21] At this level, principles are closest to values.[22] Where constitutional rights are concerned, principles have the character of constitutional permissive norms as well as the character of constitutional prohibitions of interferences.[23] Here only the permissive norm addressed to the *Titanic* shall be considered. It can be expressed as follows:

(6) $$\forall x\left(S_1 x \rightarrow \mathrm{P_i}\, Rx\right)$$

(6) may be read as follows: For all x ($\forall x$), if x is an expression of opinion (S_1), then ($\rightarrow$) its performance or realization (R) is *prima facie* constitutionally permitted ($\mathrm{P_i}$). The Federal Constitutional Court has justifiably classified the description of the paraplegic reserve officer as a 'born murderer' and as a 'cripple' as an expression of opinion. Letting 'a' stand for the description 'born murderer' yields

(7) $$S_1 a$$

From (6) and (7), one arrives at

(8) $$\mathrm{P_i}\, Ra$$

(8) follows logically, according to the basic scheme of subsumption, from (6) and (7). (8) states: it is *prima facie* permitted that the paraplegic reserve officer is described as a 'born murderer'. The special feature of (8) is that it has a concrete as well as an ideal character, expressed by the index.

The principle of freedom of expression (6) collides in our case with the personality right. This principle has a complex structure. A gross simplification will suffice here. It leads to a counterpart to the competing principle of freedom of expression:

(9) $$\forall x\left(S_2 x \rightarrow \neg \mathrm{P_i}\, Rx\right)$$

[20] See Alexy, *A Theory of Constitutional Rights* (n. 1 above), 92.
[21] Ibid., 354.
[22] See ibid., 92–3.
[23] See ibid., 196–200.

(9) may be read as follows: For all x ($\forall x$), if x is an interference with the personality right (S_2), then ($\rightarrow$) its performance or realization (R) is *prima facie* constitutionally not permitted ($\neg P_i$), that is, it is forbidden. If one classifies the description of the paraplegic reserve officer as a 'born murderer' as an interference with the personality right (S_2), expressed as (10):

(10) $$S_2 a$$

then

(11) $$\neg P_i\, Ra$$

follows logically, again according to the basic scheme of subsumption, from (9) and (10). This, however, means that the application of the two principles to the *Titanic* case leads to a contradiction between two concrete instances of the ideal 'ought'. According to the first axiom, this contradiction is possible without any loss of validity. But this does not mean that this contradiction does not exist. It exists because the two rights colliding in the *Titanic* case are both valid, that is, both exist, and it is therefore incumbent on me to explain what a collision of rights is. It is a collision or conflict not of empirical entities,[24] but of norms, more exactly, of norms that have the character of principles. The collision consists of a contradiction, which has to be resolved by balancing according to the third sub-principle of proportionality. Establishing a collision is only the first step in the balancing process. The second axiom shows that the collision must be resolved if one is going to arrive at the level of the real or definitive 'ought'. That is, the ideal contradiction cannot be transformed into a real contradiction. If such a transformation were possible, the law would lose its power to regulate human behaviour. For this reason, only one of the two contradicting instances of the ideal 'ought', in our case either the permission to describe the paraplegic reserve officer as a 'born murderer', as expressed in (8) P_i Ra, or the prohibition to do so, as expressed in (11) $\neg P_i\, Ra$, can pass to the level of the real 'ought'. This selection is regulated by the two basic laws of principles theory, the Law of Competing Principles and the Law of Balancing, the latter in the form familiar from the Weight Formula.

The Law of Competing Principles says what it means to transform an ideal or *prima facie* 'ought' to a real or definitive 'ought'. The Weight Formula establishes the criteria for this transformation. In order to demonstrate how, according to

[24] Collisions or conflicts of rights cannot be explained at a purely descriptive or empirical level. At a purely empirical level, only causal effects are possible. That p causes q does not represent, as such, a conflict. A drill that penetrates into a wall produces, indeed, a drilled hole, but this is not a case of a conflict between the drill and the wall. See Robert Alexy, 'Jörn Ipsens Konstruktion der Grundrechte', *Der Staat* 52 (2013), 87–98, at 91.

the Law of Competing Principles, the transformation is performed, the principle of freedom of expression, as formulated above in (6), shall be given the short notation P_1, whereas the personality right (9) is designated as P_2. Now, the Federal Constitutional Court, with respect to the description of the paraplegic reserve officer as a 'born murderer', gives precedence to freedom of expression owing to the satirical context. The condition 'description of a paraplegic reserve officer as a "born murderer" in a satirical context' stands for the variable 'C' in the Law of Competing Principles, where it expresses the condition of preference. The condition in our case just mentioned shall be designated by 'C_1'. This yields the following preferential statement:

(12) $$(P_1 \mathbf{P} P_2)C_1$$

The point of the Law of Competing Principles is that this preferential statement (12) implies a rule that has C_1 as its *protasis* and the legal consequences to which P_1 gives rise in our case, that is, the permission of the description 'born murderer', as its *apodosis*. It is of the utmost importance that this permission is no longer an ideal permission. It is a real or definitive permission, which can be noted as 'P_r', for it derives from the solution to the collision of the two principles by the establishing of the conditional relation of precedence expressed by (12). In this way, (8), that is, $\mathrm{P}_i\,Ra$, is transformed into

(13) $$\mathrm{P}_r\,Ra$$

This transition from the ideal level to the real level would not be possible if principles did not exist, for it is not possible to derive something from something that does not exist. Without understanding, first, what a conflict of *prima facie* or ideal obligations is, and second, how it is resolved by a transformation of the ideal 'ought' into a real 'ought' by means of a conditional relation of precedence, one cannot understand what balancing is. This suffices to establish the existence and necessity of principles *qua* ideal 'ought'.

To be sure, all this is necessary but not yet sufficient for understanding or constructing balancing. A complete understanding is not possible without the second law of principles theory, the Law of Balancing.

III. The Weight Formula

The Law of Balancing, which is identical with the third sub-principle of the principle of proportionality, the principle of proportionality in the narrower sense, states:

> The greater the degree of non-satisfaction of, or detriment to, one principle, the greater must be the importance of satisfying the other.[25]

Nearly everywhere in constitutional adjudication, the Law of Balancing is found in various different formulations. It expresses the essence of balancing and is of great practical importance. If, however, one wishes to achieve a precise and complete analysis of the structure of balancing, the Law of Balancing has to be elaborated further. The result of such a further elaboration is the Weight Formula.[26] It runs as follows:

$$W_{i,j} = \frac{I_i \cdot W_i \cdot R_i}{I_j \cdot W_j \cdot R_j}$$

'$W_{i,j}$' represents the concrete weight of the principle P_i relative to the colliding principle P_j. The Weight Formula defines this concrete weight as the quotient of three factors standing, so to speak, on each side of balancing. I_i and I_j are of special importance. 'I_i' stands for the intensity of interference with P_i. 'I_j' represents the importance of satisfying the colliding principle. I_j, too, can be understood as intensity of interference, that is, as the intensity of interference with P_j through non-interference with P_i. 'W_i' and 'W_j' stand for the abstract weights of the colliding principles P_i and P_j. When the abstract weights are equal, which is often the case in collisions between constitutional rights, they cancel each other out. 'R_i' and 'R_j' represent two factors that have received ever greater attention in recent discussions on constitutional rights. They refer to the reliability of the empirical and normative assumptions concerning the question of how intensive the interference with P_i is, and how intensive the interference with P_j would be if the interference with P_i were omitted.

IV. Law of Competing Principles and Law of Balancing

The Weight Formula stands in the centre of the debate over principles theory. Nevertheless, it will not be discussed here.[27] Only its relation to the Law of Competing Principles shall be considered. This relation is a justification relation. The Weight Formula makes explicit the form of the justification of the preferential statement $(P_i\mathbf{P}P_j)C$, which makes possible the transition from the ideal to the real 'ought'. Three preferential relations are possible: (1) P_i takes precedence over P_j, (2) P_j takes precedence over P_i, and (3) neither takes precedence over the other.

[25] Alexy, *A Theory of Constitutional Rights* (n. 1 above), 102.

[26] Robert Alexy, 'The Weight Formula', trans. Bartosz Brożek and Stanley L. Paulson, in *Studies in the Philosophy of Law*, vol. 3, eds Jerzy Stelmach, Bartosz Brożek, and Wojciech Załuski (Kraków: Jagiellonian University Press, 2007), 9–27, at 25 (in this volume: Chapter 11, 154–74, at 172).

[27] See ibid., 20–7 (Chapter 11, 165–73).

To these three precedence possibilities there correspond three possible concrete weights: (1) $W_{i,j}$ can be greater than 1, (2) it can be less than 1, and (3) it can be 1. If it is greater than 1, P_i takes precedence over P_j, if it is less than 1, P_j takes precedence over P_i, and if it is 1, a stalemate exists. In this case, neither does P_i take precedence over P_j nor does P_j take precedence over P_i. This means that the state, in particular the legislator, has discretion. This can be described by three rules that be called the 'connection rules':

(14) (a) $W_{i,j} > 1 \rightarrow (P_i \mathbf{P} P_j)C$

(b) $W_{i,j} < 1 \rightarrow (P_j \mathbf{P} P_i)C$

(c) $W_{i,j} = 1 \rightarrow \neg(P_i \mathbf{P} P_j)C \& \neg(P_j \mathbf{P} P_i)C$ (stalemate).

The connection rules show that the connection between the Law of Competing Principles and the Weight Formula, and thus the connection to the Law of Balancing, is as close as possible. This, in turn, means that there exists an intrinsic connection between the two axioms and the two laws of principles theory. They form a system. Without the ideal 'ought', the system would be incomplete. This is the core of the proof of the existence of principles as well as the proof of their necessity.

V. A Fundamental Equivalence

On the basis of the two axioms and the two laws, a fundamental equivalence can be formulated:

(15) $\mathrm{O_r}\, Opt\, p \leftrightarrow \mathrm{O_i}\, p$

'$\mathrm{O_i} p$' represents the ideal 'ought'. It says that it is ideally or *prima facie* obligatory that p. '$\mathrm{O_r}$ *Opt* p' expresses an optimization requirement. The obligation to optimize is a definitive or real obligation. Therefore, it starts with '$\mathrm{O_r}$'. The subject of this real obligation is not the complete realization of p, as in the case of the ideal 'ought', but only the optimization of p.

In my 2009 article on the ideal 'ought', I formalized the equivalence between the ideal 'ought' and the optimization requirement in the following way:

(16) $\mathrm{O}\, Opt\, \mathrm{O}\, p \leftrightarrow \mathrm{O_i}\, p$[28]

[28] Alexy, 'Ideales Sollen' (n. 10 above), 25.

The subject of optimization, however, is the same as the subject of the ideal 'ought', and this is a state of affairs in the broadest sense, represented by *p*. In the earlier article on the ideal 'ought', I said that optimization requirements can be expressed by

(17) $O Opt\, p$

as well as by

(18) $O Opt\, O\, p$ [29]

This must be corrected. Only the first formalization (17) is adequate. In this point, Poscher's critique[30] is correct. A second correction of the old formula is that 'O' at the beginning of the equivalence is replaced by 'O_r'. These two corrections of the fundamental equivalence do not mean, however, that the central thesis of my reply to Aarnio and Sieckmann in 2000, which says that the ideal 'ought' implies the optimization requirement and vice versa,[31] has to be corrected. On the contrary, embedded in the system of the two axioms and the two laws of principles theory, this thesis of mine is corroborated.

VI. Poscher's Argument from Identity

One of Poscher's main arguments for his thesis that 'principles that do not have the character of rules [do] not exist'[32] is his argument from identity. The argument claims that an analysis of 'collision[s] between norms shows ... that rules and principles are structured identically and differ only in their contingent contents within a single normative structure'.[33] The reason for this, Poscher continues, is that first, all norms have the structure of rules and that, second, only the content of those 'exception clauses'[34] that solve the conflict is different. As a means of demonstrating this, he uses the following example:

> $N1_c$: If an action endangers foreign interests of the state that *outweigh it*, this action can be prohibited.
>
> $N2_c$: If an action serves the press *and does not endanger foreign interests of the state that outweigh it*, the state must refrain from prohibitions.[35]

[29] Ibid., 24.
[30] Poscher, 'Theorie eines Phantoms—Die erfolglose Suche der Prinzipientheorie nach ihrem Gegenstand' (n. 11 above), 359.
[31] Alexy, 'On the Structure of Legal Principles' (n.5 above), 301
[32] Poscher, 'The Principles Theory. How Many Theories and What is their Merit?' (n. 8 above), 235.
[33] Ibid., 230.
[34] Ibid.
[35] Ibid., 231.

The exception clauses in these two norms refer, without question, to balancing and the two norms have, indeed, the character of rules. But this presents no problem for principles theory, which incorporates this with its concept of 'double aspect constitutional rights norms'.[36] Double aspect constitutional rights norms are constitutional rights norms that have a limitation clause 'referring to competing principles'.[37] This is exactly the type of norm to which Poscher refers with $N1_c$ and $N2_c$. He misses the point, however, when he maintains that the step from a norm with an exemption clause that does not require balancing to a norm with an exemption clause that does require balancing is 'only a small step'.[38] It is in fact 'a great step, indeed, a leap from subsumption to balancing'.[39] It is impossible to grasp the nature of a limiting clause that refers to balancing and, with it, the structure of the rule that contains it, without having recourse to the concept of collision between principles or rights. Collisions of principles, however, can exist only if principles exist. Optimization requirements do not suffice to reconstruct collisions between principles or rights, for optimization requirements as such cannot collide. Only the ideal 'ought', connected with them by the fundamental equation, can do this. In short, Poscher's attempt to reconstruct collisions between constitutional rights exclusively at the level of rules is doomed to fail.[40]

VII. Sieckmann's Reiterated Validity Obligations

By contrast with Poscher, Sieckmann defends the thesis that principles express an ideal 'ought'.[41] Nevertheless, he radically criticizes the index model defended here. His critique culminates in the thesis that 'the Alexyian conception . . . seems to be a principles theory without principles'.[42] Thus, he arrives from a point of view inside principles theory at the same result as Poscher from a point of view outside principles theory.

Sieckmann's critique is based on two theses. The first says that principles *qua* ideal 'ought' have to be constructed as infinitely reiterated validity obligations.[43] The second thesis claims that the distinction between rules and principles has to

[36] Alexy, *A Theory of Constitutional Rights* (n. 1 above), 85.

[37] Ibid.

[38] Poscher, 'The Principles Theory. How Many Theories and What is their Merit?' (n. 8 above), 231.

[39] Robert Alexy, 'Comments and Responses', in *Institutionalized Reason. The Jurisprudence of Robert Alexy*, ed. Matthias Klatt (Oxford: Oxford University Press, 2012), 319–56, at 343.

[40] To this, an argument might be added that refers to the construction of constitutional rights. I shall not, however, discuss this here; see ibid., 345, and Alexy, 'Ideales Sollen' (n. 10 above), 31–2.

[41] Sieckmann, ' Prinzipien, ideales Sollen und normative Argumente' (n. 12 above), 180.

[42] Jan-Reinard Sieckmann, 'Zur Prinzipientheorie Robert Alexys. Gemeinsamkeiten und Differenzen', in *Prinzipientheorie und Theorie der Abwägung*, ed. Matthias Klatt (Tübingen: Mohr Siebeck, 2013), 271–95, at 273 (trans. R. A.).

[43] Sieckmann, 'Prinzipien, ideales Sollen und normative Argumente' (n. 12 above), 183–92.

be based on the distinction between normative propositions and normative arguments.[44] I will begin with the argument of infinite reiteration.

The starting point of the thesis of infinite reiteration of validity obligations is plausible. The analysis of the *Titanic* Decision presented earlier can be interpreted in the sense that principles require the validity of certain norms. In our case the norms in question are that the description of the paraplegic reserve officer as a 'born murderer' is permitted (8), and that the description of the paraplegic reserve officer as a 'born murderer' is prohibited (11). For this reason, the idea of a validity obligation presents one possibility for reconstructing the normative impact of principles. And Sieckmann is also right when he says that 'the "ought" that is contained in validity obligations'[45] cannot, on the one hand, be definitely valid, for this would preclude the possibility of 'colliding principles also claiming validity',[46] but this 'ought' must, on the other hand, 'possess some form of validity'.[47] That is to say that validity obligations must be neither definitively valid nor invalid. In my first critique of Sieckmann's reiteration thesis, published in 2000, I characterized this thesis as a 'middle course',[48] that is, as an attempt to establish some kind of validity between definitive validity and lack of validity. The ideal 'ought' of the index model can be understood just in this sense. And I agreed with Sieckmann up to this point. But I cannot agree with his thesis that infinitely reiterated validity obligations count as an adequate construction of the special validity of principles.

The reiteration model begins with the thesis that validity obligations have the following structure:

(19) $$\mathrm{O\,VAL_{DEF}N}$$ [49]

In the *Titanic* case, a validity obligation of this structure would require that it shall be definitively valid that all expressions of opinion are permitted. Now, Sieckmann's formula $\mathrm{O\ VAL_{DEF}N}$ can neither express a definitive obligation nor a non-obligation if it is supposed to express an ideal 'ought'. And here the problem begins. Sieckmann attempts to make the middle course explicit by means of reiteration. With this, the first validity obligation is, at a second level, transformed into a validity obligation that requires that '[i]t shall be definitively valid that it shall be definitively valid that all expressions of opinion are permitted'.[50] At this

[44] Sieckmann, 'Zur Prinzipientheorie Robert Alexys. Gemeinsamkeiten und Differenzen' (n. 42 above), 274.

[45] Sieckmann, 'Prinzipien, ideales Sollen und normative Argumente' (n. 12 above), 190 (trans. R. A.).

[46] Ibid., (trans. R. A.).

[47] Ibid., (trans. R. A.).

[48] Alexy, 'On the Structure of Legal Principles' (n. 4 above), 302.

[49] Sieckmann, 'Prinzipien, ideales Sollen und normative Argumente' (n. 12 above), 190.

[50] Ibid., (trans. R. A.).

second level, the problem of definitiveness arises again, which results from the fact that a definitive 'ought' is never an ideal 'ought'. Sieckmann's 'solution'[51] consists in adding a third level to the second one: 'It shall be definitively valid that it shall be definitively valid that it shall be definitively valid that all expressions of opinion are permitted',[52] and this has to be continued infinitely. Sieckmann's formal reconstruction of all of this looks like this:

(20) $$(1)\ O\,VAL_{DEF}N$$

$$(2)\ O\,VAL_{DEF}\,O\,VAL_{DEF}\,N$$

$$(3)\ O\,VAL_{DEF}\,O\,VAL_{DEF}\,O\,VAL_{DEF}\,N,$$

etc.[53]

In my first objection, I classified this as a 'continuous oscillation' that 'describes in a relatively complicated way the notion that principles stand somewhere between definitive validity and non-obligation',[54] and I argued that this is not enough to serve 'as an explanation of the character of the principle'.[55]

Sieckmann has replied that this objection fails because it is based on an incomplete description of the model of infinite reiteration. It separates the different levels on which definitive validity stands on the one side and non-obligation on the other. With this, 'the infinite structure of reiterated validity obligations and the possibilities of argumentation resulting from it... are not seen'.[56] I answer here that I do see the infinite structure, but I do not see that it adds anything to the understanding of the structure of principles. Sieckmann points in his reply to possibilities of argumentation resulting from the infinite structure. This leads to his second thesis, which says that for the distinction between rules and principles one has to substitute the distinction between 'normative propositions and normative arguments'.[57]

Sieckmann's thesis is that the index model of the ideal 'ought' does not 'allow the construction of reasons with the character of principles that can justify definitive balancing judgements'.[58] His reason for this is that the ideal 'ought' expressed by $O_i\,p$ is an 'ought' that abstracts from any countervailing 'ought'. This

[51] Ibid., (trans. R. A.).
[52] Ibid., (trans. R. A.).
[53] Ibid.
[54] Alexy, 'On the Structure of Legal Principles' (n. 4 above), 303.
[55] Ibid.
[56] Sieckmann, 'Prinzipien, ideales Sollen und normative Argumente' (n. 12 above), 193 (trans. R. A.).
[57] Sieckmann, 'Zur Prinzipientheorie Robert Alexys. Gemeinsamkeiten und Differenzen' (n. 42 above), 274 (trans. R. A.).
[58] Sieckmann, 'Prinzipien, ideales Sollen und normative Argumente' (n. 12 above), 183 (trans. R. A.).

abstraction implies that it is only a *prima facie* or *pro tanto* 'ought'. Sieckmann maintains that it is impossible to 'construct reasons for balancing'[59] on this basis. This is said to result from the necessity of 'including counter reasons in balancing'.[60] Now I completely agree with Sieckmann that counter reasons must be included in balancing. Balancing without competing reasons would not be balancing. But I contest the thesis that the abstract character of the ideal 'ought' in the index model precludes the inclusion of the competing ideal norms in balancing. Quite the opposite is the case.

The *Titanic* case can once again serve as an example. If one applies the two abstract principles of freedom of expression and protection of personality, formalized above as (6) and (9), to the case, one acquires two concrete ideal norms, (8) and (11), that contradict each other. In the index model, with this contradiction, which is, according to axiom 1, possible, balancing begins and it begins in order to select, as required by axiom 2, one of the two concrete norms[61] for the level of the real 'ought'. All of this is carried out by applying the two laws of principles theory, the Law of Competing Principles and the Balancing Law, the latter as explicated by the Weight Formula. Thus, the colliding reasons are closely and systematically connected.

The basis of Sieckmann's critique is his concept of argument. According to Sieckmann, 'the relation between balancing reasons and balancing results is not a logical inference but has the structure of a normative demand'.[62] Balancing reasons demand that the norm in question is acknowledged as definitively valid. With this, they do not concern the correctness or truth of a judgement or proposition, but require the performance of an action, for, so Sieckmann, the 'determination of a balancing result is an action'.[63]

I agree with Sieckmann that the institutional or authoritative striking of a balancing, as performed by judges, is an action. But if this action is to be rational, it must be preceded by a judgment in form of a proposition. In the *Titanic* case, this judgment can take the following form: 'The freedom of expression has a higher concrete weight than the personality right as far as the description of the paraplegic reserve officer as a "born murderer" in a satirical context is concerned.' This is a proposition that raises a claim to correctness, a claim that has to be justified in legal discourse. In *A Theory of Legal Argumentation*, I defined the concept of argument as follows: 'An *argument* consists of the propositions belonging to a single argument form which are adduced in support of a further proposition.'[64] This is

[59] Ibid., 184 (trans. R. A.).
[60] Ibid., (trans. R. A.).
[61] The possibility of a stalemate, see (14)(c), shall not be considered here.
[62] Ibid., 188 (trans. R. A.).
[63] Ibid., (trans. R. A.).
[64] Robert Alexy, *A Theory of Legal Argumentation* (1978), trans. Ruth Adler and Neil MacCormick (Oxford: Clarendon Press, 1989), 92.

an expression of the propositionality thesis. Sieckmann defends a pragmatically orientated non-propositionality thesis.[65] I agree with Sieckmann that the pragmatic dimension of argumentation must be taken seriously. Discourse theory attempts to make the pragmatic dimension explicit by means of a system of rules and forms of general practical and legal discourse. But this does not imply that propositions, which can be true or false, correct or incorrect, thereby lose their central role. On the contrary, discursive rationality presupposes propositionality.

[65] Sieckmann, 'Prinzipien, ideales Sollen und normative Argumente' (n. 12 above), 195.

14
Human Dignity and Proportionality

I. Absolute and Relative Conceptions of Human Dignity

The relation between proportionality analysis and human dignity is one of the most contested questions in the debate about the normative structure of human dignity. Two conceptions stand in opposition: an absolute and a relative conception. According to the absolute conception, the guarantee of human dignity counts as a norm that takes precedence over all other norms in all cases. Taking precedence over all other norms in all cases implies that balancing is precluded. This, in turn, means that each and every interference with human dignity is a violation of human dignity. Thus, justified interference with human dignity becomes impossible. By contrast, proportionality analysis is intrinsically connected to the distinction between justified and unjustified interferences. A proportional interference is justified and is, therefore, constitutional. The opposite applies in the case of disproportional interference. The absolute conception is incompatible with this conceptual framework. For this reason, it is incompatible with proportionality analysis. According to the relative conception, precisely the opposite is true. The relative conception says that the question of whether human dignity is violated is a question of proportionality. With this, the relative conception is not only compatible with proportionality analysis but it presupposes it.

II. Practical Significance

The question of whether the absolute or the relative conception is right, one might well thing, is no more than a highly abstract theoretical question. Just the opposite, however, is the case. This can be illustrated by turning to the adjudication of the German Federal Constitutional Court, which is characterized by a number of inconsistencies. Sometimes the Court points in the direction of the absolute conception, sometimes it follows the relative line. An example of a decision with a strong absolute touch is the decision from 1973 on secret tape-recordings. The Court emphasizes that human dignity requires an 'absolutely protected core area of private self-determination'[1], and determines the relationship between the concept of absolute protection and the concept of balancing in the following way:

[1] Decisions of the German Federal Constitutional Court (BVerfGE) 34, 238 (245) (trans. R. A.).

Law's Ideal Dimension. Robert Alexy, Oxford University Press. © Robert Alexy 2021.
DOI: 10.1093/oso/9780198796831.003.0015

> Even outweighing public interests cannot justify an infringement of the absolutely protected core area of private self-determination; no balancing in accordance with the principle of proportionality takes place.[2]

In its opinion on the acoustic observation of accommodation, decided more than thirty years later, the Court confirmed this.[3] Nevertheless, this claim strikes one as puzzling.[4] Is it to be understood that human dignity takes precedence even in those cases where, *from the perspective of constitutional law*, a competing principle has greater weight? This would boil down to a contradiction. Having greater weight from the perspective of constitutional law implies precedence over whatever has lesser weight from the standpoint of constitutional law. In this interpretation, the claim quoted says that the colliding principle takes precedence and does not take precedence. To avoid this contradiction, the phrase 'outweighing public interests' must be understood as referring to interests that outweigh from some perspective other than that of constitutional law, say, from a political perspective. But then the thesis of the absolutely protected core area would become superfluous. Reasons that have no constitutional status[5] cannot outweigh reasons that have constitutional status.

On the level of self-characterization, the absolute line dominates. As soon as one turns to the details, however, the relative side emerges more and more clearly. An example is the decision on life imprisonment from 1977. The Court states:

> Human dignity is also not violated if the completion of the sentence is rendered necessary by the continued danger represented by the prisoner and if on this basis early release is excluded... In cases where the danger represented by the criminal offender has to be determined ... there is no need for further substantiation that the principle of proportionality has to be observed.[6]

This is a clear case of proportionality analysis. Human dignity is considered as a principle that collides with the principle of public security. The collision has to be resolved by giving adequate weight to both, that is to say, by balancing. This has been corroborated in an opinion concerned with preventive detention, decided in 2004.[7]

Many more examples could be adduced.[8] Here only one further case shall be considered, a case that is perhaps the judicial opinion in the adjudication of the German Federal Constitutional Court that connects human dignity with

[2] Ibid., (trans. R. A.).

[3] BVerfGE 109, 279 (313).

[4] Robert Alexy, *A Theory of Constitutional Rights* (1985), trans. Julian Rivers (Oxford: Oxford University Press, 2002), 63, n. 64.

[5] See ibid., 81.

[6] BVerfGE 45, 187 (242) (trans. R. A.).

[7] BVerfGE 109, 133 (151).

[8] See on them Nils Teifke, *Das Prinzip Menschenwürde. Zur Abwägungsfähigkeit des Höchstrangigen* (Tübingen: Mohr Siebeck, 2011), 16–25; Manfred Baldus, 'Menschenwürdegarantie und

proportionality most closely. The case, decided in 1978, concerns the question of whether human dignity is violated when one's hair and beard, which an accused allowed to grow ever since the time of his imprisonment, are altered under compulsion in order to confront him with witnesses who, if they had seen him earlier, would have seen him looking altogether different. The Court denies that there was a violation of human dignity with three arguments. The first is that the interference is of 'relatively low intensity'.[9] Such an assessment of the intensity of interference is the first step of proportionality analysis. The second argument says that the clearing up of criminal offences and the investigation of offenders is a 'preponderant public interest'.[10] With this, human dignity is balanced with public interest. The third argument concludes the justification of the interference by stating that its purpose had nothing to do with 'humiliation'[11] and that it was not connected with any other 'aims that would have to be disapproved by law'.[12] This implies that the question of whether human dignity is violated does not depend alone on the act performed as such but also on the reasons standing behind the act. Under other circumstances the interference might well be disproportional and would therefore count as a violation of human dignity. This interplay of reasons and counter-reasons is the essence of proportionality.

Up to this point, nothing has been said other than to introduce briefly the distinction between the absolute and the relative conception or construction of human dignity and to demonstrate that the adjudication of the German Federal Constitutional Court is, with respect to this distinction, highly unsatisfactory. The question that arises is whether the absolute or the relative conception is correct. My thesis is that the relative construction is, indeed, the correct one but that there exist some features of human dignity that move in the direction of absoluteness. The basis of my argument is principles theory. Therefore, I shall begin with a presentation of some basic elements of principles theory.

III. Some Basic Elements of Principles Theory

A. Rules and Principles

The basis of principles theory is the norm-theoretic distinction between rules and principles.[13] Rules are norms that require something determinate. They are

Absolutheitsthese. Zwischenbericht zu einer zukunftsweisenden Debatte', *Archiv des öffentlichen Rechts* 136 (2011), 529–52, at 536–40.

[9] BVerfGE 47, 239 (247) (trans. R. A.).
[10] BVerfGE 47, 239 (248) (trans. R. A.).
[11] BVerfGE 47, 239 (247) (trans. R. A.).
[12] BVerfGE 47, 239 (247–8) (trans. R. A.).
[13] Alexy, *A Theory of Constitutional Rights* (n. 4 above), 47–8.

definitive commands. Their form of application is subsumption. By contrast, principles are *optimization requirements*. As such, they demand 'that something be realized to the greatest extent possible given the legal and factual possibilities'.[14] Rules aside, the legal possibilities are determined essentially by opposing principles. For this reason, principles, each taken alone, always comprise merely *prima facie* requirements. The determination of the appropriate degree of satisfaction of one principle relative to the requirements of other principles is brought about by means of balancing. Thus, balancing is the specific form of application of principles. If the guarantee of human dignity were absolute, it would have to be considered as a definitive command, that is, as a rule. As a relative guarantee it has the character of a principle, that is, of a norm that requires balancing.

B. Proportionality

The nature of principles as optimization requirements leads immediately to a necessary connection between principles and proportionality analysis. The principle of proportionality, which in the last decades has received ever greater international recognition in the practice and the theory of constitutional review,[15] consists of three sub-principles: the principle of suitability, of necessity, and of proportionality in the narrower sense. All three sub-principles express the idea of optimization. For this reason, the nature of principles implies the principle of proportionality and vice versa.

The principles of suitability and necessity refer to optimization relative to the factual possibilities. Optimization relative to the factual possibilities consists in avoiding avoidable costs.[16] Costs, however, are unavoidable when principles collide. Balancing then becomes necessary. Balancing is the subject of the third sub-principle of the principle of proportionality, namely, the principle of proportionality in the narrower sense. This principle expresses what optimization relative to the legal possibilities means. It is identical with a rule that can be called the 'Law of Balancing'.[17] It states:

> The greater the degree of non-satisfaction of, or detriment to, one principle, the greater must be the importance of satisfying the other.

[14] Ibid., 47.

[15] See, for instance, David M. Beatty, *The Ultimate Rule of Law* (Oxford: Oxford University Press, 2004); Alec Stone Sweet and Jud Mathews, 'Proportionality Balancing and Global Constitutionalism', *Columbia Journal of Transnational Law* 47 (2008), 72–164; Aharon Barak, *Proportionality. Constitutional Rights and their Limitations* (Cambridge: Cambridge University Press, 2012).

[16] See on this Robert Alexy, 'Constitutional Rights and Proportionality', *Chinese Yearbook of Constitutional Law* (2010), 221–35, at 222–4.

[17] Alexy, *A Theory of Constitutional Rights* (n. 4 above), 102.

C. Weight Formula

Nearly everywhere in constitutional adjudication, the Law of Balancing is found in various different formulations. It expresses the essence of balancing and is of great practical importance. The analysis of complex problems of constitutional rights, like that of human dignity, requires, however, a more precise and complete description of the structure of balancing. In order to achieve this, the Law of Balancing has to be elaborated further. The result of such a further elaboration is the Weight Formula.[18] It runs as follows:

$$W_{i,j} = \frac{I_i \cdot W_i \cdot R_i}{I_j \cdot W_j \cdot R_j}$$

$W_{i,j}$ represents the concrete weight of the principle P_i relative to the colliding principle P_j. The Weight Formula defines this concrete weight as the quotient of three factors standing, so to speak, on each side of balancing. I_i and I_j are of special importance. I_i stands for the intensity of interference with P_i. I_j represents the importance of satisfying the colliding principle P_j. I_j, too, can be understood as intensity of interference, that is, as the intensity of interference with P_j through non-interference with P_i. W_i and W_j stand for the abstract weights of the colliding principles P_i and P_j. When the abstract weights are equal, which is the case in many collisions of constitutional rights, they cancel each other out, that is, they play no role. By contrast, the abstract weight of human dignity plays a pivotal role because it is regularly[19] deemed to be greater than that of the colliding principle. This is one of the features of human dignity from which a certain tendency towards absoluteness stems.

I_i and I_j, and also W_i and W_j, concern the substantive dimension of balancing. R_i and R_j have a completely different character. They refer to the reliability of the empirical and normative assumptions concerning, first and foremost, the question of how intensive the interference with P_i is, and how intensive the interference with P_j would be if the interference with P_i were omitted. Over and above this, the reliability of empirical and normative assumptions can also relate to the classification of the abstract weights, that is, to W_i and W_j. The decisive point is that reliability is a factor that does not refer to the things—in our case the intensities of interference and the abstract weights. That is, it is not an ontic factor. Rather, it is a factor that refers to one's knowledge of things. That is, it is an epistemic factor. The

[18] Robert Alexy, 'The Weight Formula', trans. Bartosz Brożek and Stanley L. Paulson, in *Studies in the Philosophy of Law*, vol. 3, eds Jerzy Stelmach, Bartosz Brożek, and Wojciech Załuski (Kraków: Jagiellonian University Press, 2007), 9–27, at 25 (in this volume: Chapter 11, 154–74, at 172).

[19] If one assumes that human dignity is the highest principle of law, its abstract weight is cancelled out only in collisions in which human dignity stands on both sides.

inclusion of this epistemic factor in the Weight Formula is required by a second Law of Balancing, the epistemic Law of Balancing, which runs as follows:

> The more heavily an interference in a constitutional right weighs, the greater must be the certainty of its underlying premises.[20]

The concept of underlying premises used in this formulation comprises normative premises as well as empirical premises. R_i and R_j must therefore be understood as referring to empirical premises as well as to normative premises. This can be expressed by the following equation:

$$R_i = R_i^e \cdot R_i^n$$

This equation might be called 'reliability equation'. In cases in which both empirical and normative reliability are in question, R_i and R_j have to be substituted by the respective products on the right side of the reliability equation. In this way, a refined version of the Weight Formula[21] enters the stage:

$$W_{i,j} = \frac{I_i \cdot W_i \cdot R_i^e \cdot R_i^n}{I_j \cdot W_j \cdot R_j^e \cdot R_j^n}$$

Here only one point is of interest. In the debate over human dignity extreme or tragic collisions play an important role. Examples are the use of torture to force a suspect to reveal the location of a ticking nuclear bomb and bringing down an airplane full of passengers that has been hijacked by terrorists who plan to use it as a weapon to kill as many persons as possible. Torture in the ticking bomb scenario concerns, without any doubt, human dignity. Accepting the death of the passengers is, obviously and profoundly, an interference with their right to life. Whether it is also an interference with their right to human dignity, as the German Federal Constitutional Court assumed, can remain open here. The decisive point is that in both cases the question of whether the interference is justified depends essentially on the reliability of numerous empirical assumptions,[22] that is, on R_j^e. To give it expression in the words of the Court:

> The uncertainties ... necessarily have effects on the prognosis of how long persons on board an airplane which has been transformed into an attack weapon still have

[20] Alexy, *A Theory of Constitutional Rights* (n. 4 above), 418.

[21] See on this Robert Alexy, 'Formal Principles: Some Replies to Critics', *International Journal of Constitutional Law* 12 (2014), 511–24, at 514 (in this volume: Chapter 12, 175–89, at 178).

[22] Martin Borowski, 'Abwehrrechte als grundrechtliche Prinzipien', in *Die Prinzipientheorie der Grundrechte. Studien zur Grundrechtstheorie Robert Alexys*, ed. Jan-Reinard Sieckmann (Baden-Baden: Nomos, 2007), 81–104, at 101–4.

> to live, and whether there is still a chance of saving them. For this reason, it will normally not be possible to make a reliable judgment which says that the lives of these persons are 'anyway already lost'.[23]

A formula like the Weight Formula, which expresses a quotient of two products, is sensible only if all of the factors can be represented by numbers. This is the problem of graduation. Elsewhere,[24] I have proposed a discrete, that is, a non-continuous triadic scale, in which geometric sequences are implemented. This scale assigns the values 'light' (*l*), 'moderate' (*m*), and 'serious' (*s*) to the intensity of interference and to the abstract weights. These values are expressed by the numbers 2^0, 2^1, and 2^2, that is, by 1, 2, and 4. Where the epistemic side is concerned, that is R_i and R_j, or, in the refined version of the Weight Formula, R_i^e and R_i^n as well as R_j^e and R_j^n, one can work with the stages 'reliable' or 'certain' (*r*), 'plausible' (*p*), and 'not evidently false' (*e*), to which the numbers 2^0, 2^{-1}, and 2^{-2}, that is, 1, ½, and ¼, are to be assigned.[25] By means of these triads, most of the decisions of constitutional courts can be grasped. Where they do not suffice, that is, where one has to introduce a still more attenuated graduation, they can be extended to double-triadic scales.[26] A good deal more could be said about the Weight Formula. For a discussion of the relation between human dignity and proportionality, however, what has been said here ought to suffice.

IV. The Concept of Human Dignity

A. Descriptive and Normative Elements

If the guarantee of human dignity can and should have the structure of a principle, then the relative construction is correct. Principles are optimization requirements. The answer to the question of whether the guarantee of human dignity can have the structure of a principle, therefore, boils down to the question of whether human dignity is 'something' that can 'be realized to the greatest extent possible given the legal and factual possibilities'.[27] This, again, depends on what human dignity is, that is to say, it depends on the concept of human dignity. The concept of human dignity is a highly complex concept that connects descriptive or empirical with evaluative or normative elements. The descriptive element most often mentioned is autonomy, and the most prominent formulation stems from Kant: '*Autonomy*

[23] BVerfGE 115, 118 (158) (trans. R. A.).

[24] Alexy, *A Theory of Constitutional Rights* (n. 4 above), 409–10, 419; Alexy, 'The Weight Formula' (n. 18 above), 20–6 (in this volume: Chapter 11, 165–73).

[25] Alexy, 'The Weight Formula' (n. 18 above), 25 in this volume: (Chapter 11, 171).

[26] Ibid., 22–3 (Chapter 11, 168–9).

[27] Alexy, *A Theory of Constitutional Rights* (n. 4 above), 47.

is therefore the ground of the dignity of human nature and of every rational nature.'[28] From the point of view of moral theory, Kant is right. From the point of view of legal theory, however, a broader empirical basis seems to be preferable because the legal protection of human dignity is not confined to the protection of autonomy in the sense of moral self-legislation. It also includes, for instance, the right to exist and the right to make choices of whatever kind.[29] For this reason the concept of human dignity has to be connected with a broader descriptive basis. Such a broader descriptive or empirical basis is provided by the concept of person, which, as including autonomy, in Kant's writings also plays a pivotal role.[30]

B. The 'Double-Triadic' Concept of Person

My main thesis about the concept of person is that this concept has a double-triadic structure.[31] In order to be a person, one has to fulfil three conditions twice around. The first condition of the first triad is intelligence, the second sentiment, and the third consciousness. Intelligence alone does not suffice, for computers have, in a certain sense, intelligence, but they are, at least at the present stage of their development, not persons. The connection of intelligence and sentiment, too, is not enough. Animals can have, at least to a certain degree, intelligence and sentiment, but they are not persons. For this reason, the third condition of the first triad, consciousness or, more precisely, self-consciousness, is the pivotal condition. Self-consciousness is defined by reflexivity. In order to determine what reflexivity is, three kinds of reflexivity have to be distinguished: cognitive, volitive, and normative reflexivity. This is to say that the third element of the concept of person, self-consciousness, again comprises three elements. This is the reason why the concept of person, presented here, can be designated as 'double-triadic'.

Cognitive reflexivity consists in making oneself the object of knowledge. One could also speak of 'self-knowledge'. The most elementary piece of self-knowledge is knowledge of the fact that we have been born and that we will die. To be a person, cognitive reflexivity is necessary, but it is not sufficient. Volitive and normative reflexivity must be added. Volitive reflexivity consists in the ability to direct one's behaviour and, with this, oneself by acts of will. As far as single acts are concerned, this is self-direction. With respect to the whole of life one can speak of 'self-formation'.

[28] Immanuel Kant, *Groundwork of the Metaphysic of Morals*, trans. H. J. Paton (New York, N. Y.: Harper & Row, 1964), 103; AA 4, 436.

[29] Alexy, *A Theory of Constitutional Rights* (n. 4 above), 232–6; Robert Alexy, 'Ralf Dreiers Interpretation der Kantischen Rechtsdefinition', in *Integratives Verstehen. Zur Rechtsphilosophie Ralf Dreiers*, ed. Robert Alexy (Tübingen: Mohr Siebeck, 2005), 95–109, at 101–2, n. 37.

[30] Kant, *Groundwork of the Metaphysic of Morals* (n. 28 above), 96; AA IV, 428–9.

[31] Robert Alexy, 'Data y los derechos humanos. Mente positrónica y concepto dobletriádico de persona', in *Star Trek y los derechos humanos*, eds Robert Alexy and Alfonso Garcia Figueroa (Valencia: Tirant lo Blanch, 2007), 85–100, at 94–100.

It is exactly this capacity of self-formation that Pico della Mirandola considers as the decisive reason for the dignity of human beings when he characterizes man as his 'own ... creative sculptor' ('*ipsius ... plastes et fictor*').[32]

The result of self-formation can be good or bad. Pico talks about the possibilities both of brutal degeneration ('*bruta degenerare*') and of development into a higher dimension ('*in superiora*').[33] This shows that volitive reflexivity as such does not yet include normativity. Normativity enters the stage with the third kind of reflexivity, normative reflexivity. Normative reflexivity is concerned with self-assessment under the aspect of correctness. Here the question is of whether an action one has performed or wants to perform is right or wrong, and whether the life one leads or has led is, or was, a good life. This is the dimension of Kantian autonomy.

C. Human Dignity as a Bridge Concept

One who fulfils the conditions of first, intelligence, second, sentiment, and third, reflexivity in the form of cognitive, volitive, and normative reflexivity is a person. This is the descriptive side of human dignity. The shift to the normative side begins with a connection between the concept of person and the concept of human dignity. This connection can be expressed in the following way: all persons possess human dignity. If '*P*' represents the predicate 'person' and '*D*' the predicate 'possessing human dignity', this sentence can be rendered in the following form:

(1) $$\forall x(Px \to Dx).$$

The sentence that all persons possess human dignity is certainly in need of justification. Here I will assume that it is justifiable and, therefore, true. But (1) does not render explicit the normative dimension of human dignity. This can be done either by connecting the concept of human dignity with the concept of value, as Ronald Dworkin does with his 'principle of intrinsic value',[34] or by connecting the concept of human dignity with the concepts of obligation and rights.[35] In law, the latter seems to be preferable. The connection of human dignity with rights can be expressed in the following way. Every individual who possesses human dignity has the right to be taken seriously as a person. If '*S*' represents the predicate 'having

[32] Giovanni Pico della Mirandola, *De hominis dignitate. Über die Würde des Menschen*, trans. Norbert Baumgarten, ed. August Buck (Hamburg: Felix Meiner, 1990), 6.

[33] Ibid.

[34] Ronald Dworkin, *Is Democracy Possible Here? Principles for a New Political Debate* (Princeton, N. J.: Princeton University Press, 2006), 9.

[35] On the relation between the concepts of rights and obligations or duties, see Alexy, *A Theory of Constitutional Rights* (n. 4 above), 128–38.

the right to be taken seriously as a person', this sentence can be rendered in the following form:

(2) $$\forall x(Dx \rightarrow Sx).$$

It appears to be an analytical truth that to be taken seriously as a person means that human rights are to be attributed. For this reason, a third sentence, containing '*R*' as 'having human rights' is true:

(3) $$\forall x(Sx \rightarrow Rx).$$

Now, (2) and (3) imply

(4) $$\forall x(Dx \rightarrow Rx),$$

that is: all individuals possessing human dignity (*D*) possess human rights (*R*). (4) is a simplification, for it renders the concept represented by '*S*', namely the concept of having the right to be taken seriously as a person, superfluous. A second simplification is far more important. (1) and (4) imply

(5) $$\forall x(Px \rightarrow Rx),$$

that is: all persons have human rights.

The possibility of connecting *Px* directly with *Rx* brings to light a very important formal characteristic of the concept of human dignity, which may well explain many of the difficulties in the analysis of human dignity. Human dignity is what one might call a 'bridge concept'. A bridge concept is a concept that connects an empirical or descriptive concept with a normative or evaluative concept. In our case, the descriptive concept is the concept of person. The normative concepts are, in (2), the right to be taken seriously as a person (*S*), and, in (3), the possession of human rights (*R*). These two formulations express what one might call the 'operative human dignity norms'.

V. Human Dignity as Principle and as Rule

A. Human Dignity as Principle

Now we are in a position to answer the question of whether the absolute or the relative conception or construction of human dignity is correct. If the content of the guarantee of human dignity can be expressed by the duty norm 'all persons have to be taken seriously as persons' as well as by the rights norm 'all persons have the right to be taken seriously as persons', then human dignity can participate in balancing. For reasons of simplification only the rights norm shall be considered in what follows. An interference with the right to be taken seriously as a person, P_i, can be more or less intensive. Life imprisonment without a legal regulation concerning the possibility to regain one's freedom after a certain period of time is a more intensive interference with the right to be taken seriously as a person than life imprisonment with such a regulation,[36] and in cases of continued danger represented by the prisoner the principle of public security, P_j, has a greater weight than in cases without such a danger. Thus, values for the variables concerning the intensity of interference, I_i and I_j, can be inserted into the Weight Formula. The same applies to the abstract weights. The abstract weight on the side of human dignity, W_i, receives the highest value, that on the side of public security, W_j, a medium one. In such a situation, the values of the reliability variables, R_i and R_j, are of the greatest importance. All of this fits perfectly with the Weight Formula, and therefore with balancing, and therefore with proportionality, and, therefore with the relative construction. Many more examples could be adduced but this shall suffice here.

B. Human Dignity as a Rule

In *A Theory of Constitutional Rights*, I have argued that there exists, alongside the human dignity norm as a principle, a human dignity norm as a rule. Article 1(1)(1) of the Basic Law of the Federal Republic of Germany and Article 1(1) of the European Charter of Fundamental Rights state: 'Human dignity is inviolable.' One can understand this as an expression of a rule that is violated if and only if the human dignity principle takes precedence over the colliding principle,[37] say, over public security, as in the life imprisonment case. This construction is possible owing to the semantic open-texture of the concept of human dignity. This semantic open texture allows one to use balancing as a means of interpreting this concept.

Against this dual construction, Niels Teifke has objected that the human dignity rule has 'no independent significance'.[38] This is true. The content at the level of rule depends completely on the content at the level of principle. One might call this the 'theorem of domination'. But the domination theorem is the point of the dual construction.[39] It shows that a rule construction of the human dignity norm

36 See BVerfGE 45, 187 (242–52).

37 Alexy, *A Theory of Constitutional Rights* (n. 4 above), 64.

38 Teifke, *Das Prinzip Menschenwürde* (n. 8 above), 119 (trans. R. A.).

39 Borowski has argued against the dual construction that it 'has the definitive right at centre stage'; Martin Borowski, Absolute Rights and Proportionality, *German Yearbook of International Law* 56 (2013), 385–423, at 422. The domination theorem expresses that this is not the case. It is, however, true that the dual construction can be used 'to hide the fact that proportionality analysis takes place in the

is possible, but empty. The rule construction implies the absolute conception of human dignity, whereas the principle construction implies the relative conception. The domination theorem shows that the essential feature of the normative structure of human dignity is its status as a principle. For this reason, only the relative conception can be correct.

VI. Devaluation of Human Dignity?

A critic of the relative conception might object that all this only shows that one *can* conceive of the human dignity norm as a principle which has to be applied by way of balancing. It does, however, not show that one *should* do so. On the contrary, there are good normative reasons for the absolute conception. These normative reasons focus on the thesis that the relative construction leads to a devaluation of human dignity. A fixed border ceases to exist because everything or nearly everything becomes possible. The guarantee of human dignity would no longer be a real guarantee. It would be degraded to a mere point of consideration. One might call this objection the 'devaluation objection'. The devaluation objection, however, does not apply for four reasons.

A. Clear Cases

The first reason is that there exist a considerable number of cases in which it is altogether clear that human dignity is violated. Examples are persecution for racial or religious reasons, degrading prison conditions, failure to provide protection against sexual assault, exclusion from every educational opportunity, and a life below the existential minimum. These are conditions in which there exists a strong degree of normative certainty that human dignity will take precedence over colliding principles.[40] According to the Law of Competing Principles,[41] this precedence implies that there exist concrete rules that have these conditions as their *protases* and the requirements of human dignity as their *apodoses*. In cases of these concrete rules subsumption is possible. Balancing will enter the stage only in borderline cases. This shows that the relative construction by no means implies that everything or nearly everything becomes possible.

assessment of rights claims'; ibid. But this would be an abuse of the dual model. It would violate the domination theorem, which is constitutive for the dual construction, by turning it in its opposite. The main advantage of not completely abandoning the rule dimension is that the dual construction takes, at the same time, seriously the wording of the constitution and scientific truth. This is one element, among others, of reconstructing the tendency of the guarantee of human dignity to absoluteness.

40 Alexy, *A Theory of Constitutional Rights* (n. 4 above), 63.
41 Ibid., 54.

B. Object Formula

The second argument against the devaluation objection concerns the object formula. The object formula, which plays a considerable role in the adjudication of the German Federal Constitutional Court, says that 'it is not compatible with human dignity that a human being be made into a mere object of state power'.[42] This does not preclude the treatment of human beings as objects to a certain degree. But it precludes that 'the quality as a subject … be fundamentally challenged'.[43] Now the quality as a subject is fundamentally challenged when the quality as a person is fundamentally challenged. In this case the principle of human dignity takes precedence over principles that collide with it.

The precedence in the clear cases mentioned above counts as a concrete precedence. By contrast, turning a 'human being … into a mere object' expresses an abstract concept, and it is, therefore, an abstract condition of precedence.[44] Certainly the Law of Colliding Principles is not compatible with abstract relations of precedence,[45] but it is altogether compatible with abstract conditions of preference. That concrete and abstract conditions both establish a conditional and not an unconditional relation of precedence is something they have in common. For this reason, the Law of Colliding Principles is applicable in cases of abstract conditions as well as in cases of concrete conditions. This implies that the object formula is an abstract rule resulting from balancing, which makes it possible to resolve a certain number of cases by means of subsumption. This contributes, in turn, to the stability of the guarantee of human dignity. As soon as it becomes unclear, however, whether someone is being treated as a mere object, balancing becomes indispensable.

C. Abstract Weight and Epistemic Reliability

The third argument refers to the abstract weight of the principle of human dignity, W_i, and the values of epistemic reliability, that is, of R_i or $R_i^e \cdot R_i^n$ on the side of human dignity, and of R_j or $R_j^e \cdot R_j^n$ on the side of the colliding principle, say, public security. I presented, above, the Weight Formula in its two versions, the unrefined and the refined version. I already mentioned there the high abstract value of human dignity and the importance of epistemic reliability on the side of the colliding principle. One point has to be added here. The epistemic reliability on the side of human dignity is, normally, rather high. In extreme or tragic collisions as in the cases of torture in a ticking nuclear bomb scenario or bringing down an

42 BVerfGE 109, 279 (312) (trans. R. A.).
43 BVerfGE 109, 279 (313) (trans. R. A.).
44 Teifke, *Das Prinzip Menschenwürde* (n. 8 above), 31.
45 Alexy, *A Theory of Constitutional Rights* (n. 4 above), 52.

airplane hijacked by terrorists who plan to use it as a weapon in order to kill as many persons as possible, the values of empirical and normative reliability on the side of human dignity are both unusually high. If one assumes that in such tragic cases all the variables on the side of human dignity have the highest value, then an interference with human dignity will only be allowed when all the variables on the side of the opposing principle also have the highest value. This is the most extreme of all 6561 constellations—that is, of all 3^8 constellations[46]—possible on the basis of the refined Weight Formula. This number stems from the fact that 81 constellations—that is, 3^4 constellations—are on each side possible and that each of these 81 constellations can be combined with 81 constellations on the other side, say, on the side of public security. This implies that in extreme or tragic cases, in which the highest values have to be substituted on the side of human dignity, the interference with human dignity is only proportional in one of 81 constellations on the other side. In all the other constellations, namely the 80 that remain, the interference with human dignity is disproportional, and therefore unconstitutional, and therefore forbidden. It would seem to be difficult to describe this as a 'devaluation of human dignity'.

D. Rationality

The fourth argument is that there exists no alternative to balancing, where the application of the guarantee of human dignity in an equally rational way is concerned. The most promising candidate for such an alternative has one turning to the classical canons of interpretation. It is, however, easy to see that they are of low value if they do not comprise balancing. Here only the four main canons of interpretation shall be considered: the semantic, the genetic, the teleological, and the systematic argument. The semantic argument,[47] owing to the open texture of the concept of human dignity, is of low significance in hard cases. The genetic argument,[48] which refers to the original intent of the framers of the constitution, can sometimes be helpful. But the broadness, the complexity, and the moral content of the concept of human dignity rule out the possibility that a significant number of hard cases in the field of human dignity can be resolved by mere reference to original intent. The teleological argument[49] is without any import in cases of human dignity. Human dignity is, as the highest value of the legal system, its highest purpose. What should the purpose of the highest purpose be, if not just this purpose? Where this applies, then where it is unclear what the highest purpose requires it

[46] Alexy, 'Formal Principles: Some Replies to Critics' (n. 21 above), 522 (in this volume: Chapter 12, 187).

[47] Robert Alexy, *A Theory of Legal Argumentation* (1978), trans Ruth Adler and Neil MacCormick (Oxford: Clarendon Press, 1989), 235–6.

[48] Ibid., 236–9.

[49] Ibid., 240–4.

makes no sense to answer the question what it requires with a mere hint as to what it requires. This would beg the question. The systematic argument[50] is of special interest. It refers to the relation of the norm to be interpreted to other norms of the legal system. If the guarantee of human dignity were to be conceived as a rule, not as a principle, the systematic argument would be of no value for the interpretation of this guarantee. The guarantee of human dignity as the highest substantive norm of the legal system[51] can play a considerable role in the interpretation of lower-level norms, and this is a form of systematic interpretation. But when the question is that of whether the highest-level norm is violated by a lower-level norm, the lower-level norm cannot be adduced as an argument for a violation or lack of violation, if both, the highest-level norm and the lower-level norm are considered as rules. The picture changes completely when the guarantee of human dignity is understood as a principle. Then balancing with all other principles becomes possible. This, too, is a systematic argument.[52] But as soon as the canons of interpretation include this form of systematic argument, which finds its most precise expression in the Weight Formula, they cease to be an alternative to balancing.

With this conclusion, we come to the end. Every attempt to present the classical canons of interpretation as an alternative to balancing where human dignity is concerned is condemned to failure. Balancing, a point I cannot elaborate here, is a form of rational legal argumentation.[53] By contrast, the non-balancing alternatives are relegated to something like 'human dignity intuitionism'.[54] Argumentation is an expression of rationality, intuitionism is a confession of irrationality. Ultimately, it is this reason that shows us why the relative construction alone can be considered as correct.

[50] Ibid., 240.

[51] Alexy, *A Theory of Constitutional Rights* (n. 4 above) 232, 299.

[52] Robert Alexy, *Recht, Vernunft, Diskurs*, 2nd edn (Frankfurt: Suhrkamp, 2016), 87.

[53] Robert Alexy, 'The Construction of Constitutional Rights', *Law & Ethics of Human Rights* 4 (2010), 20–32, at 32 (in this volume: Chapter 8, 121–32, at 132).

[54] See Robert Alexy, 'Grundrechtsnorm und Grundrecht', *Rechtstheorie*, supplement 13 (2000), 101–15, at 108.

15
Proportionality and Rationality

I. Empirical and Analytical Approaches

Below the level of normative questions there are two approaches to proportionality and its relation to constitutional rights and constitutional review. The first is descriptive or empirical in nature, whereas the second is broadly analytical. Certainly, each of these approaches presupposes the other. It is not possible to describe, for instance, the dissemination of the idea of proportionality around the world without any assumptions about the structure of the proportionality test. Furthermore, every analysis of the formal structure of proportionality must be confronted with cases drawn from the practice of constitutional review, just as every theory of physics must withstand the tests stemming from experiments and new facts. This is not to deny, however, that enquiries on proportionality can have either an empirical or an analytical focus. I will concentrate on analytical considerations in connection with cases. This, however, is not to be understood as an end in itself. The overarching question is the normative problem of how proportionality must be constructed if it is to animate rationality to the greatest extent possible. The basis of my answer to this question is principles theory.

II. Proportionality and Principles Theory

A. Rules and Principles

Principles theory begins with the norm-theoretic distinction between rules and principles.[1] Rules are norms that require something definitively. They are *definitive commands*. Their form of application is subsumption. If a rule is valid and if its conditions of application are fulfilled, it is definitively required that exactly what it demands be done. If this is done, the rule is complied with; if this is not done, the rule is not complied with. By contrast, principles are *optimization requirements*. As such, they demand that something be realized 'to the greatest extent possible given the legal and factual possibilities'.[2] Rules aside, the legal possibilities are determined

[1] See Robert Alexy, *A Theory of Constitutional Rights* (1985) trans. Julian Rivers (Oxford: Oxford University Press, 2002), 47–9.
[2] Ibid., 47.

Law's Ideal Dimension. Robert Alexy, Oxford University Press. © Robert Alexy 2021.
DOI: 10.1093/oso/9780198796831.003.0016

essentially by opposing principles. For this reason, principles, each taken alone, always comprise a merely *prima facie* requirement. The determination of the appropriate degree of satisfaction of one principle relative to the requirements of other principles is brought about by balancing. Thus, balancing is the specific form of application of principles.

B. Proportionality

The nature of principles as optimization requirements leads immediately to a necessary connection between principles and proportionality. The principle of proportionality (*Verhältnismäßigkeitsgrundsatz*) consists of three sub-principles: the principles of suitability, of necessity, and of proportionality in the narrower sense. Often, a fourth component is added to these three elements, the requirement of a proper purpose that defines the first step of the proportionality test. Aharon Barak's reconstruction of proportionality is an example.[3] I will argue here that such a first step is superfluous and may even pose a danger for the rationality of the proportionality test. But this requires, first, that the three components just mentioned are analysed. The analysis will show that all three sub-principles express the idea of optimization. Principles *qua* optimization requirements require optimization relative both to what is factually possible and to what is legally possible. The principles of suitability and necessity refer to optimization relative to the factual possibilities. The principle of proportionality in the narrower sense concerns optimization relative to the legal possibilities.

1. Suitability

The first sub-principle, the principle of suitability, precludes the adoption of means that obstruct the realization of at least one principle without promoting any principle or goal for which it has been adopted. If a means M, adopted in order to promote the principle P_1, is not suitable for this purpose, but obstructs the realization of P_2, then there are no costs either to P_1 or P_2 if M is omitted, but there are costs to P_2 if M is adopted. Thus, P_1 and P_2 taken together may be realized to a higher degree relative to what is factually possible if M is abandoned. P_1 and P_2, when *taken together*—that is, as elements of a single system—proscribe the use of M. This shows that the principle of suitability is nothing other than an expression of the idea of Pareto-optimality. One position can be improved without detriment to the other.

An example of the violation of the principle of suitability is found in a decision of the German Federal Constitutional Court. The law in question required that a

[3] See Aharon Barak, *Proportionality. Constitutional Rights and their Limitations* (Cambridge: Cambridge University Press, 2012), 245–302, 529–39.

weapons examination had to be passed not only by persons who apply for a general hunting licence but also by persons who apply solely for a falconry licence. The Court argued that the weapons examination for falconers is not suitable for promoting the 'proper exercise of these activities as intended by the legislator'.[4] Therefore, 'no substantially clear reason'[5] existed for the infringement of the general freedom of action on the part of the falconer, as guaranteed by Article 2(1) of the German Basic Law. For that reason, the regulation was declared disproportional[6] and, consequently, unconstitutional.

2. Necessity

Cases in which laws are declared unconstitutional for reasons of unsuitability are rare. Normally, the measure applied by the legislator will at least promote his aims to a certain degree. This suffices for suitability. For this reason, the practical relevance of the sub-principle of suitability is relatively low. The situation is completely different with regard to the second sub-principle of the principle of proportionality, the principle of necessity. This principle requires that of two means promoting P_1 that are, broadly speaking, equally suitable, the one that interferes less intensively with P_2 has to be chosen. If there exists a less intensively interfering and equally suitable means, one position can be improved at no cost to the other.[7] Under this condition, P_1 and P_2, *taken together*, require that the less intensively interfering means be applied. This is, again, a case of Pareto-optimality.

An example is the decision of the Federal Constitutional Court on sweets, especially in the form of Easter rabbits and Santa Claus figures that consist of puffed rice. In order to protect consumers from mistakenly taking those puffed rice sweets to be chocolate products, a ban on puffed rice sweets was issued. The Court argued that consumer protection could be achieved 'in an equally effective but less incisive way by a duty of labelling'.[8] For this reason, the ban was declared to be a violation of the principle of necessity and, therefore, disproportional.

3. Proportionality in the Narrower Sense

Just as with the principle of suitability, the principle of necessity concerns optimization relative to the factual possibilities. Optimization relative to the factual possibilities consists in avoiding avoidable costs. Costs, however, are unavoidable when principles collide. Then balancing becomes necessary. Balancing is the

[4] Decisions of the German Federal Constitutional Court (BVerfGE) 55, 159 (166) (trans. R. A.).

[5] BVerfGE 55, 159 (167) (trans. R. A.).

[6] BVerfGE 55, 159 (166).

[7] Where the question of whether the less or the more intensively interfering means is chosen arises, the principle of necessity presupposes that all other principles or goals are indifferent with respect to this choice. If, however, there exists a third principle or goal, P_3, that is affected negatively by the adoption of the means interfering less intensively with P_2, than the case cannot be decided by considerations concerning Pareto-optimality. When costs are unavoidable, balancing becomes necessary.

[8] BVerfGE 53, 135 (146) (trans. R. A.).

subject of the third sub-principle of the principle of proportionality, the principle of proportionality in the narrower sense. This principle tells us what optimization relative to the legal possibilities is. In *A Theory of Constitutional Rights* I expressed the requirement of optimization relative to the legal possibilities by means of a rule that I called the 'Law of Balancing'.[9] This rule states:

> The greater the degree of non-satisfaction of, or detriment to, one principle, the greater must be the importance of satisfying the other.

The Law of Balancing excludes, *inter alia*, an intensive interference with principle P_1 that is justified only by a low importance assigned to the satisfaction of the colliding principle P_2. Such a solution would not be an optimization of P_1 *together with* P_2.

4. Weight Formula

The Law of Balancing has been criticized by Barak for considering on the side of the limited right only 'the extent of the constitutional right's limitation',[10] that is, 'the degree of its limitation',[11] whereas on the side of the justification of the limitation or interference, the importance of the colliding principle is to be found. He proposes that the concept of importance be employed on both sides, and he qualifies, at the same time, this importance as 'social importance',[12] that is to say, as not having constitutional importance as such. I shall not take up the latter point here. The first point, however, is undoubtedly correct. The formulation of the Law of Balancing has been developed with an eye to a standard situation that appears with great frequency.[13] For a deeper, more precise, and complete analysis, the Law of Balancing has to be elaborated further. This further elaboration amounts to the Weight Formula.[14] The Weight Formula defines the weight of a principle P_i in a concrete case, that is, the concrete weight of P_i relative to a colliding principle P_j ($W_{i,j}$), as the quotient first, of the product of the intensity of the interference with P_i(I_i) and the abstract weight of P_i(W_i) and the degree of reliability of the assumptions concerning what the measure in question means for the non-realization of P_i(R_i), and, second, the product of the corresponding values with respect to P_j, now related to the realization of P_j. It runs as follows:

[9] Alexy, *A Theory of Constitutional Rights* (n. 1 above), 102.

[10] Barak, *Proportionality* (n. 3 above), 6.

[11] Ibid., 364.

[12] Ibid., 349.

[13] See Robert Alexy, 'The Weight Formula', trans. Bartosz Brożek and Stanley L. Paulson, in *Studies in the Philosophy of Law*, vol. 3, eds Jerzy Stelmach, Bartosz Brożek, and Wojciech Załuski (Kraków: Jagiellonian University Press, 2007), 9–27, at 15–17 (in this volume: Chapter 11, 154–74, at 160–2).

[14] See Robert Alexy, 'On Balancing and Subsumption. A Structural Comparison', *Ratio Juris* 16 (2003), 433–49, at 443–8

$$W_{i,j} = \frac{I_i \cdot W_i \cdot R_i}{I_j \cdot W_j \cdot R_j}$$

It appears that Barak's 'importance of preventing the limitation of the constitutional right'[15] is the same as the product of I_i and W_i, whereas his 'importance of the proper purpose'[16] is the same as the product of I_j and W_j. If this should be the case, Barak's critique applies to the original formulation of the Law of Balancing but not to its elaboration by means of the Weight Formula.[17]

A formula like the Weight Formula, which expresses a quotient of two products, is sensible only if all of the factors can be represented by numbers. This is the problem of graduation. Elsewhere,[18] I have proposed a discrete, that is, a non-continuous triadic scale, in which geometric sequences are implemented. This scale assigns the values 'light' (l), 'moderate' (m), and 'serious' (s) to the intensity of interference and to the abstract weights. These values are expressed by the numbers 2^0, 2^1, and 2^2, respectively, that is, by 1, 2, and 4. Where the epistemic side is concerned, that is, R_i and R_j, one can work with the stages 'reliable' or 'certain' (r), 'plausible' (p), and 'not evidently false' (e), to which the numbers 2^0, 2^{-1}, and 2^{-2}, that is, 1, ½, and ¼, are to be assigned.[19] By means of these triads, most of the decisions of constitutional courts can be grasped. Where they do not suffice, that is, where one has to introduce still more attenuated graduations, they can be extended to double-triadic scales.[20]

The epistemic variables R_i and R_j refer to empirical premises as well as to normative premises. This can be expressed by the following equation:

$$R_i = R_i^e \cdot R_i^n$$

This equation might be called the 'reliability equation'. In cases in which both empirical and normative reliability are in question, R_i and R_j have to be substituted by the respective products on the right side of the reliability equation. In this way, a refined version of the Weight Formula[21] appears on stage:

15 Barak, *Proportionality* (n. 3 above), 6.

16 Ibid.

17 A further element in Barak's reconstruction of balancing is probability; ibid., 362. It is a deep question as to whether probability has to be distinguished from reliability or certainty (R) as an epistemic modality, or whether each of them can be reduced to the other. If, as I assume, they cannot be reduced to each other, it is conceivable, that probability is exclusively an element of I_i and of I_j and that the variable 'R' refers exclusively to reliability as an epistemic modality. The latter would give sense to sentences like: 'It is clear that the danger for the right is 20 per cent', 'It is plausible that the danger for the right is 20 per cent', and 'It is not excluded that the danger for the right is 20 per cent.'

18 Alexy, 'The Weight Formula' (n. 13 above), 20–6 (in this volume: Chapter 11, 165–73).

19 Ibid., 25 (Chapter 11, 172).

20 Ibid., 22–3 (Chapter 11, 168–9).

21 See on this Robert Alexy, 'Formal Principles: Some Replies to Critics', *International Journal of Constitutional Law* 12 (2014), 511–24, at 513–5 (in this volume: Chapter 12, 175–89, at 177–9).

$$W_{i,j} = \frac{I_i \cdot W_i \cdot R_i^e \cdot R_i^n}{I_j \cdot W_j \cdot R_j^e \cdot R_j^n}$$

The two Weight Formulas show how many constellations are possible in balancing. If one takes the refined Weight Formula with four variables on each side, that is, with eight variables altogether, one acquires, on the basis of the two triadic scales, 3^8, that is, 6561 constellations.[22] In case of the elementary Weight Formula with three variables on each side, one acquires, again on the basis of the two triadic scales, 3^6, that is, 729 constellations. It is an important point concerning the rationality of balancing that this diversity has a well-ordered, rather than a chaotic, character. This plays a great role in the answer to the question of whether at least some constitutional rights, such as human dignity, have an absolute character.[23]

5. Proper Purpose

At least as important as these numerical relations is the identification of the factors that play a role in balancing. It is a pivotal requirement of the formal rationality of balancing that first, all relevant factors and only relevant factors—and not, for instance, the reasons for the values of the factors—are represented by the variables of the formula, and second, that the factors do not overlap with each other. This requirement of formal rationality is the yardstick by which the proposal to give balancing a four-pronged structure is to be measured, that is, the proposal to introduce the question of a proper purpose as the first step of proportionality analysis, preceding suitability, necessity, and proportionality in the narrower sense.

According to Barak, the nature of rights as 'shields'[24] demands a proper purpose as a 'threshold requirement'[25] when an interference with a constitutional right is based on a public interest: 'the very existence of a public interest, in and of itself, would not suffice in justifying a limitation on a constitutional right'.[26] In cases of 'constitutional rights of the highest level',[27] in order to pass the proper purpose test the public interest must be 'either "compelling" or "pressing" '.[28] All rights below the highest level are, according to Barak, to be 'grouped into a second level. Here, the requirement should be that the law's purpose be "important" '.[29]

The problem with this construction is that all these requirements are already at home on the level of proportionality in the narrower sense. Compelling or pressing as well as important public interests as reasons for an interference with constitutional

22 Ibid., 522 (Chapter 12, 187).

23 Robert Alexy, 'Human Dignity and Proportionality', this volume, Chapter 14, 205–19, at 217–8.

24 Barak, *Proportionality* (n. 3 above), 530.

25 Ibid.

26 Ibid.

27 Ibid., 533.

28 Ibid.

29 Ibid.

rights can and must be completely expressed in the Weight Formula by attributing high values to either one or both of the variables I_j and W_j. This means that the installation of a proper purpose as the first step of proportionality analysis is superfluous, implying that it violates the requirement of formal rationality of balancing by introducing an overlapping factor. Furthermore, the Weight Formula allows the impact of the public interest to be set in relation to all other factors that are relevant for the question of whether the interference with the constitutional right is proportional in the narrower sense. An abstract classification of the importance of public interests at the beginning of the proportionality analysis cannot achieve this level of formal rationality. For this reason, the only question that should be asked at the beginning is whether the purpose pursued by the legislator is excluded by the constitution. This, however, does not concern balancing; it only points out one of its presuppositions.[30]

All this concerns the formal analysis of proportionality and, in this sense, its 'logic'. Barak seems also to make a heuristic point when he says that '[t]he public interest must be of a special character in order to examine the nature of the limitation and decide whether it is constitutional'.[31] This can be read as saying that there must be some reasons in order to commence a proportionality test at all. In principle, little can be said against this. Still, one has to be careful. The Weight Formula shows that there can be rather light interferences ($I_i = l = 1$) with constitutional rights of relatively high abstract values ($W_i = m = 2$)—with both, however, backed only by rather uncertain empirical and normative premises ($R_i^e = e = ¼$; $R_i^n = e = ¼$). Now it is possible, on the other side, that not to allow the contested decision of the parliament would, indeed, only be a light interference ($I_j = l = 1$) with a public interest of low importance ($W_j = l = 1$), that is to say, the public interest, without any doubt, would have no 'special character'.[32] Nevertheless, if the epistemic variables on the side of the public interest have good values ($R_j^e = r = 1$; $R_j^n = r = 1$), the concrete weight on the side of the public interest would be greater (1) than the concrete weight on the side of the constitutional right (0,125). In this constellation, and in many others, a public interest without any special character would justify the interference with the right.

III. Balancing and Argumentation

A. The Formal and the Substantive Dimension of Rationality

Up until now, I have considered only the formal rationality of balancing, expressed especially by the Weight Formula. A series of objections has been raised against

[30] Alexy, *A Theory of Constitutional Rights* (n. 1 above), 62.
[31] Barak, *Proportionality* (n. 3 above), 530.
[32] Ibid.

the formal character of the Weight Formula. Matthias Jestaedt, for example, has objected to the Weight Formula on the ground that it 'holds out the promise of a degree of certainty and precision in application which it is quite unable to keep'.[33] '[I]ts claimed, or at least implied, precision is revealed to be a mere illusion, a methodological chimera.'[34] Stavros Tsakyrakis speaks of 'the myth of mathematical precision', which must be rejected where 'judicial reasoning' is concerned.[35] Alexander Somek objects that the balancing model of principles theory does not go beyond 'an analytically careful formalization of moral intuitionism'.[36] And, just to mention a fourth voice, Kai Möller, in his book *The Global Model of Constitutional Rights*, begins with a juxtaposition of his theory as a '*substantive moral approach* ... with a formal theory such as Robert Alexy's ... theory of rights as principles or optimization requirements'.[37]

If principles theory were only a formal theory, these objections would indeed apply. But principles theory is a theory that intrinsically connects the formal and the substantive dimension of constitutional rights, and also connects both dimensions with respect to law in general. Ralf Posher says, albeit with a critical undertone, that principles theory comprises 'a theory about the concept of law, another about the structure of norms, a theory of adjudication, one of argumentation, and finally, different doctrinal theories'.[38]

A formal theory that is in need of being supplemented by a substantive theory is as such, one might well think, of no value at all. This, however, is not the case. A purely formal theory would, indeed, be empty. A purely substantive theory has, however, another defect. It would be blind in all questions concerning the structure of balancing, and this defect would be a serious one because the structure of balancing is complex. Even the best substantive theory would always remain vulnerable to error for reasons of lack of conceptual clarity, lack of system, and lack of argumentative conclusiveness. Such a state of affairs would amount to a serious restriction of rationality.

Gottlob Frege compares in his *Conceptual Notation* ('*Begriffsschrift*') the relation of his 'Formula Language'[39] to 'ordinary language'[40] with

[33] Matthias Jestaedt, 'The Doctrine of Balancing—its Strengths and Weaknesses', in *Institutionalized Reason. The Jurisprudence of Robert Alexy*, ed. Matthias Klatt (Oxford: Oxford University Press, 2012), 152–72, at 163.

[34] Ibid., 165.

[35] Stavros Tsakyrakis, 'Proportionality: An Assault on Human Rights?', *International Journal of Constitutional Law* 7 (2009), 468–93, at 472.

[36] Alexander Somek, *Rechtliches Wissen* (Frankfurt: Suhrkamp, 2006), 135 (trans. R. A.).

[37] Kai Möller, *The Global Model of Constitutional Rights* (Oxford: Oxford University Press, 2012), 1–2.

[38] Ralf Poscher, 'The Principles Theory. How Many Theories and What is their Merit?', in *Institutionalized Reason. The Jurisprudence of Robert Alexy*, ed. Matthias Klatt (Oxford: Oxford University Press, 2012), 218–47, at 221.

[39] Gottlob Frege, 'Conceptual Notation. A Formula Language of Pure Thought Modelled upon the Formula Language of Arithmetic' (1879), trans. and ed. Terrell Ward Bynum in Frege, *Conceptual Notation and Related Articles* (Oxford: Clarendon Press, 1972), 101–208, 101.

[40] Ibid,. 104.

> the relation of the microscope to the eye. The latter, because of the range of its applicability and because of the ease with which it can adapt itself to the most varied circumstances, has a great superiority over the microscope. Of course, viewed as an optical instrument it reveals many imperfections.[41]

This directly applies to the formal analysis of proportionality. The ordinary language, the eye, must remain the language of the courts in cases of balancing as well as in cases of subsumption. In the scientific analysis of subsumption as well as of balancing, however, a formula language, the microscope, is indispensable in order to achieve as precise, as deep, and as easily comprehensible as possible insight into the structure of these two forms of the application of law.[42]

The question remains: how can the formal dimension be connected with the substantive dimension? The answer consists in embedding the Weight Formula in a theory of rational legal argumentation.

B. Numbers, Classification Propositions, and their Justification

At first glance, such an embedding seems to be excluded by the nature of the Weight Formula on the one hand, and by the nature of legal argumentation or discourse on the other. The basic elements of the Weight Formula are numbers, the basic elements of legal discourse are arguments. Numbers can be connected with measuring instruments, say, with thermometers, but how can they be linked with arguments? Alongside the thermometer, there exists no argumeter. The answer is this. The numbers that have to be substituted in the variables of the Weight Formula represent classifications, in case of the variables I_i and W_i, as well as of their counterparts, the classifications as 'light', 'moderate', and 'serious'. One example is an interference with the freedom of speech (P_i), which serves to protect the personality right (P_j). If interference with the freedom of speech is classified as serious, that is, if I_i receives the value 4, then the number 4 stands for nothing other than the proposition 'this interference with the freedom of speech is serious'. The same applies if the intensity of the interference with the personality right through non-protection is classified as light. The number 1, then, stands for the proposition 'this interference with the personality right through non-protection would be light'. The pivotal point, now, is that such propositions—one might call them 'classification propositions'—are as propositions or assertions in general in need of justification. The question is whether they are capable of justification.

41 Ibid., 105

42 On a third form see Robert Alexy, 'Two or Three?' *Archives for Philosophy of Law and Social Philosophy*, supplement 119 (2010), 9–18.

Authors who contest the rationality of balancing must deny the justifiability of classification propositions. Examples of such denials are Jürgen Habermas's argument from arbitrariness,[43] Bernhard Schlink's argument from decisionism,[44] and Poscher's argument from intuitionism.[45] Against all of these positions I set out the argumentation thesis. The argumentation thesis says that propositions about intensity of interference and degrees of importance lend themselves to rational justification. An example is presented by a 1997 decision of the German Federal Constitutional Court on the duty of manufacturers of tobacco goods to place health warnings respecting the dangers of smoking on their products.[46] This is a minor or light interference with the freedom to pursue one's profession. By contrast, a total ban on all such products would count as serious interference. Between such minor and serious cases, others of moderate intensity of interference can be found. An example would be a ban on cigarette machines along with the introduction of provisions restricting the sale of tobacco to selected shops. If it were true, as Poscher maintains, that balancing depends on nothing other than 'our intuition',[47] then every interpreter of a constitution would be free to say, appealing to his intuitions, that the duty to set down health warnings is a serious interference and the total tobacco ban a light interference with the tobacco producers' freedom of profession. But it would not be easy to take such an approach seriously. In any case, it would be easy to give cogent reasons as to why these classifications are mistaken. If, in this way, the intensity of interference, as in the tobacco case, is established as minor and the importance of protecting the population from health risks as high,[48] the result is easily recognizable. The reason that weighs heavily on behalf of interference justifies the minor interference.

C. Disagreement, Discourse, and Rationality

A balancing sceptic might concede that it is possible to justify classifications of the intensity of interference in the case considered but nevertheless insist that there are cases in which different classifications can be justified equally well, which, so the objection continues, is to say that none of them is justifiable. As an example, the sceptic might refer to the decision of the German Federal Constitutional Court in 2006 on electronic data-screening. A student with Moroccan citizenship brought a constitutional complaint against an order of a court, upheld in the higher courts,

[43] Jürgen Habermas, *Between Facts and Norms. Contributions to a Discourse Theory of Law and Democracy* (1992), trans. William Rehg (Cambridge: Polity Press, 1996), 259.

[44] Bernhard Schlink, 'Freiheit durch Eingriffsabwehr—Rekonstruktion der klassischen Grundrechtsfunktion', *Europäische Grundrechte-Zeitschrift* 11 (1984), 457–68, at 462.

[45] Poscher, 'The Principles Theory. How Many Theories and What is their Merit?' (n. 38 above), 241.

[46] BVerfGE 95, 173.

[47] Poscher, 'The Principles Theory. How Many Theories and What is their Merit?' (n. 38 above), 241.

[48] BVerfGE 95, 173 (183–7).

concerning electronic data-screening. This order required residents' registration offices, the central aliens' registry, and universities to transmit data to the police concerning male persons between eighteen and forty years regarding, *inter alia*, their faith, native country, and subject of study. These data were submitted to automatic data processing with an eye to identifying potential Islamist terrorists. The majority of the First Panel of the Federal Constitutional Court classified the measure as an interference of 'considerable weight',[49] that is, as a serious interference with the complainant's right to data self-determination. Such a serious interference would be justified in cases of concrete danger but not in cases of abstract danger, characterized by a 'generally threatening situation' as it has existed 'at the latest since September 11, 2001'.[50] It was deemed, however, that no concrete danger was at hand. Therefore, the constitutional complaint was considered to be justified. Completely different is the classification stemming from the dissenting opinion of Judge Haas. According to her assessment, the interference is 'of low weight' and has to be accepted as being in the 'public interest'.[51] From this point of view, the constitutional complaint would not be justified.

Two points are of interest here. The first is that both sides presented numerous arguments for their classifications. The arguments of the majority on the assessment of the interference as serious ran over eleven pages,[52] those of Justice Haas for her assessment as light ran over four pages.[53] This shows that balancing is not a matter of naked classification. It is, essentially, a matter of argumentation. Thus, if rational legal argumentation is possible, rational balancing is possible, too.

The second point is that disagreement does not count as an argument for irrationality if 'reasonable disagreement'[54] can be distinguished from unreasonable disagreement. Here only normative or practical argumentation is of interest. Now the decisive point is that there exist criteria of the rationality of practical arguments and practical argumentation or discourse. The conditions of discursive rationality can be made explicit by means of a system of principles, rules, and forms of general practical discourse.[55] This system comprises criteria that demand non-contradiction, clarity of language, reliability of empirical premises, and sincerity, as well as rules and forms that speak to the consequences, to universalizability, and to the genesis of normative convictions.

A sceptic might concede that there are, indeed, some criteria of the rationality of practical arguments but insist that this does not suffice to establish rationality in cases like the *Electronic Data-Screening* case. The issue has not been resolved

[49] BVerfGE 115, 320 (348) (trans. R. A.).
[50] BVerfGE 115, 320 (364) (trans. R. A.).
[51] BVerfGE 115, 320 (379) (trans. R. A.).
[52] BVerfGE 115, 320 (347–57).
[53] BVerfGE 115, 320 (371–4).
[54] See John Rawls, *Political Liberalism* (New York, N.Y.: Columbia University Press, 1993), 55.
[55] Robert Alexy, *A Theory of Legal Argumentation* (1978), trans. Ruth Adler and Neil MacCormick (Oxford: Clarendon Press, 1989), 188–206.

discursively by the power of the better argument but institutionally by a majority decision. The point is correct, but it does not amount to a complete analysis of the situation. Both sides raise a claim that is not a claim to majority but a claim to correctness, necessarily connected with law.[56] This claim remains alive even after the authoritative majority decision has been taken. This implies the possibility of changes by way of future argumentation. In this respect, rationality has an ideal dimension.

IV. Balancing, Universalizability, and Legal Certainty

A. The ad hoc Problem

An opponent of balancing might grant the point that rational legal argumentation is, in general, possible to the degree just described but nevertheless maintain that this does not resolve a serious special rationality problem of balancing, the ad hoc problem. Indeed, not only opponents of balancing but also committed proponents can conceive of the ad hoc problem as a serious problem. Barak is an example.[57] The ad hoc problem stems from the fact that balancing takes place with respect to cases. This is an implication of the Weight Formula. This implication stems from the fact that, in the elementary form of the Weight Formula, two of the three variables on each side (I_i and R_i as well as I_j and R_j) refer to concrete values or weights, that is, to values or weights that depend on the case at hand. In the refined version of the Weight Formula even more variables, that is, three of the four on each side (I_i, R_i^e, and R_i^n as well as I_j, R_j^e, and R_j^n) refer to concrete values or weights. Now the ad hoc objection maintains that this has the consequence that one can never be sure, before balancing has been performed, what the result will be. In this sense, balancing is said to be, so to speak, ruleless. This lack of rules, the objection continues, is incompatible with rationality. It violates one of the most fundamental requirements of practical rationality, the requirement of universalizability, as elaborated, for instance, by Richard Mervin Hare.[58] As a necessary requirement of practical rationality, it is included in the system of rules and forms of rational practical discourse, which define practical rationality.[59] What is more, the lack of rules is not only incompatible with practical rationality in general, it also violates such fundamental principles of law as the principle of legal certainty and the principle of equality.

[56] Robert Alexy, *The Argument from Injustice. A Reply to Positivism* (1992), trans. Bonnie Litschewski Paulson and Stanley L. Paulson (Oxford: Clarendon Press, 2002), 35–9.

[57] Barak, *Proportionality* (n. 3 above), 41, where the argument is put forward against my theory of derivative constitutional rights norms that it 'reflects a case-by-case (ad hoc) balancing approach'.

[58] R. M. Hare, *Freedom and Reason* (Oxford: Clarendon Press, 1963), 30–5.

[59] Alexy, *A Theory of Legal Argumentation* (n. 55 above), 190.

B. The Law of Competing Principles

The ad hoc objection would apply if its basic assumption, the thesis that balancing is necessarily connected with a lack of rules, were true. This is not the case, however. Thus far I have considered only the first law of principles theory, the Law of Balancing, which is nothing other than a rudimentary form of the Weight Formula. In order to reply to the ad hoc objection, one has to consider the second law of principles theory, the Law of Competing Principles. Two concepts are constitutive for this law. The first is the relation of precedence, symbolized by '**P**'. The second is the condition of precedence, symbolized by '*C*'. The result of each application of the Weight Formula can be expressed on this basis.[60] The standard form is:

$$(P_i \mathbf{P} P_j)\ C$$

This formula expresses a conditional relation of precedence. It is to be read as follows: 'Principle P_i precedes principle P_j under the condition C'. The decisive point is that this conditional relation of precedence implies a rule. Precisely this is expressed by the Law of Competing Principles, which runs as follows:

> If principle P_i takes precedence over principle P_j in circumstances C: $(P_i \mathbf{P} P_j)C$, and if P_i gives rise to legal consequences Q in circumstances C, then a valid rule applies which has C as its protasis and Q as its apodosis: $C \rightarrow Q$.[61]

This will be illustrated by means of two cases, the first of which is the *Lebach* Judgment of the German Federal Constitutional Court from 1973. A television channel had planned to broadcast a documentary, '*The Soldier's Murder at Lebach*'. This concerned a crime in which four sleeping soldiers at the munitions depot of the Federal Army at Lebach were murdered and weapons were stolen for the purpose of committing further crimes. At the time of the intended broadcast, a person who has been convicted as an accomplice was shortly to be released from prison. He was of the view that the broadcast of the programme in which he was named and in which his picture was given, would violate his personality right, mainly because it would endanger his entry back into society following his prison term. The Federal Constitutional Court established a competition between the protection of personality and the freedom of media and resolved the matter by balancing

[60] There exist three possibilities:

(1) $W_{i,j} > 1 \rightarrow (P_i \mathbf{P} P_j)C$
(2) $W_{i,j} < 1 \rightarrow (P_j \mathbf{P} P_i)C$
(3) $W_{i,j} = 1 \rightarrow \neg (P_i \mathbf{P} P_j)C \,\&\, \neg (P_j \mathbf{P} P_i)C$ (stalemate)

These three rules establish the relation between the Weight Formula and the Law of Competing Principles.

[61] Alexy, *A Theory of Constitutional Rights* (n. 1 above), 54.

these two principles in the light of the facts of the case. The result is the precedence of the protection of personality over the freedom of media reporting under a condition that connects four elements or sub-conditions: first, a repeated report, second, of a serious criminal act, which is, third, no longer covered by the interest in up-to-date information, and which, fourth, endangers the resocialization of the criminal.[62] This conditional relation of precedence implies, according to the Law of Competing Principles, a rule that runs as follows: '[A] repeated media report, no longer required by the interest in current information, concerning a serious criminal offence, which endangers the resocialization of the offender is constitutionally prohibited.'[63] This is a highly specific rule, but it is a rule that has the force of a precedent of a Constitutional Court.[64]

The second example is the *Electronic Data-Screening* case, already mentioned. The majority of the First Panel of the Federal Constitutional Court establishes that in cases of 'concrete danger' public security takes precedence over the right to data self-determination, whereas in cases of merely abstract danger the opposite is the case.[65] The decision implies two rules. The first says that in cases of concrete danger, electronic data-screening is constitutionally permitted, the second that in cases of abstract danger, electronic data-screening is constitutionally prohibited. This shows that balancing can lead not only, as in the *Lebach* case, to rather concrete rules but also to rather abstract rules.

The level of abstractness of the *Electronic Data-Screening* case can even be exceeded. Cases concerning human dignity offer some examples of this. According

[62] BVerfGE 35, 202 (237).

[63] Alexy, *A Theory of Constitutional Rights* (n. 1 above), 56 (symbols omitted).

[64] I have characterized this rule as a 'derivative constitutional rights norm' (ibid.). As a constitutional rights norm it has to be located at the level of the constitution. It expresses a definitive limitation of the *prima facie* right of the television channel established by the principle of freedom of media (ibid., 60, 181). Barak has objected that 'this derivative constitutional rule can only operate within the sub-constitutional level. It affects only the realization of the constitutional right on the sub-constitutional level. It has no effect at the constitutional level' (Barak, *Proportionality* (n. 3 above), 40). There can be no doubt that the derivative constitutional rights norm operates at the sub-constitutional level. It establishes the constitutionality or unconstitutionality of what is to be found there. But can it do so without belonging to the constitutional level? Barak assumes that the extent of protection of a constitutional right is a matter of proportionality, and I agree with this. But the result of proportionality analysis is always a rule according to the Law of Competing Principles. This rule exists. And it cannot be a rule at the sub-constitutional level if it is to have the power to invalidate norms at the sub-constitutional level. And if it belongs to the constitutional level, it will have effects on this level, too. It establishes a definitive no-right (Alexy, *A Theory of Constitutional Rights* (n. 1 above), 133) of the television channel. It is a central point of Barak's that proportionality does not 'reduce[s] the scope of the constitutional right' (Barak, *Proportionality* (n. 3 above), 6). Indeed, the scope of the right as a *prima facie* right is not reduced at all. To this extent, the derivative constitutional rule has no 'effect on the scope of the right' and, in this sense, 'no effect at the constitutional level' (ibid., 40). The scope of a constitutional right always remains the same. But it has to be connected with the definitive rules produced by balancing. This is required by the concept of the constitution. A constitution consists not exclusively of invariable rights connected with proportionality. The practice of proportionality gives the constitution concrete content in a process of development. In order to understand this, the constitutional rights must be conceived as *prima facie* rights and not as 'definite right[s]', as Barak maintains (ibid.).

[65] BVerfGE 115, 320 (364) (trans. R. A.).

to the German Federal Constitutional Court, 'it is not compatible with human dignity that a human being be made into a mere object'.[66] This can be understood as saying that in cases in which human beings are turned into mere objects, the principle of human dignity takes precedence over all other principles.[67] It is difficult to imagine a condition of precedence with a still higher degree of abstractness.

C. Rules and Conditions

Barak has assessed his basic rule of balancing[68]—corresponding, as I have attempted to show above, in decisive aspects to the Law of Balancing as interpreted by the Weight Formula—as 'too abstract'.[69] He speaks, at the same time, of a 'specific rule of balancing [which] is at too low a level of abstraction'.[70] Against this backdrop he proposes the idea of a 'third rule of balancing'[71] which is located at an 'intermediate level of abstraction'.[72] If he is saying, with this, that besides the basic rule of balancing there exist less abstract rules relating to balancing as an argumentative procedure, I disagree. There are only two rules *about* balancing, the Law of Balancing, as explicated by the Weight Formula, and the Law of Competing Principles. Their abstract nature is a condition of the rationality of balancing. If, however, the reference to lower levels of abstractness can be construed as a reference to different levels of abstractness of the conditions of preference (C)—Barak occasionally speaks here of 'conditions'[73]—I could agree. That the rules produced by balancing according to the Law of Competing Principles have an adequate level of abstractness as well as an adequate level of concreteness is an important requirement of the rationality of balancing. This requirement might be called the 'requirement of adequate abstractness and concreteness'. The requirement of adequate abstractness and concreteness of the rules produced by balancing is, indeed, connected with the requirement of the abstract character of the two fundamental rules about balancing, but the one cannot replace the other.

66 BVerfGE 109, 279 (312) (trans. R. A.).
67 Alexy, 'Human Dignity and Proportionality', this volume, Chapter 14, 205–19, at 217.
68 Barak, Proportionality (n. 3 above), 11.
69 Ibid., 542.
70 Ibid.
71 Ibid.
72 Ibid., 543.
73 Ibid.

16
The Absolute and the Relative Dimension of Constitutional Rights

I. The Absolute and the Relative

In the contemporary debate over the structure of constitutional rights, the phrase 'migration of proportionality', be it across Europe[1] or across the whole world, has become an oft-encountered metaphor.[2] A detailed picture has been drawn by Aharon Barak. As he writes, proportionality first migrated from Germany into European law, from here further into the law of the western and southern European states and into Turkey, then from continental Europe to Canada, Ireland, and England, from Canada on to New Zealand and Australia, then from Canada and Germany to South Africa, and, after the collapse of communism, to central and eastern Europe, and, alongside all this, to Asia, South America, and Israel.[3] With respect to the United States, however, Barak ends his report with a question: 'Is American constitutional law ready for this change?'[4]

A more precise analysis of this process of dissemination would be the object of comparative constitutional law. Here only the phenomenon as such is of interest. Is it a process that might well have gone in a different direction, and that, like a fad, might well pass away altogether? Is it, that is to say, something that is merely contingent, or do we observe something that is necessary, which, like Aristotle's syllogistic, can, indeed, be refined, deepened, and analysed where its peculiarities are concerned,[5] but in its core endures in time and space?

The principle of proportionality is necessary if it can claim validity in all legal systems. What can claim validity in all legal systems has absolute validity.[6] On the

[1] Carlos Bernal Pulido, 'The Migration of Proportionality Across Europe', *New Zealand Journal of Public and International Law* 11 (2013), 483–515.

[2] A more general version of this metaphor is expressed by the concept of the migration of constitutional ideas. See on this *The Migration of Constitutional Ideas*, ed. Sujit Choudhry (Cambridge: Cambridge University Press 2006).

[3] Aharon Barak, *Proportionality. Constitutional Rights and their Limitations* (Cambridge: Cambridge University Press, 2012), 181–210.

[4] Ibid., 208.

[5] See Günther Patzig, *Aristotle's Theory of the Syllogism* (1959), trans. Jonathan Barnes (Dordrecht: Reidel, 1968).

[6] With respect to constitutional rights, the concept of absoluteness is used in different senses. Often, especially in adjudication, it refers to the absolute *structure* of rights. A right has an absolute structure if 'no possible legal reason can ever restrict' it; Robert Alexy, *A Theory of Constitutional Rights* (1985), trans. Julian Rivers (Oxford: Oxford University Press, 2002), 195. This reading means that exceptions

Law's Ideal Dimension. Robert Alexy, Oxford University Press. © Robert Alexy 2021.
DOI: 10.1093/oso/9780198796831.003.0017

other hand, what can only claim to have validity in some legal systems has merely relative validity. This distinction is applicable not only to the principle of proportionality as a norm about the application of constitutional rights but also to the constitutional rights themselves and to the institutionalization of the protection of constitutional rights by means of constitutional review. This leads to three questions, which are systematically closely connected: (1) Do constitutional rights have an absolute character? (2) Does the principle of proportionality have an absolute character? (3) Does constitutional review have an absolute character? Only the first two questions will be discussed here.[7]

In order to answer these questions, the distinction between the absolute and the relative has to bear a connection with the concept of the extent or degree of the absolute and the relative. If the highest degree of the absolute has to be assumed at all three stages, then all constitutions will have to contain the same constitutional rights, all applications of constitutional rights will have to lead to the same results, and the institutionalization of the protection of constitutional rights will have to be arranged in the same way everywhere. By contrast, if the highest degree of the relative has to be assumed at all three stages, then everything is possible everywhere. The assumption that these two extremes have to be precluded suggests itself. This implies that the correct solution is going to consists in a connection of the absolute with the relative dimension. The main features of the construction of this connection with regard to constitutional rights and proportionality are the objects of my consideration.

II. Constitutional Rights

A. Constitutional and Human Rights

The absolute dimension of constitutional rights consists in the necessity of their validity. Whether constitutional rights are necessarily valid, depends on what constitutional rights are, that is, on the nature of constitutional rights. Two fundamentally different conceptions of the nature of constitutional rights stand in opposition: a positivistic and a non-positivistic one.[8] According to both, constitutional rights are

are excluded, and that the right in question is not subject to being overridden. Human dignity is the most important and most discussed candidate as a right with an absolute structure; see on this ibid., 62–4. In contrast to this, the concept of absolute *validity* refers to the validity of rights in all legal systems, regardless of whether these rights have a relative or an absolute structure. All rights that are subject to proportionality analysis have, at least to a certain degree, a relative structure, though they can, nevertheless, have absolute validity. The right to religious freedom is an example. It can claim validity in all legal systems, but, as will be argued below, it can also be limited to different degrees.

[7] On the third question see Robert Alexy, 'Constitutional Rights, Democracy, and Representation', *Rivista di filosofia del diritto* 4 (2015), 23–36.

[8] Robert Alexy, 'A Non-Positivistic Concept of Constitutional Rights', in *The Quest for Rights. Ideal and Normative Dimensions*, eds Massimo La Torre, Leone Niglia, and Mart Susi (Cheltenham: Edward Elgar, 2019), 13–26, at 18–21.

part of the positive law—namely, positive law at the level of the constitution. The difference is that, according to the positivistic conception, the constitutional rights are merely positive law. Their validity depends exclusively on what has been duly enacted and is socially effective. For this reason, they are not necessary but only possible or contingent. One can call this the 'contingency thesis'. In contrast, according to the non-positivistic conception, positivity represents but one side of constitutional rights—that is to say, their real or factual side. Over and above this, they also have an ideal or critical dimension. Thus, constitutional rights have a dual nature.[9] The reason for this is that, with constitutional rights, not just any political decision is transformed into positive law; rather, it is human rights *qua* supra-positive rights that are rendered positive. This is the basis of the necessity thesis.

Human rights are characterized by five properties.[10] They are first, moral, second, universal, third, fundamental, and fourth, abstract rights, that, fifth, with respect to their moral validity, take priority over all other norms. Here only the first of these five properties is of interest: the moral character of human rights.

The moral character of human rights consists in their having, *qua* moral rights, only moral validity. A right is morally valid if it can be justified. Rights exist, as norms in general,[11] if they are valid. Thus, the existence of human rights depends on their justifiability, and on nothing else. Elsewhere, I have attempted to show that human rights are justifiable and, therefore, exist.[12] This cannot be undertaken here. In our present context, the only question to be addressed is the necessity of the connection between human rights and constitutional rights and, with this, between human rights and constitutions.

The key to the necessary connection is the concept of correctness. Constitutions, as law in general,[13] necessarily raise a claim to correctness. This is the one side of the argument. The other is that human rights—since their existence consists in their justifiability—are necessarily connected with the concept of correctness because what is justifiable is correct. If one adds to these two poles of correctness the fundamental character and the priority of human rights that, when taken together, require to be transformed into positive law at the

[9] Robert Alexy, 'Constitutional Rights and Proportionality', *Chinese Yearbook of Constitutional Law* (2010), 221–35, at 231–4.

[10] Robert Alexy, 'Die Institutionalisierung der Menschenrechte im demokratischen Verfassungsstaat', in *Philosophie der Menschenrechte*, eds Stefan Gosepath and Georg Lohmann (Frankfurt: Suhrkamp, 1998), 244–64, at 246–54.

[11] Hans Kelsen, *Pure Theory of Law*, 2nd edn (1960), trans. Max Knight (Berkeley, Calif.: University of California Press, 1967), 10.

[12] Robert Alexy, 'The Existence of Human Rights', *Archives for Philosophy of Law and Social Philosophie*, supplement 136 (2013), 9–18, at 13–18 (in this volume: Chapter 10, 142–53, at 147–53). The justifiabiliy of human rights leads to the universality of their moral validity, which must be distinguished from the universality of their structure, to which the second element of their definition refers; see Alexy, 'Die Institutionalisierung der Menschenrechte im demokratischen Verfassungsstaats' (n. 10 above), 249.

[13] Robert Alexy, *The Argument from Injustice. A Reply to Legal Positivism* (1992), trans. Bonnie Litschewski Paulson and Stanley L. Paulson (Oxford: Clarendon Press, 2002), 35–39.

constitutional level, then constitutions that do not contain human rights in the form of constitutional rights do not meet the claim to correctness raised by them. They are defective, and the defect, owing to the necessity of the claim, is not only a moral defect but also a legal defect.[14] Therefore, the validity of constitutional rights that positivize human rights is necessary, too. That is the absolute dimension of constitutional rights.

B. The Degree of the Absolute Dimension of Constitutional Rights

The degree or extent of the absolute dimension of constitutional rights, however, is limited. The main reason for this takes us to the fourth element of the definition of human rights, their abstractness. Human rights refer to abstract subject matters like liberty and equality, life and property, and freedom of speech and protection of personality. This is both a strength and a weakness. It is a strength because it is easier to justify abstract principles than their application. Two persons can agree that freedom of speech as well as protection of personality are human rights, but nevertheless determine their weights in a concrete case quite differently. The latter is the weak point of abstractness. As abstract rights, human rights leave a great many things open. They are in need of being made concrete. This is achieved, as will be explained below, first and foremost by means of proportionality analysis.

Therefore, the framer of a constitution has considerable discretion where laying down constitutional rights is concerned. Everything that falls within the scope of this discretion belongs to the relative dimension of constitutional rights. Thus, constitutional rights can be shaped very abstractly as well as rather concretely. They can contain elements of well-established rules, and they can be pure principles completely in need of balancing. A general limitation clause applicable to all constitutional rights is possible as well as a series of specific limitation clauses. A catalogue of constitutional rights can include the guarantee of human dignity, but human dignity can also be protected by a bundle of rights implied by it.

The constitutional framer's discretion is not, however, unlimited. It is exceeded, first, when the constitution contains no constitutional rights at all or practically no constitutional rights, second, when single constitutional rights that are required by human rights are lacking, and third, when a constitution contains limiting clauses that represent or allow violations of human rights.

[14] Ibid., 26.

An example of the first possibility is the Australian Constitution which contains, besides norms concerning the organization of the state, only mere fragments of constitutional rights.[15] This did not keep the High Court from assigning 'implied rights'[16] to the Constitution. An example is the 'right of freedom of political communication',[17] which is a special case of the right of freedom of speech. Drawing on the non-positivistic dual-nature thesis as background, this is, in principle, correct. The inclusion of the general right of freedom of speech, however, would have been a preferable solution. At the supranational level, the adjudication of the European Court of Justice offers an example of the comprehensive judicial creation of constitutional or fundamental rights that has led to the protection of fundamental rights. As the German Federal Constitutional Court in its *Solange II* Decision puts it, this 'has to be considered as essentially equal to the protection of constitutional rights indispensably required by the Basic Law'.[18]

The second limitation of discretion concerns the insertion of a constitutional right, required by constitutional correctness, into a catalogue of constitutional rights that is otherwise comprehensive. Here the right to an existential minimum might be mentioned, which the German Federal Constitutional Court added in its *Hartz IV* Decision, in 2010, to the catalogue of constitutional rights, a catalogue that renounces social constitutional rights with only one exception, namely, the right of every mother to the protection and care of the community, as laid down in Article 6(4) of the German Basic Law. The justification is based essentially on human dignity,[19] which, to be sure, in the *War Widow* Decision of 1951 did not yet have the power to require 'protection against material hardship'.[20] Perhaps one can speak here of a strengthening of the interpretation of human dignity required by human rights. A friend of paradoxical formulations might remark, with an eye to the examples illustrating the first two limitations of the constitutional framer's discretion, that constitutions contain constitutional rights even if they do not contain them.

Finally, the third limitation of the constitutional framer's discretion is transgressed, for instance, when constitutional rights are placed under a religious, ideological, or collectivistic reservation free from balancing. But this cannot be explored here.

[15] See Adrienne Stone, 'Australia's Constitutional Rights and the Problem of Interpretive Disagreement', *University of Melbourne Law School Research Series* 3 (2005), 1–17, at 2: http://www.austlii.edu.au/au/journals/UMelbLRS/2005/3.html.

[16] Ibid., 3

[17] *Lange v Australian Broadcasting Commission* (1997) HCA 53; (1997) 189 CLR 520.

[18] Decisions of the German Federal Constitutional Court (BVerfGE) 73, 339 (387) (trans. R. A.).

[19] BVerfGE 125, 175 (222).

[20] BVerfGE 1, 97 (104) (trans. R. A.).

III. Proportionality

The relation between necessity and contingency also arises with the problem of the absoluteness of proportionality. This problem comprises two questions: first, the question of the absoluteness and relativity of the principle of proportionality as such, and second, the question of the absoluteness and relativity of the application of the principle of proportionality. The respective answers to these two questions presuppose an analysis, as precise as possible, of proportionality. The tools for this are provided by principles theory.

A. The Absoluteness of the Principle of Proportionality

1. Principles Theory

The basis of principles theory is the norm-theoretic distinction between rules and principles.[21] Rules are norms that require something determinate. They are *definitive commands*. Their form of application is subsumption. By contrast, principles are *optimization requirements*. As such, they demand 'that something be realized to the greatest extent possible given the legal and factual possibilities'.[22] Rules aside, the legal possibilities are determined essentially by opposing principles. For this reason, principles, each taken alone, always comprise merely *prima facie* requirements. The determination of the appropriate degree of satisfaction of one principle relative to the requirements of other principles is brought about by means of balancing. Thus, balancing is the specific form of application of principles.

The nature of principles as optimization requirements leads straightaway to a necessary connection between principles and proportionality. The principle of proportionality consists of three sub-principles: the principles of suitability, of necessity, and of proportionality in the narrower sense. All three sub-principles express the idea of optimization. For this reason, the nature of principles implies the principle of proportionality and vice versa. One who accepts the principle of proportionality must accept the character of constitutional rights as principles, and one who accepts the character of constitutional rights as principles must accept the principle of proportionality.

Principles as optimization requirements demand an optimization relative to the factual possibilities as well as relative to the legal possibilities. The principles of suitability and necessity refer to optimization relative to the factual possibilities. Optimization relative to the factual possibilities concerns the question of whether one position can be enhanced without detriment to the other.[23] Thus, the first two sub-principles require Pareto-optimality.

21 Alexy, *A Theory of Constitutional Rights* (n. 6 above), 47–8.
22 Ibid., 47.
23 Ibid., 67–9.

Optimization relative to the factual possibilities consists in avoiding avoidable costs. Costs, however, are unavoidable when principles collide. Balancing then becomes necessary. Balancing is the subject of the third sub-principle of proportionality: the principle of proportionality in the narrower sense. This principle expresses what optimization relative to the legal possibilities means. It is identical with a rule that can be called the 'Law of Balancing'.[24] It states:

> The greater the degree of non-satisfaction of, or detriment to, one principle, the greater must be the importance of satisfying the other.

The Law of Balancing excludes, *inter alia*, an intensive interference with principle P_1 that can only be justified by assigning a low importance to the satisfaction of the colliding principle P_2. To allow the interference under these conditions would not be an optimization of P_1 *together with* P_2.

2. Weight Formula

Nearly everywhere in constitutional adjudication, the Law of Balancing is found in various different formulations. It expresses the essence of balancing and is of great practical importance. If, however, one wishes to achieve a precise and complete analysis of the structure of balancing, the Law of Balancing has to be elaborated further. The result of such a further elaboration is the Weight Formula.[25] It runs as follows:

$$W_{i,j} = \frac{I_i \cdot W_i \cdot R_i}{I_j \cdot W_j \cdot R_j}$$

'$W_{i,j}$' represents the concrete weight of the principle P_i relative to the colliding principle P_j. The Weight Formula defines this concrete weight as the quotient of three factors standing, so to speak, on each side of balancing. I_i and I_j are of special importance. 'I_i' stands for the intensity of interference with P_i. 'I_j' represents the importance of satisfying the colliding principle. I_j, too, can be understood as intensity of interference, that is, as the intensity of interference with P_j through non-interference with P_i. 'W_i' and 'W_j' stand for the abstract weights of the colliding principles P_i and P_j. When the abstract weights are equal, which is often the case in collisions between constitutional rights, they cancel each other out. 'R_i' and 'R_j'

[24] Ibid., 102.

[25] See Robert Alexy, 'The Weight Formula', trans. Bartosz Brożek and Stanley L. Paulson, in *Studies in the Philosophy of Law*, vol. 3, eds Jerzy Stelmach, Bartosz Brożek, and Wojciech Załuski (Kraków: Jagiellonian University Press, 2007), 9–27, at 25 (in this volume: Chapter 11, 154–74, at 172).

represent two factors that have received ever greater attention in recent discussions on constitutional rights. They refer to the reliability of the empirical and normative assumptions[26] concerning the question of how intensive the interference with P_i is, and how intensive the interference with P_j would be if the interference with P_i were omitted. This is a factor that does not refer to such things as the interference with the right in question, that is, it is not an ontic factor. Rather, it is a factor that refers to knowledge, that is, it is an epistemic factor. Beyond that, the reliability of the empirical and normative assumptions can also relate to the classification of the abstract weights, that is, to W_i and W_j.[27]

A formula like the Weight Formula, which expresses a quotient of two products, is sensible only if all of the factors can be represented by numbers. This is the problem of graduation. Elsewhere[28] I have proposed a discrete, that is, a non-continuous, triadic scale, in which geometric sequences are implemented. This scale assigns the values 'light' (*l*), 'moderate' (*m*), and 'serious' (*s*) to the intensity of interference and to the abstract weights. These values are expressed by the numbers 2^0, 2^1, and 2^2, that is, by 1, 2, and 4. Where the epistemic side is concerned, that is, R_i and R_j, one can work with the stages 'reliable' or 'certain' (r), 'plausible' (*p*), and 'not evidently false' (*e*), to which the numbers 2^0, 2^{-1}, and 2^{-2}, that is, 1, ½, and ¼, are to be assigned.[29] By means of these triads, most of the decisions of constitutional courts can be grasped. Where they do not suffice, that is, where one has to introduce more attenuated graduations, they can be extended to double-triadic scales.[30]

[26] That R_i and R_j refer to empirical as well as to normative assumptions can be expressed by the following equation:

$$R_i = R_i^e \cdot R_i^n$$

This equation might be called 'reliability equation'. In cases in which both the empirical and the normative reliability are in question, R_i und R_j are to be substituted by the respective products on the right side of the reliability equation. In this way, the following refined version of the Weight Formula enters the stage:

$$W_{i,j} = \frac{I_i \cdot W_i \cdot R_i^e \cdot R_i^n}{I_j \cdot W_j \cdot R_j^e \cdot R_j^n}$$

See on this Robert Alexy, 'Formal Principles: Some Replies to Critics', *International Journal of Constitutional Law* 12 (2014), 511–24, at 514 (in this volume: Chapter 12, 175–89, at 178).

[27] It might be possible that this can be captured by the following refinement of the reliability equation, which would lead to a refinement of the refined Weight Formula:

$$R_i = R_{Ii}^e \cdot R_{Ii}^n \cdot R_{Wi}^e \cdot R_{Wi}^n$$

But this shall not be pursued further here.

[28] Alexy, 'The Weight Formula' (n. 25 above), 20–6 (in this volume, Chapter 11, 165–73).

[29] Ibid., 25 (Chapter 11, 171).

[30] Ibid., 22–3 (Chapter 11, 168–9).

If the concrete weight ($W_{i,j}$) of P_i is greater than 1, P_i takes precedence over P_j; if it is smaller than 1, P_j takes precedence over P_i. If, however, the concrete weight ($W_{i,j}$) is 1, a stalemate exists. In this case, it is permitted either to perform the measure in question or not to perform it.[31] This means that the state—in particular, the legislator—has discretion. This will play a considerable role in the discussion of the relative dimension of the application of the principle of proportionality.

3. Balancing and Argumentation

Matthias Jestaedt has objected to the Weight Formula on the ground that 'its claimed, or at least implied, precision is', on closer inspection, 'revealed to be a mere illusion, a methodological chimera'.[32] Along similar lines, Stavros Tsakyrakis speaks of 'the myth of mathematical precision', which must be rejected where 'judicial reasoning' is concerned.[33] At first glance, the objection that the Weight Formula represents an attempt to replace argumentation by calculation, and that this is doomed to failure, and that the formula, therefore, can never ascend to the absolute dimension, does indeed suggest itself. The basic elements of the Weight Formula are numbers; the basic elements of legal discourse are arguments. Numbers can well be connected with measuring instruments, say, with thermometers. Alongside the thermometer, however, there exists no argumeter. The answer is this. The numbers that have to be substituted in the variables of the Weight Formula represent classifications, in the case of the variables I_i and W_i as well as in that of their counterparts, the classifications as 'light', 'moderate', and 'serious'. An example is an interference with the freedom of speech (P_i), which serves to protect the personality right (P_j). If the interference with the freedom of speech has to be classified as serious, that is, if I_i receives the value 4, then the number 4 stands for nothing other than the proposition 'the interference with the freedom of speech is serious'. The same applies if the interference with the personality right through non-protection has to be classified as light. The number 1, then, stands for the proposition 'the interference with the personality right through non-protection would be light'. The pivotal point, now, is that such propositions—one might call them 'classification propositions'—are, as propositions or assertions in general, in need of justification. The question is whether they are capable of justification.

Ralf Poscher, like Alexander Somek,[34] is of the opinion that 'the balancing process itself depends on our intuition as to the relative weight of the conflicting

[31] Robert Alexy, 'Verfassungsrecht und einfaches Recht—Verfassungsgerichtsbarkeit und Fachgerichtsbarkeit', *Veröffentlichungen der Vereinigung der Deutschen Staatsrechtslehrer* 61 (2002), 7–30, at 22–6.

[32] Matthias Jestaedt, 'The Doctrine of Balancing—its Strengths and Weaknesses', in *Institutionalized Reason. The Jurisprudence of Robert Alexy*, ed. Matthias Klatt (Oxford: Oxford University Press, 2012), 152–72, at 165.

[33] Stavros Tsakyrakis, 'Proportionality: An assault on human rights?' *International Journal of Constitutional Law* 7 (2009), 468–93, at 472.

[34] See Alexander Somek, *Rechtliches Wissen* (Frankfurt: Suhrkamp, 2006), 135.

principles'.[35] One can call this the 'intuition thesis'. The reply to the intuition argument just as to Bernhard Schlink's argument from decisionism[36] and to Jürgen Habermas's argument from arbitrariness[37]—is the argumentation thesis.

The argumentation thesis says that propositions about intensity of interference and degrees of importance lend themselves to rational justification. An example is presented by a decision of the German Federal Constitutional Court in 1997 on the duty of manufacturers of tobacco products to place health warnings on those products respecting the dangers of smoking.[38] This is a minor or light interference with the freedom to pursue one`s profession. By contrast, a total ban on all tobacco products would count as serious interference. Between such minor and serious cases, others of moderate intensity of interference can be found. An example would be a ban on cigarette machines along with the introduction of provisions restricting the sale of tobacco to selected shops. If classification propositions merely expressed intuitions, decisions, or arbitrary acts, then one could only respond to a classification of the duty to place health warning as a serious interference or to a classification of the total ban on tobacco products as a light interference with counter-intuitions, anti-decisions, or opposite arbitrary acts. It is of vital importance for the rationality of balancing that absurd classifications such as these can be countered with arguments. These are not always as striking as in our examples. However, this issue belongs to the field of the absoluteness and relativity of the application of the principle of proportionality. In any case, under the aspect of the justification of the absoluteness of the principle of proportionality as such, an important first step is taken with the finding that the Weight Formula is an argument form[39] of legal discourse.

The mere reference to the argumentative character of balancing as part of proportionality analysis does not yet, however, suffice to establish the necessity, and with it the absoluteness, of proportionality. There might exist other forms of argumentation which are more rational then balancing, as explicated by the Weight Formula, or at least as rational.[40] This is the problem of alternativity. Three alternatives shall be considered: (1) subsumption or classification, (2) the reasonableness test, and (3) the protection of minimum positions.

The subsumption alternative attempts to shift the examination of violations of constitutional rights completely into the interpretation of the words used in the

[35] Ralf Poscher, 'The Principles Theory. How Many Theories and What is their Merit?' in *Institutionalized Reason. The Jurisprudence of Robert Alexy*, ed. Matthias Klatt (Oxford: Oxford University Press, 2012), 218–47, at 241.

[36] See Bernhard Schlink, 'Freiheit durch Eingriffsabwehr—Rekonstruktion der klassischen Grundrechtsfunktion', *Europäische Grundrechte-Zeitschrift* 11 (1984), 457–68, at 462.

[37] See Jürgen Habermas, *Between Facts and Norms. Contributions to a Discourse Theory of Law and Democracy* (1992), trans. William Rehg (Cambridge: Polity Press, 1996), 259.

[38] BVerfGE 95, 173.

[39] On this concept, see Robert Alexy, *A Theory of Legal Argumentation* (1978), trans. Ruth Adler and Neil MacCormick (Oxford: Clarendon Press, 1989), 92.

[40] Bernal, 'The Migration of Proportionality Across Europe' (n. 1, above), 508.

constitutional rights provisions. Article 5(3) of the German Basic Law guarantees freedom of science without a limiting clause and Article 20a of the same law obligates the state to protect the animals 'within the framework of the constitutional order'. This gives rise to norm conflicts in the case of animal experiments. Take an animal experiment that is 'according to content and form a serious methodical attempt to discover the truth',[41] although the truth is about a question that is quite unimportant for science as well as for society. On the other side, the experiment requires that a great many animals of high evolutionary development have to be exposed to very serious pain. How is this case to be resolved merely by the appeal to subsumption? The concern of science can scarcely be doubted in the light of the fact that there exists a host of more or less important questions that are pursued by scientists in their serious and methodical search for truth. On the other side, Article 20a of the German Basic Law embeds the obligation to protect animals into the framework of the constitutional order, and this order includes the freedom of science, which is guaranteed, without reservation, by Article 5(3) of the German Basic Law. Thus, if both provisions are conceived as rules under which the case has to be subsumed, the experiment would have to be permitted. Now it shall be assumed that in our case a prohibition would be an admissible limitation of the freedom of science. Given this background, the subsumption alternative would have to be confined to a classification of less important scientific questions as not scientific at all or to a declaration of the clause 'within the framework of the constitutional order' in Article 20a of the German Basic Law, first, as non-existent and then, on this basis, of Article 20a of the German Basic Law either as an exception to Article 5(3) of the German Basic Law or as higher-ranking vis-à-vis Article 5(3) of the German Basic Law. All this would have virtually nothing to do with rational argumentation. It would be no more than an attempt to justify something by means of subsumption that can well be rationally justified by means of balancing[42] but not by means of subsumption. The open play of argument and counter-argument according to the Weight Formula is altogether superior to such quibbling.

The second alternative is the reasonableness test. The concept of reasonableness is understood in very different ways. A narrow version is to be found in the British *Wednesbury* Judgment from 1948. According to it, a decision is unreasonable when it contains 'something so absurd that no sensible person could ever dream that it lay within the powers of the authority'.[43] An absurdity test such as this is, however, too weak if it is conceived as an alternative to proportionality analysis. There are cases which require a much closer review than an absurdity test can provide. If, however, the absurdity test is understood as a special case of proportionality analysis, say, as a case located on the lowest level of empirical or normative reliability—'not

[41] BVerfGE 35, 79 (113) (trans. R. A.).

[42] See on this OVG Bremen, DVBl 2013, 669.

[43] *Associated Provincial Picture Houses v Wednesbury Corporation* (1948) 1 KB 223.

evidently false' (*e*)—then the absurdity test is not an alternative to proportionality analysis but is, rather, an extreme case of its application. A broad version of reasonableness or *ragionevolezza* includes in this concept everything, in principle, that can count as a criterion of practical correctness. If this comprises proportionality, and if the relation of proportionality to the further elements is clearly determined, the reasonableness test is no real alternative to proportionality analysis. It is the point of the argumentation thesis that proportionality analysis is connected with the further rules and forms of rational legal discourse. A broad version of the reasonable test, however, is a poor alternative to proportionality analysis if it simply makes indistinct reference to a bundle of topics. The Weight Formula makes explicit which elements—one might even say, which powers—are significant for the limitation of constitutional rights and how they are related to each other. With this, it introduces, in Barak's words, 'order into legal thought'.[44]

The third alternative to be considered here is the protection of minimum positions, as brought into play by Schlink[45] and Poscher.[46] This alternative would make possible in constitutional law such propositions as the following: 'The interference with the constitutional right is constitutional, even though it is serious and justified only by a reason with a low or light weight, for the minimal position is observed.' For the thesis of the minimum position, it is sufficient for the constitutionality of a suitable and necessary interference that the minimal position not be infringed. Constitutional interferences, however, are justified interferences.[47] Now it seems to be true that an interference with a constitutional right is unjustified when it is certain that the interference is serious from the point of view of the constitution and the reason justifying the interference has, again from the point of view of the constitution, only a light weight. This implies that, according to the thesis of the minimal position, there exist unjustified justified interferences. This leads into the '*regno delle assurdità*',[48] the kingdom of absurdity.

Under the aspect of finality, no list of alternatives is complete; something new can always appear. Nevertheless, the previous considerations give rise to the assumption that proportionality as such will have a stability over time that compares with Aristotle's syllogistic. Should this assumption be true, the principle of proportionality would have absolute validity and, therefore, as a principle, an absolute character.

[44] See Aharon Barak, *The Judge in a Democracy* (Princeton, N. J.: Princeton University Press, 2006), 173.

[45] Bernhard Schlink, *Abwägung im Verfassungsrecht* (Berlin: Duncker & Humblot, 1976), 76–8, 192–9.

[46] Poscher, 'The Principles Theory. How Many Theories and What is their Merit?' (n. 35 above), 232, 237.

[47] Or shall there exist unjustified interferences that are constitutional where 'unjustified' means 'constitutionally unjustified'?

[48] Federico Pedrini, 'Colloquio su Princìpi, Diritto e Giustizia. Intervista al Robert Alexy', *Lo Stato* 2 (2014), 125–64, at 151.

B. The Relativity and Absoluteness of the Application of the Principle of Proportionality

That the principle of proportionality has an absolute character does not mean that its application must also possess such a character. One who thinks that everything can always be brought within the variables of the Weight Formula, that is, that all classifications are always possible, supports the thesis of the complete relativity of the application of the principle of proportionality. Schlink comes quite close to this thesis when he says that 'the optimization requirement is such an open concept that it allows for the justification of every not completely nonsensical state interference with freedom.'[49] If the thesis of complete relativity applied, the third sub-principle of proportionality, as explicated by the Weight Formula, would be a criterion that is no criterion. This would have the systematic consequence that the third sub-principle has to be rejected. It would lose its necessary validity and, with this, its absolute character. Now one could think of setting against the thesis of complete relativity of the application of the principle of proportionality the thesis of complete absoluteness of the application of the principle of proportionality. This would imply that all constitutional courts and all supranational and international courts concerned with supranational or international human rights would have to arrive, in all sufficiently similar cases, at the same decision. The plausibility of this assumption, however, appears to be no greater than the plausibility of its counterpart, the thesis of complete relativity of the application of the principle of proportionality. The principle of proportionality as such, as I have argued above, has absolute validity. Things are more complex with respect to the application of the principle of proportionality. Neither complete relativity nor complete absoluteness of the application of the principle of proportionality can be right. Therefore, a middle course has to be pursued. But this statement, as with middle-course theses in general, has little value apart from the construction of this middle course.

1. Discretion

The basis on which the relation between relativity and absoluteness in the application of the principle of proportionality has to be determined is the theory of discretion. Discretion is connected with proportionality in all cases in which proportionality analysis leads to the result that two contradictory measures are equally proportional. Discretion theory cannot be presented here in any detail.[50] Instead, I will confine myself to indicating by means of an example taken from the jurisdiction of the European Court of Human Rights how the relativity of the application

[49] Bernhard Schlink, 'Grundrechte als Prinzipien?' *Osaka University Law Review* 39 (1992), 41–58, at 54 (trans. R. A.).

[50] See on this Alexy, 'Verfassungsrecht und einfaches Recht—Verfassungsgerichtsbarkeit und Fachgerichtsbarkeit' (n. 31 above), 15–30.

of the third sub-principle of proportionality—that is, of balancing—can be constructed with the help of the Weight Formula.

The basic distinction of discretion theory is the distinction between substantive[51] and epistemic discretion. Substantive discretion exists when something is neither commanded nor prohibited by the constitution. By contrast, epistemic discretion arises when knowledge of what the constitution commands or prohibits is uncertain. Here, only substantive discretion shall be considered.[52]

There are three kinds of substantive discretion: (1) end-setting discretion, (2) means-selecting discretion, and (3) discretion in balancing. The legislator has end-setting discretion to the extent that the constitution gives him the free choice of the reasons for interferences with constitutional rights, say, by explicit reservation clauses.[53] The *Lautsi* Judgment of the Grand Chamber of the European Court of Human Rights presents an example of end-setting discretion. The decision concerns the question of whether crucifixes in Italian state-school classrooms violate the religious right to education on the part of the parents in Article 2(2) of Protocol No. 1 to the European Convention on Human Rights and, as concerns the children, their right to education in Article 2(1) of Protocol No. 1 or their religious freedom under Article 9 of the European Convention on Human Rights. After classifying the measure as interference,[54] the Court identifies as the reason for this interference the end sought by the Italian government, namely, to perpetuate a tradition it conceives to be important for the identity of Italy.[55] With regard to this purpose, end-setting discretion is clearly assumed: 'The Court takes the view that the decision whether or not to perpetuate a tradition falls in principle within the margin

[51] Instead of 'substantive' discretion one can also speak of 'structural' discretion. See Alexy, 'Verfassungsrecht und einfaches Recht—Verfassungsgerichtsbarkeit und Fachgerichtsbarkeit' (n. 31 above), 16.

[52] Epistemic discretion occurs when the empirical or normative premises on which the classification of the intensity of interference (I_i, I_j) and the abstract weights (W_i, W_j) are based are not certain or reliable (*r*), but only plausible (*p*) or not evidently false (*e*). In case of certainty, R_i, respectively R_j, receives the value 2^0, that is, 1. This means that the epistemic level has no influence on the substantive level. If, however, the premises are merely plausible (*p*), the value 2^{-1}, that is ½, has to be substituted, and when they are only not evidently false (*e*), the value 2^{-2}, that is ¼. With this, the epistemic level affects the substantive level by reducing the substantive result in case of *p* to ½ and in case of *e* to ¼. It shall be assumed that the abstract weights, as so often, are equal so that they can be reduced. Now, if I_i has the value 2 and I_j the value 4, than there exists no substantive stalemate. If one adds to this R_i with the value 1 and R_j with the value ½, a stalemate results, which can be designated as 'substantive-epistemic stalemate'. The substantive-epistemic stalemate has to be distinguished from the purely epistemic stalemate. A purely epistemic stalemate exists when two contradictory premises that stand in competition with respect to the same substantive variable are equally plausible (*p*) or equally not evidently false (*e*). Then, the legislator has free choice. The *Cannabis* Judgment of the German Federal Constitutional Court (BVerfGE 90, 145) is an example of this; see Alexy, 'The Weight Formula' (n. 25 above), 26 (in this volume, Chapter 11, 172–3). If, however, one of the premises competing with respect to the same substantive variable has the value *p* and the other the value *e*, no purely epistemic stalemate exists. For a closer analysis of the epistemic dimension of balancing see Alexy, 'Formal principles: Some replies to Critics' (n. 26 above), 519–24 (in this volume: Chapter 12, 184-9).

[53] Alexy, 'Verfassungsrecht und einfaches Recht—Verfassungsgerichtsbarkeit und Fachgerichtsbarkeit' (n. 31 above), 17.

[54] ECHR, 18.3.2011–30814/06, *Lautsi and Others v. Italy (Grand Chamber)*, § 65.

[55] Ibid., § 67.

of appreciation of the respondent State.'[56] With this, the tradition is elevated to the rank of a countervailing principle.[57] This principle, P_j, has to be balanced against the religious freedom as connected with education, P_i. Now the European Court of Human Rights classifies, in marked contrast to the German Federal Constitutional Court,[58] the interference with religious freedom as light,[59] that is, I_i receives the value 1. The intensity of the hypothetical interference with the tradition principle through a prohibition of crucifixes is not clearly determined. Much in the decision, however, indicates that the European Court of Human Rights assumes a moderate intensity of interference here. Thus, I_j receives the value 2. It can be assumed that the values of the two other variables of the Weight Formula are equal in the present case. Therefore, they play no role in the determination of the concrete weight of P_i, that is, of $W_{i,j}$. For this reason, $W_{i,j}$ receives the value ½. That this value is lower than 1 implies that P_j, the tradition principle, takes precedence over P_i, the principle of religious freedom. Thus, the interference is proportional. Much more could be said about this decision. Here, however, only one point needs to be emphasized and generalized. The relativity generated by end-setting discretion consists in the fact that when, due to a case of the state's end-setting, the concrete weight ($W_{i,j}$) of the right affected is not greater than 1, then whether the holder of the right must suffer the interference or not depends on the decision of the state.

The means-selecting discretion, which plays a key role in connection with rights to positive state action,[60] shall not be considered here, and only a brief glance can be cast at the third kind of substantive discretion, discretion in balancing. Discretion in balancing exists when there is a balancing stalemate. That is the case when the products on both sides of the Weight Formula are equal, that is, when the concrete weight ($W_{i,j}$) of P_i is 1. As long as the triadic scale is used, three stalemate constellations exist: (1) *l*/*l*, (2) *m*/*m*, and (3) *s*/*s*.[61] In these situations, the legislator is free to decide as he wishes. Again, the relativity consists in the fact that it depends on the decision of the state as to whether the holder of the right must suffer the interference or not. The discretion in balancing can be connected with other kinds of discretion, for instance, with end-setting discretion. If in the *Lautsi* case I_j, that is, the hypothetical interference with the tradition principle by means of a prohibition of crucifixes in classrooms, is classified not as moderate but as light, which implies

56 Ibid., § 68.

57 Alexy, *A Theory of Constitutional Rights* (n. 6 above), 81–2.

58 BVerfGE 93, 1 (18).

59 ECHR, *Lautsi and Others v. Italy* (n. 54 above), § 72.

60 Robert Alexy, 'On Constitutional Rights to Protection', *Legisprudence* 3 (2009), 1–17, at 5, 16.

61 It is of prime importance for the theory of discretion that the stalemate constellations decrease with the refinement of the scale. With the triadic scale a third of all constellations are stalemate constellations. With a nine-stage double-triadic scale, that is, with a scale which starts with *l*/*l*, proceeds with *l*/*m*, and ends with *s*/*s*, the stalemate constellations shrink to a ninth. Thus, the choice of a rough scale increases the discretion of the state. On this see Julian Rivers, 'Proportionality, Discretion and the Second Law of Balancing', in *Law, Rights and Discourse. The Legal Philosophy of Robert Alexy*, ed. George Pavlakos (Oxford: Hart, 2007), 167–88, at 184.

that the value 1 and not 2 is assigned to it, then, with the stalemate, there occurs discretion in balancing based on end-setting discretion, which is to say that the freedom of decision on the part of the Italian government is preserved.

2. Discursively Necessary Classifications

Up until now, the point has been the construction of elements of the relative dimension in the application of the principle of proportionality by means of the Weight Formula. There, the concept of discretion stood at the centre. Now the question is whether such a construction is also possible on the side of the absolute dimension. Here the argumentation thesis is paramount. This thesis says that propositions about intensities of interference and degrees of importance are rationally justifiable. Now classification propositions are concerned with the question of what is forbidden, commanded, and permitted by constitutional rights,[62] that is, they are concerned with practical questions. At this point, radical scepticism—based on forms of emotivism, decisionism, subjectivism, relativism, naturalism, or deconstructivism—claims that rational practical argumentation is not possible. The objection to this is that there exist criteria of practical rationality which constitute a system of rules and forms of rational practical discourse.[63] Therefore, the question cannot be that of whether rational practical argumentation exists but only what force it has. In order to grasp this, the distinction between discursive necessity, discursive impossibility, and discursive possibility is indispensable.[64] What is required by the rules of discourse is discursively necessary. Human rights and democracy belong here.[65] What is excluded by the rules of discourse is discursively impossible. The racial principle (*Rassenprinzip*) and the leader principle (*Führerprinzip*), as constitutive for the Third Reich, belong here. What can be justified without violation of discourse rules, although the contrary can also be justified without violation of discourse rules, is discursively merely possible.

The decisive question for the dimension of absoluteness in the application of the principle of proportionality is whether there exists besides the abstract discursive necessity of human rights also a concrete discursive necessity of classification propositions and, with this, of certain results of proportionality analysis. This is to be answered in the affirmative. The *Tobacco* case offers an example. Another example is found in the *Titanic* Decision of the German Federal Constitutional Court. Here the public characterization of a seriously disabled person in a disparaging

[62] The way from the classification propositions to the prohibitions, obligations, and permissions of constitutional rights runs past the connection of the two laws of principles theory, the Law of Balancing, as explicated by the Weight Formula, and the Law of Colliding Principles. See on this Robert Alexy, 'Proportionality and Rationality', in: *Proportionality. New Frontiers, New Challenges*, eds Vicki C. Jackson and Mark Tushnet (Cambridge: Cambridge University Press, 2017), 13–29, at 26–8 (in this volume: Chapter 15, 220–34, at 232–4).

[63] For such a system of twenty-eight rules and forms, see Alexy, *A Theory of Legal Argumentation* (n. 39 above), 188–206.

[64] Ibid., 207.

[65] Robert Alexy, 'Discourse Theory and Human Rights', *Ratio Juris* 9 (1996), 209–35, at 220–33.

context as a 'cripple' is classified by the Court as a 'serious' violation of his personality right.[66] It is not easy to contest this. And for how long would we be willing to enter into discussion with someone who classifies life imprisonment[67] as a light interference and, by contrast with this, a local ban on feeding pigeons[68] as a serious interference?

For all of that it must be taken into consideration that cases in which discursively necessary classifications are possible—one might call them 'clear balancing cases'—rarely reach the constitutional courts. Nevertheless, these clear cases are of great importance systematically. The system of proportionality does not hang in the air. It rests on a massive fundament of clear cases. One could talk here about the 'proportionality basis'.

3. Real Relativity and Ideal Absoluteness

Against this it might be objected that, while there certainly exists a certain basis of clear cases, beyond this basis the realm of pure relativity begins. Thus, proportionality analysis, where it is really needed, is without value. In order to counter this objection, I shall take up briefly a decision of the German Federal Constitutional Court in 2006 on electronic data-screening. A student with Moroccan citizenship brought a constitutional complaint against an order of electronic data-screening. This order required residents' registration offices, the central aliens' registry, and universities to transmit data to the police concerning male persons between eighteen and forty years regarding, *inter alia*, their faith, native country, and subject of study. These data were submitted to automatic data processing with an eye to identifying potential Islamist terrorists. The majority of the First Panel of the Federal Constitutional Court classified the measure as an interference of 'considerable weight',[69] that is, as a serious interference with the complainant's right to data self-determination. Such a serious interference would be justified in cases of concrete danger but not in cases of abstract danger, characterized by a 'generally threatening situation' as has existed 'at the latest since September 11, 2001'.[70] It was deemed, however, that no concrete danger was at hand. Therefore, the constitutional complaint was considered to be justified. The classification stemming from the dissenting opinion of Judge Haas is completely different. According to her assessment, the interference is 'of low weight' and has to be accepted as being in the 'public interest'.[71] From this point of view, the constitutional complaint would not be justified.

[66] BVerfGE 86, 1 (13).
[67] BVerfGE 45, 143 (238): 'serious interferences with constitutional rights' (trans. R. A.).
[68] BVerfGE 54, 143 (147): 'only very limited interference' (trans. R. A.).
[69] BVerfGE 115, 320 (348) (trans. R. A.).
[70] Ibid., 364 (trans. R. A.).
[71] Ibid., 379 (trans. R. A.).

One who focuses on the fact that the case has been resolved by a majority decision can easily gain the impression of relativity, and, indeed, with an eye to the decision-making procedure, one can speak of 'real relativity'. With this, however, the phenomenon is only partially grasped. In order to grasp it completely, ideal absoluteness has to be set next to real relativity. The ideal absoluteness stems from the fact that both sides raise a claim to correctness for their classifications and attempt to discharge it by means of arguments. With the claim to correctness, reference is made to correctness as a regulative idea. Correctness as a regulative idea means that the actually existing, and by majority rule institutionally resolved, disagreement remains open for future argumentation. With this, correctness as a regulative idea strives towards the dimension of the absolute. For this reason, even beyond the basis of clear cases, the dimension of the absolute does not perish. It lives on in the connection of real relativity and ideal absoluteness.

PART III

ARGUMENTATION, CORRECTNESS, AND LAW

The central theme of Part III is argumentation. Two questions are discussed. The first is the general question of whether rational argumentation about normative questions is possible or not possible. The positive answer is based on discourse theory. The second question is of whether the idea of rational discourse can be applied in law. The answer is that legal discourse is a special case of general practical discourse. This is the special case thesis. The special case thesis connects the real dimension of law with law's ideal dimension.

17

A Discourse-Theoretical Conception of Practical Reason

I. Introduction

The theme legal system and practical reason, would appear to presuppose what must first be proven, namely that there is such a thing as practical reason because it is only if practical reason exists, at least in the sense that there is a possibility of reason being brought to bear on practical questions, that it is meaningful to inquire into its relationship to the legal system. A brief look at twentieth-century literature in legal philosophy shows that there is considerable doubt as to this possibility and thus as to the existence of practical reason. No lesser figures than Alf Ross and Hans Kelsen considered the concept of practical reason to be 'a self-contradictory concept'.[1] According to them, reason relates to cognition, while by contrast the realm of the practical embraces only volition. It is argued that cognition is defined precisely by the fact that it is not volition and for something to constitute a volition it is necessary that it does not have the character of cognition. The concept of practical reason is therefore a 'logically untenable concept'.[2]

All advocates of a non-cognitivist ethics, all emotivists for example,[3] would agree with the general thrust[4] of this view. According to emotivist theories, normative statements such as 'all human beings have a right to freedom and dignity' only have the function of expressing or arousing feelings or attitudes. As mere vehicles for the expression of feelings and influencing of the human psyche, such expressions are said to have nothing to do with truth or correctness and therefore nothing to do with practical reason either. Virulent critics of reason such as Nietzsche are in broad agreement with the stark meta-ethical school of the emotivists. For Nietzsche, reason in general, and practical reason in particular, is 'a deceitful

[1] Hans Kelsen, 'Das Problem der Gerechtigkeit', in Kelsen, *Reine Rechtslehre*, 2nd edn (Vienna: Franz Deuticke, 1960), 355–444, at 415; Alf Ross, *Kritik der sogenannten praktischen Erkenntnis* (Leipzig: Felix Meiner, 1933), 19.

[2] Kelsen, 'Das Problem der Gerechtigkeit' (n. 1 above), 419.

[3] Compare the most significant emotivist, Charles L. Stevenson, *Ethics and Language* (New Haven, Conn.: Yale University Press, 1944).

[4] This qualification is necessary since Stevenson does after all distinguish between rational and non-rational methods of justification. See Stevenson, *Ethics and Language* (n. 3 above), 115–30, 139–40.

Law's Ideal Dimension. Robert Alexy, Oxford University Press. © Robert Alexy 2021.
DOI: 10.1093/oso/9780198796831.003.0018

old woman',[5] who stands in the way of a healthy morality, that is, according to Nietzsche, one governed 'by an instinct of life'.[6]

Is it really necessary to conclude that we are dealing with a self-contradictory concept which can at best be used as a semantic weapon in a permanent process of mutual manipulation and at worst deceives us about life? My response is an emphatic 'no'. The question is how my thesis can be justified.

II. In Defence of the Concept of Practical Reason

One of the first problems which presents itself to anyone who wishes to expound the view that practical reason is possible and in this sense exists lies in the fact that the concept of practical reason is indeterminate to a high degree. In addition, terminology fluctuates considerably. People often speak of 'practical rationality' rather than of 'practical reason'. In order to avoid prejudicing the argument, these two expressions will be used synonymously.

The argument now becomes more intense. The multiplicity of what may be regarded as practical rationality would appear to be almost unlimited. Thus Lenk distinguishes twenty types of rationality.[7] In this situation one can attempt to track down the most general features of the concept of practical rationality.[8] In this process one will come up against things such as consistency, coherence, justifiability, empirical truth, effectiveness, optimization, and reflexivity. Yet even if it were possible to single out such concepts as the most general features of the concept of practical rationality and to determine their relationship to one another, little would be achieved. The real dispute about the concept of practical reason takes place beneath this level of abstraction. It is not a dispute about the most general characteristics of rationality, but rather a conflict between different conceptions of practical rationality.

Three main conceptions of practical reason or practical rationality are in competition with one another in current discussions. These can be named as follows by reference to their historical models: Aristotelian, Hobbesian, and Kantian. Taking the position of a radical critic of the concept of practical reason as adopted by Nietzsche, one is faced by a common opponent to all three views. The arguments of contemporary advocates of these views show that the dispute about different conceptions of rationality embraces far more than purely academic

[5] Friedrich Nietzsche, *Twilight of the Idols*, trans. R. J. Hollingdale (Harmondsworth: Penguin Books, 1968), 48.

[6] Ibid., 55.

[7] Hans Lenk, 'Rationalitätstypen', in *Rationalität und Wissenschaft*, ed. Gerhard Pasternak (Bremen: Zentrum philosophische Grundlagen der Wissenschaft, 1988), 9–22, at 11–18.

[8] Delf Buchwald, *Der Begriff der rationalen juristischen Begründung* (Baden-Baden: Nomos, 1990), 58–68

concerns. It concerns the normative foundation of human coexistence and one's perception of the individual and of society. Thus, according to Alasdair MacIntyre who is probably the most widely discussed advocate of an Aristotelian conception,[9] 'the Enlightenment project' has foundered.[10] All variants of liberal individualism are to be rejected.[11] Every universalistic morality appears as a spectre to haunt us.[12] The belief in human rights is said to be on a level with that in witches and unicorns.[13] In their place, MacIntyre recommends an orientation to the idea of the good life as bound up with the local and the specific.[14] Advocates of the Hobbesian conception such as Buchanan[15] and Gauthier[16] have broadened Weber's idea of 'purpose-rationality'[17] into the concept of the maximization of individual utility and have reformulated classical theories of contract within the framework of modern theories of rational choice and rational negotiation.[18]

[9] For a general exposition of the Aristotelian conception, compare Herbert Schnädelbach, 'Was ist Neoaristotelismus?' in *Moralität und Sittlichkeit*, ed. Wolfgang Kuhlmann (Frankfurt: Suhrkamp, 1986), 38–63, at 42, 50–4, and also Jürgen-Eckardt Pleines, 'Zur Sache des sogenannten Neoaristotelismus, *Zeitschrift für philosophische Forschung* 43 (1989), 133–79. Both articles are interesting from the point of view of a classification of conceptions of rationality, in that they count neo-Hegelianism in the field of political philosophy as belonging to neo-Aristotelianism. This thesis underlies the classification advocated here.

[10] Alasdair MacIntyre, *After Virtue*, 2nd edn (London: Duckworth, 1985), 271.

[11] Ibid., 220–1, 259.

[12] Ibid., 43, 60, 256–9.

[13] Ibid., 69.

[14] Ibid., 126–7, 219.

[15] James M. Buchanan, *The Limits of Liberty* (Chicago, Ill.: University of Chicago Press, 1975).

[16] David Gauthier, *Morals by Agreement* (Oxford: Clarendon Press, 1986).

[17] The concept of purpose-rationality does not as such define a conception of rationality. Every rational human action has a teleological structure. It is for this reason that the logic of teleological action is valid for every conception of rationality. As Max Weber stressed, this is not limited to the question of whether a means is necessary to achieve the purpose or goal sought through it; Max Weber, *The Theory of Social and Economic Organisation*, trans. A. M. Henderson and Talcott Parsons (New York, N.Y.: Free Press, 1964), 117. Much more than this it requires a threefold balancing process over and beyond this: first, that of the means against the purpose or goal, second, that of the purpose or goal as against any unavoidable side effects, and, third, that of goal or purpose being pursued as against other possible ends; Max Weber, 'The Meaning of "Ethical Neutrality" in Sociology and Economics', , trans. E. A. Shils and H. A. Finch, in Weber, *The Methodology of the Social Sciences* (New York, N.Y.: Free Press, 1968), 1–47. The idea of purpose-rationality develops into an actual conception of rationality only when combined with the non-cognitivist thesis to the effect that the choice of goals or purposes together with the weighing and balancing of those purposes against means, side-effects, and alternative ends ultimately depends on subjective preferences which are themselves no longer amenable to rational justification. This is Max Weber's view: 'It is really a question not only of alternatives between values but of an irreconcilable death-struggle, like that between "God" and the "Devil"'; ibid., 17; Weber, 'Science as a Vocation', , trans. H. H. Gerth and C. Wright Mills, in *From Max Weber. Essays in Sociology* (New York, N.Y.: Oxford University Press, 1958), 129–55.

[18] Rawls' theory of justice does not belong to the Hobbesian, but rather to the Kantian conceptions. In Rawls' account individuals are denied all information about themselves by means of the original position and its veil of ignorance. Having set up the parameters it is only possible to take any decisions from the point of view of any person whatsoever and hence impartially and justly. Rawls' original position thereby contains a normative decision in favour of a universalistic and hence a Kantian conception of rationality. It is for this reason that Rawls came to see his earlier thesis, that his theory of justice should be viewed as part of the theory of rational choice, John Rawls, *A Theory of Justice* (Cambridge Mass.: Harvard University Press, 1971), 16, 583, as an 'error' and withdrew it; John Rawls, 'Justice as Fairness: Political not Metaphysical', *Philosophy and Public Affairs* 14 (1985), 223–51, at 237.

Buchanan's thesis to the effect that a contract for slavery is a possible result of rational negotiation shows that even these theories may involve contestable normative implications.[19] Foucault may be cited as a sceptic following in the tracks left by Nietzsche. According to him behind the 'will to truth' and discourse are concealed 'desire and power'.[20] It all depends on 'exposing instinct, passion, inquisitorial rage, cruel refinement, malevolence ... [and] violence' as 'forms and reformulations of the will to knowledge'.[21]

I shall attempt to defend a discourse-theoretical version of the Kantian conception. Limitations of time and space will not permit me to present and criticize the opposing positions in any great detail. I shall merely refer to some objections from these quarters.

III. A Kantian Conception of Practical Rationality: Discourse Theory

The idea of universalizability forms the basis of every Kantian conception of practical rationality. This idea can be interpreted in very different ways. Only the interpretation given by discourse theory will be of interest here.[22]

[19] Buchanan, *The Limits of Liberty* (n. 15 above), 59–60; James M. Buchanan, 'The Gauthier Enterprise', *Social Philosophy and Policy* 5 (1988), 75–94, at 84–94. Gauthier attempts to avoid results of this kind by formulating a proviso for the initial bargaining position which is aimed to exclude the possibility that an individual should bring something to the bargaining table which had previously been obtained at the cost of someone else; Gauthier, *Morals by Agreement* (n. 16 above), 200–1. Buchanan has correctly pointed out that in this way Gauthier's theory of bargaining has adopted moral premises in contrast to its Hobbesian starting point, for in the case of utility-maximization, it is in no way always required necessarily to forego all the advantages of any exploitation; Buchanan, 'The Gauthier Enterprise', (n. 19), 84–94; compare also Gilbert Harman, 'Rationality in Agreement', *Social Philosophy and Policy* 5 (1988), 1–16, at 11. The objection that he adopts too much from morality in his initial bargaining position, brings Gauthier close to Rawls whose theory is to be classified as Kantian. On the other hand, from the point of view of the weak and disadvantaged, who can bring only little or nothing at all to the bargaining table, Gauthier's conception can be said to contain too little morality; James S. Fishkin, 'Bargaining, Justice, and Justification: Towards a Reconstruction', *Social Philosophy and Policy* 5 (1988), 46–64, at 52. Taking both views together shows that Gauthier's suggestion embraces a decision in favour of a particular morality, which cannot be justified through the idea of utility-maximization alone.

[20] Michel Foucault, *L'ordre du discours* (Paris: Gallimard, 1971), 15.

[21] Michel Foucault, 'Nietzsche, Genealogy, History', in *Language, Counter-Memory, Practice*, trans. D. F. Bouchard and S. Simon, ed. D. F. Bouchard (Oxford: Blackwell, 1977), 164.

[22] For an evaluation of discourse theory as Kantian, see Robert Alexy, *A Theory of Legal Argumentation* (1978), trans. Ruth Adler and Neil MacCormick (Oxford: Clarendon Press, 1989), 117; Jürgen Habermas, 'Moralität und Sittlichkeit. Treffen Hegels Einwände gegen Kant auch auf die Diskursethik zu?' in *Moralität und Sittlichkeit*, ed. Wolfgang Kuhlmann (Frankfurt: Suhrkamp, 1986), 16–37; Otfried Höffe, *Kategorische Rechtsprinzipien* (Frankfurt: Suhrkamp, 1990), 343–4.

A. The Basic Idea of Discourse Theory

Discourse theory is a procedural theory. The conception of rationality applicable to discourse theory is thus a procedural, universalistic rationality. The contract theories of Buchanan and Gauthier being in the Hobbesian tradition are also procedural theories. In these theories just as in discourse theory, a norm is said to be a correct one precisely when it is or might be the outcome of a specific procedure.[23] The distinction between these theories lies in how the procedure is set up. In contract theories the procedure is one of negotiation, while in discourse theory it is one of argumentation. At the centre of contract theory lies the concept of the rational decision. This is determined by the idea of the maximization of individual utility. The key concept of discourse theory is that of rational judgment. This is defined by means of the concept of rational justification or argumentation. The latter in its turn is then determined by the concept of rational discourse.

A practical discourse is rational when it meets the conditions of rational practical argumentation. These conditions can be summarized into a system of rules[24] of discourse.[25] Practical reason can be defined as the ability to arrive at practical judgments according to this system of rules.

Rules of discourse may be classified in many different ways. A division into two groups will be recommended here: those rules which relate directly to the structure of arguments and those rules whose immediate subject-matter is the procedure of discourse. Rules in the first group, that is rules relating directly to the structure of arguments, demand, among other things, freedom from contradiction (l. l),[26] universalizability in the sense of a consistent use of applied predicates (1.3), (1.3'), linguistic and conceptual clarity (6.2), the truth of applied empirical premises (6.1), deductive completeness of arguments (4), consideration of consequences (4.2), (4.3), prioritization (4.5), (4.6), the assumption of an exchange of roles or role reversal (5.1.1), and the analysis of the genesis of moral convictions (5.2.1), (5.2.2). All these rules are also applicable in the context of monologues, and it can be assumed that no theory of rational practical argumentation or justification can dispense with them. This makes it clear that discourse theory in no way replaces justification by merely producing consensus. It fully embraces those rules

[23] Robert Alexy, 'Die Idee einer prozeduralen Theorie der juristischen Argumentation', *Rechtstheorie*, supplement 2 (1981), 177–88, at 178.

[24] The concept of a rule of discourse is taken here to include both rules and principles in the sense of a general theory of norms. On this distinction, compare Robert Alexy, *A Theory of Constitutional Rights* (1985), trans. Julian Rivers (Oxford: Oxford University Press, 2002), 47–8.

[25] Such a system of twenty-eight discourse rules is to be found in Alexy, *A Theory of Legal Argumentation* (n. 22 above), 187–206.

[26] The numbering refers to the formulation of the rules in Alexy, *A Theory of Legal Argumentation* (n. 22 above), 188–206.

of rational argumentation which are applicable to arguments. Its distinctive feature lies exclusively in the fact that it adds a second level to this one, namely that of rules referring to the procedure of discourse.

This second group of rules is not applicable to monologues. Its main purpose is to secure the impartiality of practical argumentation and therewith of any practical opinions resting on it. Rules serving this particular purpose may be designated 'specific rules of discourse'. The most important are as follows:

(2.1) Everyone who can speak may take part in discourse.
(2.2) (a) Everyone may problematize any assertion.
(b) Everyone may introduce any assertion into the discourse.
(c) Everyone may express his or her attitudes, wishes, and needs.
(2.3) No speaker may be prevented from exercising the rights laid down in (2.1) and (2.2) by any kind of coercion internal or external to the discourse.

These rules express the universalistic character of the discourse-theoretical conception of practical rationality in the cloak of a theory of argumentation. If these rules are valid then the following condition of universal agreement (UA) is also valid:

> UA: In any discourse a norm can only find universal agreement when the consequences of generally following that norm for the satisfaction of the interests of each and every individual are acceptable to all by reason of arguments.[27]

A norm which finds universal agreement under this condition is, in an ideal sense, correct. It therefore has ideal moral validity. This concept of ideal moral validity corresponds to the Kantian principle of legislative power:

> Therefore only the concurring and united will of all, insofar as each decides the same thing for all and all for each, and so only the general united will of the people, can be legislative.[28]

[27] The condition of universal agreement becomes a rule of discourse when its establishment is viewed as mandatory. Compare rule (5.1.2) in Alexy, *A Theory of Legal Argumentation* (n. 22 above), 203, and Habermas's principle of universalization; Jürgen Habermas, 'Diskursethik—Notizen zu einem Begründungsprogramm', in Habermas, *Moralbewußtsein und kommunikatives Handeln* (Frankfurt: Suhrkamp, 1983), 53–125, at 75–6, 103.

[28] Immanuel Kant, *The Metaphysics of Morals*, trans. and ed. Mary J. Gregor, in *The Cambridge Edition of the Works of Immanuel Kant. Practical Philosophy* (Cambridge: Cambridge University Press, 1996), 353–603, at 457; AA 6, 313–4.

B. The Status of Discourse Theory as a Theory of Practical Correctness and Rationality

1. Discourse and Good Reasons

Weinberger has the following objection to discourse theory as a theory of practical correctness. He holds the view that the correctness of a thesis does not depend on whether it could be the result of a discourse but only on whether or not good reasons can be adduced in its favour.[29] It is further argued that a consensus cannot be a criterion of truth since such a consensus might quickly come to prevail in situations of mass psychosis.[30]

It can be pointed out here that the situation of mass psychosis is precisely the opposite of the situation of rational discourse. I have already explained that discourse theory includes the rules of rational argumentation which are applicable to arguments.[31] To be sure, it must be conceded that mere adherence to the rules of discourse does not guarantee the soundness of the arguments. This brings us to a fundamental premise for discourse theory which has, on the whole, been inadequately stressed.[32] Discourse theory presupposes that the participants in discourse, that is human beings as they actually exist, are in principle capable of distinguishing between good and bad reasons. Its starting point therefore is that of a presumption of a fundamental competence to judge on the part of the participants.[33] This does not mean that the competence to judge is a requirement of the procedure.[34] The relationship between the procedure of discourse and the competence to judge on the part of its participants instead corresponds to that between the constitution of a democratic constitutional state and the capability of its citizens to participate in political, economic, and social activities. The latter is not required by the norms of the constitution but is instead presupposed by the constitution itself.[35]

[29] Ota Weinberger, 'Logische Analyse als Basis der juristischen Argumentation', in *Metatheorie juristischer Argumentation*, eds Werner Krawietz and Robert Alexy (Berlin: Dunker & Humblot, 1983), 159–232, at 188–9.

[30] Ibid., 192.

[31] Spaemann asks how discourse 'is to be distinguished from any other processes of group dynamics'; Robert Spaemann, *Glück und Wohlwollen*, 2nd edn (Stuttgart: Klett-Cotta, 1990), 177. The answer is the observance of rules of rational argumentation.

[32] Robert Alexy, 'Problems of Discourse Theory', *Crítica* 20 (1988), 43–65, at 56 (in this volume: Chapter 18, 275–87, at 283).

[33] We are dealing here with something like a 'missing link' between the rules of discourse and the correctness of the outcome, a shortcoming to which frequent objection is made. Compare Otfried Höffe, 'Kritische Überlegungen zur Konsensustheorie der Wahrheit (Habermas)', *Philosophisches Jahrbuch* 83 (1976), 313–32, at 330; Karl-Heinz Ilting, 'Geltung als Konsens', *Neue Hefte für Philosophie* 10 (1976), 20–50, at 34; Arthur Kaufmann, 'Recht und Rationalität', in *Rechtsstaat und Menschenwürde. Festschrift für Werner Maihofer*, eds Arthur Kaufmann, Ernst-Joachim Mestmäcker, and Hans F. Zacher (Frankfurt: Klostermann,1988), 11–39, at 36.

[34] On this variant, see Albrecht Wellmer, *Ethik und Dialog* (Frankfurt: Suhrkamp, 1986), 72.

[35] The presupposition of competence to judge is a weak premise in a twofold sense. On the one hand there is hardly an ethical theory which can dispense with it. For this reason discourse theory need not fall back on to a special and in this sense strong premise. On the other hand, taken on its own, the

2. The Necessity of Communication

A second objection goes as follows, namely that the concept of rational justification is not necessarily linked with that of rational discourse. Thus Tugendhat objects to discourse theory as follows: 'all justification ... is ... not intrinsically communicative, because it can be equally well achieved by an individual alone and in this sense through monologue'.[36]

The counter objection to this is that it is necessary for the framing of one's practical judgment to be embedded in a communicative structure if rationality is to be achieved in the fullest measure. Contrary to Habermas's view,[37] the framing of practical judgment does not look only to determining common interests, that is, interests shared by all. In practice, the more significant judgments are those concerning the just reconciliation of interests which are not common but particular to different parties.[38] A reconciliation of interests is at core a matter of the weighing and balancing of interests. Since there exists no general, strictly applicable criterion for the weighing of different interests, the process of weighing and balancing which is necessary to reconcile them can only take place in relation to the existing interests of others. However, the relative weight or relative legitimacy of interests is in itself contestable. Determination through argument of the relative weights of conflicting interests has, from the point of view of rationality and thus of correctness, priority over agreement reached without arguments.

The decisive point is that the interpretation and weighing and balancing of particular interests is a matter for those affected by them at the time.[39] Whoever disputes this fails to respect the autonomy of others and takes only him or herself seriously. This makes it plain that there are two factors which lead to a necessarily communicative structure of practical justification: first the possibility of arguing about the relative weight of interests, which becomes a necessity if one wishes to arrive at a just and hence correct reconciliation of interests, and

concept of a competence to judge is too devoid of substance to form the basis of an ethical theory. It contains neither criteria for correct judgments nor procedures for arriving at them. Discourse theory so to say circumscribes the competence to judge with requirements of argumentation. The underlying idea is that through argumentation which meets these requirements, optimal control and development of the competence to judge will become possible.

[36] Ernst Tugendhat, 'Zur Entwicklung von moralischen Begründungsstrukturen im modernen Recht', in *Argumentation und Recht*, eds Winfried Hassemer, Arthur Kaufmann, and Ulfrid Neumann (Wiesbaden: Steiner, 1980), 1–20, at 6.

[37] Habermas, 'Diskursethik—Notizen zu einem Begründungsprogramm' (n. 27 above), 83.

[38] For more detail on this, see Robert Alexy, 'Nachwort (1991): Antwort auf einige Kritiker', in Alexy, *Theorie der juristischen Argumentation*, 2nd edn (Frankfurt: Suhrkamp, 1991), 399–435, at 406–7.

[39] Compare Günther Patzig, 'Zur Begründung sozialer Verhaltensnormen', in Patzig, *Tatsachen, Normen, Sätze* (Stuttgart: Reclam, 1980), 98–118, at 116: 'Every justification of a norm must start out from the actual needs, interests, and wishes of those individuals affected by it... From this it also follows that no one can be justified in playing off against one another, above the heads of the participant individuals, their "objective" that is essential and true needs and interests as against their subjective needs... The justification of norms is thus not possible in a once and for all manner, but rather only in a continual rational discourse.'

second the requirement to genuinely accept others as individuals in their own right.[40]

C. Towards the Justification of the Rules of Discourse

The requirement mentioned above genuinely to accept others as individuals expresses a normative premise underlying the whole of discourse theory. It is reflected in the specific rules of discourse which guarantee everyone's right to participate in discourse as well as the freedom and equality of all the participants in discourses. The question arises how this premise or these rules can be justified. This question calls for nothing less than the justification of the universalistic character of practical rationality.

An objection to the conception of rationality underlying discourse theory states that it is only the expression of a particular form of life,[41] namely that of European rationality in a variant moulded by the concept of practical reason. On this ground alone, it cannot claim any universal validity. A post-modernist critique is apt to point to the problems of modernity and add that in the process of enlightenment, rationality has not only reached its peak but has in fact gone beyond it. Paul Feyerabend for example stresses that other forms of life are at bottom equally defensible.[42] It is therefore not permissible to establish a necessary connection between the idea of discourse and concepts such as truth, correctness or rationality. The rules of discourse are, on the contrary, historically conditioned and to this extent relative. To accept the underlying postulate of their rationality is a matter of personal decision.[43]

These objections make it clear that there is a need to distinguish two aspects of universality. The one concerns the content of the rules of discourse, the other, their validity. The rules are substantively universal to the extent that they demand equal

[40] Spaemann claimed that discourse is not an 'instance of normative decision-making'; Spaemann, *Glück und Wohlwollen* (n. 31 above), 179. This is true in the sense that the competence to form a judgment must stay with the individual, however it is equally true that the execution of discourse is a necessary condition of the correct and therefore of the rational formation of practical judgments.

[41] Carl Braun, 'Diskurstheoretische Normenbegründung in der Rechtswissenschaft', *Rechtstheorie* 19 (1988), 238–61, at 254.

[42] Feyerabend terms 'Western rationalism' a 'tribal creed'; Paul Feyerabend, *Farewell to Reason* (London: Verso, 1987), 297, 301. It will be shown that discourse theory is to be distinguished from mere tribal creeds in that it formulates the conditions for the co-existence of what Feyerabend probably understands by 'tribal creeds'. Discourse theory leads to basic and human rights which secure space for different forms of life and thereby give a legal form to Feyerabend's postulate of 'equality of traditions'; ibid., 308. To be sure, there is a fundamental difference between Feyerabend and discourse ethics in that the latter attempts to justify basic and human rights and does not leave decisions on these rights to 'attitudes', 'inclinations', 'personal opinions', and 'powers of rhetoric and self-righteousness'; ibid., 309–10.

[43] Helmut Rüßmann, 'Review of R. Alexy, Theorie der juristischen Argumentation', *Rechtstheorie* 10 (1979), 110–20, at 112.

rights for all those in the discourse. The question is whether this substantive universality can claim universal validity.

My thesis is that the universal validity of the rules of discourse can be substantiated by means of a three-part argument.[44] The first part consists of a very weak version of a transcendental-pragmatic argument. Then comes the second part—an argument which takes account of the maximization of individual utility. This combination presupposes the third part in the form of an empirical premise.

The universalistic character of discourse theory rests primarily on the first part of the whole argument, namely the transcendental-pragmatic argument. This forms the core of its justification. Transcendental-pragmatic arguments are a variant of a more general type of argument, namely transcendental arguments. Every transcendental argument consists of at least two premises.[45] The first premise identifies the starting point of the argument which consists of such things as perceptions, ideas, or speech acts. Starting from the chosen subject-matter, the first premise proceeds to claim that it is in some sense necessary. The second premise then goes on to say that some categories or rules are necessary if the subject-matter chosen in the first premise is to be possible. Finally, the conclusion states that these categories or rules are necessarily valid.

My chosen starting point and thus the subject-matter of the version of a transcendental-pragmatic argument to be put forward here, is the speech act of assertion and I begin with the second premise, that is with theses concerning what is necessarily presupposed by assertions. The first thesis states that asserting is only possible where there exist some valid rules for making assertions. This is hardly contestable. Argument centres round the question of the nature of these rules.[46] If the transcendental-pragmatic argument is to succeed, these rules must be shown to be necessary presuppositions of the possibility of making assertions. There must be no alternatives to them.[47]

[44] The whole argument does not lead to an ultimate justification in the sense that it forces everyone not only to acknowledge that the discourse rules are correct but also to follow them. However it does attempt to expound the view that a universalistic practice admits of a better justification than any other practice. On dispensing with an ultimate justification compare Günther Patzig, '"Principium diiudicationis" und "Principium executionis"', in *Handlungstheorie und Transzendentalphilosophie*, ed. Gerold Prauss (Frankfurt: Klostermann, 1986), 204–218, at 218: 'But dispensing with an ultimate justification is as acceptable in ethics as it is in science: we have procedures for distinguishing better from less good reasons and we can accept whatever proves to be the best justification as the basis of our practice for the time being.'

[45] On the structure of transcendental arguments, see Roderick Chisholm, 'What is a Transcendental Argument?' *Neue Hefte für Philosophie* 14 (1978), 19–22; Stanley L. Paulson, 'Läßt sich die Reine Rechtslehre transzendental begründen?' *Rechtstheorie* 21 (1990), 155–79, at 171–3.

[46] Herbert Keuth, 'Fallibilismus versus transzendentalpragmatische Letztbegründung', *Zeitschrift für allgemeine Wissenschaftstheorie* 14 (1983), 320–37, at 334–7; Patzig, '"Principium diiudicationis" und "Principium executionis"' (n. 44 above), 213.

[47] Hans Albert, 'Die angebliche Paradoxie des konsequenten Fallibilismus und die Ansprüche der Transzendentalpragmatik', *Zeitschrift für philosophische Forschung* 41 (1987), 421–8, at 427; Paulson, 'Läßt sich die Reine Rechtslehre transzendental begründen?' (n. 45 above) 174, 176.

The problem would be insoluble were one to include whatever one pleased under the term 'assertion'. It would then be possible to distinguish numerous conceptions of assertion and to define each according to its own system of rules.[48] An indication that this is certainly not possible in an unbridled way lies in recognition of the fact that assertions can at least be distinguished from other speech acts such as expressions of emotional reactions[49] or mere opinions.[50] There exists a core meaning of the expression 'assertion'.[51] Assertions are only those speech acts which raise an implicit claim to truth or correctness.[52]

The claim to truth or correctness carries with it an implied claim to justifiability. Whoever presents something as an assertion and at the same time remarks that no grounds or reasons at all exist for what is being asserted is perhaps not even putting up a genuine assertion. In any case such an assertion is necessarily faulty. Corresponding to the claim of justifiability is a requirement of argumentation that one has to justify on request anything one asserts or to give reasons for refusing to give a justification.[53]

Whoever asserts something to someone else thus has a *prima facie* duty to the second party to justify his or her assertion when asked to do so. To this extent, expressing an assertion is an entry into the domain of argumentation. Whoever justifies something to someone else at the very least pretends to accept the other as an equal partner in the exchange, at least as far as the justification is concerned, and neither to practice coercion him or herself nor to rely on coercion exercised by others. Furthermore he or she is making the claim that the assertions are not

[48] Keuth, 'Fallibilismus versus transzendentalpragmatische Letztbegründung' (n. 46 above), 334.

[49] Günther Patzig, 'Relativismus und Objektivität moralischer Normen', in Patzig, *Gesammelte Schriften*, vol. 1 (Göttingen: Wallstein, 1994), 9–43, at 21.

[50] Keuth, 'Fallibilismus versus transzendentalpragmatische Letztbegründung' (n. 46 above), 332,

[51] This corresponds to Kuhlmann's thesis 'that there exists a central core of basic rules of argumentation and assertion'; Wolfgang Kuhlmann, Reflexive Letztbegründung versus radikaler Fallibilismus, *Zeitschrift für allgemeine Wissenschaftstheorie* 16 (1985), 357–74, at 373.

[52] Compare Donald Davidson, *Inquiries into Truth and Interpretation* (Oxford: Clarendon Press, 1984), 268: 'Someone who makes an assertion represents himself as believing what he says, and perhaps as being justified in his belief. And since we want our beliefs to be true, it seems right ... that when someone makes an assertion, he represents himself as intending to say what is true.' Fusfield objected to the transcendental-pragmatic argument on the grounds that it was either circular or ended in an infinite regress or rested on untestable intuitions, that is it founders on the third horn of the famous Münchhausen Trilemma, on dogmatism; William D. Fusfield, 'Can Jürgen Habermas' "Begründungsprogramm" Escape Hans Albert's *Münchhausen Trilemma*?' *Jahrbuch Rhetorik* 8 (1989), 73–82, at 77–80. He objects in particular to *grounding* or *justifying* rules of discourse by means of performative contradictions; ibid., 77. Fusfield is right inasmuch as pointing out a performative contradiction does not involve justifying a sentence by means of another independent sentence because a performative contradiction occurs only in those instances where a rule of discourse is already valid. It is therefore only a matter of a means for *showing* that rules of discourse are valid. It is thus only a question of making explicit something which is assumed to be generally presupposed. This assumption, like any assumption, can be false and the explication therefore inadequate. The same holds for assumptions about the core meaning of the concept of assertion and its explication.

[53] This corresponds to the general justification rule (2): 'Every speaker must give reasons for what he or she asserts when asked to do so, unless he or she can cite reasons which justify a refusal to provide a justification.' On this see Alexy, *A Theory of Legal Argumentation* (n. 22 above), 127–9, 192.

only justifiable to those participating in the particular exchange but far beyond this are justifiable to anyone at all. The specific rules of discourse which correspond to these claims are those which guarantee the right of all to participate in discourse as well as their freedom and equality in discourse.

It might be objected here that this is no more than a trick of definition. It could be said that the path from the concept of assertion to the specific rules of discourse via the claim to correctness, the claim to justifiability, and a *prima facie* duty to justify, consists of no more than a chain of definitions. By introducing such a strong concept of assertion, there really is no alternative to the specific rules of discourse. However, it would be possible to put forward a weaker concept for which this would not be valid. This objection takes us back to the first premise of the transcendental-pragmatic argument, which can now be formulated in such a way that assertions in the sense defined here are necessary in some respect.[54] The question arises whether this thesis can be justified.

According to Apel and Habermas the renunciation of assertions as defined above has far-reaching consequences, assuming that it includes the abandonment of argumentation. Thus Apel speaks of the loss 'of the very possibility of self-understanding and self-identification' even of 'self-destruction',[55] and Habermas of 'schizophrenia and suicide'.[56] These are contestable empirical assumptions.[57] A weaker conceptual thesis will suffice for present purposes. This states that it is necessary to make assertions and to put forward arguments in the following sense: whosoever fails *ever* to make an assertion (in the sense defined here) and *ever* to put forward an argument (in the sense defined here) fails to participate in what can be termed 'the most general form of life of human beings'. In this way the transcendental argument is radically toned down. For example, it no longer grounds the duty of the stronger to justify to a weaker person whatever he or she may require of that person. He or she can simply issue a straightforward order and carry it through with a threat of force and nevertheless participate in the most general form of life of human beings provided he or she resolves to make assertions and found arguments in some other contexts. What remains however, is a systematically highly significant normative residue. Whenever there exist no extremely unusual circumstances, such as growing up in complete isolation, it ought to be more or less impossible to refrain from participating in the most general form of life of human beings, at least to the extent of never making any assertion at all however weak, or never putting forward any argument in any way at all and similarly

[54] Watt appositely observed that there exists a strong relationship between the two premises of the transcendental argument. The greater the normative content of the second premise, the more doubtful the necessity of the first becomes. Conversely, the normative content of the second premise goes down with the increasing certainty of the necessity of the first. Compare A. J. Watt, 'Transcendental Arguments and Moral Principles', *The Philosophical Quarterly* 25 (1975), 40–57, at 43–5.

[55] Karl-Otto Apel, *Transformation der Philosophie*, vol. 2 (Frankfurt: Suhrkamp, 1973), 414.

[56] Habermas, 'Diskursethik—Notizen zu einem Begründungsprogramm' (n. 27 above), 112.

[57] Patzig, '"Principium diiudicationis" und "Principium executionis"' (n. 44 above), 213.

with reference to the counterpart to assertions and the founding of arguments, never asking the question: 'Why?' Everyone has the fundamental capacity to ask this question, to express assertions, and to give a reason, even if it is not a good one, and everyone—exceptional circumstances apart—has used these abilities even if only to a minimal degree.

The thesis concerning the most general form of life of human beings is quite compatible with the view that there exist different forms of life. It does however state that all human forms of life necessarily include universals of argumentation which can be expressed through rules of discourse. These universals may in reality hardly be apparent because of the existence of taboos, traditions, or terror, however they would only disappear completely once the participants in any given form of life finally and completely lost the capacity to pose the question: 'Why?' It is for this reason that the rules of discourse do not define a particular form of life but rather something which has validity or relevance in any form of life whatsoever, albeit to a very variable degree.[58] To this extent discourse theory is an indication of the potential for reason in human reality. In this sense it is, to use an expression of Höffe's, 'enlightenment shed upon human existence'.[59]

Of course, this achieves little by way of moral justification. It does not follow from the fact that someone has the capacity to resolve conflicts of interests through argument, that he or she ought to make use of such a capacity in every conflict of interest with respect to anyone affected by it. It might appear rather more advantageous to the stronger to limit matters to rituals of domination, the issuing of orders, and the exercise of power. In so doing they would not need to dispense with the most general form of life of human beings. They can engage in discourse with members of their own group. The situation would be different only if it were possible to presuppose the existence of an overriding interest on the part of every human being to resolve conflicts correctly, that is, justly. Experience teaches us that such an assumption would be untenable. It would therefore seem that the transcendental argument can only be used to justify the hypothetical validity of the discourse rules as follows: they are valid wherever and to the extent that there prevails an interest in correctness.[60]

We now come to the second part of the justification. This is based on the maximization of individual utility and to this extent is Hobbesian in character. It will

[58] This implies that discourse is also possible in principle between members of different forms of life. On this see Robert Alexy, 'Aamio, Perelman und Wittgenstein', in *Reasoning on Legal Reasoning*, eds Aleksander Peczenik and Jyrki Uusitalo (Vammala: Society of Finnish Lawyers, 1979), 121–37, at 128–34.

[59] Höffe, *Kategorische Rechtsprinzipien* (n. 22 above). 336.

[60] On this see Patzig, '"Principium diiudicationis" und "Principium executionis"' (n. 44 above), 212, 216–17. Such a purely hypothetical validity is sometimes discernible in Habermas: 'because everyone *who wishes to argue seriously* must be drawn into the idealised imputation of an exacting form of communication'; Jürgen Habermas, 'Wie ist Legitimität durch Legalität möglich?' *Kritische Justiz* 20 (1987), 1–16, at 12–13 (italics mine).

be assumed that the prime concern of a ruling elite defined, say, by racial features, would be to maintain the advantages accrued by exploiting the subject group. The members of the ruling elite might attempt to establish a natural equilibrium of their own interests by brute strength. This would not be the best line for them to take for a number of reasons, however.

I shall consider only one reason here. This reason rests on an empirical thesis which forms the third part of my justification. This runs as follows: that it is always the case that there exists such a large number of people with an interest in correctness, that it is, at least in the long run, more advantageous for the members of the ruling elite to justify their domination than to rely exclusively on might. This thesis holds true both for the relationship between the rulers and their subjects and that between the members of the ruling group.[61] The arguments rehearsed in justification of the rulers' position do not have to be good arguments. They might be pure propaganda. What is decisive is that an argument takes place at all. In this way, provided account has to be taken of a sufficient interest in correctness, the maximization of individual utility leads one into the domain of argumentation.

It might be objected that this position is inadequate as a justification for the discourse rules. Those who enter into discourse merely for reasons of strategy, only have to behave *as though* they accept the freedom and equality of their discourse partners. But this would only be an objection if it were necessary to view the generation of motivation as a necessary constituent of any justification of the discourse rules. This, however, is not the case. Even in the realm of speech, it is possible to make a distinction between subjective validity, that is one based on motivation, and objective validity, based on outward behaviour.[62] The justification presented here is aimed at the objective or institutional validity of the rules of discourse. A subjective validity, one based on motives, exists only where there is an interest in correctness. This is presupposed by some, but not by all and cannot be established by justification alone. The fact that the justification of the rules of discourse is limited to their objective or institutional validity shows that they should be classed as belonging primarily to the realm of legality and thereby to that of law.[63]

This does not fully answer the case put up by critics of discourse theory. They can assert that the discussion so far has only been about rules for speaking. It has nothing to say about acting. This objection points to the problem of application to which we must now turn our attention.

Our interim findings show that the discourse rules can be justified in a threefold sense. First the rules of discourse put into words a competence which belongs to

[61] Alexy, 'Nachwort (1991): Antwort auf einige Kritiker' (n. 38 above), 424–5.

[62] This distinction corresponds to Kant's between morality and legality; Kant, *The Metaphysics of Morals* (n. 28 above), 383; AA 6, 219.

[63] Compare this with Höffe's thesis that discourse ethics presents less problems from an argumentative perspective when conceived as an 'ethics of law and state'; Höffe, *Kategorische Rechtsprinzipien* (n. 22 above), 379.

the most general form of life of human beings. Anyone who participates in it will at some time or other express an assertion vis-à-vis someone, will at some time or other pose the question 'Why?" to someone, and will at some time or other give a reason in response to some person. To the extent that this is the case, he or she has exercised this competence at least to a rudimentary degree. Second, everyone who has an interest in correctness must make use of this competence. Third, for those who have no interest in correctness, it remains advantageous in the long run, from the point of view of maximization of individual utility, to observe the discourse rules at an objective level.

D. The Application of Discourse Theory

The discussion so far has focused on the justification of the rules of discourse as rules relating to the realm of speech. Practical rationality is aimed at correct practical action. The question arises what bearing the discourse rules have on action. It is necessary to distinguish two problems here, one of substance and one of enforcement. The substantive problem raises the question whether and to what extent norms for correct action can be distinguished on the basis of the rules of discourse. The subject-matter relating to the problem of enforcement is the question of how one can assure that norms which are recognized as being correct are complied with in practice. I shall begin with the problem of enforcement.

The problem of enforcement arises because acknowledgement of the correctness of a norm is quite distinct from compliance with that norm.[64] Thus a unanimous assessment of a norm as a just norm does not necessarily lead to general compliance with it. However if it is open to some to contravene a norm others cannot be expected to comply with it. From this fact, that insights can be generated through discourse without always creating the corresponding motivation to act on them, follows the necessity of rules backed by force and hence the necessity of law.[65] This

[64] This corresponds to Kant's distinction between the 'principium diiudicationis' and the 'principium executionis'. 'When the question is: what is morally good or not, then it is a matter of the principium of diiudication according to which I judge the worthiness and depravity of actions. But when the question is what moves me to live according to this law? Then it is the principium of motivation'; Immanuel Kant, *Moralphilosophie Collins*, in *Kant's gesammelte Schriften*, vol. 27, ed. Academy of Sciences, German Democratic Republic and Academy of Sciences, Göttingen (Berlin: Walter de Gruyter, 1974), 237–473, at 274. Compare also Patzig, '"Principium diiudicationis" und "Principium executionis"' (n. 44 above), 205–7.

[65] This argument basically corresponds to one of Kant's arguments for the transition from the state of nature to the civil state. See Kant *The Metaphysics of Morals* (n. 28 above), 456; AA 6, 312. On the application of this argument in the framework of discourse theory see Jürgen Habermas, 'Law and Morality', *The Tanner Lectures on Human Values* 8 (1988), 217–79, at 245. The text names only one premise for the justification of the necessity of law. A second premise is presupposed, namely that it is required that norms which are generally viewed as correct, be generally followed. Furthermore the premise cited in the text can be strengthened in that given the motivational weakness of discourse, law is at least a necessary means for securing general compliance. The formulation contained in the conclusion 'necessity of law' means that it is required to introduce legal regulations that is, to move into a state of law or legality.

shows for the first time what will be confirmed below, namely that discourse theory can only achieve practical significance when it is embedded in a theory of law.

The problem of substance presents far greater difficulties. The origin of these lies in the fact that the system of rules of discourse does not offer a procedure of finite operations through which one can always arrive at precisely one result. There are three reasons for this. First, the rules of discourse do not prescribe arrangements with regard to the starting points of the procedure. The starting points are the participants' currently existing normative convictions and interpretations of their interests. Second, the discourse rules do not lay down all the steps of argumentation. Third, a number of discourse rules can only be met to an approximate degree. To this extent discourse theory does not offer determinate decisions. This certainly holds true for actual discourses and to a certain extent probably for ideal ones too.[66]

The fact, however, that discourse theory does not lead to just one solution in every case does not entail that it fails to establish a solution in any case.[67] The question therefore arises whether there are at least some outcomes which are discursively necessary and others which are discursively impossible.[68]

In order to answer this question, it is necessary to distinguish two kinds of behavioural rules or norms: the procedural kind and the substantive kind. Examples of procedural rules of behaviour or conduct can be found in the organizational norms of a democratic constitutional state; the main example of the substantive kind of behavioural rules are laws about human rights. We shall now turn to the question of whether human rights can be justified on the basis of discourse theory.

It is not possible to infer human rights directly from the rules of discourse.[69] The rules of discourse are only rules of speech. Adhering to them only means treating

[66] On the latter compare Alexy, 'Problems of Discourse Theory' (n. 32 above), 50–1 (in this volume: Chapter 18, 279–80).

[67] On the thesis that discourse theory never leads to precisely one solution, see Lucian Kern, 'Von Habermas zu Rawls. Praktischer Diskurs und Vertragsmodell im entscheidungslogischen Vergleich', in *Gerechtigkeit. Diskurs oder Markt?* eds Lucian Kern and Hans-Peter Müller (Opladen: Westdeutscher Verlag, 1986), 83–95, at 91. Habermas seems close to this view when he pleads for a 'modest self-conception of moral theory' and merely assigns to it the task of 'elucidating and justifying the moral point of view'. Discourse theory must 'dispense with its own substantive contributions'; Habermas, 'Moralität und Sittlichkeit' (n. 22 above), 32. It is said not to give any 'substantive orientation'; Habermas, 'Diskursethik—Notizen zu einem Begründungsprogramm' (n. 27 above), 113.

[68] On the concepts of discursive possibility, impossibility, and necessity see Alexy, 'Die Idee einer prozeduralen Theorie der juristischen Argumentation' (n. 23 above), 180–5.

[69] Adela Cortina attempts to justify human rights discourse-theoretically by means of direct inference. Cortina starts out from the premise that 'every potential participant in a practical discourse [must] be recognised as a person' and directly concludes that one 'must ascribe *certain rights* to this real and potential discourse partner'; Adela Cortina, 'Diskursethik und Menschenrechte', *Archives for Philosophy of Law and Social Philosophy* 76 (1990) 37–49, at 44. The problem with this inference lies in the premise, in particular with the concept of recognition as a person. The discourse rules only require recognition of the other as a discourse partner, as a rule of speech. From this nothing follows about recognition as a person in the realm of action. Cortina can only make her inference by normatively loading the concept of practical discourse. It is said to include the goal of communication as a teleological schema; ibid., 40–1. It has been explained above that such motivational requirements cannot be justified from the transcendental-pragmatic viewpoint. What can be justified in this way, is only the objective validity of the rules of discourse.

the other party *to the discourse* as an equal partner.[70] From this it does not follow that the other person must simply be recognized as a person *in the realm of action.* In order to arrive at rules of behaviour or conduct from the discourse rules, there is a need for assumptions about the outcomes of discourses. These assumptions must have as their content that certain rules of conduct, in the foregoing case those which yield human rights, are a necessary outcome of discourse. It will now be asked whether it is possible to justify human rights in this sense, when one adds to the objective validity of discourse rules the premise that all participants have an interest in correctness. If this could be achieved then human rights could be justified given the presupposition of an interest in correctness, and in this sense, hypothetically.

Human rights regulate fundamental conflicts of interest. Where fundamental conflicts of interest are to be resolved exclusively through negotiations between individual utility maximizers and several parties to the negotiations are in an unfavourable position at the outset, the result may be, for example, the one not excluded by Buchanan, namely the status of slavery. In this situation, what are generally understood as human rights are no longer capable of being justified. In the realm of practical discourses, and thus also discourses about human rights, interests also form the basis of argumentation. In this area too, it can be assumed that everyone strives for maximum advantage.[71] The difference lies in the fact that here we are dealing with *a justified* maximum advantage. This is because in the realm of discourses, whatever an individual desires for himself and wishes to deny others, must be justified. Decisions about individual rights are made not on the basis of power or traditions, but rather through a justificatory process characterized by freedom of argument and equality of argument, that is under conditions of impartial argument.

I wish to assert that under these conditions and given a presupposition of an interest in correctness, certain human rights can be shown to be discursively necessary, and their negation discursively impossible. Amongst these are the right to life and freedom from bodily harm and the rights to integrity of person, to basic freedom of action, of belief, of opinion, and of assembly, to freedom of occupation and ownership, the right to basic equal treatment and participation in the process of the formation of political objectives. Minimal basic social rights[72] should also be added here, such as the right to a subsistence level.

[70] Leist speaks appositely about 'language-pragmatic recognition', which must be distinguished from general moral recognition relating to action; Anton Leist 'Diesseits der "Transzendentalpragmatik": Gibt es sprachpragmatische Argumente für Moral?' *Zeitschrift für philosophische Forschung* 43 (1989) 301–17, at 303–4.

[71] On the thesis that discourse ethics cannot manage without the concept of advantage see Höffe, *Kategorische Rechtsprinzipien* (n. 22 above), 386.

[72] On this concept see Alexy, *A Theory of Constitutional Rights* (n. 24 above), 336, 343–8. According to Honneth the normative implications of discourse ethics are not limited to human rights as fundamental rights and to procedural requirements. Discourse ethics as such is said to include a 'concept of social justice'; Axel Honneth, 'Diskursethik und implizites Gerechtigkeitskonzept', in *Moralität*

Whoever wishes to dispute this must show that it is possible for someone to observe the rules of discourse and have an interest in correctness and yet not agree with some or all human rights. An example which has been cited as an objection against discourse theory is that of the racist who believes that members of other races, by virtue of their race alone, have none or only some of the human rights cited above or have them to a lesser extent.[73] If the racist has an interest in correctness and observes the rules of discourse, he or she must adduce arguments in support of these claims and subject them to criticism. Assume the racist is a National Socialist who views his or her theory of race as a scientific theory. Such a theory would already founder on empirical grounds. The case becomes serious when the racist rests his or her theories on religious revelations, on metaphysical assertions which are not amenable to proof or on magical views. Nevertheless, this does not invalidate the discourse-theoretical justification of human rights. Whoever disputes the existence of human rights on the basis of unprovable religious, metaphysical, or magical grounds may have an interest in correctness from a subjective perspective, however such an individual does not observe the rules of discourse from an objective point of view. Wherever there is a question of resolving a conflict of interest, as in the case of human rights, these rules only admit arguments which are amenable to proof by everyone.[74]

Until now I have only outlined one argument for human rights under the presupposition of an interest in correctness. A completely new situation arises where this interest is absent. Take the individual mentioned above, who always maximizes utility, who only participates in discourses for strategic reasons in order to maximize utility by legitimizing his domination. He does this solely because a domination which is recognized as just is, in the long run, more advantageous than a regime based solely on force. Such an individual must count the recognition of human rights as the price for legitimation of his domination. All participants in discourse wish for maximum advantage. Only a justified advantage is discursively possible. An advantage based on the cost of the human rights of others cannot be shown through discourse to be a justified advantage. It is for this reason that for the individual utility maximizer human rights are indirectly discursively necessary on grounds of purpose-rationality.

It has so far been explained that the existence of human rights can be justified or substantiated through discourse theory. This achieves something but not everything. Whoever has dealt with the question of the application of human rights, that

und Sittlichkeit, ed. Wolfgang Kuhlmann (Frankfurt: Suhrkamp. 1986), 183–93, at 189. Clearly Adela Cortina also assumes stronger implications than those put forward here; Cortina, 'Diskursethik und Menschenrechte' (n. 69 above) 46–7.

[73] See Leist, 'Diesseits der "Transzendentalpragmatik": Gibt es sprachpragmatische Argumente für Moral?' (n. 70 above), 307–8.

[74] Compare rules (6.1) and (6.2) in Alexy, *A Theory of Legal Argumentation* (n. 22 above) 206.

is with the question of what they yield in specific contexts and cases, knows that this raises countless problems of interpretation and weighing and balancing. In the case of most of these problems, no solution can be shown to be discursively necessary or impossible on the basis of discourse theory alone.[75] The discourse ethics as such does establish some substantive points, however a great deal is left open. Not everything which is merely discursively possible can at the same time be legally valid. This would mean that social conflicts could be resolved by means of contradictory rules. Thus the substantive problem leads to the necessity of legal procedures which guarantee a determinate outcome.[76] Discourse theory thus presupposes the necessity of law not only because of the problem of enforcement but also because of the problem of substance.

Legal norms can be generated and applied in quite different procedures. This raises the question of whether the discourse ethics at least requires procedural rules in those areas in which it fails to establish substantive rules of behaviour. Some procedural rules do indeed arise out of the human rights which can be justified through the discourse ethics. Amongst these is the right to participation in the process of the formation of political objectives. The process of the creation of laws must be democratic. However, the majority principle should not be upheld without limits. There must be institutional precautions which ensure that majority decisions do not infringe discursively necessary human rights. Of particular significance is that the claim to correctness should not be abandoned with the transfer of decision-making to legal proceedings.[77] From this follows the necessity of institutionalizing justification and criticism in legal procedures and of securing them constitutionally out with these procedures. Discourse theory is thus shown to be the basic theory of the democratic constitutional state[78] founded on discussion.[79]

At the beginning, the Kantian conception of practical reason was contrasted with three concurrent conceptions. It is now clear what can be said in favour of its superiority. It can show the sceptic following Nietzsche that and how practical reason is possible. Countering the Hobbesian conception, it can show that the idea

[75] The case of blasphemy as examined by MacCormick shows that while several solutions of the problem of blasphemy are discursively impossible, nevertheless more than one form of regulation is discursively possible. Discursively impossible are the prohibition against serious, factual arguments for and against religious teaching and the protection of only one or some religions through a prohibition on blasphemy. By contrast both a total rejection of a prohibition on blasphemy as well as the protection of all religions from blasphemy are discursively possible; Neil MacCormick, 'Moral Disestablishment and Rational Discourse', in *Recht und Moral*, eds Heike Jung, Heinz Müller-Dietz, and Ulfrid Neumann (Baden-Baden: Nomos, 1991), 219–31, at 226–9.

[76] Alexy, 'Die Idee einer prozeduralen Theorie der juristischen Argumentation' (n. 23 above), 186; Habermas, 'Wie ist Legitimität durch Legalität möglich?' (n. 60 above), 13–14; Habermas, 'Law and Morality' (n. 65 above), 245.

[77] Compare MacCormick, 'Moral Disestablishment and Rational Discourse' (n. 75 above), 224–5.

[78] Martin Kriele, *Recht und praktische Vernunft* (Göttingen: Vandenhoeck & Ruprecht, 1979), 30–4; Alexy, 'Problems of Discourse Theory' (n. 32 above), 63–4 (in this volume: Chapter 18, 287); Jürgen Habermas, 'Interview mit Hans Peter Krüger', in Habermas, *Die nachholende Revolution* (Frankfurt: Suhrkamp, 1990), 82–98, at 84.

[79] Decisions of the German Federal Constitutional Court (BVerfGE) 5, 85 (197–200).

of the maximization of individual utility must be complemented by that of universalizability, if only because account must be taken of the interest in correctness. The idea of practical correctness includes the idea of universalizability. Advocates of the Aristotelian position can be shown that the discourse-theoretical variant of the Kantian conception is by no means devoid of substance and purely formal. It does after all lead to human rights and democracy. Furthermore, the weakness of its substantive requirements appears as an advantage. Human rights, as basic rights, guarantee space for different forms of life and different conceptions of the good life, and the democratic process creates the possibility of a just settlement in which the multiplicity of voices can be heard. In this way discourse theory shows how practical reason can become a reality without denying respect to different forms of life and conceptions of the good life.

18

Problems of Discourse Theory

There are three categories of problems in discourse theory. The first group of problems arises if discourse theory is regarded as a theory of truth. The second group investigates the practical applicability of discourse theory, and the third group concerns the justification of discourse theory. We talk about the *status* of discourse theory as theory of truth when we discuss the relationship between the concepts of truth and correctness on the one side and the concepts of consensus, unlimited discussion, and rationality on the other side.[1] The problem of *applicability* is at stake if discourse theory is claimed to be without content and merely formal. The claim is thought to be apparent, for discourse theory does not lead to any definitive result.[2] The problem of *justification* is the problem of establishing conclusive reasons for discourse rules and principles.[3]

I shall confine my discussion to the first two problems, namely the status and applicability problems. My subject will be limited in another respect, too. Both problems pertain to all forms of discourse, which is to say that they appear, for instance, in theoretical, practical, and aesthetic discourse. I will only consider practical discourse here.

I. Discourse Theory as a Procedural Theory

Discourse theory belongs to the class of procedural theories.[4] According to all procedural theories, the correctness of a norm or the truth of a proposition depends upon whether or not the norm or proposition is or can be the result of a certain procedure. The actual result of a procedure *can* of course be the result of that procedure, but this is not the case in reverse. The 'can' version does, therefore, embrace more. The 'can' version embraces both the mere possibility and the actuality. It will be the starting point of my considerations. If *a* is the exponent of a procedural

[1] See Herbert Scheit, *Wahrheit-Diskurs-Demokratie* (Freiburg: Alber, 1987), 123–32; Albrecht Wellmer, *Ethik und Dialog* (Frankfurt: Suhrkamp, 1986), 70–81.

[2] Wellmer, *Ethik und Dialog* (n. 1 above), 72.

[3] See Jürgen Habermas, 'Diskursethik–Notizen zu einem Begründungsprogramm', in Habermas, *Moralbewußtsein und kommunikatives Handeln* (Frankfurt: Suhrkamp, 1983), 53–125, at 67–78; Wolfgang Kuhlmann, *Reflexive Letztbegründung* (Freiburg: Alber, 1985), 181–215.

[4] See Robert Alexy, 'Die Idee einer prozeduralen Theorie der juristischen Argumentation', *Rechtstheorie*, supplement 2 (1981), 178–80.

Law's Ideal Dimension. Robert Alexy, Oxford University Press. © Robert Alexy 2021.
DOI: 10.1093/oso/9780198796831.003.0019

theory of the 'can' version, according to which the procedure *P* is to be applied, then *a* will answer the question as to whether or not a norm *N* is correct with:

D: A norm *N* is correct if and only if it can be the result of the procedure *P*.

There are various ways of constructing the procedure *P*. The differences may relate first, to those concerning the individuals, and second, to those concerning the requirements of the procedure. Third, its character depends upon how the procedure is constructed with regard to the individuals and the requirements.

As to the *individuals*, one has to distinguish between number and characteristics. *P* can be carried out by one individual, but it is also possible that several or all individuals of a more or less wide class may take part. Concerning the characteristics of the individuals, one can work with actually existing individuals or with constructed or ideal individuals. The ideal observer theory proposed by Firth[5] is an example of a procedure that uses only one individual, namely, an ideal individual. By contrast with this, discourse theory is characterized by the fact that an unlimited number of individuals, in the state in which they actually exist, can participate in *P*.

The *requirements* can be of various kinds. Thus, it is possible to establish certain cognitive and motivational characteristics of the individuals, or to fix conditions or circumstances in which argumentation and decision have to take place, or to formulate rules according to which the procedure has to be performed. The most important differences arise from variations in the strength of the requirements.

The procedure's *character* depends on the number of individuals and the kinds of requirements. Determining the character of the procedure, the question of whether the possibility of a change in empirical and normative convictions of the participants is or is not provided is decisive. Where such is not provided, one can decide on the basis of the empirical and normative material at *one* point in time. Such a model of *decision theory* is suggested by Rawls in order to choose his principles of justice, which he calls 'the only choice consistent with the full description of the original position'[6] that can be made from the 'standpoint of one person selected at random'.[7] In contrast to this, discourse theory as a model of *argumentation theory* is characterized by the possibility that the empirical and the normative convictions as well as the interests of the individuals can change owing to arguments presented in the course of the procedure. In the following, I will only be discussing this version of a procedural theory.

[5] Roderick Firth, 'Ethical Absolutism and the Ideal Observer', *Philosophy and Phenomenological Research* 12 (1952), 317–45, at 321.

[6] John Rawls, *A Theory of Justice* (Cambridge, Mass.: Harvard University Press, 1971), 121.

[7] Ibid., 139.

II. Rules of Discourse

The requirements of discourse theory can be formulated solely by rules because there is no prescription concerning individuals. I have tried elsewhere to set out the system of discourse rules as completely as possible.[8] The system consists of rules that require, for example, non-contradiction, clarity of language, empirical truth, and sincerity, along with rules that express the idea of universalizability, for example, by giving everyone the right to participate in the discourse and by granting everyone equal consideration in the discourse, and, finally, along with rules that concern the consideration of consequences, the weighing of reasons, and the analysis of the genesis of normative convictions.

An objection to this repertoire of requirements has been raised, namely, that it expresses a 'mixed concept of rationality'[9] that does not actually promote the clarity of analysis. To this one can reply that practical rationality is a complex matter. The result of an analysis of a complex matter can only be a complex model. The decisive issue is whether the model is in a position to cope with the crucial problems that arise in the field in question. Furthermore, it has been critically remarked that some rules have a moral content.[10] This could be a valid objection, however, only if at least one of three preconditions were true. The first would be that the concept of practical rationality as explicated by the rules must not have any moral content. In my opinion it is at least allowed, and perhaps even necessary, to incorporate moral contents into a fully fledged concept of practical rationality. The second precondition would be fulfilled if those rules that have moral content, such as those that express non-trivial demands for universalizability, were not justifiable. I cannot take up here the thesis that they are capable of a transcendental-pragmatic justification by way of a presupposition analysis.[11] At any rate the idea that they cannot be justified is uncertain. A third precondition required to sustain the objection mentioned above would be that the moral content of some of the discourse rules would deprive the entire system of its practical applicability. This leads one back to the general question of practical applicability.

From the standpoint of applicability, the main flaw of discourse theory lies in the fact that its rule system provides no procedure that makes it possible for one to arrive at exactly one result in a finite number of operations. There are three reasons for this. First, the rules of discourse contain no prescriptions concerning the starting points of the procedure. The starting points are the participants' normative

[8] Robert Alexy, *A Theory of Legal Argumentation* (1978), trans. Ruth Adler and Neil MacCormick (Oxford: Clarendon Press, 1989), 187–206.

[9] Ota Weinberger, 'Logische Analyse als Basis der juristischen Argumentation', in *Metatheorie juristischer Argumentation*, eds Werner Krawietz and Robert Alexy (Berlin: Dunker & Humblot, 1983), 159–232, at 200: 'Mischbegriff der Rationalität'.

[10] Ibid., 195.

[11] Habermas, 'Diskursethik—Notizen zu einem Begründungsprogramm' (n. 3 above), 93–6; Alexy, *A Theory of Legal Argumentation* (n. 8 above), 185–7.

convictions and interpretations of their interests, just as these convictions and interests appear. Second, the rules of discourse do not prescribe all the steps at the argumentation. Third, a number of the rules can be fulfilled only approximatively.[12] Thus, discourse theory does not guarantee a definite decision in every case.

One might think that already here, the inapplicability of discourse theory is shown. To meet this objection, one has to distinguish between real and ideal discourses. I shall turn first to the latter.

III. The Ideal Discourse

Discourse can be ideal in some or all respects. Here I take up only the discourse that is ideal in all aspects. It is defined by the search for an answer to a practical question under the conditions of unlimited time, unlimited participation, and complete freedom of constraints, thereby achieving complete linguistic conceptual clarity, complete empirical information, complete ability and willingness to change roles, and complete freedom from prejudice. The concept of a discourse that is ideal in all respects poses many problems, of which the four most important are the problem of construction, of consensus, of the criterion, and of correctness.

A. The Problem of Construction

The problem of construction stems from the fact that discourse theory works with real, actually existing persons as participants. To prolong their participation into an unlimited period of time leads the real, actually existing participants to become partially ideal or constructed, that is, immortal, participants. This is not the only idealization. One could imagine that a person who is immortal may take part in discourses eternally and still learn little or nothing. This is why the concept of a discourse that is ideal in all respects implies that its participants fulfil all the rules of discourse completely. This is to say that they achieve, regardless of how much time is involved, complete clarity, information, ability and willingness to change roles, and freedom from prejudices. That this is not in fact actually possible does not raise any problems as long as only the concept of ideal discourse is being discussed. To be taken seriously in this context is the question of whether or not the state of affairs described is conceptually possible at all. Thus, the question arises of whether linguistic-conceptual clarity is achievable in a discourse with participants from very different cultures with very different languages. Questions of this kind

[12] The concept of rule is used in a wide sense here, embracing both definite obligations and obligations concerning optimization; on this distinction see Robert Alexy, 'Rechtsregeln und Rechtsprinzipien', *Archives for Philosophy of Law and Social Philosophy*, supplement 25 (1985), 13–20, at 19–21.

cannot be taken up here. At any rate, it is clear that participants in the ideal discourse undergo a nearly total change from real and actually existing participants into ideal and constructed ones. This seems to contradict the basic idea of discourse theory mentioned above, namely, that discourse is a procedure performed by non-fictitious, that is, real individuals. Considering, however, that the ideal discourse is at the beginning not perfect, but rather becomes perfect by means of a construed, potentially eternal prolongation and owing to learning processes that initially take place with real individuals, this problem can be resolved.

B. The Problem of Consensus

With the problem of consensus, the question arises of whether an ideal discourse leads to a consensus on every practical question. Such a consensus does not follow logically from the statement that the conditions of ideal discourse are fulfilled. A consensus on a certain normative question is a substantive matter. In relation thereto, the conditions listed above have a formal character. Therefore, a consensus on every question could be guaranteed only if it could be assumed that the empirical premise, that the fulfilment of the conditions of ideal discourse would make all differences of opinion on practical issues vanish, holds true. This premise presupposes that there are no discourse-resistant anthropological differences that could preclude a consensus on questions of value, even under the ideal conditions listed above. I believe this question cannot be decided. This is the case because there exist no methods that could accurately predict the behaviour of real persons under the forementioned non-real conditions. This means that the guarantee of a consensus can neither be precluded nor assumed. This has the following consequence. It has to be considered as possible that even after a discourse that lasts for an eternity, participants will adhere to norms that are incompatible with each other. The result of the procedure would then be both N and $\neg N$. This means, according to the definition D given at the beginning, that both N and $\neg N$ would have to be labelled as 'correct'. The question that stems from this will be addressed in the discussion of the problem of correctness.

The question of whether a consensus reached after potentially infinite duration and under ideal conditions would necessarily be a final or definite consensus leads to a second aspect of the problem of consensus. A stable consensus would be reached only if no additional argument that could lead to a change in the normative convictions in question in the case of at least one participant were possible. In this context, I think it does not matter whether the class of normatively relevant arguments is finite or infinite. As long as the participants are not assumed to been equipped with the characteristic of not overlooking any possible normatively relevant argument, then even a potentially infinite discourse, in which the participants achieve the ideal conditions mentioned, would not assure that no new argument could destroy the consensus that is reached. Things would be different only if an infinite discourse were interpreted as actual[13] infinity in such a way that all possible arguments were brought up and considered, which shall be not done here. A consensus could then, by definition, no longer be destroyed by means of a new argument.

Summing up what has been said about the problem of consensus, two points are of special importance: (1) Even in the case of a potentially infinite ideal discourse, it cannot be excluded that there will be no consensus at all. (2) And, even in the case of a potentially infinite ideal discourse, it is never certain whether a consensus once reached is final or definitive.

C. The Problem of the Criterion

The matters discussed above have serious consequences with respect to the third problem, the problem of the criterion. This problem concerns the question of the extent to which the ideal discourse will work as a criterion of correctness when substituted for *P* in the definition D given above. Since the ideal discourse, by definition, cannot be carried out, it can only be used as a criterion by asking whether a norm *N could* be the result of an ideal discourse. Three problems are of special interest here.

The first problem stems from the fact that in order to use the ideal discourse as a criterion of correctness, a procedure, that is essentially a collective endeavour involving several persons, must be carried out in the mind of one person, and in this sense, *monologically.* It is of the essence of a practical discourse that several persons are involved, and this for the following reasons. In a practical discourse, correct answers to practical questions are sought that concern the interests of several persons. Thus, the correct solution of a conflict of interests is at stake. For this purpose, the respective actually existing normative convictions of the participants, convictions concerning the right solution, are exposed to rational scrutiny. In this process, the respective interpretations of the participants' interests and the changes thereto, that are brought about by arguments, play a decisive part. How an interpretation of interests eventually has to be changed owing to arguments, is in the end everyone's own concern. From this it follows that if the correctness of the results of discourse depends on the correctness of the interpretation of interests, and if the correctness of the interpretation of interests is a matter of argumentative investigation, then the discourse is *essentially non-monological.*

For someone who asks himself whether something can be the outcome of a discourse the consequences resulting from this are, however, less fatal than they

[13] On the concepts of potential and actual infinity compare Paul Lorenzen, 'Das Aktual-Unendliche in der Mathematik', in Lorenzen, *Methodisches Denken* (Frankfurt: Suhrkamp, 1974), 94–103, at 100.

appear to be at first glance. Though discourses are essentially non-monological, a discourse carried out by one person can nevertheless approximate a discourse conducted by several persons. One can never be sure of the arguments, the interpretation of interests, and the changes in the interpretations of other persons, but it is to a considerable degree possible to make well-grounded conjectures about them. Manifold arguments have been adduced, by various persons, about almost any practical question. Everyday life, literature, and science provide numerous forms of information about possible ways in the interpretation and changes of interests. From the monological conduct of discourse there arises a considerable amount of uncertainty. Nevertheless, for this reason, the virtual discourse carried out in one person's reflections would be an inappropriate criterion only if from the uncertainty of a criterion its inappropriateness would follow.

The second sub-problem of the problem of the criterion stems from the *ideal* character of the ideal discourse's requirements. Neither a real discourse nor a virtual discourse, carried out in one person's reflections, can fulfil these demands completely. It is possible, however, to fulfil the ideal requirements approximately. A result that meets the requirements of the procedure only approximately is necessarily an uncertain criterion. Still, as mentioned above, uncertainty does not imply uselessness.

The third sub-problem of the problem of the criterion stems from the *internal structure* of the ideal discourse. When I took up the problem of consensus, I stated that first of all, even in a potentially infinite ideal discourse, no one can be certain about whether a once-reached consensus is finite or definite, Second, it cannot be ruled out that there is, even in such a discourse, no consensus at all, which is to say that two contradicting norms can be the result of the ideal procedure. The problem of definiteness gives rise to fewer difficulties. A consensus that stems from a potentially infinite ideal discourse does not yield final certainty but may nevertheless yield such a high rate of certainty that it can be accepted as a criterion. The problem of contradiction is more serious. A criterion that does not preclude the possibility that two contradicting norms are counted as correct seems to fail owing to the most basic semantic demands of the term 'correct'. This problem shall be pursued further in the following discussion of the problem of correctness.

D. The Problem of Correctness

In considering the problem of correctness, three questions arise: (1) the problem of the concept of correctness, (2) the problem of objectivity, and (3) the aforementioned problem of contradiction. I wish to emphasize that my considerations apply only to practical discourses and therefore only to practical correctness or truth. How far what is said here is transferable to theoretic discourse and the problems of theoretic truth must remain as an open question.

1. Concept and Criterion of Correctness

The standard objection to the discourse theory, concerning the concept of correctness, is that it conflates the distinction between concept and criterion. To meet this objection, one has to distinguish between a criteria-free and a criteria-laden definition of the concept of practical correctness. A criteria-free definition is achieved if one develops a semantic conception of practical correctness, using ideas of Tarski.[14] It is oriented towards the following equivalence: The sentence 'X is obligatory' is correct if and only if X is obligatory. Such a conception of practical correctness sheds light on an important aspect of the concept of practical correctness. There are, however, further aspects of this concept, which can only be grasped by means of a criteria-laden procedural definition, as suggested here. The two conceptions are compatible. They are not in a relation of competition but, rather, in a relation of complementarity.[15] For each of these, there are purposes that justify it.

2. The Problem of Objectivity

More important is the second sub-problem of the problem of correctness, the problem of objectivity. It concerns the objection that the links between the concepts of correctness and truth with those of discourse and consensus suggested by discourse theory are inappropriate. Correctness and truth are objective, while discourse and consensus, for their part, belong to the realm of subjective conviction and mere belief and acceptance.[16] The discourse theory does not distinguish sufficiently clearly between being regarded as true and being true.[17] The fact that all agree to a statement does not mean that it is correct or true, for all can be mistaken. This also applies to the result of ideal discourses.[18]

This objection expresses in part misunderstandings and leads in part to very basic questions. It would be a misunderstanding to think that according to discourse theory, something is already true when all think it is true. It is not the consensus that is decisive but rather the performance of the discourse procedure. This goes so far as to grant that even in a dissent, the contradicting opinions can be labelled as 'correct' in a sense to be specified later, provided that they have survived the discourse procedure. It is therefore incorrect to blame discourse theory for taking the consensus as a *reason* for correctness or truth.[19]

It is not the consensus but the performance of the procedure, according to the discourse rules, that counts as the real criterion of correctness in discourse theory.

[14] See Alfred Tarski, 'The Semantic Conception of Truth and the Foundations of Semantics' *Philosophy and Phenomenological Research* 4 (1943/4), 341–75, at 343.

[15] On the thesis that various truth and correctness theories do not necessarily stand in a competitive relation, but can also stand in a complementary relation, see Otfried Höffe, 'Kritische Überlegungen zur Konsensustheorie der Wahrheit (Habermas)', *Philosophisches Jahrbuch* 83 (1976), 313–32.

[16] Weinberger, 'Logische Analyse als Basis der juristischen Argumentation' (n. 9 above), 188.

[17] Karl-Heinz Ilting, 'Geltung als Konsens', *Neue Hefte für Philosophie* 10 (1976), 20–50, at 36.

[18] Weinberger, 'Logische Analyse als Basis der juristischen Argumentation' (n. 9 above), 192.

[19] So Wellmer, *Ethik und Dialog* (n. 1 above), 72.

The decisive question is whether performing a procedure according to the basically formal discourse rules is related to the substantive correctness of normative propositions at all. This question formulates the main problem concerning the relation between procedure and correctness. The answer depends on a premise essential for discourse theory. Discourse theory presupposes that the participants to a discourse, that is, human beings, as they actually exist, are generally able to distinguish between good and bad reasons for substantive normative propositions. It assumes that there is, in general, a sufficient ability or power to form considered judgments on the part of the participants.[20] This does not mean that a sufficient power of judgment is a requirement of the procedure.[21] The relation between the discourse procedure and the sufficient power of judgment on the part of the participants is, rather analogous, to that between the constitution of a democratic state and the ability of its citizens to take part in political, economic, and social activities. The latter is not demanded by norms of the constitution but is presupposed by the constitution. Further, it should be added here that sufficient power of judgement is presupposed only *in general*. It is one of the purposes of the procedure of the discourse to develop this faculty.

If the presupposition of a generally existing sufficient power of judgment, that is, an ability to distinguish between good and bad reasons for substantive propositions, is introduced in this way as a link between procedure and correctness, then one arrives at the question: why is it still the procedure that is decisive and not simply good reasons or sufficient justifications?[22] The reason is this. There are, at least in practical questions essentially concerned with the interpretation and reconciliation of interests, no good reasons as such. What actually counts as a good reason can only emerge in the process of discursive investigation. Applying the concepts of subjectivity and objectivity, one might say that the result of the discourse procedure is neither simply subjective nor simply objective. It is subjective in so far as it is based on characteristics of the participants. It is objective in so far as it has proven itself resistant to a discursive investigation, resting on the general power of judgment on the part of the participants. In this way, discourse theory avoids the flaws of both subjectivistic or relativistic and objectivistic moral theories.

3. The Problem of Contradiction

There remains a third sub-problem of the problem of correctness, the problem of contradiction. This stems from the fact that one cannot preclude the state of affairs in which even an ideal practical discourse can have two contradictory norms as its

[20] The absence of such a 'missing link' between the discourse rules and the correctness of results has often been criticized. See Höffe, 'Kritische Überlegungen zur Konsensustheorie der Wahrheit (Habermas)' (n. 15 above), 330; Ilting, 'Geltung als Konsens' (n. 17 above), 34.

[21] On this version see Wellmer, *Ethik und Dialog* (n. 1 above), 72.

[22] See ibid., 70, 72; Weinberger, 'Logische Analyse als Basis der juristischen Argumentation' (n. 9 above), 190.

result. According to the definition of 'correct' given here, this means that the two contradictory norms can be simultaneously correct. This is not to say that one and the same person can maintain contradictory norms. For the system of norms of every individual, the postulate of non-contradiction remains valid. It is only the incompatible norm systems of different persons that are recognized. The question remains as to whether incompatible parts of the norm systems of different persons, if and because they have survived the procedure, can be equally labelled as 'correct'.

This would not be admissible if there were just one right answer to each practical question,[23] apart from whether there is any procedure to discover or to prove it. Those who adhere to this thesis separate the concept of correctness from the concepts of justifiability and probability. From this an *absolute* concept of correctness arises, which has a *non-procedural* character. This approach would indeed preclude the possibility of labelling both N and $\neg N$ as 'correct'. The underlying problem is ontological in nature. That is, the assumption that there exists one right answer to every practical question, apart from any procedure, is an ontological thesis, a thesis that is not only difficult to justify but is also not very plausible. Answers to practical questions turn essentially on the interpretation and weighing of interests. It cannot be assumed, on this basis, that there is just one right answer to each practical question. As far as practical questions are concerned, the thesis respecting the existence of one right answer to each question is a non-justifiable ontological fiction. Such a fiction is not helpful in determining how the term 'correct' is to be used.

That the thesis of the existence of one right or correct answer to each practical question must be abandoned does not entail that the concept of correctness has no absolute character whatsoever. It has an absolute character as a regulative idea. The concept of correctness as a regulative idea does not presuppose that there will always exist a right or correct answer to each practical question, which only has to be found.[24] The idea of the one correct answer acquires, then, the character of a goal to be strived towards.[25] If the statements and justifications of those who are participating in a practical discourse are supposed to make sense, they have to claim that their answers are the only correct ones, and this apart from whether there is in fact a single correct answer. This merely presupposes that there are practical questions for which it is possible that one single correct answer can be found in a discourse. Since it is not certain what these questions are, it is worthwhile to

[23] See Ronald Dworkin, *A Matter of Principle* (Cambridge, Mass.: Harvard University Press, 1985), 119–22.

[24] See Immanuel Kant, *Critique of Pure Reason*, trans. Werner S. Pluhar (Indianapolis, Ind.: Hackett, 1996), 518; A 509, B 537: 'Thus it is a principle of reason that, qua *rule*, postulates what is to be done by us in the regression, and *does not anticipate* what is given in itself in the *object* prior to all regression. I therefore call this principle a *regulative* principle of reason' (trans. altered).

[25] Ibid., 619; A 644, B 672: 'On the other hand, the transcendental ideas have a superb and indispensably necessary *regulative* use, namely, to direct the understanding to a certain goal by reference to which the directional lines of all the understanding's concepts converge in one point' (trans. altered).

try to find the one single correct answer to each of them. This expresses an *absolute procedural* conception of correctness. It squares with the meaning of the term 'correct' as it is used in ordinary language.

The problem of contradiction thereby leads to a splitting up of the concept of correctness into an absolute and a relative one. If both N and $\neg N$ are results of the procedure, then they are both correct relative to this procedure.[26] Again, the absolute procedural concept of correctness demands that the search for only one answer be sustained. The concept of relative procedural correctness plays its most important role as far as real discourses are concerned. This will be made clear in the course of the following discussion.

IV. The Real Discourse

A. The Discursive Modalities

To discuss the problem of real discourse, it is useful to adopt a simple model. We may assume that two persons, a_1 and a_2, are trying to answer a practical question by means of the procedure defined by the discourse rules. At time t_1, a_1 maintains N_1, and a_2 maintains N_2, N_1 and N_2 being incompatible. At time t_2, which marks the end of the procedure, the following assignments of solutions to the participants are possible: (1) Both agree on N_i, which may be identical with N_1 or N_2, but need not be; (2) both reject N_i; (3) a_1 supports N_i and a_2 supports N_j, $i \neq j$. It makes sense to spell out these three cases. In the first case, N_i is, relative to the discourse rules, the degree of their fulfilment, the participants, and the time t_2, *discursively necessary.* In the second case N_i, accordingly, is *discursively impossible.* In the third case, N_i and N_j are, relative to the discourse rules, the degree of their fulfilment, the participants, and the time t_2, neither discursively impossible nor discursively necessary but only *discursively possible.* It is important to note here, that the picture in time t_3 and with participation of other individuals can look different.

According to the definition D of correctness given above, both what is discursively necessary at the end of the procedure as well as what is at this point in time only discursively possible must be labelled as 'correct'. The introduction of the concept of discursive possibility, however, renders the problem of contradiction less severe. The fact that both N and $\neg N$ can be correct merely means that both N and $\neg N$ are possible in a specific way, namely discursively possible. That the parts of a contradictory conjunction are possible is logically unobjectionable. What at first

[26] The conception of relative correctness proposed here is not the only one possible. A conception oriented towards the idea of different cognitive processing mechanism has recently been proposed by Nicholas Unwin, 'Beyond Truth: Towards a New Conception of Knowledge and Communication', *Mind* 96 (1987), 299–317.

glance strikes one as an altogether counterintuitive result, namely that two contradictory norms can be equally correct, thereby loses some of its bite.

B. The Relative Concept of Correctness

The relativity of the concept of correctness raises the most severe problems of discourse theory. The relativity of correctness has four aspects: (1) the discourse rules, (2) the degree of their fulfilment, (3) the participants, and (4) points of time.

I shall not discuss the first problem here, relativity with respect to the *discourse rules*. This problem does not concern either the applicability or status problems; rather it concerns the justification problem, which is not to be investigated here. It should be apparent that, and how, this problem pertains to the problem of correctness.

Second, the fulfilment of some rules is an all-or-nothing affair, while other rules can be fulfilled only approximately owing to their ideal character. In the latter case, fulfilment is a matter of degree. This gives rise to the second problem of relativity, the problem of relativity with respect to the *degree of fulfilment*. What is essential here has already been said in connection with the problem of the criterion in discussing the ideal discourse. Merely approximate satisfiability leads necessarily to uncertainty of the discourse as a criterion, although, as has already been noted, uncertainty does not imply uselessness.

Third, relativity with respect to the *participants* also gives rise to uncertainty. Moreover, it leads, at least in so far as real discourses limited in time are concerned, to a broadening of the scope of what is only discursively possible. On the other hand, owing to the structure of practical problems, uncertainty cannot be avoided. It demands, as shown above, a non-monological procedure. Furthermore, every discourse must have a starting point. It cannot begin from nothing. Its starting points are the factually existing normative convictions of the participants, whatever they may be. The discourse is nothing other than a procedure of rational enquiry into these convictions. In this process, any normatively relevant conviction counts as a candidate for a change arising from rational argument. This restriction to the rational structuring of the process of argumentation is an important advantage of discourse theory. A more demanding theoretical alternative might try to determine the outcome of the procedure. To this end it would have to establish certain substantive normative tenets as starting premises instead of merely structuring the process of argumentation or decision. This more demanding alternative would have to overcome at least two severe obstacles. First, objections to the theorist's substantive starting premises are usually harder to answer than objections against the basically formal discourse rules. Second, this alternative would have to come to grips with the general objection that the theorist would be treading on ground that he ought to leave to the participants of the discourse because his substantive normative convictions cannot generally be assumed to be more correct than those of the participants themselves. Furthermore, it should be noticed that the role of the participant is open to the theorist, too, at any time.

Fourth, relativity with respect to *points of time* is inescapable owing to the limits of every real discourse. As far as merely discursively possible results—that is, dissent—are concerned, the regulative idea of correctness demands the non-final character of the results. With discursively necessary results—that is, consensus—the necessarily non-final character is brought about by the necessary imperfection of any real discourse.

One may be tempted to think that in the light of the fulfilment, the participants, and the relativity respecting points of time, one ought to abandon the concept of correctness. In this connection it would be helpful to suggest that concepts such as that of warranted assertability, plausibility, justifiability, and reasonableness might be used. Indeed, this would have the advantage of not having to proceed with a bifurcated concept of correctness, that of absolute procedural correctness, which has the character of a merely regulative idea, and that of relative procedural correctness, which includes a high degree of uncertainty. As is so often the case, the terminological issues reflect serious substantive questions. At least it can be said on behalf of the terminology introduced here, that colloquial speech leaves open the possibility of saying that the proponents of two well-grounded but incompatible normative opinions are both correct *in their way* (relative correctness), in order thereby to continue by asking who is *really* right (absolute correctness), while at the same time granting that it is very likely no-one is going to find out. The substantive reason on behalf of the terminology chosen here is that the discourse leads, if not to certainty, at least away from the realm of mere opinion and subjective belief. If one takes into account that on practical questions more cannot be achieved, the use of the concept of relative correctness seems appropriate.

Although many objections to discourse theory can be met, the result remains curiously unsatisfying. On the one hand, the concept of correctness survives only as a regulative idea, on the other, it is highly relativized and overburdened with uncertainties. This need not be the last word, however. It may be true that the practical value of discourse theory will show itself in the best light only if it is taken as the basic theory of the institutions of a democratic constitution that incorporate the idea of discussion.[27] To address these questions,[28] however, would require another paper.

[27] Compare Decisions of the German Federal Constitutional Court (BVerfGE) 5, 85 (197–200).

[28] See Martin Kriele, *Recht und praktische Vernunft* (Göttingen: Vandenhoeck & Ruprecht, 1979), 30–4; Alexy, 'Die Idee einer prozeduralen Theorie der juristischen Argumentation' (n. 4 above), 185–8.

19
Legal Argumentation as Rational Discourse

In a decision from 1990, the German Federal Constitutional Court expressed the opinion that '[t]he interpretation of the constitutional law in particular has the character of a discourse, in which ... reasons and counter-reasons are offered, and, ultimately, the better reasons shall yield a decision'.[1] This hints at the thesis that legal argumentation ought to be regarded as a rational discourse. The question is how to understand this thesis and how to substantiate it. In answering it here, I shall take three steps. First of all, I will present four models that oppose the theory of legal discourse. Then I shall sketch a discourse theory of the law that forms a framework for the theory of legal discourse. Finally, I intend to offer the main elements of a theory of legal argumentation that is orientated to the idea of discourse.

I. Models

The discourse model of legal argumentation represents a reaction to the weaknesses or deficiencies of alternative models and conceptions. The most important alternative models are the model of deduction, the model of decision, the hermeneutic model, and the model of coherence.

A. The Model of Deduction

The true model of deduction says that the decision in every legal case follows logically from valid norms, together with definitions of legal concepts that are presupposed as certain, along with empirical sentences. Many statements from the heyday of conceptual jurisprudence are not far from this model.[2] One has doubts, however, about whether this was at any time more than a programme or an ideal. It is too easily proven wrong. With an eye to a shorthand demonstration

[1] Decisions of the German Federal Constitutional Court (BVerfGE) 82, 30 (38–9).

[2] See, for instance, Bernhard Windscheid, *Lehrbuch des Pandektenrechts*, 9th edn, ed. Theodor Kipp, vol. 1 (Frankfurt: Rütten & Loening, 1906), 111: '[D]ie Endentscheidung ist das Resultat einer Rechnung, bei welcher die Rechtsbegriffe die Faktoren sind.' ('The final decision is the result of a calculation in which the legal concepts are the factors.')

Law's Ideal Dimension. Robert Alexy, Oxford University Press. © Robert Alexy 2021.
DOI: 10.1093/oso/9780198796831.003.0020

of the point, the following will suffice: reference to the vagueness of the language of the law, to the possibility of conflicts between or collisions of norms, to the fact that there might well be no norm at all for the decision at hand, and to the possibility of a development of the law against the wording of a norm, which cannot be totally excluded in most legal systems. For this reason, the model of deduction is no longer being proposed as a comprehensive model of the application of the law by anyone. The creative role of those who apply the law is emphasized or at least recognized everywhere. All that remains to argue about is whether at least simple cases ought to be resolved by a deduction and whether one should postulate that the solution of a difficult case found by non-deductive means might be presented as a deduction.[3] Those questions, however, are concerned with the structure of legal argumentation and no longer with the model of deduction in the sense defined here.

B. The Model of Decision

The model of decision is a reaction to the collapse of the model of deduction. It exists in vastly differing forms. They range from a '*freirechtlichen*' (free law) approach to realist and analytical conceptions, and they all share the thesis that the judge, if authoritative reasons like statutes and precedents leave some issues open, must then decide on the basis of extra-legal standards.[4] This is very clearly formulated by Kelsen, who says that in a difficult case the judge, like a legislator, has to resolve a problem of 'legal politics'.[5] In doing so, the judge is deciding in accordance with 'free' discretion. His decision is based on an 'act of will'.[6]

All this is contradicted by the self-understanding and the internal point of view of judicial decision-making. Even in difficult cases judges try to decide on the basis of legal reasons and to give rational legal explanations, or at least they ought to do so. They raise the claim that their decision, if not the only correct one, is at least correct overall.[7] All of the further models to be taken up here strive to prove that this is no illusion.

[3] See, on the one hand, Hans-Joachim Koch and Helmut Rüßmann, *Juristische Begründungslehre* (München: C. H. Beck, 1982), 48–58, 112–3, as well as, on the other, Ulfrid Neumann, *Juristische Argumentationslehre* (Darmstadt: Wissenschaftliche Buchgesellschaft, 1986), 16–37.

[4] John Austin, *Lectures on Jurisprudence or the Philosophy of Positive Law*, 5th edn. (London: John Murry, 1885), vol. 2, 664: 'So far as the judge's *arbitrium* extends, there is no law at all.'

[5] Hans Kelsen, *Pure Theory of Law*, 2nd edn (1960), trans. Max Knight (Berkeley, Calif.: University of California Press, 1967), 353.

[6] Ibid., (n. 5 above), 354. Less radically formulated but similar in content is Hart's attitude; see H. L. A. Hart, *The Concept of Law*, 2nd edn (Oxford: Clarendon Press, 1994), 127–8, 135, 204.

[7] Robert Alexy, *The Argument from Injustice. A Reply to Legal Positivism* (1992), trans. Bonnie Litschewski Paulson and Stanley L. Paulson (Oxford: Clarendon Press, 2002), 35–9.

C. The Hermeneutic Model

At the centre of the hermeneutic model, developed in the twentieth century mainly by Gadamer and Betti and taken up in German jurisprudence by, for instance, Larenz, Kaufmann, and Esser, there is the structure of interpretation and understanding. The key concept is that of the hermeneutic circle. For jurisprudence, three types of hermeneutic circle are important.[8]

The first concerns the relation of the so-called *preconception* and the *text*.[9] A 'preconception' is a hypothesis held by the interpreter who is approaching the text. This hypothesis gives expression to the interpreter's supposition or expectation concerning the correct resolution of the legal problem to be decided. Its content is determined by the interpreter's general conception of society and his professional experiences. The image of the circle is intended to point out the interaction between the text of the norm and the hypothesis of interpretation. On the one hand, without a hypothesis of interpretation, the text of the norm cannot even be seen to be problematic or unproblematic. On the other hand, the hypothesis of interpretation has to be examined on the basis of text of the norm along with the help of the rules of legal methodology. The decisive point here is that the theory of the hermeneutic circle as such does not say anything about the criteria for affirming or rejecting the hypothesis of interpretation. This question can only be decided on the basis of argument, and this by itself is enough to show that the theory of the hermeneutic circle cannot replace the theory of legal argumentation. It is, however, not worthless. It directs one's attention to the problem of the productive contribution made by the interpreter to the interpretation, thereby making possible and indeed promoting a critical attitude. One can therefore say that the circle of preconception corresponds to the '*postulate of reflexivity*', which is of great importance for the theory of legal argumentation.

The same is true for the two other types of hermeneutic circle. The second of these is concerned with the relation between the *part* and the *whole*. On the one hand, to understand a norm one has to understand the system of norms it belongs to, and on the other, it is not possible to understand a system of norms without understanding the individual norms it consists of. Again, we simply find a problem formulated but without criteria for its solution. The problem here is the creation of unity or coherence. This is the task of systemic argumentation. One can call the postulate that stands behind the second circle the '*postulate of coherence*'. Thus, the

[8] For further types see Wolfgang Stegmüller, 'Walther von der Vogelweides Lied von der Traumliebe und Quasar 3 C 273', in Stegmüller, *Rationale Rekonstruktion von Wissenschaft und ihrem Wandel* (Stuttgart: Philipp Reclam, 1979), 27–86, at 35–46.

[9] See Josef Esser, *Vorverständnis und Methodenwahl in der Rechtsfindung*, 2nd edn (Frankfurt: Athenäum Fischer, 1972), 136–41, as well as Martin Heidegger, *Sein und Zeit*, 11th edn (Tübingen: Max Niemeyer, 1967), 148–53, and Hans-Georg Gadamer, *Wahrheit und Methode*, 4th edn (Tübingen: Mohr Siebeck, 1975), 250–61.

hermeneutic model includes the basic idea of the model of coherence, which to be considered below.

The third type of hermeneutic circle is concerned with the relation between the *norm* and the *facts*. Norms are abstract and universal. The facts they are meant to be applied to are concrete and individual. Norms contain few features, whereas facts contain a potentially unlimited number. On the one hand, facts are described by the features in the statement of facts provided by the norm, and on the other, aspects of the actual facts can give reasons not to apply the norm originally intended, but another norm or to give the norm a new interpretation, for instance, by deleting, adding, or changing features in the statement of facts provided by the norm. Here the language of the *Hin- und Herwandern des Blickes*[10] ('to-and-fro movement of one's view') coined by Karl Engisch is instructive. Like the others, this circle, too, illustrates a problem but without offering criteria for its resolution. At any rate, it is at least clear that the problem can only be resolved if all aspects of the facts as well as all the norms that lend themselves to possible application are considered. The postulate behind the third circle can therefore be called the '*postulate of completeness*'. It requires that all relevant aspects be considered, thereby stating a fundamental criterion of rationality.

In the light of what has been said here, one has to conclude that the hermeneutic model, although offering important insights into the structure of legal interpretation and yielding the three fundamental postulates of rationality mentioned above, does not suffice as a solution to the problem of the correct interpretation.[11] The correctness of an interpretation can only be demonstrated by naming reasons that count in its favour and rejecting those opposed to it. The claim that interpretation is argumentation is true.

D. The Model of Coherence

The fourth model is centred around an idea that has already been turned up as a focus of interest in the hermeneutic conception: the idea of systemic unity or coherence. Coherence is indeed an essential element of rationality and cannot be ignored in a theory of rational legal discourse, as will be shown.[12] The idea of coherence becomes an independent model only if it arises as the dominant idea. In the history of jurisprudence, this has happened again and again. The historically

[10] Karl Engisch, *Logische Studien zur Gesetzesanwendung* (Heidelberg: Carl Winter, 1943), 15.

[11] If one regards hermeneutics as a theory of the structure of understanding, this is not its aim; see Arthur Kaufmann, 'Problemgeschichte der Rechtsphilosophie', in *Einführung in Rechtsphilosophie und Rechtstheorie der Gegenwart*, 5th edn, eds Kaufmann and Winfried Hassemer (Heidelberg: C.F. Müller, 1989), 25–142, at 130.

[12] Robert Alexy and Aleksander Peczenik, 'The Concept of Coherence and Its Significance for Discoursive Rationality', *Ratio Juris* 3 (1990), 130–47, at 143–6

most important example is Friedrich Carl von Savigny's theory of the 'organic whole' and the 'internal interdependence or relation by means of which individual legal concepts and rules are brought together in a larger unit'.[13] Of all recent views one should mention, in particular, Ronald Dworkin's theory of integrity, which, in its methodological dimension, is identical with the theory of coherence: 'Law as integrity, then, requires a judge to test his interpretation of any part of the great network of political structures and decisions of his community by asking whether it could form part of a coherent theory justifying the network as a whole.'[14]

A model in which coherence is the only criterion—or the most important and therefore decisive criterion—for the correctness of an interpretation would represent in its consequence the idea of legal holism, according to which all premises are already included or hidden in the legal system and need only to be discovered.[15] In reply, however, one can say, that what has been institutionalized as the legal system is always necessarily incomplete. Just as rules cannot apply themselves so likewise a system cannot create completeness and coherence all by itself. To do this, persons and procedures are necessary. The necessary procedure is that of legal argumentation.

II. A Discourse Theory of the Law

A look at the four alternative models shows that a theory of legal argumentation that resolves the problem of the correct interpretation or at the very least leads in the direction of a resolution is desirable. Its being desirable does not necessarily mean, however, that it is also possible. There is no difficulty in pointing to two different types of theories of legal argumentation: empirical and analytical theories. Empirical theories describe legal argumentation that has actually taken place. Analytical theories attempt to arrive at a classification of the arguments used in legal argumentation and an analysis of their structure. Doubtlessly, these measures are of immense importance. They do not suffice, however, to answer the question of the correctness of an interpretation or of the rationality of its justification. These questions require a normative theory that provides for at least some determination of the power or weight of the different arguments and the rationality of a legal argumentation. The theory of legal discourse purports to be such a theory. The

[13] Friedrich Carl von Savigny, *System des heutigen Römischen Rechts*, vol. 1 (Berlin: Veit and Company, 1840) XXXVI–XXXVII (trans. R. A.); Savigny, *Vom Beruf unsrer Zeit für Gesetzgebung und Rechtswissenschaft* (Heidelberg: Mohr and Zimmer, 1814), 22.

[14] Ronald Dworkin, *Law's Empire* (Cambridge Mass.: Harvard University Press, 1986), 245. See also Klaus Günther, 'Ein normativer Begriff der Kohärenz für eine Theorie der juristischen Argumentation', *Rechtstheorie* 20 (1989), 163–90, at 175, 181.

[15] This idea has especially been stressed in the romantic movement. A poetic expression is found in Joseph von Eichendorff's 'Wünschelrute': 'Schläft ein Lied in allen Dingen, / Die da träumen fort und fort, / Und die Welt hebt an zu singen, / Triffst du nur das Zauberwort.'

theory of rational legal discourse is created by incorporating the theory of general practical discourse into a theory of the legal system. This incorporation is no mere application of general discourse theory to the law but an unfolding of discourse theory that is necessary for systematic reasons.

A. General Practical Discourse

The basic idea of discourse theory is that one can—with a claim to correctness—rationally argue about practical questions. Thus, discourse theory attempts to steer a middle course between objectivist and cognitivist theories on the one hand and subjectivist and non-cognitivist theories on the other. General practical discourses are not institutionalized argumentation about what is obligatory, prohibited, or permitted, or about what is good or bad.[16] A practical discourse is rational only if it fulfils the conditions of rational practical argumentation. If these conditions are fulfilled, the result of the discourse is correct. Discourse theory is therefore a procedural theory of practical correctness.[17]

The conditions of the rationality of the discourse procedure can be summarized in a system of rules and forms of discourse.[18] Practical rationality can be defined as the capacity of reaching practical decisions by means of this system of rules and forms.

The rules and forms of discourse can be classified in many different ways. The introduction of two groups seems to make sense here: rules and forms that refer directly to the structure of arguments, and rules whose direct concern is the procedure of the discourse. To the first group belongs, for example, the demand for freedom from contradiction (1.1),[19] for universalizability in the sense of a consistent use of applied predicates (1.3), (1.3'), for linguistic and conceptual clarity (6.2), for the truth of the applied empirical premises (6.1), for the deductive completeness of the arguments (4), for the consideration of consequences (4.2), (4.3),

[16] Habermas distinguishes between moral, ethical, and pragmatic discourses; see Jürgen Habermas, 'Vom pragmatischen, ethischen und moralischen Gebrauch der praktischen Vernunft', in Habermas, *Erläuterungen zur Diskursethik* (Frankfurt: Suhrkamp, 1991), 100–18, at 101–8. This distinction presupposes a theory of the relationship between the deontological and the teleological, which cannot be taken up here. The concept of general practical discourse used here comprises what Habermas calls 'moral', 'ethical', and 'pragmatic' questions and reasons. Such an overarching concept of practical discourse is necessary, for in practice there exists between these three kinds of practical reason not only a relation of supplementation but also of permeation; see Robert Alexy, 'Jürgen Habermas's Theory of Legal Discourse', *Cardozo Law Review* 17 (1996), 1027–34, at 1033–4.

[17] Robert Alexy, 'Die Idee einer prozeduralen Theorie der juristischen Argumentation', *Rechtstheorie*, supplement 2 (1981), 177–88.

[18] For such a system of twenty-eight rules and forms of discourse, see Robert Alexy, *A Theory of Legal Argumentation* (1978), trans. Ruth Adler and Neil MacCormick (Oxford: Clarendon Press, 1989), 187–206.

[19] The numbers refer to the formulation of the rules and forms in Alexy, *A Theory of Legal Argumentation* (n. 18 above), 188–206.

for weighing and prioritization (4.5), (4.6), for the assumption of an exchange of roles or role reversal (5.1.1), and for an analysis of the genesis of moral convictions (5.2.1), (5.2.2). All of these rules can also be applied monologically, and a good bit can be said on behalf of the opinion that no theory of rational practical argumentation or justification can do without them. Thus, one can make quite clear that discourse theory in no way, as some would have us believe,[20] replace justification by the mere creation of consensus. Rather, it includes the rules of rational argumentation that refer directly to arguments. Its distinctive feature lies solely in the fact that it adds a second level to the first one, that is to say, the level of rules referring to the procedure of the discourse.

The second group of rules is non-monological. Its main purpose is to secure the impartiality of the practical argumentation. Rules serving this purpose can be called 'specific rules of discourse'. The most important of these are:

(2.1) Everyone who can speak may take part in discourse.
(2.2) (a) Everyone may problematize any assertion.
(b) Everyone may introduce any assertion into the discourse.
(c) Everyone may express his or her attitudes, wishes, and needs.
(2.3) No speaker may be prevented from exercising the rights laid down in (2.1) and (2.2) by any kind of coercion internal or external to the discourse.[21]

These rules grant every individual the right to participate in discourses along with freedom and equality in discourse. They express the universal character of discourse theory. It is not possible to substantiate those rules here.[22] One can say, however, that they correspond to the basic principles of democratic constitutionalism, that is, to freedom and equality.

One of the main problems of discourse theory is that its system of rules does not offer a procedure of finite operations by means of which one can always arrive at precisely one result. For this state of affairs, there are three reasons. First, the discourse rules do not contain definitions as to the starting points of the procedure. Starting points comprise the participant's normative convictions and interpretations of interests. Second, the discourse rules do not define all the steps that are to be taken in the argumentation. Third, a number of discourse rules have an ideal character and can therefore only be fulfilled approximatively. To this extent, discourse theory is a theory that does not offer determinate decisions.

[20] Ota Weinberger, 'Logische Analyse als Basis der juristischen Argumentation', in *Metatheorie juristischer Argumentation*, eds Werner Krawietz and Robert Alexy (Berlin: Duncker & Humblot, 1983), 159–232, at 192, 203.

[21] Alexy, *A Theory of Legal Argumentation* (n. 18 above), 193.

[22] See Robert Alexy, 'A Discourse-Theoretical Conception of Practical Reason', *Ratio Juris* 5 (1992), 231–51, at 238–44 (in this volume: Chapter 17, 255–74, at 263–9).

B. Institutionalization

The ideal character of discourse theory leads to the necessity of its being incorporated into a theory of the state and the law. This connection amounts to far more than mere compensation for its weaknesses. A legal system that elects to meet the demands of practical rationality can come into existence only by means of a connection of institutional or real elements with those of an ideal and non-institutional nature.

The connection in question is found at three levels: philosophical, political, and legal levels. On the *philosophical* level, the necessity of the existence of a legal system and the necessary basic demands with respect to its contents and structure are substantiated by means of general practical arguments. The existence of a legal system is necessary owing to the weaknesses of the general practical discourse. General practical argumentation does not lead in all cases to results that all can agree upon,[23] and even if it leads to a result that all do agree upon, general agreement in the discourse does not secure general observance. Social conflicts, however, cannot be solved by means of conflicting rules, and the observance of rules that everyone can be violate without fear of sanctions, cannot be asked of anyone. This Hobbesian argument must be supplemented by a Kantian one. It says that in a rational discourse not all legal systems can be justified but only those that fulfil the elementary demands of practical rationality. Among these are the guarantee of fundamental human rights, the institutionalization of democratic procedures, and the rule of law. Thus, discourse theory turns out to be the basic theory of the democratic constitutional state.

The importance of discourse theory on the *political* level stems from the fact that in a democratic constitutional state the creation of law is based not only on compromises and institutional acts but on informal argument that is conducted both within and outside the formal procedures of law creation. Legality can be connected with legitimacy in the sense of rational acceptance only in this way.

On the *legal* level, the connection of the institutional with the discursive is necessary for two reasons. On the one hand, as mentioned vis-à-vis the model of deduction, no legal system can be so perfect and complete that its norms necessarily define the solution to every possible case. On the other hand, the claim to correctness and rationality is raised with every decision, and one has to try to fulfil this claim if, in the long run, the legal system is to retain its legitimacy and consequently its acceptance. This has far-reaching consequences for the character of legal argumentation.

[23] This corresponds to Rawls's assumptions about the 'burdens of judgements'; see John Rawls, *Political Liberalism* (New York, N.Y.: Columbia University Press, 1993), 54–8.

III. Legal Argumentation

A. The Different Kinds of Legal Arguments

The arguments which that may be employed in legal justification can be classified in many different ways. The choice of a classification turns primarily on the purpose in question. With this in mind, four categories suggest themselves, namely linguistic, genetic, systematic, and general practical arguments.

Linguistic arguments are based on the ascertainment of usage that actually exists. Often, especially in the so-called simple cases, it leads to a definite result. The decision is than fixed, and another decision is possible only if the law is developed against the wording. Often, however, one can only state that the norm is vague or in some other way indefinite. Then a decision can only be substantiated with the help of other arguments.

Genetic arguments aim at the factual will of the historical legislator. Often, they are not applicable because the factual will cannot be ascertained or because it is too indefinite or contradictory. Also, the application of genetic arguments is disputed owing to the unresolved controversy between the subjective and the objective theories of interpretation.

Systematic arguments are based on the idea of the unity or coherence of the legal system. They represent the correct, central point of the idea expressed in a somewhat exaggerated form in the model of coherence. They can be divided into eight sub-groups that can only be named but not explicated here. They comprise (1) arguments securing consistence, (2) contextual and (3) conceptual-systematic arguments, (4) arguments of principle as well as (5) special legal forms of argument like analogy, (6) arguments of precedent as well as (7) historical and (8) comparative arguments. Most important in our context are the arguments of principle. In democratic constitutional states, arguments of principle are essentially based on constitutional principles.[24] In hard cases, their application regularly requires balancing. This indicates that principles have the character of optimization requirements.[25] Within the scope of balancing, however, general practical arguments play an important part. For this reason, the most important part of systematic argumentation is necessarily connected with general practical argumentation.

General practical arguments form the fourth category. They can be divided into teleological and deontological arguments. Teleological arguments look at the consequences of an interpretation and are based ultimately on an idea of what is good. Deontological arguments express what is legally right or wrong without looking at the consequences.

[24] Robert Alexy, *A Theory of Constitutional Rights* (1985), trans. Julian Rivers (Oxford: Oxford University Press, 2002), 351–4.

[25] Ibid., 47.

B. The Strength of the Arguments

The classification does not yet tell us anything about the strength of the arguments. Their strength can only be based on the reasons that justify their employment. Those reasons stem from the discourse theory of the law sketched above.

The linguistic, genetic, and systematic arguments are directly or indirectly supported by the authority of the positive law. They are, therefore, *institutional* arguments. The general practical arguments, on the other hand, derive their strength solely from their correct content. They are, therefore, *substantive* arguments. I shall confine myself to the relation between these two groups of arguments. To turn to rankings within the groups would go beyond of the scope of the present chapter.

The discourse theory of the law leads, as explained earlier, to the necessary institutionalization of a legal system. This implies the authority of the positive law. A successful institutionalization—according to the criteria of discourse theory—includes the principles of the democratic constitutional state, among others, those of democracy, of the separation of powers, and of the rule of law. The principle of the authority of the positive law, supported by these principles, requires that the institutional reasons be seen as enjoying priority over the substantive reasons. This, however, is merely a *prima facie* priority. Substantive reasons can be of such great weight in individual cases that they prevail over the institutional reasons. This not only corresponds to the general practice and to widespread opinion but is also justifiable systematically. If the legal system as a whole represents the attempt to realize practical reason, then the tension between authority and substantive correctness is preserved with all of its ramifications.

The fact that institutional arguments have merely a *prima facie* priority means that legal argumentation remains dependent on substantive or general practical argumentation even where institutional arguments alone lead to a certain result. This becomes obvious not only in the dramatic case of a judge who decides against the wording of a statute but also in the evaluation of a case of plain subsumption as unproblematic. Such an evaluation includes the judgment that there are no important substantive reasons that count against the decision. The dependence becomes altogether obvious if institutional arguments lead to no result, or to differing results, or if they—as happens regularly when weighing opposing principles—must be supplemented by general practical arguments.

All of this shows that the idea of discourse can and must remain alive notwithstanding institutionalization. Thus, calling legal argumentation a *special case* of general practical discourse is justified.[26] This is not to say that discourse theory can

[26] Alexy, *A Theory of Legal Argumentation* (n. 18 above), 212–20. The special case thesis is highly controversial. Opposing it are, among others, Jürgen Habermas, 'Theorie der Gesellschaft oder Sozialtechnologie? Eine Auseinandersetzung mit Niklas Luhmann', in *Theorie der Gesellschaft oder Sozialtechnologie—Was leistet die Systemforschung?* eds Habermas and Niklas Luhmann (Frankfurt: Suhrkamp, 1971), 142–290, at 200–1; Habermas, *Between Facts and Norms. Contributions to*

determine the strength of the substantive arguments employed in legal argumentation either generally or definitively. The special case thesis says, however, that discourse theory can define the conditions according to which the power of the better argument can, also in legal argumentation, be unfolded. These are the conditions of an open and impartial rational discourse. The theoretical gain is rationality, the political gain is, on an optimistic reading, lasting legitimacy.

a Discourse Theory of Law and Democracy (1992), trans. William Rehg (Cambridge: Polity Press, 1996), 230–3; Gerd-Walter Küsters, 'Rechtskritik ohne Recht', *Rechtstheorie* 14 (1983), 95–114, at 98–9; Werner Krawietz, 'Juridisch-institutionelle Rationalität des Rechts versus Rationalität der Wissenschaften?' *Rechtstheorie* 15 (1984), 423–52, at 438; Arthur Kaufmann, 'Über die Wissenschaftlichkeit der Rechtswissenschaft', *Archives for Philosophy of Law and Social Philosophy* 72 (1986), 425–42, at 435–7; Neumann, *Juristische Argumentationslehre* (n. 3 above), 86–91; Carl Braun, 'Diskurstheoretische Normenbegründung in der Rechtswissenschaft', *Rechtstheorie* 19 (1988), 238–61, at 258–60; Günther, 'Ein normativer Begriff der Kohärenz für eine Theorie der juristischen Argumentation' (n. 14 above), 184–8. Among those who have argued in its favour: Neil MacCormick, *Legal Reasoning and Legal Theory* (Oxford: Clarendon Press, 1978), 272; MacCormick, 'Legal Reasoning and Practical Reason', *Midwest Studies in Philosophy* 7 (1982), 271–86, at 282; Martin Kriele, *Recht und praktische Vernunft* (Göttingen: Vandenhoeck and Ruprecht, 1979), 33–4; Jürgen Habermas, *Theorie des kommunikativen Handelns*, vol. 1 (Frankfurt: Suhrkamp, 1981), 62–3; Maarten Henket, 'Towards a Code of Practical Reason?' *Archives for Philosophy of Law and Social Philosophy*, supplement 25 (1985), 36–42, at 41; Ingrid Dwars, 'Application Discourse and the Special Case-Thesis', *Ratio Juris* 5 (1992), 67–78, at 77.

20
Jürgen Habermas's Theory of the Indeterminacy of Law and the Rationality of Adjudication

Habermas's discourse theory of law turns on the tension between facticity and validity. This tension appears in different forms in different contexts. Chapter 5 of *Between Facts and Norms* is concerned with the '*theory of adjudication* and legal discourse'.[1] Here, the 'immanent tension in law between facticity and validity' is said to manifest 'itself as a tension between the principle of legal certainty and the claim to a legitimate application of law, that is, to render correct or right decisions'.[2] In short, the reader is confronted with a tension between '*the certainty of law* and its *rightness*'.[3] At the very latest since Gustav Radbruch[4] this tension defines one of the main problems of legal philosophy.[5]

I. The Problem of Rationality in Adjudication

The principle of legal certainty requires that legal decisions be oriented to valid positive law, that is, to what is duly issued and socially effective. This means that the 'institutional history of law' has to form 'the background of the ordinary practice of decision-making'.[6] This institutional history comprises not only decisions by the legislature but also customary law and decisions of the judiciary.[7] Thus, each practice of legal decision-making is embedded in 'the contingencies of this original context of emergence'.[8] This, however, is only the one side of the story. The claim to correctness raised by law requires more than mere compliance with statutes, precedents, and customary law. Over and above this, it demands that legal decisions be

[1] Jürgen Habermas, *Between Facts and Norms. Contributions to a Discourse Theory of Law and Democracy* (1992), trans. William Rehg (Cambridge: Polity Press, 1996), 197.
[2] Ibid.
[3] Ibid., 199.
[4] Gustav Radbruch, *Legal Philosophy* (1932), trans. Kurt Wilk, in *The Legal Philosophies of Lask, Radbruch, and Dabin* (Cambridge, Mass: Harvard University Press, 1950), 43–224, at 107–12.
[5] See Robert Alexy, 'Legal Certainty and Correctness', *Ratio Juris* 28 (2015), 441–51, at 443–4.
[6] Habermas, *Between Facts and Norms* (n. 1 above), 198.
[7] Ibid.
[8] Ibid.

Law's Ideal Dimension. Robert Alexy, Oxford University Press. © Robert Alexy 2021.
DOI: 10.1093/oso/9780198796831.003.0021

'rationally grounded in the matter at issue'.[9] Following a terminology introduced by Wróblewski in a not altogether happy way—Wróblewski refers exclusively to the formal distinction between deduction and the justification of the premises used in the deduction, premises of whatever kind[10]—Habermas designates the justification of a legal decision on the basis of premises provided by positive law as the 'internal justification of a verdict',[11] and, by contrast, the rational justification of the premises provided by positive law as 'external justification'.[12] Against this background, he formulates the 'problem of rationality in adjudication'.[13] 'The rationality problem thus consists in this: how can the application of a contingently emergent law be carried out with both internal consistency and rational external justification, so as to guarantee simultaneously the *certainty of law* and its *rightness*?'[14]

II. Three Insufficient Answers

In order to undertake a solution to the rationality problem, Habermas casts a short glance at the answers of legal hermeneutics, legal realism, and legal positivism, as a prelude to discussing, in greater detail, the position of Ronald Dworkin.

Habermas first grants to legal hermeneutics the merit of having described the relation between norm and case as circular, thereby inviting attention to a methodological problem that every theory of the application of law has to elucidate. From the standpoint of hermeneutics, proposals have been made to resolve this problem by means of recourse to historically corroborated standards or 'to a prevailing ethos developed through interpretation'.[15] Habermas aptly replies that recourse to something historical or dominant is not sufficient to solve the rationality problem in 'a pluralistic society'.[16]

Against legal realism, which essentially has reference to psychological or sociological descriptions, explanations, and predictions, Habermas objects that it misses '[t]he participants' idealistic notion, that all (or most) cases can be decided on the basis of established law both consistently and rightly'.[17] With this, it loses the possibility of explaining 'the very function of law, to stabilize expectations'.[18] Habermas, however, refers in this context only to 'guarantees of legal certainty'.[19] With this,

[9] Ibid.

[10] Jerzy Wróblewski, 'Legal Syllogism and Rationality of Judicial Decision', *Rechtstheorie* 5 (1974), 33–46, at 39.

[11] Habermas, *Between Facts and Norms* (n. 1, above), 199.

[12] Ibid.

[13] Ibid., 197.

[14] Ibid., 199.

[15] Ibid., 200.

[16] Ibid.

[17] Ibid., 201.

[18] Ibid.

[19] Ibid.

a possible connection between the clearly more idealistic substantive correctness and the 'functionally necessary accomplishments of the legal system'[20] remains undetermined.

Where legal positivism, as represented by Hans Kelsen and H. L. A. Hart, is concerned Habermas concedes that this view is able 'to account for the function of stabilizing expectations'[21] because it 'facilitate[s] the consistency of rule-bound decisions'.[22] But he reproaches legal positivism for providing 'an asymmetrical solution of the rationality problem',[23] for 'the positivist reading of judicial decision making privileges the certainty guarantee at the expense of the rightness guarantee'.[24] This becomes evident in the positivist's treatment of hard cases. A hard case occurs, for instance, when the vagueness of the wording of a norm allows for more than one decision to be made. According to Kelsen and Hart, the judge in such cases has 'discretionary leeway', which he is empowered to fill out 'with extra-legal preferences'.[25] Habermas designates this as a 'decisionistic conclusion'.[26] This reproach can be understood as saying that positivism scarcely exhausts the rationality postulates implicit in law. Much, indeed, speaks in favour of this.

III. Ronald Dworkins's Theory of Rights

According to Habermas, it is Dworkin's theory of rights which 'can be seen as an attempt to avoid the deficits of the realist, positivist, and hermeneutical solutions'[27] and, therefore, points in the right direction. The basic assumption of this theory is that 'positive law has unavoidably absorbed a moral content',[28] the core of which can be 'articulated in the principle of equal concern and respect for each person'[29] or the 'basic right to equal concern and respect'.[30] The proximity of Habermas's theory to Dworkin's basic assumption finds exemplary expression when Habermas remarks that this assumption 'harbors no surprise for a discourse theory'.[31]

It is striking that Habermas immediately goes on to add an 'explanation'[32] to his approval of Dworkin's thesis of the necessary inclusion of moral contents into the positive law. This 'Excursus on the Moral Content of Law'[33] is concerned with the

20 Ibid.
21 Ibid.
22 Ibid., 202.
23 Ibid.
24 Ibid.
25 Ibid., 203.
26 Ibid.
27 Ibid.
28 Ibid., 204.
29 Ibid., 203.
30 Ibid., 204.
31 Ibid.
32 Ibid.
33 Ibid.

avoidance of 'natural-law connotations'.[34] The core thesis is that 'the migration of moral contents into law does not signify any *immediate* moralization of law'.[35] With the inclusion of moral contents into the law, these contents 'are translated into the legal code and furnished with a different mode of validity'.[36] It seems to be easy to say what is meant by a clause that provides moral contents with a different mode of validity. The moral norms receive legal validity, which implies that the motivation of their compliance becomes irrelevant and non-compliance is sanctioned. Not so easy, however, is the question of what is to be understood by the transfer into the legal code. Habermas says that the moral contents 'undergo a change in meaning that is specific to the legal form'.[37] In the German edition of his book, Habermas mentions human dignity[38] as an example of a legal principle or 'general legal standard'.[39] Now there is little doubt that the principle of human dignity is also a moral principle. Shall 'change in meaning' mean that the meaning of the expression 'human dignity' changes when a guarantee of human dignity is incorporated into a constitution? This cannot be the case. With this, human dignity is, indeed, placed into the context of a legal system, which increases its enforceability and facilitates its being rendered concrete. The content of the moral principle of human dignity, however, is not changed by means of this transformation into positive law. Habermas says 'that the basic norms of both law and morality, which are grounded in the same discourse principle, *substantively* intersect'.[40] Perhaps this makes a solution possible. To the extent to which moral norms, such as the norm of human dignity, are at the same time also valid as legal norms, one can speak of an *immediate* and *substantive* rendering the law moral. This rendering is solely substantive because it does not extend to the 'mode of validity'[41] which can be considered as formal. And, above all, to render the law moral in no way concerns all legal norms because most of them are not located in the space of moral impossibility, that is, the space of what is morally prohibited, or in the space of moral necessity, that is, the space of what is morally obligatory. Rather, most legal norms are located in the wide space of mere moral possibility, that is, the space of what is morally merely permitted.

In Dworkin's theory of interpretation as a theory that connects law and morality, the distinction between rules and principles plays a particular role, in any case in its earlier form, to which Habermas refers. Habermas presents Dworkin's

[34] Ibid.
[35] Ibid., 206.
[36] Ibid.
[37] Ibid., 204.
[38] Jürgen Habermas, *Faktizität und Geltung. Beiträge zur Diskurstheorie des Rechts und des demokratischen Rechtsstaats*, 4th edn (Frankfurt: Suhrkamp, 1994), 255: 'Menschenwürde'. In the English translation, 'human dignity' is substituted by 'human rights'. See Habermas, *Between Facts and Norms* (n. 1 above), 208.
[39] Habermas, *Between Facts and Norms* (n. 1, above), 208.
[40] Ibid., 207.
[41] Ibid., 206.

distinction, but he does so without referring to a feature that plays a pivotal role in Dworkin's earlier work, the 'dimension of weight or importance'.[42] This dimension of weight suggests that competing principles are resolved by means of balancing according to the principle of proportionality.[43] This, in turn, speaks in favour of conceiving principles as optimization requirements.[44] Habermas, however, rejects this emphatically. If principles are 'understood as optimizing prescriptions', they would thereby receive a 'teleological structure',[45] and this, in turn, 'would eradicate their deontological character'.[46] Rights would no longer be Dworkinian 'trumps' to which one can appeal in overriding policy arguments in legal discourse,[47] and with this a 'firewall'[48] collapses. The reason for this, we are told, is that optimization requirements, owing to their teleological structure, have to be understood as values. Because principles as norms, 'in virtue of their deontological character, can claim to be *universally binding* and not just *specially preferred*, they possess a greater justificatory force than values',[49] for values 'must be brought into a transitive order with other values from case to case'.[50] For such balancing, however, there exist 'no rational standards'.[51] To all of this I have already replied,[52] and there is no need to repeat any of this here. Only one point is of interest. In Chapter 6, where Habermas discusses the relation between the judiciary and the legislature, he explains the ostensibly lower justificatory force of optimization requirements by means of the fact that, as values, they 'must be brought into a transitive order with other values from case to case'.[53] Exactly this, however, Habermas attributes in Chapter 5 to principles interpreted—in contrast to optimization requirements—deontologically: 'Depending on the case to be decided, one of the prima facie relevant principles takes precedence over the others. Because the appropriate principle can change from case to case, different transitive orders are set up between the same principles without thereby affecting their validity.'[54] This sounds like balancing the 'deontological'. What is more, the explication of the concept of being '*specially preferred*'[55] by means of the formulation 'from case to case'[56] seems to be

[42] Ronald Dworkin, *Taking Rights Seriously* (London: Duckworth, 1977), 26.
[43] Robert Alexy, *A Theory of Constitutional Rights* (1985), trans. Julian Rivers (Oxford: Oxford University Press, 2002), 50, 66.
[44] Ibid., 47–8.
[45] Habermas, *Between Facts and Norms* (n. 1, above), 208.
[46] Ibid.
[47] Ibid., 259.
[48] Ibid., 258.
[49] Ibid., 259.
[50] Ibid.
[51] Ibid.
[52] Robert Alexy, 'Jürgen Habermas's Theory of Legal Discourse', *Cardozo Law Review* 17 (1996), 1027–34, at 1028–31; Alexy, 'The Construction of Constitutional Rights', *Law & Ethics of Human Rights* 4 (2010), 20–32, at 26–32 (in this volume: Chapter 8, 121–32, at 126–32).
[53] Habermas, *Between Facts and Norms* (n. 1 above), 259.
[54] Ibid., 209.
[55] Ibid., 259.
[56] Ibid.

too narrow. Not cases *qua* individuals in space and time rule the 'precedence',[57] but the properties of the cases that justify the precedence along with the requirement that these properties are not referred to either by individual names or by definite descriptions but by predicates that have, in spite of their relative concreteness or specificity, a universal dimension.[58]

IV. Law as an Ideally Coherent System of Norms

Habermas takes up Dworkin's idea of 'an ambitious theory that enables one, especially in hard cases, to justify the individual decision by its coherence with a rationally reconstructed history of existing law',[59] while raising, at the same time, the question of whether the conception of existing law 'as an ideally coherent system of norms'[60] does not 'hold up a false ideal as the standard for judicial decision making'.[61] From the standpoint of Critical Legal Studies the objection has been raised 'that existing law in general is shot through with *contradictory* principles and policies; consequently, every attempt at a rational reconstruction is doomed to failure'.[62] Habermas's reply consists in a connection of Dworkin's distinction between rules and principles with Klaus Günther's distinction between discourses of justification and discourses of application. By contrast with conflicts of rules, competing principles do not concern 'contradictory prescriptions, each claiming equal validity'.[63] That is to say, it is not a matter of genuine contradictions, but of the competition between two norms that are, prima facie, both applicable. Which of them is definitively applicable has to be clarified in a discourse of application that, in contrast to a discourse of justification, does not concern the validity of norms but solely their applicability. Definitively applicable is the norm that is appropriate. According to Günther, a norm is appropriate if it has to be preferred after 'the consideration of all features of the application situation'[64] and the consideration of 'all the other principles applicable in the situation'.[65] This postulate of the consideration of all features of the application situation and of all norms that come into question corresponds to the old hermeneutic maxim of considering all circumstances, which is not wrong but says too little. A more serious defect of Günther's approach is the separation of discourses of application and discourses of

[57] Ibid., 209.
[58] Alexy, *A Theory of Constitutional Rights* (n. 43 above), 53–4.
[59] Habermas, *Between Facts and Norms* (n. 1 above), 211.
[60] Ibid., 220.
[61] Ibid., 213.
[62] Ibid., 216.
[63] Ibid., 217.
[64] Klaus Günther, *The Sense of Appropriateness. Application Discourses in Morality and Law* (1988), trans. John Farrell (Albany, N.Y.: State University of New York Press, 1993), 69.
[65] Ibid., 216.

justification. The rational application of norms requires, in hard cases, the determination of new norms related to the case, be it, for instance, in the form of 'word usage or semantic rules'[66] or in the form of rules that express 'conditional relations of precedence'.[67] Any renunciation of this would endanger the consistency of legal decision-making and, with this, of legal certainty.

Habermas seems to see this when he says that the Dworkinian theory of 'ideally justified coherence', connected with 'Günther's elegant proposal',[68] becomes a theory that 'merely provides guidelines for a *flexible* set of principles and policies',[69] and when he asks: 'Yet how can such a theory inform a decision-making practice intended to guarantee the certainty of law?'[70] Habermas begins his answer to this question with the statement that 'legal certainty … is itself a principle that must be weighed against other principles in the case at hand'.[71] This is true.[72] In a second step, Habermas locates legal certainty '*at a different level*'.[73] This different level is the level of procedures that shall guarantee 'a discursive clarification of the pertinent facts and legal questions'.[74] In principle, one can agree with this, although one is less than clear on what is to be understood by '*procedure-dependent certainty of law*'.[75] It seems that even with Habermas there persists a certain scepticism when he says that 'the orientation towards such a demanding ideal will, as a rule, overtax even professional adjudication'.[76] In a third step, Habermas sees a possible solution in legal paradigms.[77] Here he distinguishes the paradigm of 'bourgeois formal law' from that of 'welfare-state materialized law',[78] and from both, again, a '*proceduralist understanding of law*',[79] which, according to Habermas, 'provides a specific interpretation of the other two and goes beyond them'.[80] Thus, it is from the outset a matter of a connection of paradigms. Now there are tensions within the first two paradigms as well as between them. How can one resolve tensions by something that is essentially characterized by tensions? It is no surprise when Habermas notes that already owing to the competition of alternative legal paradigms, a proceduralist understanding of law must 'distinguish a level at which reflective legal paradigms can open up *for one another*'.[81] With this, the burden of reconciling legal certainty and correctness lies with procedure.

66 Robert Alexy, 'Justification and Application of Norms', *Ratio Juris* 6 (1993), 157–70, at 164.
67 Alexy, *A Theory of Constitutional Rights* (n. 43 above), 53.
68 Habermas, *Between Facts and Norms* (n. 1 above), 219.
69 Ibid.
70 Ibid.
71 Ibid., 220.
72 Alexy, 'Legal Certainty and Correctness' (n. 5 above), 444.
73 Habermas, *Between Facts and Norms* (n. 1, above), 220.
74 Ibid.
75 Ibid.
76 Ibid.
77 Ibid., 220–1.
78 Ibid., 221.
79 Ibid.
80 Ibid., 195.
81 Ibid., 221–2.

V. Theory of Legal Argumentation

With the step to procedure, Habermas rejects Dworkin's '*monological* approach'[82] which finds its most manifest expression in judge Hercules, 'a lawyer of superhuman skill, learning, patience and acumen'.[83] To be sure, the task remains of 'reconstructing the practice of interpretation in terms of legal theory, and not just along narrow, doctrinal lines',[84] but the ideal individual is replaced by the ideals of discourse: 'The critique of Dworkin's solipsistic theory of law must begin at the *same* level and, in the shape of a *theory of legal argumentation*, ground the procedural principles that henceforth bear the brunt of the ideal demands previously directed at Hercules.'[85]

At the centre of each theory of argumentation stands the concept of argument. Habermas defines arguments as 'reasons proffered in discourse that redeem a validity claim'.[86] With this, the ideal, which was considered by Dworkin as a requirement directed at the theory, is now relocated in the conditions of discourse described by Habermas as 'ideal demands on a *cooperative procedure of theory formation*'.[87] The idea of coherence persists, subordinated, however, to discourse. It shall refer 'to the pragmatic presuppositions of the argumentative process'.[88] With this, the establishing of a 'coherent whole' is connected with the idea of an 'uncoerced agreement'.[89] One could speak here of a 'discursive coherence theory'. Also, the idea of 'just one right answer' receives a discourse theoretic transformation. It is downgraded from an ontological assumption to a 'regulative ideal'[90] and, as such, is connected to the 'fallibility of actual decision-making'.[91] This, again, leads to the 'idea of an unending process of argumentation'[92] in which 'we presume that we sufficiently approximate the ideal conditions'[93] of discourse. These ideal conditions comprise the exclusion of 'repression and inequality',[94] that is, freedom and equality, 'endless time, unlimited participation, and perfect freedom from coercion',[95] as well as 'best information'.[96] In practical discourses, a 'universalized ideal role-taking practiced in common'[97] is of particular importance. 'This is how

82 Ibid., 222.
83 Dworkin, *Taking Rights Seriously* (n. 42 above), 105.
84 Habermas, *Between Facts and Norms* (n. 1 above), 225.
85 Ibid.
86 Ibid.
87 Ibid., 226.
88 Ibid., 229.
89 Ibid., 227.
90 Ibid.
91 Ibid., 226.
92 Ibid., 227.
93 Ibid., 228.
94 Ibid.
95 Ibid., 230.
96 Ibid., 228.
97 Ibid.

discourse ethics captures Dworkin's basic norm of equal concern and respect.'[98] With all of this, the discourse theoretic foundations of a theory of legal argumentation are established.

VI. The Special Case Thesis

The foundations of a theory, however, are something other than the theory itself. Each theory of legal argumentation has to determine the relation between legal certainty and correctness. This, in turn, requires that the specific character of legal argumentation be expounded. The special case thesis, developed in my book, *A Theory of Legal Argumentation*,[99] is an attempt to achieve both. Habermas criticizes the special case thesis. Four of his objections shall be considered here.

A. Moral, General Practical, and Legal Discourse

Habermas's first objection turns on the relation between legal and moral discourse. The answer to the question of whether his critique is justified under this aspect essentially depends on how one understands the special case thesis. According to Habermas, the special case thesis 'that Robert Alexy proposes' says 'that legal discourse should be conceived as a special case of moral discourse'.[100] Legal discourses, however, 'do not represent special cases of moral argumentation'.[101] They should not 'be conceived as a subset of moral argumentation'.[102]

If one looks at the wording of the special case thesis, it says 'that legal discourse is a special case of general practical discourse'.[103] If one considers the expression 'general practical discourse' as synonymous with the expression 'moral discourse' and if one defines moral discourse, as Habermas does, as a discourse about universalizability and only about universalizability[104] in the form of the question of whether the respective norm proposals 'express a common interest of all concerned',[105] the special case thesis immediately proves to be mistaken. Legal discourse is open not only for moral reasons but also for ethical-political and pragmatic reasons.[106] The

[98] Ibid., 230.

[99] Robert Alexy, *A Theory of Legal Argumentation* (1978), trans. Ruth Adler and Neil MacCormick (Oxford: Clarendon Press, 1989), 212–20.

[100] Habermas, *Between Facts and Norms* (n. 1 above), 197.

[101] Ibid., 234.

[102] Ibid., 230.

[103] Alexy, *A Theory of Legal Argumentation* (n. 99 above), 212.

[104] Habermas, *Between Facts and Norms* (n. 1 above), 108, 153.

[105] Jürgen Habermas, 'Vom pragmatischen, ethischen und moralischen Gebrauch der praktischen Vernunft', in Habermas, *Erläuterungen zur Diskursethik* (Frankfurt: Suhrkamp, 1991), 100–18, at 113 (trans. R. A.).

[106] Habermas, *Between Facts and Norms* (n. 1 above), 154, 230.

former 'express an authentic, collective self-understanding' based on 'traditions and strong evaluations'.[107] The latter concern the selection of 'suitable means for realizing goals and preferences that are already given'.[108] For systematic reasons, this openness to moral as well as to ethical and pragmatic arguments is necessary. In a democracy, statutes that are created in the democratic process represent the most important starting point of legal argumentation. The democratic process of law-making, however, is concerned with 'those action norms that appear in legal form. Such norms can be justified by calling on pragmatic, ethical-political, and moral reasons—here justification is not restricted to moral reasons alone'.[109] If legal argumentation shall be connected with what has been decided in the democratic process, then it has to take seriously all three kinds of reasons linked to its results.

For this reason, the special case thesis would be obviously mistaken if it were necessary to conceive the expression 'general practical discourse' as synonymous with the expression 'moral discourse'. There are, however, not only other possibilities but they are also more suggestive. General practical discourses are discourses that connect moral, ethical, and pragmatic questions and arguments. An example is the discussion in the general public of a draft law.

Against this concept of general practical discourse, the objection might be raised that it endangers the priorities between what is just, what is good, and what is expedient. This, however, is not the case. The priority of the good over what is merely expedient is already established as stemming from the fact that even the highest degree of the expediency of a means to an end counts for nothing if the end has no value. The priority of the just over the good cannot be established as easily. The good concerns non-universal individual and collective values, the just universal norms. Thus, it is a matter of the priority of the universal over the non-universal. The question of how this priority can be justified will not be discussed here. In order to reject the objection that the priorities are endangered, it suffices to state that the priority of the universal over the non-universal, if it can be justified, that is, if it is valid, is likewise valid with respect to 'different types of discourse'[110] just as it is with respect to different types of argument in one type of discourse. That is to say, it is valid for Habermas's construction just as it is for my construction, the general practical discourse.

It is of no less importance that there are not only priorities between moral, ethical, and pragmatic arguments, but also connections. Consider human rights, which define the core of justice. Human rights are abstract rights that are morally valid if they are justifiable.[111] If they are justifiable as abstract rights, they have

[107] Ibid., 108.
[108] Ibid., 159.
[109] Ibid., 108.
[110] Ibid., 159.
[111] Robert Alexy, 'The Existence of Human Rights', *Archives for Philosophy of Law and Social Philosophy*, supplement 136 (2013), 9–18, at 11 (in this volume: Chapter 10, 142–53, at 144–5).

absolute priority. No constitutional assembly and no parliament can ignore them for ethical or pragmatic reasons. If, however, one arrives at the question of what they require in a concrete case, ethical and pragmatic arguments may well play a role alongside moral arguments. This becomes most evident if one looks at proportionality analysis. In its first two steps, that is, the suitability and necessity tests, pragmatic arguments play the decisive role. In the third step, that is, the test of proportionality in the narrower sense, ethical arguments can come into play as reasons for imposing limitations on rights. If an interference with a human right is very light and the ethical reasons for it have a very high weight, then the latter can justify the interference. In this way, what is absolute at an abstract level can undergo a relativization in its concrete dimension.[112] All this shows that general practical discourse is by no means a mere mixture or combination. On the contrary, it consists of a systematically necessary connection that expresses the unity of practical reason.[113]

B. The Rules and Forms of Legal Discourse

Habermas's second objection to the special case thesis states that in order to demonstrate that this thesis is sound, 'Alexy would have to show' that the special rules and forms of legal discourse 'merely specify the universal requirements for moral-practical discourses in view of the connection with existing law'.[114] For this, however, Alexy's 'brief allusion to structural similarities in the rules and forms of argument respectively deployed in the two types of discourse is not sufficient'.[115]

My reply is that this requirement can, indeed, never be satisfied, but this—and here is the rub—does not raise questions about the special case thesis. Some rules and forms of legal discourse correspond to those of general practical discourse.[116] That this does not apply, however, to all rules and forms of legal discourse is not a merely innocuous point. The point stands, indeed, for a necessity. This necessity stems from the necessity of positive law, which, again, is the result of the 'decisional uncertainty'[117] or indefiniteness[118] of general practical discourses.[119] Legal discourses are essentially defined by authoritative or institutional reasons

[112] See Robert Alexy, 'The Absolute and the Relative Dimension of Constitutional Rights', *Oxford Journal of Legal Studies* 37 (2017), 31–47, at 42–7 (in this volume: Chapter 16, 235–52, at 247–52).

[113] See Robert Alexy, 'The Special Case Thesis', *Ratio Juris* 12 (1999), 374–84, at 378.

[114] Habermas, *Between Facts and Norms* (n. 1 above), 231.

[115] Ibid.

[116] Alexy, *A Theory of Legal Argumentation* (n. 99 above), 289–91.

[117] Habermas, *Between Facts and Norms* (n. 1 above), 234.

[118] Jürgen Habermas, 'Erläuterungen zur Diskursethik', in *Erläuterungen zur Diskursethik* (Frankfurt: Suhrkamp, 1991), 119–226, at 164.

[119] Alexy, 'Legal Certainty and Correctness' (n. 5 above), 443–4.

that give expression to the binding character of statutes, precedents, and the system itself. For this reason, the rules and forms of semantic, genetic, prejudiced, and systematic interpretation express more than just 'established canons of legal interpretation'.[120] They participate in the necessity of positivity. This implies that, with respect to their content as well as their structure, they cannot be specifications of the rules and forms of general practical discourse. Nevertheless, the rules and forms of legal discourse are connected with them. The existence of positive law is a requirement of practical reason. Thus, the existence of positive law can be justified in general practical discourse.[121] For this reason, those rules and forms of legal discourse that are concerned with the authoritative dimension are indirectly connected with the rules and forms of the general practical discourse.

C. Unjust Law

Habermas's third objection to the special case thesis states that 'the harmony between law and morality assumed by Alexy has the unpleasant consequence not only of relativizing the rightness of a legal decision but calling it into question as such'.[122] The reason for this, Habermas continues, is that '[v]alidity claims are binarily coded and do not admit of degrees of validity'.[123] '[H]armony between law and morality' cannot mean that according to the special case thesis, the law always actually comports with morality. This formulation can only be understood as a reference to the claim to correctness necessarily raised by legal norms and legal decisions. The claim to correctness raised in moral discourses is a claim to moral correctness. The claim to correctness raised in general practical discourses is a claim to general practical correctness. In both cases, the point is material or substantive correctness. One can speak here of first-order correctness. First-order correctness refers to the ideal dimension. In law, the ideal dimension is connected with the real dimension of positivity. For this reason, the claim raised in legal discourses is complex. It refers to the ideal as well as to the real dimension. One can speak here of second-order correctness. The claim to second-order correctness necessarily connects both the principle of substantive correctness, especially that of justice, and the principle of legal certainty, with law.[124] This implies that in cases in which it is required that an unjust statute be

[120] Habermas, *Between Facts and Norms* (n. 1, above), 231.

[121] Georgios Pavlakos, 'The Special Case Thesis. An Assessment of R. Alexy's Discursive Theory of Law', *Ratio Juris* 11 (1998), 126–54, at 152.

[122] Habermas, *Between Facts and Norms* (n. 1 above), 232.

[123] Ibid.

[124] Alexy, 'Legal Certainty and Correctness' (n. 5 above), 444.

applied, the formal principle of legal certainty has to be balanced against the substantive principle of justice. I shall, however, not elaborate on this here. Only two points matter. If the principle of legal certainty has to be given precedence, the claim to second-order correctness is met, and the validity claim of law which is, indeed, binarily coded, is not questioned. On the other hand, the second-order claim to correctness is also met if the principle of justice has to be given precedence, and, furthermore, in this case, too, the binary coding is not questioned. Thus, Habermas's supposition is groundless, namely that for the binary coding a graduated scheme of legal validity is substituted. This is the first point. The second point is that an unjust legal decision, backed by the principle of legal certainty, is, despite its legal validity, a legally defective decision. It is an advantage of the special case thesis that it can represent this divergence between legal validity and mere legal defectiveness.

D. Specific Legal Nature?

A fourth objection to the special case thesis could be formulated with Habermas's thesis that 'legal discourses not only refer to legal norms but, together with their institutionalized forms of communication, are themselves *embedded* in the legal system'[125] and 'do not represent special cases of moral argumentation' but rather 'refer *from the outset* to democratically enacted law'.[126] With the expressions '*embedded*' and '*from the outset*' Habermas might be saying that the general practical arguments—that is, the moral, ethical, and pragmatic arguments in the legal discourse—lose their general character and acquire a specific legal nature. This would fit Habermas's thesis, already mentioned in connection with his 'Excursus on the Moral Content of Law', that 'moral contents, once *translated* into the legal code, undergo a change in meaning that is specific to the legal form'.[127] The thesis of a specific legal nature, however, is diametrically opposed to the thesis, also held by Habermas, that 'legal discourse cannot operate self-sufficiently inside a hermetically sealed universe of existing norms but must rather remain open to arguments from other sources', whereby Habermas refers to 'pragmatic, ethical, and moral reasons'.[128] The solution, I suggest, could be that the general practical arguments applied in legal discourse remain what they are, that is, general practical arguments, but that, on the other hand, the legal discourse as a whole has a specific legal nature. This would correspond to the special case thesis.

[125] Habermas, *Between Facts and Norms* (n. 1 above), 234.
[126] Ibid.
[127] Ibid., 204.
[128] Ibid., 230.

21
Law and Correctness

Currently positivists as well as non-positivists largely agree that law consists of more than the pure facticity of a variety of regularities in acting, in ordering, in mental dispositions, or in the exercise of coercion. Law carries, besides this factual or real dimension, a critical or reflexive side that goes further.[1] Accordingly, there are authors who deny that there is a conceptually necessary relation between law and morality, as well as authors who assert such a relation, which support the thesis that law raises a claim to correctness or justice.[2] The old dispute between positivism and non-positivism can therefore proceed in a new setting, one that is characterized by the question of meaning and by the question of consequences stemming from the claim to correctness connected with or raised in law. The centre of this dispute remains unchanged and focuses on the relation of law and morality. This relation is approached by questioning whether the claim to correctness can serve to produce a link between law and morality that goes beyond the scope of the positivistic concept of law. In order to consider an answer to this question it is necessary first to discuss what is meant by a claim to correctness connected with or raised in law. Section II of this chapter will then deal with the question of whether such a claim is in fact necessarily connected with law. In section III, I shall take up the consequences of the claim to correctness for the relation of law and morality.

I. The Concept of the Claim to Correctness

A. The Subjects

Talk about law's raising a claim to correctness sounds familiar enough, but given a closer look, it seems, at first glance, peculiar. That people or legal subjects have the ability to raise claims based on law is self-evident. But how can such a claim possibly be raised by law itself? Claims can only be raised in a fully qualified or strict sense by subjects having the capacity to take action. But the law has no such capacity—neither its individual legal norms nor the legal system as a whole. If one

[1] See H. L. A. Hart, *The Concept of Law*, 2nd edn (Oxford: Clarendon Press, 1994), 57, 87–91.

[2] See, on the one hand, Neil MacCormick, 'The Concept of Law and *The Concept of Law*', in *The Autonomy of Law*, ed. Robert P. George (Oxford, Clarendon Press, 1996), 163–93, at 172, 175, 189, and, on the other, Robert Alexy, 'On Necessary Relations Between Law and Morality', *Ratio Juris* 2 (1989), 167–83, at 169, 177–80.

Law's Ideal Dimension. Robert Alexy, Oxford University Press. © Robert Alexy 2021.
DOI: 10.1093/oso/9780198796831.003.0022

does not want to focus on abstract subjects or entities such as the state or the legal community, which would create new problems, the only remaining possibility is to connect the claim to correctness to those subjects who act for and in law, those who create, interpret, use, and enforce it. In the last resort, this can only be done by single individuals or persons. It could be objected that this reference to persons renders subjective the claim to correctness too much. Whether or not someone raises any such claims could be said to be his own business. A judge could say no to the question of whether he thinks his judgment is correct and call it catastrophic. To answer this objection, a distinction has to be drawn between a subjective and an objective raising of the claim.[3] A person raises a claim subjectively if he wants to raise it. In this regard it can also be called 'personal' claim to correctness. On the other hand, there is an objective claim to correctness if everyone who decides or discusses the matter in a legal system must necessarily raise this claim. The objective claim is not a private matter but is necessarily connected to the role of a participant in the legal system. It could also be designated as 'official'. The objective or official character becomes most evident in the case of the judge who, as a representative of the legal system, raises the claim to correctness. The distinction between a subjective or personal and an objective or official claim clarifies why talking about the claim to correctness of law is intuitively quite plausible. The claim is raised by persons, but on behalf of law. Therefore, it can be said that law raises this claim through the persons who work for and in it.

B. The Addressees

The counterpart of the question of who raises the claim to correctness is provided by the question towards whom this claim is raised. One circle of addressees is identified quickly. It is the circle of addressees of the respective legal acts. These legal acts include the legislator's acts in, for example, raising a claim to correctness as against the addressees of the laws, the judge's acts addressed to the parties in trials, and the administrative officer's acts vis-à-vis the addressees of his acts of administration. This circle of addressees can be called 'institutional'. It is of great importance that the circle of addressees of the claim to correctness in law be broader than that of the respective legal act. Besides the institutional circle there is a non-institutional circle of addressees. It includes everyone who takes the point of view of a participant in the legal system. Such an inner perspective or internal point of view[4] is adopted in posing the question about what is obligatory, prohibited, or permitted in the legal system and what it authorizes. This question

[3] Also in this direction Philip Soper, 'Law's Normative Claims', in *The Autonomy of Law*, ed. Robert P. George (Oxford, Clarendon Press, 1996), 215–47, at 218.

[4] See Hart, *The Concept of Law* (n. 1 above), 89.

can be posed by everyone, and everyone can try to answer this question and try to substantiate it or may criticize answers given by others. These acts of questioning, judging, and asserting and of arguing and reasoning that are in general connected to the claim to correctness or truth define the circle of addressees of the claim to correctness in law. It therefore has a universal character in law, too. The only qualification, albeit a decisive qualification, is that only those belong to the non-institutional circle of addressees who take the point of view of the legal system. This is the difference between the claim to correctness in law and a universal morality. In the latter, the question is not what is valid in a specific system but what is valid in general. The particulars need to be specified further owing to the possibility that universal substantive or formal requirements relating to legal systems on such matters as human rights or the postulate of legal certainty exist. Yet for a first and general determination of the circle of addressees the aforesaid should suffice.

C. Raising a Claim

So far, we have only dealt with the question of who raises the claim to correctness against whom. The question of what this raising of a claim means has been left open. In the literature, even where claims connected to law are discussed in detail, little attention is directed to the question of what action or actions are necessary for the claim to correctness to be raised.[5] Again, there is a distinction to be made between the institutional and the non-institutional. Institutional acts are performed by virtue of norms granting power or authority. Examples are the legislative act, the judicial decision, or the issuance of an administrative act. The core of the argument of correctness is the thesis that such institutional acts are always connected to the non-institutional act of *asserting* that the legal act is substantially and procedurally correct. This assertion of correctness has consequences. Correctness implies justifiability. Therefore, in raising the claim to correctness, law also raises the claim to justifiability. In recognizing this claim, it not only accepts a general obligation to justification in principle; it also maintains that this obligation is complied with or could be complied with as far as possible. The claim to correctness therefore includes not only a mere assertion of correctness but also a *guarantee* of justifiability. Moreover, there is a third element besides assertion and guarantee. It is the *expectation* that all addressees of the claim will accept the legal act as correct for as long as they take the standpoint of the respective legal system and for as long as they are reasonable. This expectation comes closest to

[5] See, for instance, Soper, 'Law's Normative Claims' (n. 3 above), 237, who plainly and without further discussion talks about a law that 'insists', 'believes', and 'thinks' that its legal norms are 'just' or 'correct'.

what is meant legally by a claim. According to Article 194(1) of the BGB (German Civil Code), a claim (*Anspruch*) is the right to demand an action or an omission from another person. The concept of expectation can be specified such that whoever raises a claim to correctness also sets up the right against the addressee of the claim to accept the legal act in question as correct. This is to say that the expectation implied by the claim to correctness is a normative expectation. Summing up what has been said about the claim to correctness, it consists of three elements: (1) the assertion of correctness, (2) the guarantee of justifiability, and (3) the expectation of the acceptance of correctness.

These three elements are not only connected to the institutional acts discussed so far, for example, judicial decisions. Everyone who, as a participant in a legal system, for example, as a lawyer in court or as a citizen at a public discussion, makes an assertion about what is obligatory, prohibited, or permitted in the legal system and what it authorizes raises a claim that consists of the assertion of correctness, the guarantee of justifiability, and the expectation of acceptance.

The trilogy of assertion, guarantee, and expectation does not say anything about the content of the claim to correctness, and it does not say anything about what it intended to accomplish either. It is a genuine characteristic of the claim to correctness that the criteria of correctness are open. Otherwise, the claim could not be raised everywhere in law. Not only do the criteria of correctness of different legal systems differ from one another but also within a given legal system the criteria that are valid for correctness, for example, of statutes, judicial decisions, and acts of administration may be of quite distinct kind. The question is whether, despite all the differences, there exists a commonality that produces a necessary connection between law and morality. Before we discuss this problem, however, we have to ask whether the nexus between law and the claim to correctness has a necessary character. If this should turn out not to be the case, our claim could not produce a necessary connection between law and morality.

II. The Necessity of Connecting Law and Correctness

Ostensibly counting against the thesis that the claim to correctness is necessarily raised in law, it has been pointed out that the question of what kinds of claims are raised by law is an empirical one.[6] If this should prove correct, the connection of law and correctness would not have a necessary character but only a contingent one. Accordingly, the law might raise this claim, and then again, it might not. If it is possible to forbear from raising the claim to correctness that would imply that it is not necessary. To examine this possibility, I will consider two examples.

[6] Soper, 'Law's Normative Claims' (n. 3 above), 217, 230–1.

A. An Absurd Constitutional Article

One example concerns the first article of a new constitution for state *X*, where a minority oppresses the majority. The minority would like to continue to enjoy the advantages of its oppression but would like also to be honest. The constitutional assembly therefore adopts as the first article of the constitution the following proposition:

X is a sovereign, federal, and unjust republic.

There is something defective about this constitutional article. The question is where the defect lies. Doubtlessly, it violates conventions about drafting constitutions, but this alone does not explain the flaw. A basic rights catalogue of, say, 100 pages would also be most unusual or unconventional, but in spite of this, giving rise to inexpediency, it does not seem as nonsensical as the injustice clause. The same is true for the moral defect. From the moral point of view there would be no difference if the majority were to be explicitly deprived of their rights, but such a direct approach would not look defective in the same way. The injustice clause is not only immoral but it is also, in a way, absurd. It has been said that the injustice clause is only a political mistake because it is 'politically inexpedient'.[7] This is indeed so, but this, too, does not fully explain the defect. Much might be politically inexpedient in a constitution and in this sense technically defective without thereby seeming to be as strange as our first article.[8] Neither the conventional, nor the moral, nor the technical defectiveness explains the absurdity of the injustice clause. Rather, its absurdity, as is often the case with an absurdity, stems from a contradiction. Such a contradiction emerges since the act of laying down a constitution necessarily incorporates a claim to correctness, which in this case is essentially a claim to justice. Claims comprise, as mentioned, assertions. In the case of the claim to justice raised here, it is the assertion that the constituted republic is just. This assertion, being implicit in the act of passing a constitution, contradicts the explicit content of the constituent act, the injustice clause. Contradictions between the content of an act and necessary presuppositions of its execution can be designated as 'performative contradictions'. One may elect to use the term 'conceptual defect' broadly enough to relate to violations of rules that are constitutive for speech acts, that is, linguistic utterances as actions. If so, one may then conclude that a conceptual defect in form of a performative contradiction is under consideration. Accordingly, a conclusion

[7] Eugenio Bulygin, 'Alexy und das Richtigkeitsargument', in *Rechtsnorm und Rechtswirklichkeit. Festschrift für Werner Krawietz*, eds Aulis Aarnio, Stanley L. Paulson, Ota Weinberger, et al. (Berlin: Duncker & Humblot, 1993), 19–24, at 23–4 (trans. R. A.).

[8] See Robert Alexy, *The Argument from Injustice. A Reply to Legal Positivism* (1992), trans. Bonnie Litschewski Paulson and Stanley L. Paulson (Oxford: Clarendon Press, 2002), 36–7.

that begins with the conventional defect and then moves to consider the moral and the technical defect, leads to the result that only the assumption of a conceptual defect can explain the peculiar defectiveness of the injustice clause. If, however, the mistake is a conceptual one, the necessary connection between law and the claim to correctness on which it rests can be called 'conceptually necessary'.

All of this can be confirmed by means of a check test. That the injustice clause is contradictory in the sense just explained, implies that an article such as:

X is a just state

is redundant in a constitution. What is necessarily claimed does not need to be explicitly stated.

Against this line of argument regarding the absurd constitutional article, it has been said that passing a constitution by a constitutional assembly belongs to a type of legal order that developed relatively late. It cannot be ruled out that specific normative claims are only inherent in the modern constitutional state and therefore cannot be used as defining criteria for a concept of law that aims at universal applicability.[9] It is without doubt correct that the modern constitutional state is connected with claims that have not been raised in every legal order. The claim to correctness, however, is not a part of this special set of claims. It is a general claim connected to every law. This is also true of the claim to justice being comprised by it. As a general or abstract claim, the claim to justice does not aim at a specific conception of justice but only at a correct distribution of goods and burdens and the correct balance of guilt and punishment, damage and compensation. Abstract justice is nothing other than correctness concerning distribution and compensation. The criteria for justice in distribution and compensation are different, but the claim to a correct distribution and compensation is universal. And this is not restricted to modern times. One only need think of Justinian's having the famous three *iuris praecepta of* Ulpian[10] inserted into the *Corpus Juris Civilis* in the following negated form:

Iuris praecepta sunt haec: inhoneste vivere, alterum laedere, suum cuique non tribuere.[11]

[9] Ulfrid Neumann, 'Review: Robert Alexy, Begriff und Geltung des Rechts', *Protosoziologie* 6 (1994), 241–7, at 243.

[10] Ulp. D. 1, 1, 10, 1: '*Iuris praecepta sunt haec: honeste vivere, alterum non laedere, suum cuique tribuere*'. See also, Inst. 1, 1, 3.

[11] 'The commands of law are such: live dishonorably, injure others, assign no one his due.' The absurdity of this sentence corresponds to the evident character of the Ulpian formula. This should explain the 'missing originality' that is sometimes discussed. See on this Wolfgang Waldstein, 'Zur juristischen Relevanz der Gerechtigkeit bei Aristoteles, Cicero und Ulpian', in *Der Gerechtigkeitsanspruch des Rechts. Festschrift für Theo Mayer-Maly*, eds Margarethe Beck-Mannagetta, Helmut Böhm, and Georg Graf (Vienna: Springer, 1996), 1–71, at 60–1.

B. An Absurd Judgment

Not all legal systems know constitutional assemblies yet in all at least minimally developed legal systems acts of jurisdiction are to be found. They are the subject of our second example. It may be supposed that a judge hands down the following decision:

> The accused is sentenced to life imprisonment, which is an incorrect interpretation of prevailing law.

This judgment provokes a number of questions that will not be followed up here.[12] In the present context, the only matter of importance is that the assumption of a conventional, moral, or technical defect as well as of an offence against the positive law[13] is insufficient here, too, to come to terms with the peculiar character of the defectiveness. Again, the absurdity in this sentence explains itself only from the standpoint of a performative contradiction. The claim to a correct application of the law is always raised in a judicial decision, however badly this claim may be realized. The claim to correctness, necessarily raised with the institutional act of judgment, contradicts its being classified as wrong. Raising a claim to correctness means, among other things, that implicitly the assertion is made that the judgment is correct. This implicit assertion contradicts the explicit and public assertion connected with the judgment that it is wrong. This contradiction between the implicit and the explicit explains the absurdity.

It has been objected that the reference to these two examples is not a real justification of the thesis that the claim to correctness is necessary.[14] This leads to the question of whether the contradictions in the examples amount to a justification. The answer depends on what one takes to be a justification. If one requires that a sentence be substantiated by an independent sentence, the reference to a performative contradiction cannot serve as a justification.[15] This stems from the simple fact that a performative contradiction arises only if the rule that it is to justify is already valid. If the rule that with a judicial decision a claim to correctness is raised is not valid, then no performative contradiction arises. Performative contradictions are therefore only a means of *showing* that specific rules are necessarily in force. The

[12] See on this Ulfrid Neumann, *Juristische Argumentationslehre* (Darmstadt: Wissenschaftliche Buchgesellschaft, 1986), 87–90, Neumann, 'Review: Robert Alexy, Begriff und Geltung des Rechts' (n. 9 above), 244–5, and also, on the one hand, Bulygin, 'Alexy und das Richtigkeitsargument' (n. 7 above), 23, and, on the other, Alexy, *The Argument from Injustice* (n. 8 above), 38–9, and Alexy, 'Bulygins Kritik des Richtigkeitsarguments', in *Normative Systems in Legal and Moral Theory. Festschrift for Carlos E. Alchourrón and Eugenio Bulygin*, eds Ernesto Garzon Valdes, Werner Krawietz, Georg Henrik von Wright, et al. (Berlin: Duncker & Humblot, 1997), 235–50, at 247–9.

[13] See Alexy, *The Argument from Injustice* (n. 8 above), 38.

[14] Bulygin, 'Alexy und das Richtigkeitsargument' (n. 7 above), 21–3.

[15] See on this William D. Fusfield, 'Can Jürgen Habermas' "Begründungsprogramm" Escape Hans Albert's *Münchhausen Trilemma*?' *Jahrbuch Rhetorik* 8 (1989), 73–82, at 77.

demonstration consists in the reference to an inevitable absurdity that can only be explained by the necessary existence of a rule. This is an argument, even if it is not infallible. Thus, if one does not take the concept of justification too narrowly, it also counts as a justification.[16]

C. The Alternative

It could be argued that none of this shows the necessity of the claim to correctness. Absurdities are avoidable. It would only take a radical change in the present practice and self-conception of law. Once constitutions are understood by all solely as a means of power, will, and force, and judicial rulings as mixtures of emotion, decision, and commands, the claim to correctness disappears, and with it the contradiction and absurdity in our examples. The claim to correctness is then replaced by something like a claim to power. Still, something of the strangeness would remain. But this could be explained by the fact that a practice in which only power, will, and decision count lies beyond the categories of just and unjust, of correct and wrong. Our two examples, as far as they use these categories, would indeed not be contradictory but senseless.

In order to determine the weight of this objection, we might take a look at a possible extension. Claims to correctness exist by no means only in law. They are also raised with judgments about moral value and obligation. Their most general form is connected with the speech act of assertion. Moral statements that do not raise this claim are, as Günther Patzig has shown, merely 'utterances of an emotional reaction'.[17] The interpretation of moral statements as reports on individual attitudes and emotions, or as an appeal to feel as the speaker feels, formerly common in analytical philosophy,[18] fail to capture 'the real meaning of moral judgments'. Judgments about moral value and obligation are 'real assertions',[19] and assertions are speech acts that raise a claim to truth or correctness.[20] To renounce the claim to correctness would change our language, along with the way we understand

[16] It should be emphasized that this justification concerns solely the objective necessity of the claim to correctness. The objectivity consists in the claim's being raised with specific acts that are independent of the actors' thoughts or wishes. Regrettably, the claim to correctness is frequently raised by people who know that what they pretend to be correct is actually wrong, or by people who, in general, do not care about correctness. Therefore the claim is necessary only objectively and not subjectively. Objective necessity has an ambivalent character. On the one hand, it provides an opportunity for deceit and fraud, on the other, it provides an opportunity for exposure and criticism.

[17] Günther Patzig, 'Relativismus und Objektivität moralischer Normen', in Patzig, *Gesammelte Schriften*, vol. 1 (Göttingen: Wallstein, 1994), 9–43, at 21.

[18] See on this Robert Alexy, *A Theory of Legal Argumentation* (1978), trans. Ruth Adler and Neil MacCormick (Oxford: Clarendon Press, 1989), 39.

[19] Patzig, 'Relativismus und Objektivität moralischer Normen' (n. 17 above), 21.

[20] See Ernst Tugendhat, *Vorlesungen über Ethik*, 2nd edn. (Frankfurt: Suhrkamp, 1994), 19; Robert Alexy, 'Discourse Theory and Human Rights', *Ratio Juris* 9 (1996), 209–35, at 214.

ourselves, thereby changing our lives completely. Instead of judgments and assertions, there would only be emotions and opinions; with justification becoming persuasion. Successful manipulation and deeply rooted beliefs would take the place of correctness and truth. Everything would be subjective, nothing objective.

This clarifies the sense in which the claim to correctness is necessary. It is necessary relative to a practice that is essentially defined by the distinction of true or correct and false or wrong.[21] Yet this practice is of a special kind. Indeed, we can try to dismiss the categories of truth, correctness, and objectivity. But if we should succeed in doing so, our speaking and acting would be essentially different from what it is now. The price would not only be high, to a certain extent we would thereby deprive ourselves of our identity.

III. Legal and Moral Correctness

A positivist could agree with all of this, while still maintaining that it adds nothing to the effect to show a necessary connection between law and morality. That is, the positivist contends that the claim to correctness necessarily raised in law has a purely legal content without, then, any moral implications. The question therefore is whether the claim to correctness raised in law includes a claim to moral correctness. This question can be raised with reference to legislation as well as to administration and adjudication. Here, solely questions about adjudication will be examined.

A. Law's Open Texture

The starting point is an insight of legal methodology with which positivists and non-positivists generally agree. Every positive law has, as Hart says, an '*open texture*'.[22] The main reasons for this are the vagueness of legal language, the possibility of conflict between norms, the gaps that exist in law, and the possibility of deciding, in special cases, contrary to the wording of the statute.[23] To this extent, a

[21] This relativity of the necessity of the claim to correctness to a specific practice coincides, in its structure, with the thesis of Grice and Strawson, to the effect that it is one thing to grant that there is no absolute necessity to adopt or use any conceptual scheme or system whatever, and quite another thing to say that there are no necessities within whatever conceptual scheme or system we adopt or use. The latter does not follow from the former; H. P. Grice and P. F. Strawson, 'In Defence of a Dogma', *The Philosophical Review* 65 (1956), 141–58, at 157. The necessity within a specific conceptual scheme or system and also within a specific practice is in opposition to the necessity of a specific conceptual scheme or system as such, or a specific practice as such. This is altogether consistent with Quine's thesis that 'no statement is immune to revision'; W. V. O. Quine, 'Two Dogmas of Empiricism', in Quine, *From a Logical Point of View*, 2nd edn. (New York, N.Y.: Harper & Row, 1963), 20–46, at 43.

[22] Hart, *The Concept of Law* (n. 1 above), 128.

[23] See Alexy, *A Theory of Legal Argumentation* (n. 18 above), 1.

necessarily 'open' quality of positive law exists. Cases within the scope of this 'open' quality can, following a familiar terminology, be called 'hard cases'.

Cases that fall within the scope of this 'open' quality of positive law cannot, by definition, be decided by positive law. If they could, they would not fall within the scope of the 'open' quality. Positivists such as Kelsen and Hart are therefore simply following this logic when they say that within the scope of this 'open' quality the judge is authorized to create new law on the basis of standards other than legal standards, according to his own discretion, in the manner of a legislature.[24] By contrast, the claim to correctness leads to a non-positivistic reading. This claim is because of its necessary connection to the judicial judgment a legal, and not merely a moral claim. To this legal claim there corresponds a legal obligation that is necessarily connected to judicial decisions, namely, that a correct decision be handed down. Now the decision in the scope of the 'open' quality is the decision of a normative question because in the last analysis it concerns what is obligatory, prohibited, or permitted. This problem cannot be resolved solely on the basis of legal standards. If this were possible, we would not be within the scope of the 'open' quality. Thus, resorting to a standard other than the legal standard is the only course available. Non-legal standards as such give rise to general reflections on utility, traditional and common ideas of what is good and evil, as well as considerations of justice—in short, utility, custom, and morality. Considerations of utility and of the traditions and values of the community have, without doubt, a legitimate place in judicial decisions. Yet, if the claim to correctness is to be viable, the question of correct distribution and compensation must have priority. Questions of correct distribution and of correct compensation are questions of justice. Questions of justice are, however, moral questions. Therefore, the claim to correctness creates a necessary methodological or argumentative connection between law and morality. The claim to legal correctness is on no account identical with the claim to moral correctness, but it includes a claim to moral correctness.[25]

B. The Autonomy Objection

Numerous objections may be raised against this argument. Three unusually important ones shall be considered here. The first states that it is wrong to interpret the argument from necessity in hard cases as a moral argument. In so far as this objection serves only to claim that it is not only moral principles but also utility

[24] Hans Kelsen, *Pure Theory of Law*, 2nd edn (1960), trans. Max Knight (Berkeley, Calif.: University of California Press, 1967), 353–4; Hart, *The Concept of Law* (n. 1 above), 126, 135, 204.

[25] The argument sketched here can be spelled out as the 'principles argument' on the one hand (Alexy, *The Argument from Injustice* (n. 8 above) 68–81), and as the 'special case thesis' on the other (Alexy, *A Theory of Legal Argumentation* (n. 18 above), 212–20; Alexy, 'Jürgen Habermas's Theory of Legal Discourse', *Cardozo Law Review* 17 (1996), 1027–34, at 1033–4).

considerations and values of the respective community that play a legitimate role in law, it is pushing at an open door. The necessity of general practical argumentation in hard cases includes all of these,[26] although under the primacy of moral arguments. An objection arises only if the necessity of moral arguments for meeting the claim to correctness is denied altogether. The most attractive version of this objection stems from radical coherence theories of legal interpretation. Radical coherence theories do not rest content with the doubtlessly reasonable and correct thesis that systematic completeness and systematic connection are essential criteria of rationality and therefore of correctness. They assert further that coherence is a sufficient—indeed, the only—criterion in hard cases. Radical theories of coherence are, therefore, an expression of the idea of legal holism, according to which all premises are already part of or hidden in the legal system and need only to be discovered. Jurists have found this idea fascinating for its promise of the total autonomy of law. But it cannot be realized. Every formula directed to rendering it precise proves to be open and dependent on being filled with values and norms that have not already been included. Whether one takes the hermeneutic circles between preconception and text, between part and whole, between the norm and the facts of a case, or the demand for rational argumentation to take all facts of the case and all relevant norms into consideration and then balance them,[27] or the familiar maxim to search for similarities, one always has something reasonable but also something incomplete and therefore in need of supplementation. Just as norms cannot apply themselves, a legal system as a system of norms cannot produce completeness and coherence. To achieve this, persons and procedures are necessary to provide content. Content, however, includes moral content if the claim to correctness is to be realized.

C. The Objection of Impossibility

The second objection reaches deeper. It maintains that a conceptually necessary connection between law and morality is conceptually impossible. If morality is in any way necessarily connected with law, it necessarily belongs to law. But what necessarily belongs to law is law. Such necessary connections, therefore, can only exist within law and never beyond its borders. The thesis stating that there is a legal obligation to recognize and consider moral principles within the scope of the 'open' quality of law leads to a dilemma, the dilemma of non-positivism. On the one hand, the consideration of a specific principle is legally obligatory, in which case the principle would be a legal principle. For what other than the legal

[26] Alexy, 'Jürgen Habermas's Theory of Legal Discourse' (n. 25 above), 1033.

[27] See Klaus Günther, 'Critical Remarks on Robert Alexy's "Special Case Thesis"', *Ratio Juris* 6 (1993), 143–56, at 151.

obligation to recognize it would make of such a principle a legal principle? But if the principle to be recognized were a legal principle, the problem of a necessary connection between law and morality would not arise. Or, on the other hand, the principle in question is solely a moral principle. This would require that it be recognized as not legally obligatory for if it were legally obligatory, the principle would be a legal principle and not solely a moral principle. If, however, the recognition of solely moral principles were by definition not legally obligatory, the question of a necessary connection between law and morality could not arise.[28]

The solution to this dilemma lies in defining moral principles and arguments that have to be recognized legally by means of a legal obligation for their recognition that derives solely from their substantive correctness. Correctness and correctness alone connects them to law. Their argumentative power is exclusively non-institutional in character. This is precisely what leads to a delimitation of positive law and morality. Positive law can only be defined by means of institutionalization, however constituted.[29] Proper issuance and social efficacy—essentially supported by sanctions—are the main elements. Substantive correctness, alongside proper issuance and social efficacy, is the third possible element for defining law. If the question of whether substantive correctness is of importance in a legal system were to depend on what was issued along with its efficacy, the connection between law and morality would indeed be determined exclusively by positive law. If, however, the issued and efficacious law necessarily raises a claim to correctness, and therefore necessarily embraces substantive correctness and thus also morality, then morality does indeed belong to law in the sense mentioned in the dilemma of non-positivism, but the law to which it belongs is not the law of the positivists. Along with issuance and efficacy, it also embraces correctness and thus morality. This is the way in which the claim to correctness undermines the positivist concept of law and opens it up to morality. That is, if proceeding from the positivist concept of law, defined by issuance and efficacy, a nexus of law and morality arises. Under the conditions of a non-positivist concept of law, nothing is left to be connected because substantive correctness and therefore morality are already a part of law. The dilemma advanced against non-positivism is therefore completely resolved once there is clarity concerning the concept of law in question.

D. Reality and Ideal

The third objection is directed neither to the thesis that law necessarily raises a claim to correctness nor to its moral content. Rather, it disputes the possibility of anything is being gained from claims raised by law with respect to a necessary

[28] See on this Neumann, 'Review: Robert Alexy, Begriff und Geltung des Rechts' (n. 9 above), 246.
[29] See MacCormick, 'The Concept of Law and *The Concept of Law*' (n. 2 above), 164.

connection between law and morality. It is argued that the law obviously raises a claim to correctness. The mistake is to try to make too much of this. It is one thing to raise a claim but another to realize it. That the law claims to be just does not mean that it actually is just. A mere claim, therefore, cannot produce any correspondence, substantive in nature, between law and morality. Everything that has been said thus far concerning the claim to correctness can be essentially accepted without any change of the positivistic thesis that there is no necessary connection between law and morality. This can be seen most clearly where the claim to correctness is not realized without legal character or legal validity being affected in any way. Notwithstanding the claim to correctness, it remains the case that immoral law, too, can be law. The fundamental difference between the raising of a claim and compliance with it is therefore 'all that the modern positivist needs for his continued denial of a necessary connection between law and morality'.[30]

In reply to this objection, the argument may be made that the objection underestimates the impact of the claim to correctness. There are three reasons here. The first two will only be mentioned. The third reason is the one that matters.

The first reason is that the objection based on the undisputed difference between claim and compliance concentrates on non-compliance alone and does not take account of those cases in which the claim to correctness is not raised at all. Good reasons can be given for the thesis that a social order is lacking the character of a legal system if it is a system based solely on force and raises no claim to correctness at all, not even a mendacious or crazy one. If this is correct, the raising of the claim to correctness plays, with respect to the legal system as a whole, a law-defining role.[31]

The second reason concerns the consequences that follow from non-compliance with the claim to correctness. It is indeed correct that mere non-compliance with this claim does not deprive law of its legal character and thereby its legal validity. There can be a considerable number of unjust but nevertheless valid laws. Legal certainty is the predominant reason why injustice does not always lead to a loss of the legal character of the norm in question. But it does not follow from the fact that injustice is not always incompatible with law that any and every instance of injustice is compatible with it. Reasons are at hand for the position that at a certain threshold injustice becomes intolerable. This threshold can be defined by the concept of extreme injustice,[32] which essentially comports with Radbruch's Formula.[33] German courts applied the formula to instances of Nazi injustice,[34] as well as to

[30] Soper, 'Law's Normative Claims' (n. 3 above), 220.

[31] See Alexy, *The Argument from Injustice* (n. 8 above), 32–3, 127.

[32] Ibid., 40, 127.

[33] Gustav Radbruch, 'Statutory Lawlessness and Supra-Statutory Law' (1946), trans. Bonnie Litschewski Paulson and Stanley L. Paulson, *Oxford Journal of Legal Studies* 26 (2006), 1–11, at 7.

[34] Decisions of the German Federal Court of Justice in Civil Cases (BGHZ) 3, 94 (107); Decisions of the German Federal Court of Justice in Criminal Cases (BGHSt) 2, 173 (177); 2, 234 (237); 3, 357 (362); Decisions of the German Federal Constitutional Court (BVerfGE) 3, 58 (119); 3, 225 (232); 6, 132 (198); 6, 389 (414); 23, 98 (106); 54, 53 (68).

injustices perpetrated in the German Democratic Republic.[35] All of this is, to be sure, highly contested.[36] Still, it is far easier to deny the legal character of extreme injustice if all law raises the claim to correctness than if this were not the case. The claim to correctness can therefore play an important role in the substantiation of the thesis that extreme injustice is no law. If this substantiation is successful, even if only in connection with normative arguments,[37] a second law-defining meaning is acquired.

Here, it is only the third argument against the objection concerning the difference between claim and compliance that counts. This argument does not make reference to the dramatic case of a large band of robbers or to the extraordinary situation of the collapse of a wicked, unjust system but to the everyday legal routine found below the threshold of extreme injustice. Here, the claim to correctness does not have any effect on legal character and legal validity, for unjust law below this threshold is still law if it is properly issued and socially efficacious. But the claim to correctness puts everything in a different light. Unjust judgments can no longer be designated as morally questionable but nevertheless legally perfect or masterful. They are also legally defective. Hence, law is not only open to moral criticism from the outside. The critical dimension is inserted into the law itself. Despite the contingency of particular legal systems, this yields a nexus of law and the idea of correct morality. The claim to correctness, necessarily connected to law, implies in this way an ideal dimension necessarily connected to law. This matrix does not stand for a simple, substantive correspondence between law and morality. Rather, it stands for their necessary conceptual connection.[38]

[35] BGHSt 39, 1 (16); 40, 218 (232); 40, 241 (244); 41, 101 (106).

[36] These cases at least show that the question 'whether unjust laws can enjoy formal legal validity' is not, as MacCormick asserts, a 'non-question'; Neil MacCormick, 'Law, Morality and Positivism', in *An Institutional Theory of Law*, eds MacCormick and Ota Weinberger (Dordrecht: Reidel, 1986), 125–44, at 142. See, with further references, Robert Alexy, *Mauerschützen. Zum Verhältnis von Recht, Moral und Strafbarkeit* (Hamburg: Joachim Jungius-Gesellschaft der Wissenschaften, 1993), 22–30; Alexy, *Der Beschluß des Bundesverfassungsgerichts zu den Tötungen an der innerdeutschen Grenze vom 24. Oktober 1996* (Hamburg: Joachim Jungius-Gesellschaft der Wissenschaften, 1997), 26–35.

[37] See on this Alexy, *The Argument from Injustice* (n. 8 above), 40–1.

[38] MacCormick speaks of a 'necessary aspiration of actual legal process to ideal law, or of the perennial "claim to correctness" implicit in law-making and law-applying acts' (MacCormick,'The Concept of Law and *The Concept of Law*', n. 2 above, 189) on the one hand, but insists that 'there is no necessary conceptual connection between law and morality' (ibid., 175) on the other. Presumably the difference between his opinion and the opinion expressed here lies not so much in the matter as in the concept of connection or nexus. This presumption is supported by MacCormick's classifying himself as a positivist (MacCormick, 'Law, Morality and Positivism', n. 36 above, 138), while rejecting the existence of a 'sharp division' between 'legal positivism and natural law theories' (ibid., 141). This seems to be based on the opinion that the stomach of the positivist is strong enough to digest certain moral or natural law elements without any unwanted consequences. Here, by contrast, the idea is maintained that even the slightest infection of the properly issued and socially efficacious norms with a norm that stems from morality is sufficient to transform the law from positivism to something non-positivistic; see Robert Alexy, 'A Definition of Law', in *Prescriptive Formality and Normative Rationality in Modern Legal Systems. Festschrift für Robert S. Summers*, eds Werner Krawietz, Neil MacCormick, and G. H von Wright (Berlin: Duncker & Humblot, 1994), 101–7, at 102.

Index of Names

Index of Subjects